AN ATLAS OF

ANGLO-SAXON AND NORMAN COIN FINDS

AN ATLAS OF
ANGLO-SAXON AND NORMAN
COIN FINDS, *c*.973—1086

D.M. METCALF

ROYAL NUMISMATIC SOCIETY
AND ASHMOLEAN MUSEUM OXFORD
LONDON

1998

Royal Numismatic Society

Special Publication No. 32

ISBN 1 85444 110 8

British Library Cataloguing in Publication Data

Metcalf, D.M.

An Atlas of Anglo-Saxon and Norman
Coin Finds, *c.*973—1086
(Royal Numismatic Society Special
Publication, No. 32)
I/Title II. Series 737.498

Computer typeset in Monotype Plantin
Light and Semi-bold by the Ashmolean
Museum, Oxford. Printed and bound by
Cambridge University Press

Contents

MAPS

A. Distribution-maps for the whole country, imposed on a base-map of all find-spots.

B. Regional maps showing mint-towns (open squares, names in capitals), hoards (square symbols, larger type), and single finds (dots, smaller type). Mint-towns may also be the location of hoards and single finds, which however are not shown separately).

DIAGRAMS

Foreword

This is a book about English monetary history in the eleventh century. It is about how coins (of whatever kind, English or foreign) were used within the frontiers of the English state. It seeks to understand, mainly through the evidence of the coins themselves, what were the intentions and the policies of those who issued the coins and controlled the currency, and how their plans worked out in practice. It attempts to discern, behind the policies and their outcome, the constraints and the opportunities—in the availability of silver bullion, in trading opportunities with England's continental neighbours, in the necessity for military preparedness and the expediencies of buying off predatory invaders with tribute or 'danegeld'.

It is not *about the uses of coinage in Scotland, or Ireland—where Anglo-Saxon coins may have been available, but were not necessarily used in the same ways as in their country of origin—and it certainly is* not *about the uses of Anglo-Saxon coins in the Scandinavian world, which is a big topic in its own right. Nor is it a book about everything we know about Anglo-Saxon coins. Please do not expect it to be that. Anglo-Saxon numismatics has grown over the last forty years to be an intellectually impressive discipline, which has attracted a cluster of outstandingly able scholars, both in Britain and in Scandinavia. Their subject matter is also impressive, and fully deserves the research that has been devoted to it. From c.973 onwards English coins were produced, in quantities running into millions, under elaborate and sophisticated political control, mediated through the local supervision of over 1,600 'moneyers', i.e. craftsmen-entrepreneurs, all of whom are known to us by name. Their careers can be reconstructed, some lasting for much of a working lifetime, others active in one short period only. The town or towns where each one worked are also known, from the legends of the coins themselves.*

There is a vast body of information about the names of the moneyers and their linguistic origins, the exact dates of the many different varieties of coin, their weight-standards, and their alloy. This book is not primarily about any of that, although of course it utilizes the results of all the skilled and detailed numismatic research. It is not really a book about how *coins were minted, but about* why *they were minted and about what happened to them after they had been issued. In the virtual absence of contemporary written accounts of how coins were used, almost all our evidence necessarily comes from the coins themselves—and, indeed, from those coins found in England. The immensely rich finds of Anglo-Saxon coins in Scandinavia may provide a certain amount of information at one remove, about what was happening in England, but it is the finds from England, and they alone, which provide direct, localized evidence about the currency of England.*

Ideas about monetary history have often been distilled from the empirical evidence, and used by numismatists to give themselves working hypotheses about the significance of their data. There has been a tendency for ideas to be generated piece-meal, and as occasion offered.

Monetary history follows on from numismatics—or does it? For most of this century, students have been accustomed to link the two: Münz- und Geldgeschichte, *coinage history and money history. It was the task of numismatics to assemble the facts. If this was done assiduously, it would then become straightforward to pluck out the conclusions which constituted monetary history. This offered too passive an idea of writing monetary history. Certainly the subject is empirical, and relies on a great deal of numismatic spadework. But the monetary insights do not derive straightforwardly from an organized view of the history of coin production—the history of minting. To make up an imaginary example, one might know all that there was to be known about the minting of eleventh-century Anglo-Saxon coins, but if the currency of eleventh-century England had consisted mainly of imported French and German coins, (as the currency of Scandinavia in the eleventh century consisted mainly of imported Islamic, German, and Anglo-Saxon coins), one would not thereby know about Anglo-Saxon monetary history.*

Instead of a passive approach to monetary history, one needs actively to ask questions—idiot questions, technical questions, historical questions—and then to work out what arguments would best address each question as put. The answers will draw upon contemporary written sources, and on what we know about the working of the mints, but especially (for monetary history) on the patterns of stray coins lost randomly, as evidence of what was in circulation locally. This approach is question-led: we try to ask appropriate questions about the uses of coinage, and then think carefully about the arguments that would fit the questions.

The written records concerning English monetary history of the eleventh century could be transcribed upon a very few sheets of paper. If we had more documentary sources about the coins, our understanding of their history would doubtless be set into a detailed human context that would tell us what individuals thought they were doing, in their affairs, and our conviction that we had grasped the main perspectives correctly would be more confident. On the other hand, the relevance of the documents to the general outlines of monetary history is not always clear and unambiguous. In particular the laws, while they may well be pools of light in the darkness for us, still have to be considered critically. We have to judge whether the abuse that provoked a particular provision was widespread, and whether that provision had the result that seems to have been intended: whether laws were obeyed by all men everywhere, and even whether they were expected to be obeyed. For example, when Cnut's law decrees that no-one shall buy anything over four pence in value, either livestock or other property, unless he have four men as trustworthy witnesses, do we believe that the guide-lines were punctiliously observed by all men everywhere? We are entitled to take into consideration that this was a re-enactment of similar provisions dating back to the time of Edward the Elder. We are also entitled to take into consideration that something of the order of 40 million coins were minted in England in Cnut's name in the Quatrefoil type, and that they circulated briskly, as shown by the proportion of them involved in inter-regional transfers. What was fourpence in this sea of money? Were four good men and true being summoned a dozen times a day? And who could be expected to remember a particular transaction at a later date? In fact the detailed clauses of the same law then go on to speak about disputed ownership of property. If the person in possession cannot call on his original witnesses, the property is to be given up to its rightful owner, and there is to be a supplementary payment and a fine. The provision about witnesses only comes into play, that is to say, in cases of dispute over the property. It may be an offence to buy or sell without witnesses (for sums in excess of what might be £100 today), but it is not in itself a punishable offence. Friends or neighbours may well have relied on good-will, and may not have bothered to observe the letter of the law.

In a period from which little written evidence survives about the uses of coinage, many of the facts of monetary history can nevertheless be inferred from the patterns of monetary circulation. These in turn have to be built up from the detailed evidence of coin finds. Coin finds comprise hoards, and single finds. In either case, money fell out of use (by concealment or by loss) at a particular moment and a particular place. Each loss was a unique event, whether it consisted of one coin or hundreds. Perhaps surprisingly, the single finds provide the better evidence, freer from ambiguities and distortion. There are far more of them than there are hoards, and their number increases year by year. They cover the entire country, and they lie thick on the ground. The total, for the period c. 973—1086, has already passed six hundred. These six hundred coins, to each of which a find-spot attaches, are precious evidence, whereas six thousand similar coins with no provenance are well-nigh useless to the monetary historian, except as part of the background information about the history of minting.

Although this book is based primarily on the English single finds of the period c. 973—1086, and on the distribution-patterns they generate, an attempt has been made to show how other categories of evidence have a bearing on understanding the uses of coinage. The geographical spread of England's a hundred and ten mint-places, and also the location of the coin hoards of the period are examined in the light of the single finds. The approach is deliberately holistic.

There are many different questions that can be put to the finds. The answers, the many answers, ought all to fit together, or to point in the same general direction, since they are all derived from the same data and relate to an integrated monetary system. The system had to balance. The same coins were used by all sorts and conditions of men—rich and poor, farmers and merchants, officials and soldiers. As they passed from hand to hand, they were used for many kinds of transaction—the buying and selling of land, of beasts, of grain, the payment of tolls and gelds, the purchase of luxury items, gifts, alms. It lies in the nature of a region's or of a country's money economy that the coinage sums up and automatically strikes a balance at the end of the day, which takes account of all these transactions. The information on the bottom line is about the stock of currency within a region or within the country as a whole, and about the regional or national balance-of-payments situation vis-à-vis other regions or countries. Whereas the written evidence about eleventh-century money is liable to be episodic, and partial or biassed according to the interest of the writer, the patterns of the coins themselves strike a balance of all transactions, both those known to us from written records, and also the many more of which no record was made. Because the evidence of monetary circulation can best be digested in a regional framework, that is how the monetary history of the eleventh century should be studied.

The numismatic experts referred to above, who are as familiar with all the detail as with the back of their hands, will recognize straight away that this book has grown out of an earlier study, published sixteen or seventeen years ago in the pages of the British Numismatic Journal, *and entitled 'Continuity and change in English monetary history, c. 973–1086'. Its data-base of single finds contained some 270 entries. The total available has now more than doubled, partly through archaeological excavation, but thanks largely to the contributions of metal-detectorists, gathered up in the annual 'Coin Register' of the* Journal. *The present total of over 600 finds permits one to undertake a more elaborate analysis than was statistically feasible with fewer than 300. The general conclusions of the earlier work still stand, but the experts will note that two new key ideas have been developed, and it may be helpful to flag them here in the foreword. First, the case has been argued that hoards are often atypical in their mint-structure, sometimes because they were concealed far away from where they were put together, sometimes because they contain a higher proportion of coins of the local mint than was to be found in the local currency—even in the mint-town itself. The suggestion is put forward that there may have been an 'inner circle' of merchants who obtained new coins from the mint, and sometimes traded among themselves. These men were 'closer to source' than the general population from which, on a statistical basis, the stray losses derive. In any case, the single finds are certainly to be preferred to the hoards as a measure of the mint-structure of the currency. Following on from this, views are expressed on the 'multi-type' hoards which are a feature of the Confessor's reign and which, if it were really the case that they reflected a multi-type currency, would have significant implications for the velocity of circulation, in so far as stray losses had had much longer to travel from their mint of origin to where they were lost. Relying on those multi-type hoards with a local flavour, however, one can argue that, if there had indeed been a currency of extended age-structure, like that in Scandinavia, the older types should have become progressively more mixed with age, by the normal processes of inter-regional transfers, creating an age-profile of localization within the hoard. As with the second law of thermodynamics, no amount of circulation will cause the coins of different mints to separate out again, and become unmixed.*

Secondly, Bertil Petersson has recently published a study of radical importance analysing the weights, mint by mint and type by type, of a sample of no fewer than 44,350 coins. From his figures it is very clear that the national averages type by type (previously available) conceal local variations on a grand scale. In effect, the administrative control of minting was shared between central government and the shires. Each mint had its own weight-standards. This astounding system appears fully-fledged at the very moment of Eadgar's reform, and it is not finally abolished until 1083, i.e. it survived the Norman Conquest. Petersson concludes that the standards were fixed for each shire. This conclusion is unsatisfactory, in so far as those shires with more than one mint-place (mostly those south of the Thames) provide so many exceptions to his rule as to call its validity into question. Petersson's instinct was no doubt right, because the governance of England was to a large extent shire governance, but the numismatic facts do not satisfactorily prove that each shire had a single or uniform policy on weight-standards. Nevertheless it is now very clear that the history of minting, and perhaps of monetary circulation too, should be studied within the framework of the shire boundaries. (Needless to say, this book uses the county boundaries as they existed before local government reorganization in the 1970s.) Petersson's results have been employed in a fresh attempt to penetrate the enigma of weight-variation—which, it must be said, still holds its secrets.

Readers may begin by dipping into the text here and there, as the fancy takes them, and there is no harm in that. Indeed, it may make sense to begin by reading the Strategy and the Conclusions, in order to gain a general perspective into which to fit the detailed arguments; because this book is not a dictionary or encyclopedia. It is structured as a whole. The thirty-nine questions in particular (a package suggested by the thirty-nine steps of John Buchan's story) are consecutive and incremental. Each builds on, or assumes, what has been said before. Similarly the regions have been treated from north to south in order to begin with Yorkshire, of which the monetary affairs offer a relatively uncomplicated starting-point.

Finding their way about through all the arguments will be a learning process for most readers, who may need time to familiarize themselves with the layout. If one wishes to walk from Victoria Station to the British Museum, an A to Z street plan of London may save one from taking several wrong directions. The text of the thirty-nine questions is an A to Z of the arguments, marshalling them in such a way as to help the reader to grasp how they radiate out from any particular point in a complicated network. The arguments are cross-referenced and sign-posted back and forth among the thirty-nine questions, as a practical response to the need to make sense of the whole in terms of the local details, and vice versa.

The detailed maps locate the single finds within the old shire boundaries, and also show the find-spots of the hoards in relation to the mint-towns.

I am grateful for the influence and the friendship over the years of the group of scholars who from the 1960s made Anglo-Saxon numismatics such an exciting field. The British Numismatic Society and its journal were the focal point of their endeavours, and one might well speak of them as a latter-day 'nest of singing birds'. Michael Dolley was my early mentor, and with him I drew maps of Anglo-Saxon coinage thirty-six years ago, for an article on this very subject of Eadgar's reform and the monetary system it created. In 1961 it would have been quite impossible to write this book: so many of the facts did not yet exist. The new maps in this volume were likewise drawn by the author. Mark Blackbürn and Mike Bonser deserve special mention, for their major contribution to the recording of single finds over a long period. With Jens Christian Moesgard, they kindly supplied an advance copy of their latest publication of finds, which added usefully to the total available for historical analysis. More single finds are being brought to light all the time, but at some point one has to close the books and draw up the balance sheet. If, or rather when, the next specimen turns up, the question is usually not, 'What does it tell us?', but 'Now that we have 29 specimens of this category instead of 28, does the extra one affect our judgement?' On many topics, we can feel that we have reached a stable situation, which will not be changed in a hurry, if at all.

★ ★ ★ ★ ★

The author will be grateful to receive any additional information, comments, and corrections which he can digest and store away, against the day when a revised edition may be called for. Circumstantial information about the finds from a site is likely to be particularly precious: the inportance of a random sample is dwelt on in the text.

He is indebted to the Publications Committee and the Council of the Royal Numismatic Society, which agreed to accept this work in the Society's Special Publication series; to the authorities of the Ashmolean Museum, which financed the publication; and to Mrs Roslyn Britton-Strong, who typed and retyped the manuscript with impressive accuracy.

D.M.M.
Michaelmas 1997

PART ONE

THE STRATEGY

Assembling a working model of monetary circulation, from the random evidence of single finds

PART ONE

The strategy

The English coinage of the 'long' hundred years from *c.*973 to 1086—that is, from King Eadgar's coinage reform to the Domesday Survey—can be dated exceptionally precisely, because the design of the coins was changed every few years, and because the duration of each new type can be determined, usually within narrow limits of a year or two years. Thus the issues of our 113-year period can be divided, virtually without controversy, into 31 successive types, a few of which can even be subdivided. The relative chronology is completely secure, and the absolute chronology is anchored at many points along the way, permitting us to correlate the coins with political events. Such chronological precision is not available either before or subsequently in the English medieval coinage, until dateable initial marks and other such privy marks are introduced, from the late fourteenth century. Nor can one think of any other European coinage of the earlier middle ages, in studying which the historian enjoys such an advantage. Only Islamic dirhams and dinars can rival the Anglo-Saxon penny in this respect, for they are dated year by year with hijra dates.

Secondly, the same material can be divided regionally or topographically, because the English coinage was struck (to the same design) at many mint-places. Upwards of 50 towns, spread fairly evenly over England, each had their minters; and all the coins—*all* the coins—carry the name of the mint-place where they were produced. In the tenth century some of the coins had borne a mint-name, while many were silent about their town of origin. When one tries to analyse tenth-century monetary patterns, in which a significant fraction of the specimens may be of conjectural mint-attribution, the margins of uncertainty attaching to some of the attempted conclusions will be so wide that the exercise becomes vague and unsatisfactory. For our 'long' hundred years, more than 99 per cent of all the coins (other than cut halfpennies) can be securely assigned to their mint-place, without controversy. There is the potential, therefore, for historical and regional conclusions to be sharp-edged.

By combining these two modes of division into a grid, as it were across and down, we can assign virtually every coin to a small box, depending on when and where it was minted. The boxes are not all of exactly the same size. Some will refer to a period of six or seven years, others to only two years (or occasionally even just a couple of months). But the sizes are known. Thus we have in our grid at least 31 times 50, or upwards of 1,500 categories of information, securely defined. In fact, the standard list of late Anglo-Saxon mints contains 107 names, so that the potential total of boxes is 3,317.

Next, we can place all the surviving coins in their little boxes. There are tens of thousands of coins, in museums and private collections all over Europe and America. Of the 3,317 boxes, something close to half will be empty, because a particular mint-place simply did not strike coins in a particular design-period—or perhaps occasionally because very few were struck, of which none has survived. But upwards of 1,500 boxes will contain coins. Not all will contain the same number. Some will hold only one or two specimens. In others there will be a tall stack of chips. We have now assembled a three-dimensional model.

Fourthly, we can construct another similar model, in which the numbers of coins in each box are in arithmetical relation to the total numbers that were originally struck, rather than comprising the numbers that happen to have survived, perhaps erratically. This can be achieved with the help of statistical methods of estimation, which are tried and tested, and are child's play to mathematicians. Statistical estimation involves margins of uncertainty, which tend to diminish the larger the sample becomes. It is important, therefore, that we should have tens of thousands of coins to work with, because by the time they have been distributed around some 1,500 boxes, with great disparities, many boxes will hold uncomfortably few specimens for statistical accuracy. Even so, large numbers may not be satisfactory in themselves. It is much more important that the sample should be random. A random sample will give the same answers whether it is large or medium-sized, and it may well be worth sacrificing maximum numbers, in pursuit of a sample that is as nearly random as possible. By die-estimation, then, we can construct what should be a highly reliable new model, in 'virtual reality', showing the relative numbers of dies employed in each little unit of our grid of boxes. The step from numbers of dies to numbers of coins is fraught with uncertainty, but there is no reason why a hundred dies should not have been used to strike a million coins. There are many technicalities that need to be carefully discussed, including possible variation from time to time or from place to place in the average number of coins struck by each die, but in principle we can construct a detailed model of mint-output, which can be used to make comparisons and examine trends, and generally to go to and fro between one small box and another.

Stage five: we can set our improved model in motion, by introducing a new category of information, in order to discover what happened to the coins, in detail, after they left the mints and were put into circulation. To what extent did they move about? —In which directions did they move? The need for distribution-maps becomes clear, as an essential part of presenting the evidence. Without them, one cannot form a geographical idea of the national pattern of finds, and one certainly cannot compare one distribution with another. One needs to do that, and to do it accurately, if one is to ask, for example, whether the coins of some mint-places moved about more than or differently from others.

At this step in the argument, there are two important new considerations. We know (from hoards) that each of our 31 successive types was recalled from circulation at the end of its validity-period and melted down, to be replaced by a new type. This proposition is partly debateable, for the reign of Edward the Confessor, but few students would doubt that it is essentially true up to 1036. On average, therefore, coins had only three or four years, or even less, to become mingled in circulation. Even if we only accept that this conclusion is secure up to 1036, that is enough: it demonstrates the velocity and the directions of eleventh-century monetary circulation, which is unlikely to have changed its character radically after 1036. Secondly, we can analyse the evidence of hundreds of single finds of eleventh-century coins, scattered all over England, by asking how far each had been carried from its mint of origin before it was accidentally lost. This aspect of the evidence has the enormous advantage that it is thoroughly random in respect of the coin's mint-place. By definition people did not check the mint of a coin before they accidentally lost it. They did not lose coins selectively with reference to their mints of origin. Whatever was available in a locality stood a random chance of being lost. Thus the evidence in our 1,500 small boxes can be transposed into a different geographical pattern, equally precise as to both find-spot and date of loss, and without any uncertainties except the statistical margins arising from too-small samples. This transposition is at the heart of what is meant by setting the model in motion. It shows us which way the wind was blowing—and not just for the country as a whole, but town by town and region by region, in considerable detail.

Thus one can create an intellectual crystal palace,—integrated and elegant in its design, fully transparent, and bolted together section by section in all directions.

One can then usefully go over the material again, concentrating first on the chronology, and then on the regional patterns. The Reform type, struck by three kings in the years *c.*973-9, has a special place both because it was the moment when remarkable changes were made in the English coinage, and also for technical reasons which will be explained in the text. The regional survey, in which the shires are grouped into small blocks taking account of whether they were traditionally under West Saxon or Mercian law or were part of the Danelaw, allows one to consider whether trends noticed in the material as a whole are reflected in a coherent way region by region. In so far as they are, the over-all case is considerably strengthened.

Stage six: armed with all this minutely compartmentalized information, which has the merits of being systematic and comprehensive, we are in a position to bring it into the general historical debate, by asking a series of carefully-framed questions and by showing how those questions might be answered by reference to the distributional evidence, to the ranking of the mints in terms of their output, to hoards as evidence of the age-profile of the currency, and so on. The questions, or rather the answers to them, build up into a complex description of a working model.

For each question separately one needs to consider whether the available sample of coins is satisfactorily random *in that aspect*, because a sample can be random in one way, but less so or not at all in another. Thus, for example, there may be numerous finds from a particular site because it has been intensively searched or excavated. The *number* of finds will not be random, but the mints represented among them may be.

Randomness is crucial at every point. Archimedes, much taken with the principle of the lever, said, 'Just give me somewhere to stand, and I will move the earth'. We might say, 'Just give us a reliably random sample of single finds, and we will reconstruct the currency from which they were lost'.

To judge from comments on the historical significance of the coinage that the author has come across in general historical works, a systematic framework is what the non-specialist most needs to be offered. Without it, he all too often leaves various aspects of the coinage out of his consideration, or attempts to proceed in one easy move from the coins themselves to general conclusions about them, when he would have been better advised to proceed more critically, taking ten or a dozen small logical steps. Splitting the analysis up into small, carefully focussed sections will, it is hoped, make it more accessible to the reader, as well as building up a sound and sober framework of argument.

The strategy which has been sketched, in six stages, builds up progressively from numismatic detail, and by putting different kinds of evidence in conjunction, until it reaches conclusions of general historical interest, the strength of which the reader should be in a position to assess. It offers not just the answers, but the steps of argument by which they were reached.

Perhaps one may be allowed to anticipate the outcome by pointing to three large conclusions and one very large question-mark at the end of the whole exercise. First, in spite of all the uncertainties and debate around average die-output, it is clear that the Anglo-Saxon currency was measured in millions of coins, and that these quantities were briskly moving about all the time between the regions of England and, no doubt, within each region too, although that happens to be less visible in the evidence. The monetization of English political and economic life, about which the written sources tell us relatively little, should be judged against those millions of coins actively in motion. The quantities are large enough for the precise totals not, perhaps, to matter unduly.

Secondly, it is clear that our working model is not a closed system. Money flowed out of the country, particularly towards Scandinavia and particularly up until *c.*1040. The quantities involved were far greater than the recorded danegelds of the reign of Æthelred II, and the outflows continued after Cnut had taken control of England. The Anglo-Saxon money which accumulated in the Northern Lands can be roughly measured by statistical methods, and it amounted, eventually, to millions of coins, or even tens of millions. As the stock of currency in England was not diminished thereby, it follows that money also flowed in, doubtless from the near Continent.

Thirdly, the administrative control of minting seems to have been shared between central government and the shires. The weights of the coins, even though they were of a uniform national design, varied widely from mint to mint. In general the coins minted in the western half of England, west of a north-south line running through Southampton, were heavier and more uniform in weight than those from the eastern half of the country. In the east, within each validity-period there were usually two or more weight-standards at each mint. By and large they seem to reflect progressive reductions in weight. How multiple weight-standards were managed, without opening the door to large-scale fraud, remains thoroughly enigmatic. The complexities are unparalleled in any other medieval coinage. We cannot claim to have grasped the intentions of the monetary authorities, nor the constraints within which they made their decisions, nor the impact the system made on the ways in which coins would otherwise have circulated, at home or abroad. It may be that we just do not have quite enough pieces of the puzzle to reach an agreed solution. Or perhaps one day a convincing case will be made. For the present, weight-variation remains mysterious: the ghost in the machine.

PART TWO

THE QUESTIONS

Asking appropriate questions about the find-evidence, and thinking about the arguments that would fit the questions

PART TWO

The thirty-nine questions

1. Were Anglo-Saxon people careless, to lose so many valuable coins?
2. In what respects are single finds likely to be a random sample of the locally-available currency?

* * * * *

3. What was the relative mint-output of the various mint-towns?
4. How does this ranking of the mints compare with that derived from the Scandinavian material?
5. What are the implications of London's dominant role in minting?
6. What was the approximate scale of the currency, and how does it relate to the 'danegeld' tributes in the reign of Æthelred II?
7. Where did all the silver come from?
8. How are the single finds distributed through the period *c.*973—1086? Are there any sudden peaks, or longer-term trends?
9. Were stray losses more or fewer in troubled times?
10. How evenly are the stray losses distributed through England? How accurately is their pattern likely to reflect the situation at the time?
11. If, at any given moment, the stock of currency was concentrated in the towns, would the evidence of stray finds allow us to detect the imbalance?
12. Is the regional distribution of the stock of currency likely to distort our assessment of relative mint-output?
13. Do coins of the first validity-period (*c.*973—*c.*979) show signs that Eadgar's reform required a settling-in period?
14. What does the distance travelled by individual coins before they were lost tell us about the uses of coinage?
15. Did the tendency for coins to become geographically dispersed increase or decrease over the period *c.*973—1086?
16. Did coins struck at small mints behave differently from those from large mints?
17. What can regression analysis of the single finds tell us about the diffusion of the currency?
18. At any given moment, what proportion of the currency was to be found in each of the monetary zones?
19. Why were coins minted where they were minted, and in such varying quantities from place to place?

20. Can one detect any blips in the statistics of estimated mint-output, which might suggest that particular mints were, briefly, minting for special reasons, and can such reasons be identified from written sources?
21. Where a type was struck on more than one weight-standard, were the heavier and lighter coins used differently in England?

Excursus. The enigma of weight-variation: the evidence of the Reform/First Small Cross type.

22. Is there any evidence from stray finds that coinage was used to an important extent in the governance of the shires, or that it reflects the needs of taxation or of royally-controlled expenditure?
23. Did Swein's brief rule in England leave any traces in the coinage? —and did Cnut's conquest of England lead to any changes in the patterns of monetary circulation?
24. If we did not know that there had been a foreign conquest of England in 1066, could we deduce from the coins that something of the sort had happened?
25. Was the fall in mint-output during Edward the Confessor's reign accompanied by any changes in the patterns of monetary circulation in England?

⋆ ⋆ ⋆ ⋆ ⋆

26. Were pennies cut up into halves and quarters by private individuals as required, or by the mints?
27. Was the cutting done during the validity-period of the type, or subsequently?
28. Within the find-evidence as a whole, are cut halfpennies and cut farthings random in their chronological distribution?
29. Do the mint-places of the fractions show, within statistical limits, the same proportions as the pennies?
30. Did fractions circulate as freely over distances as the pennies?

⋆ ⋆ ⋆ ⋆ ⋆

31. What were gold pennies for?
32. Do coins which have been turned into brooches or jewellery show any signs of being anomalous in their chronology, mint of origin, or place of loss?

⋆ ⋆ ⋆ ⋆ ⋆

33. Were foreign coins permitted to circulate in England? Is the regional and topographical occurrence of foreign coins significantly different from that of English coins?
34. What do the single finds of foreign coins reveal about the destinations of England's overseas trade?

⋆ ⋆ ⋆ ⋆ ⋆

35. Do hoards point to the same conclusions as single finds?
36. What does the clustering of die-linked coins in hoards imply?
37. How long did coins remain in circulation?

* * * * *

38. Given that the uses of coinage were necessarily various and interlocking, can we strike any sort of balance between the public and private sectors of the monetary economy?
39. Can we strike any sort of balance between the monetary and non-monetary sectors of the economy?

How we might answer each of the 39 questions by reference to the coin finds

Q.1. Were Anglo-Saxon people careless, to lose so many valuable coins?

Losing a silver penny, which for most people in the eleventh century would be equivalent to at least a day's earnings, was at worst a once-in-a-lifetime experience. Our 685 stray finds (Map 1) are doubtless only a small fraction of the original total of stray losses. That fraction is the major uncertainty in the equation. Let us guess that for every stray find in our records there are in collections two unprovenanced coins and ninety-seven still in the soil. If the population of late Anglo-Saxon England was a million, of whom half handled coins, then over the period *c.*973—1086 there were very roughly 0.5M people x 100 years—50 million man-years to set against 68,500, or let us say, 100,000 stray losses. That works out at one stray loss per 500 man-years. Even if our guess at the original total of stray losses was too low by a factor of ten, losing a coin would still have been a once-in-a-lifetime experience.

A good many of our recorded stray finds are from controlled archaeological excavations in habitation areas, but most are now metal-detectorist's finds from ploughed fields. How did so many coins end up in what are today ploughed fields? In the absence of local authority cleansing services, rubbish accumulated around people's houses until they were tired of the sight of it. They then presumably carted it away and spread it on their fields, where it would have served quite usefully to improve the soil. (The number of single finds from a region may thus be partly a function of the proportion of arable land.)

For the monetary historian, that theory implies that many Anglo-Saxon pennies may have been lost half a mile or a mile from where they were found. Certainly, we should not postulate large numbers of ploughmen with holes (and money) in their pockets.

Q.2. In what respects are single finds likely to be a random sample of the locally-available currency?

In shopping arcades today one may find coins lying on the ground almost any day of the week. They are nearly always pennies, and rarely of larger denominations. That may be either because people take better care of more valuable coins, or because one has arrived too late on the scene, when scavengers

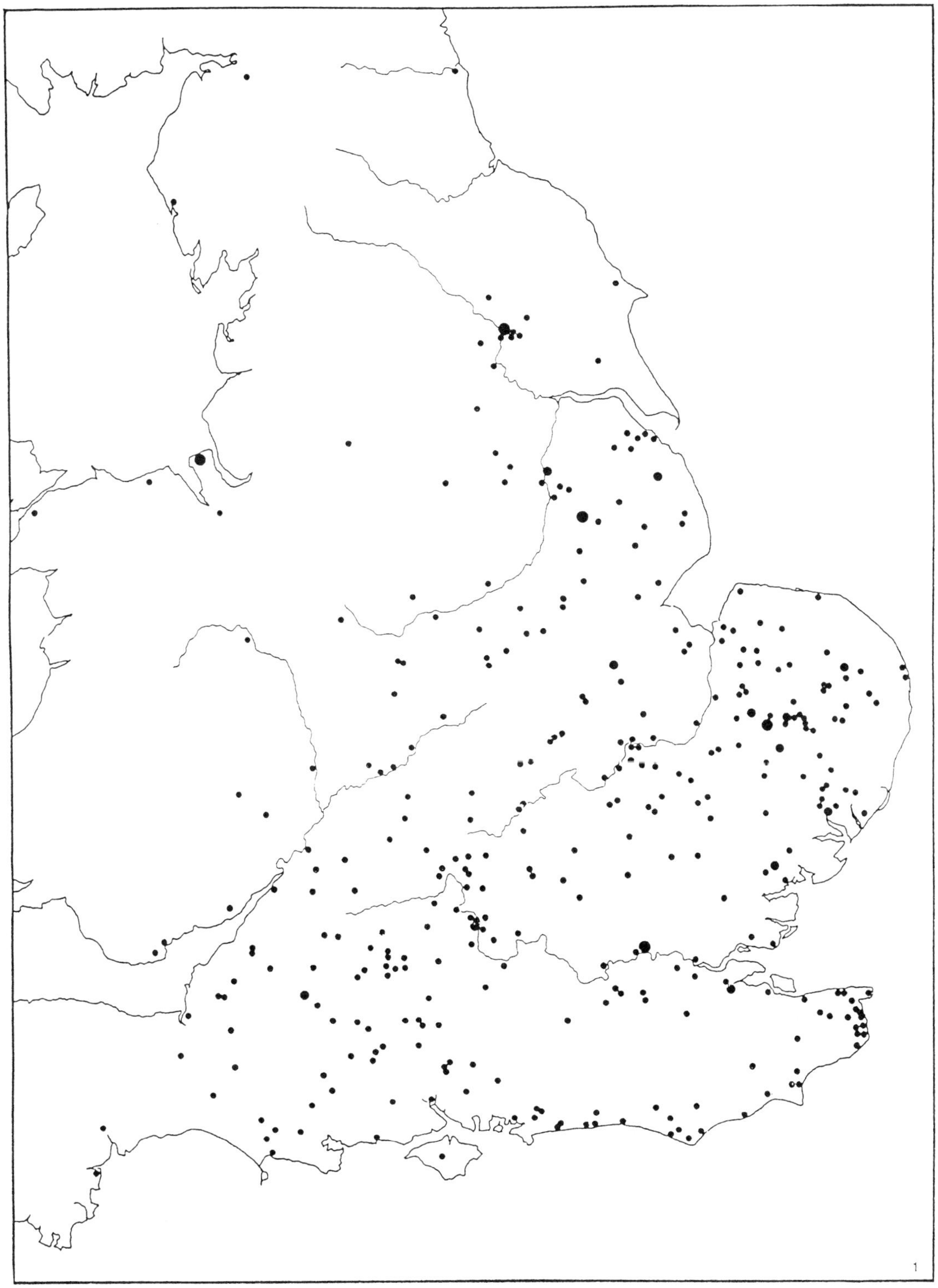

MAP 1. All finds.

have already picked up any money worth the trouble of stooping for. In archaeological excavations of the later medieval centuries, when there was a developed system of coin denominations, the finds are usually very heavily biassed towards low-value coins. The same reasons might apply, but in the much dirtier surroundings of an unpaved market-place or yard, a coin once dropped would not be as easily found by a third party. It seems likely that what is found by archaeologists will approximate to what was lost in those circumstances, and that low-value coins really had a heavier loss-rate. That might be because there were many more of them in the market-place, or on the site, or because they were more frequently used than larger coins. It seems likely that coins were most in danger of being lost when they were in active use.

In the period *c.*973–1086 there were in effect three denominations of coin in widespread use, namely the penny, halfpenny, and farthing. In answer to the question, we must assume that the sample of single finds may not be random in respect of the denominations, being biassed towards the cut fractions. On the other hand, the law *de minimis* may not have come into play, when even a halfpenny was worth something like a ten-pound note today.

In other respects, the sample may be entirely random, for example as regards the mint of origin of the coin that was lost. Coins of all mints were of essentially the same design, size, and alloy, and for many purposes they were of a standard face value. By definition people did not look through their money and decide to lose a coin of one mint rather than another (even if they could read the coins' legends). They lost coins accidentally.

A sample that is random in one respect may be far from random in another. One has to specify the kind of randomness carefully, and judge each case separately.

The question speaks of single *finds* rather than single *losses*. Again one needs to distinguish. Finding a coin is in one sense as accidental as losing it, and in respect of its mint-place, for example, the finds should be an entirely random sample of the losses. In respect of the quantities of finds from a site or from a region, they may be far from random, being dependent on the effort put into searching for them, and (particularly the tiny farthings) the skill and care of the searchers. The pattern is self-reinforcing in so far as metal detectorists concentrate their efforts where they expect to succeed. Soil conditions and land use may also distort the pattern of finds as a reflection of the pattern of losses.

One assumes that single finds are mostly accidental losses, but a few of them might be coins deliberately concealed by their owners—mini-hoards consisting of one coin. Hoards obey different historical laws from stray losses. They tend to be more frequent in troubled times, whereas the tendency with single losses, if they reflect the number of transactions taking place, will probably be the opposite.

Sudden death, whether in battle or through epidemic disease, may occasionally have generated single coin-losses. An Anglo-Saxon skeleton was found at Stockbridge Down with six coins in the area of the arm-pit—where they had no doubt been kept, wrapped in a piece of cloth fixed to the under-arm hair with beeswax. It seems that this individual had been executed as a felon. (See Part 3, section 22.)

Although it is a reasonable assumption that the stray finds are heavily dominated by accidental losses, one should be on the look-out for any localized evidence to the contrary.

There remains the question whether the single finds in our sample might have been reported selectively. At the time of writing the answer is no, but that may change in the future.

'I've been metal-detecting for eight or ten years, but this is the first Anglo-Saxon coin I've found'. The writer has heard remarks of this nature many a time. Most detectorists only show museum curators the coins which they judge to be worth-while or which they have failed to identify (as a museum curator one hesitates between 'more's the pity' and 'thank goodness for that'). Over the last twenty years a vast quantity of stray finds of late Roman coins and post-1600 coins have gone unrecorded. They form the bulk of what is found, in almost every part of the country. Relatively very few detectorists have personally found more than two or three Anglo-Saxon pennies. The lucky few are often among the most conscientious in recording and reporting all their serious finds. If there has been any systematic neglect to report such coins, it will probably have resulted in a slight under-reporting of coins of the London mint, or of major mints in general. But the distorting effect of detectorists identifying their more straightforward Anglo-Saxon pennies for themselves, and not bothering to report them, can be assumed to have been minimal. As regards its randomness in that respect, the sample reported seems likely to be almost exactly as reliable as the sample found.

There is a minority of uncooperative detectorists, including a few very rough characters with no concern except for their own pockets. Some counties have had a better record of co-operation than others.

In the future it may become advisable to use new finds selectively, relying on controlled excavations and on detectorists whose commitment to cooperation is known, even if that means a smaller sample over-all. Until now, the detectorists contributing information have in general been exemplary in their helpfulness.

The writer would like to make a plea to detectorists in the future: please do not be selective in what you report, because you cannot see that it would be interesting or worth-while. Maybe it would not; but coins may acquire extra interest as new ideas are tested, and the randomness of the sample is of the utmost historical importance.

Q.3. What was the relative output of the various mint-towns?

If stray losses were random in respect of their mint-town, and have not been selectively reported to any significant extent, should they not give a good measure of the relative output of the various mint-towns? Just over a hundred place-names occur on the coins of the period c.973—1086. Their relative output varies wildly, from 10,023 coins of London and 4,805 of York, all the way down to a dozen mint-places which are known from only a single specimen. The wide variations in mint-output are generally quite consistent type by type. What they have to tell us (by implication) about the reasons for minting (see Q.19) should be exceptionally secure historical information, quantifiable within narrow limits and precisely dated.

There is one further condition, however, which is not fully met. If the issues of all the mints had been mingled into a perfectly homogenous currency, it would not matter from where the sample was taken. But the mixing was imperfect. Finds tend to include an above-average proportion of coins of the local mint. At Lincoln, one finds coins minted at Lincoln, and so on. If the find-places and the finds were evenly distributed through England, the inconsistencies would average out. To a large extent they do. But because there are a few sites which have been very productive of late Saxon and early Norman coins, some distortions may remain. They can in practice be discounted by rule of thumb. It is fairly obvious, for example, that the statistics for the Chester mint are exaggerated by the finds from near-by Meols.

Because of the wide disparities in mint-output, there are no fewer than 50 small mints which each account for a tenth of one per cent or less of the national total. It follows that a very large sample of single finds would be needed to do justice to those small mints, because of the wide margins of statistical uncertainty attaching to small numbers. As a rough guide one may say that the difference between one stray find and four is unlikely to be statistically significant at a rigorous confidence level. For four finds to equal a tenth of one per cent, a database of 4,000 finds would be needed.

The sample on which our analysis is based currently includes 685 finds. Of these, 7 are coins that have been turned into brooches, 5 are contemporary counterfeits, and 2 are lead strikings, leaving 671. Out of 671, a few are certainly, and a few more may be coins from mini-hoards, which do not properly belong in an inventory of single finds, but which have been left in the list for procedural reasons. Another 27, or 4 per cent, are foreign coins, leaving 644 English coins. Of these, 17 are known merely to be of a particular king, but are not further described, as to either mint-place or type; they are of very limited use, except as regards their find-spots. We are left with 627 finds, namely 503 pennies and 124 fractions. Of these 29 of the pennies and 26 of the fractions are of identifiable types but their mint-places cannot be read. Conversely there are 13 pennies from identifiable mints, but of which the type is uncertain. Thus we have a series of effective samples (depending on the purpose for which they are required), varying from 685 finds of all categories, down to 588 English coins identifiable as to their mints (but these may include about a dozen coins from mini-hoards). In a sample of only 588 coins, the expectation is that there will be numerous mint-places represented by only one coin, or none.

The limitations of the sample size may to some extent be overcome by grouping the small mints. The question whether dies were under-used at small mints compared with the practice at large mints (discussed under Q.7) can, for example, be approached by the judicious grouping of the data.

Meanwhile, the evidence for the activity of the large mints is statistically much more secure. In ranking order, the top ten mints represented in the sample of 588 are:

London 133	=	23 per cent
Lincoln 73		12 per cent
York 48		8 per cent
Stamford 27		5 per cent
Thetford 27		5 per cent
Winchester 25		4 per cent
Canterbury 19		3 per cent
Norwich 19		3 per cent
Chester 18		3 per cent
Wallingford 13		3 per cent
10 mints 402		68 per cent

Although upwards of a hundred mint-places are known, just ten account for two-thirds of the coinage. London alone accounts for a quarter. The six east-coast ports and trading towns of London, Lincoln, York, Stamford, Norwich and Thetford together produced more than half the national coinage. That is one of the cardinal facts of eleventh-century monetary history.

The English currency was a controlled currency, from which foreign coins were in principle excluded (see Q.33). Merchants arriving from overseas with foreign coins were evidently required to take them to the moneyers, who melted them down and replaced them with current English coins. The persistent dominance of the half-dozen largest east-coast mint-towns suggests that the to and fro of currencies in the trade of the North Sea costlands (and the Baltic) was a major reason for the activity of the English mints.

Q.4. How does this ranking of the mints compare with that derived from the Scandinavian material?

Relative mint-output was assessed, in an article published by the present writer in 1980-1, on the basis of a sample of 16,971 coins from the period *c.*973—1066 (n.b. not 1086) found in Scandinavia. They have the particular merit of being a very large sample, from which worth-while statistics can be calculated type by type, as well as globally. For the small mints they offer evidence of far better statistical quality in that respect than the English single finds do. A mint with a one per cent share of the national output could be expected to yield 170 specimens; yet there are plenty of mints which worked regularly through a series of different types, and which contributed in total fewer than 20 specimens to the sample. Torksey, for example, contributes only 7 coins to the Scandinavian statistics, of five different types: if more had been found, they would certainly have been retained in the Scandinavian collections. The English evidence conflicts, for there are two Torksey coins among our sample of 588. One must assume that that is mere random variability unless a case can be argued on other grounds.

For the top ten mints, statistical variability in the English sample should be much less of a problem. If there are any differences in the proportions, as between the English and the Scandinavian evidence, it will be natural to begin by thinking that the English evidence is more first-hand, or closer to source, and is likely to be the more reliable. (But both samples escape the uncertainty of differences in average output per die between large mints and small mints in so far as they are based on counting coins, not dies.)

The Scandinavian material, essentially the systematic collections of Stockholm and Copenhagen combined, will exclude a certain number of die-duplicates, and may therefore be slightly biassed against the larger mints. A much bigger uncertainty concerning its randomness is the question whether the coins carried to Scandinavia were drawn from England at large, or with a slight bias towards Winchester (as seems to have been the case) or towards the large ports of eastern England.

Further, the outflows from England to Scandinavia dwindled away after 1042, to almost nothing by 1086, or at least their survival among the Scandinavian finds dwindled away, perhaps because of re-minting in Denmark. Thus, in comparing them with the English material we are not comparing like with like. Provided there were no shift in the relative importance of the mints before and after 1042, it would not matter so far as answering the present question is concerned. But there are shifts. To make a fair comparison, one needs either to weight the Norman material from Scandinavia so as to match its proportion among the English single finds or, probably better, strip the coins of William I out of the English sample, even at the price of being left with a smaller total.

There are only 71 and 146 coins of William I in the Danish and Swedish systematic collections respectively, and those of Edward the Confessor are far fewer than those from before 1042. The proportions among the English finds are likely to give a more accurate view of the changing levels of activity in the English monetary economy (which may or may not correspond with the changing levels of mint output).

	In England	In Scandinavia
*c.*973—1042	358 = 100	15,650 = 100
1042—1066	186 = 52	1,321 = 8
1066—1086	99 = 28	217 = 1.4
Sample	643	17,188

The difference is dramatic.

There were changes in the ranking order of the big mints if we compare the periods *c.*973—1066 and 1066—1086. Among the Anglo-Saxon coins the top ten mints account for much the same proportions in England and in Scandinavia, with no percentage differences worth commenting on. After 1066 the statistics are more variable, and one should hesitate to attach too much significance to the discrepancies. The heavy representation of the Winchester mint, even in Scandinavia, is intriguing. The under-representation of York may reflect the disruption caused by the harrying of the North.

	Before 1066		After 1066	
London	4,216	= 25%(24%)	42	= 19%(23%)
Lincoln	1,746	= 10%(14%)	19	= 9%(6%)
York	1,667	= 10%(9%)	3	= 1%(5%)
Stamford	682	= 4%(5%)	2	= 1%(0%)
Thetford	584	= 3%(4%)	8	= 4%(10%)
Winchester	1,019	= 6%(5%)	28	= 13%(0%)
Canterbury	435	= 3%(3%)	11	= 5%(6%)
Chester	507	= 3%(4%)	1	= 0%(0%)
Norwich	415	= 2%(3%)	10	= 5%(0%)
Wallingford	164	= 1%(1%)	2	= 1%(10%)
Ten mints	11,399	= 67%(71%)	126	= 58%(65%)
Sample	16,971	(415)	217	(81)

Q.5. What are the implications of London's dominant role in minting?

In the context of a controlled currency (see Q.3), London's position as England's wealthiest city, and a port engaged in foreign trade, generated a strong demand for moneyers' services. That is reflected in the large number of moneyers who worked there, and in their lion's share of the kingdom's mint-output.

Coins minted in London very quickly became dispersed throughout the Thames valley and the midlands, and to a lesser extent in Wessex, East Anglia, and the North (see Map 2). Because of the system of frequent type-changes, the average life of a coin, throughout the period *c.*973—1086, was probably five years or less. The regional mingling of coins from different mint-towns in our random sample of stray losses necessarily happened within that sort of time-span. That implies monetary transfers (for whatever reasons) between the shires of southern England on a large scale. No doubt there were also numerous local transactions, which involved London coins, for example, being used within London. These are less visible on the map of single finds.

Of our 685 single finds, no fewer than 76 are coins found in (modern) London, thanks to assiduous recording by Peter Stott and to the co-operation of numerous individuals. The total 76 does not tell us anything precise, but it constitutes a useful random sample of the coins that were circulating in London, drawn from a dozen different sites. Out of 47 coins of which the mints can be identified, 34 per cent are of the London mint (cf. the national average of 24 per cent), 15 per cent from Lincoln, and 11 per cent from Canterbury. There are two coins each (4 per cent) from Nottingham, Hertford, Winchester, Dover, and Lewes, and singletons from Chichester, Colchester, Derby, Hastings, Leicester, Lympne, Northampton, Shaftesbury, and Thetford. York is unrepresented, and the east-coast ports generally are under-represented. The Channel ports, on the other hand, are well represented.

We do not know how much of the national stock of currency was concentrated in London. Wealthy merchants will have held, on average, a substantial working capital in the form of coin. In 1018 the citizens of London paid £10,500 in tribute to Cnut, in addition to the £72,000 levied nationally. The 66 per cent of coins from other mints found in London will reflect a large reciprocal movement of money from the provinces to London, much of it no doubt in a commercial context.

Q.6. What was the approximate scale of the currency, and how does it relate to the 'danegeld' tributes in the reign of Æthelred II?

It is certain that the late Anglo-Saxon coinage was produced, in aggregate, from many thousands of dies, and that on average each die was capable, if fully used, of striking thousands of coins. Over a period of a hundred years, many tens of millions of coins were minted.

Calculations have been made using the corpus of coins of the Lincoln mint, in combination with the Scandinavian sample. For each of the 16 types which were valid between *c.*973 and *c.*1050, the Lincoln material allows us to make a statistical estimate of the proportion of the original output represented by the known dies—in effect, a rough estimate of the total number of dies originally used at Lincoln. In some types, most of the Lincoln dies are already known, and there is not much room for statistical uncertainty. In others the sample is less complete and the estimate correspondingly more open to error.

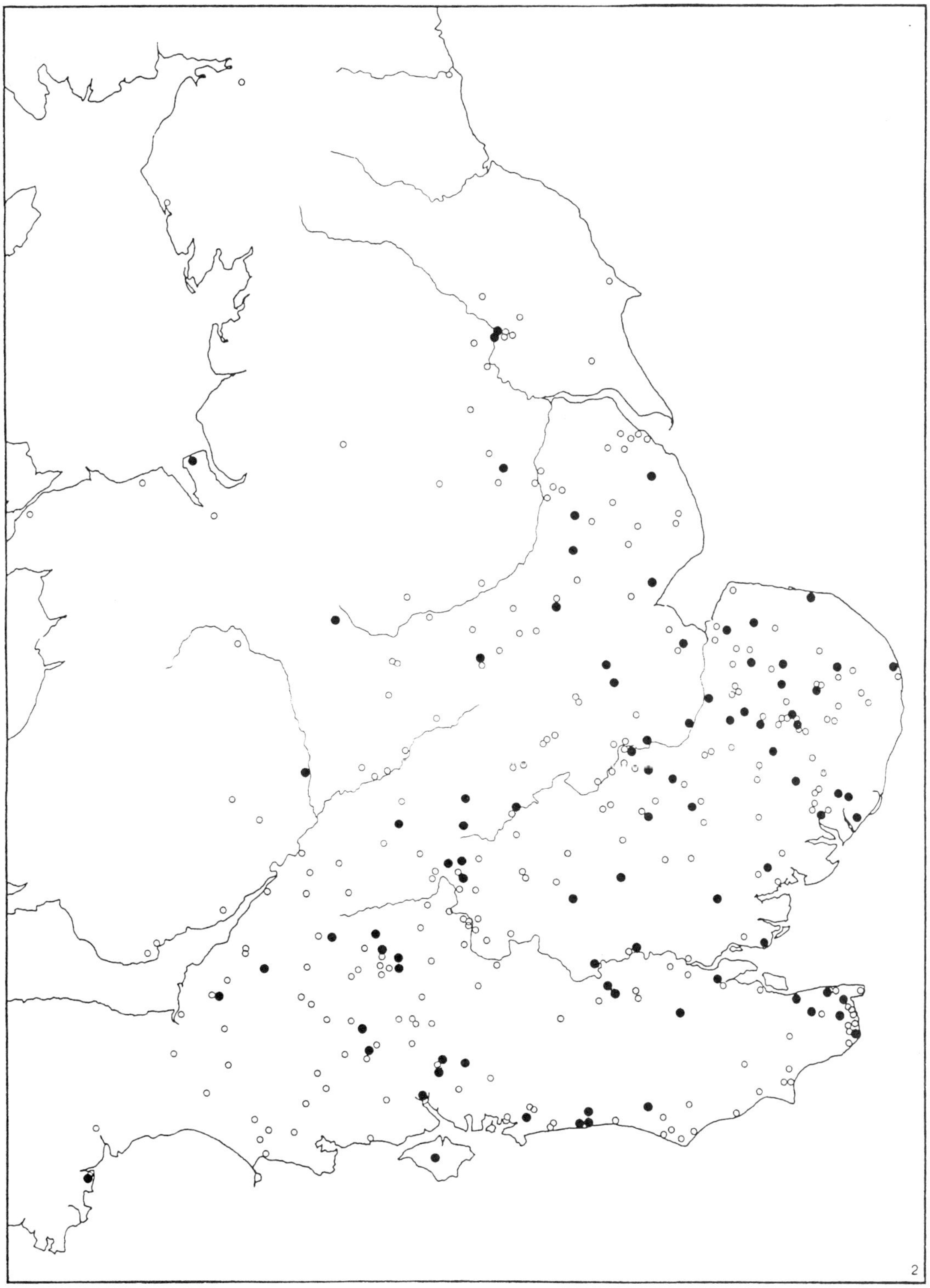

MAP 2. Coins minted in London.

The Lincoln estimates are next combined with the Scandinavian statistics, type by type, simply by calculating the percentage of Lincoln coins in the Scandinavian sample. The total number of 'Lincoln equivalent dies' (this skirts around the uncertainty whether the average output of a die was the same at Lincoln and elsewhere) originally used to produce the type (and, indeed, the total numbers for each and every mint) are easily derived, by calculating

$$\varkappa = L \times \frac{SC}{SC_L}$$

where L is the Lincoln estimate, SC is the number of coins in the Scandinavian sample, and SC_L is the number of Lincoln coins in that sample.

If the checking of the Lincoln material for die-duplication were incomplete or inaccurate, the errors would carry over into the results. For most of the 16 types, this is very unlikely to introduce major errors.

As regards the global total, the accuracy of the results is dependent on the Lincoln coins being randomly represented in Scandinavia. In so far as there was a substantially separate circulation area in the north of England, the regional origins of the money leaving England for Scandinavia may distort the results of the calculations significantly—and differently from type to type. This is the weakest link in the whole chain of reasoning. When Yvonne Harvey's corpus of the Winchester mint is published, if one substitutes Winchester for Lincoln, the figures will no doubt vary.

$$\varkappa = W \times \frac{SC}{SC_W}$$

One could substitute any other mint for which a corpus, reliably checked for die-duplication, was available, but a small mint would be unsuitable because the small numbers involved would introduce unacceptably wide margins of statistical variation.

One could also make a rough judgement about English mint-output by combining the Lincoln-based and the Winchester-based results, along the lines that 'the truth probably lies somewhere in between'. For types where the results were reasonably close, combining them might increase one's confidence in their general historical reliability.

The English single finds provide in principle an entirely independent alternative to the Scandinavian sample for the purposes of making the calculation.

$$\varkappa = L \times \frac{EF}{EF_L}$$

Unfortunately, with only six or seven hundred, there are still far too few of them for the resulting figures to be precise, type by type.

The step in the argument from numbers of dies to numbers of coins is very speculative. We know from fourteenth-century official records of the London mint that the average output of a reverse die could vary very widely, and that even annual averages vary widely, around a long-term average of 15,000-20,000. The conventional multiplier of 10,000 applied to the Anglo-Saxon statistics yields as sensible a guess as one can hope for, but it is very much a guess.

For the general historian addressing the question of the part played by coinage in eleventh-century England, estimates of ten or twenty million coins issued within a six-year validity period may seem to provide over-kill. Even if they were reduced to a half or a third, they would still be a strong argument for the extent of the monetary sector of the economy, especially when combined with the fact that coinage was diffused so rapidly between the regions of southern England.

Comparisons between the totals for one type and another should be treated with caution, in so far as the (national) average output of a die may have varied quite widely *between types*. Only if we assume that the accidental loss-rate was steadily related to the scale of the currency can we avoid that uncertainty: at least, the number of English single finds type by type should reflect numbers of coins, not of dies.

It seems to be a matter of common sense that the moneyers would not have gone to the trouble and expense of acquiring numerous dies that were, from their point of view, identical, if fewer would have served. For the more active mints or moneyers there is a presumption of sorts that dies were fully used. At the small mints, however, some or all of the dies may have been little used because demand was over-estimated. That would tend to bring down the overall average, but not dramatically if the top ten mints already account for two-thirds of the national output.

In both the Scandinavian sample and the English single finds, differences in average die-output between types and also between large and small mints will (as already mentioned) be automatically discounted, because the proportions will reflect the number of coins available to be exported or lost, not the number of dies. The question can in principle be studied by comparing corpus-based die-estimates for large and small mints with the corresponding proportions in the samples. Axbridge, Watchet, and Warwick are among the mints for which this has been attempted.

Next, there is a blurring of the arguments because the volume of mint-output and the scale of the English currency are not identical. Losses whether by export or for any other reason will reduce the currency. A study which has been made of the List hoard suggests that there was heavy wastage in the Long Cross type. Millions of Anglo-Saxon coins, certainly, were exported to Scandinavia. The sampling procedures we are using are designed to measure mint-output, and as such they are immune to wastage because they are based on counting dies. Measuring the English currency can in some centuries be approached by assessing wastage-rates from the age-structure of hoards. In a period of frequent and thorough recoinages, that is virtually impossible.

Conversely, if recoinage became less thorough after *c.*1050 (which is debateable: see Q.37), the currency may have exceeded the scale of the current issue.

The following table shows various steps in the argument, in order to give an idea of reliability, namely the number of Lincoln reverse dies recorded by Mossop, the original total of Lincoln dies by statistical estimation, the known dies as a proportion of output (a/b), the number of specimens in the Scandinavian sample, and the ratio of these specimens (x 100) to estimated dies. One may judge that the figures are at their most reliable in Types 4-18.

	Type	a	b	c	d	e
		Known rev. dies	Estimated rev. dies	a/b (%)	Coins in sample	d/b x 100 (%)
1	Small Cross	46	82	56	6	7
2	Hand	33	77	43	14	18
3	Crux	127	198	64	63	32
4	Long Cross	183	208	88	139	67
5	Helmet	80	105	76	59	56
6	Last Small Cross	277	370	75	224	61
7	Quatrefoil	276	378	73	236	62
8	Helmet	186	219	85	271	123
9	Short Cross	175	194	90	262	135
10	Jewel Cross	91	126	72	120	95
11	Fleur-de-lis	81	116	70	87	75
12	Arm & sceptre	51	72	71	64	89
13	Pacx	52	81	64	49	60
14	Radiate	51	62	82	54	87
15	Trefoil	59	88	67	25	28
16	Short Cross	21	25	83	24	96
17	Expanding cross	61	76	80	21	28
18	Helmet	34	56	61	11	20
19	Sovereign	24	73	33	5	7
20	Hammer Cross	44	68	65	4	6
21	Facing bust	24	42	57	1	2
22	Pyramids	14	23	60	4	17
23	Pax	14	16	87	0	-

Source: Mossop, Table 4; 'Continuity and Change', Appendix 4.

Because it is possible, indeed probable, that coin left England for Scandinavia separately or to some extent separately from York, Lincoln, and the south of England, there may (as already mentioned) be some distortion of the north/south ratios in the medium term. An alternative approach is a complete die-study (for all mints) of a particular type. This is possible for Harold I's Fleur-de-lis type. The results, which are set out and discussed below (in Part 3, Section 11), in fact reveal no significant bias.

According to the *Anglo-Saxon Chronicle*, it was in 991, following the ravaging of Ipswich and the death of Ealdorman Brihtnoth at Maldon, that the decision was taken for the first time to pay tribute to the Danes. Archbishop Sigeric advised the action, and the payment was £10,000. The Danes returned for more, and were, according to the *Chronicle*, paid £16,000 (£22,000?) in 994, £24,000 in 1002, £30,000 (£36,000?) in 1007, £48,000 in 1012, and £72,000 paid in 1018, plus a further £10,500 paid by the citizens of London. This crescendo of extortion was equivalent to many million silver pennies—paid probably by weight rather than tale, and equivalent to at least 2.4 million coins in 991, and subsequently 4 million, 6 million, 8 million, 12 million, and eventually perhaps as many as 25 million pennies in 1018.

Assuming that actual pennies of the current type were collected as geld, it is natural to ask how large a dent was made in the currency of England. Estimates are available for the numbers of dies used in each validity-period, but the average output of a die (10,000 pennies?) is only a guess. There is also the possibility that some tributes were paid partly in obsolete coin. And it is not always certain into which validity-period a tribute fell, because the dating of the type is subject to margins of uncertainty. All that said, the payment of perhaps 8 million pence in 1007, out of an estimated total of 12 million 'Helmet' coins (*c.*1003—1009) made very substantial inroads, for the first time, into the currency. Should we expect it to have left visible signs in the regional circulation of coinage, as revealed by single finds? If our dates are accurate, there will have been three or four years of the 'Helmet' validity-period before the tribute was collected, during which stray losses will have accumulated normally. The practical question is whether there is any difference in the ranking of the mints between the Scandinavian sample and the English single finds (see Part 3, Section 5). The tribute of 1012, which is virtually certain to have fallen within the Last Small Cross validity-period, is less problematic because of the very large scale of that issue. With Cnut's massive tribute of £72,000 imposed before peace was agreed, one wonders what was the destination of the coins collected. Much of it could have stayed in the king's treasure.

If we consider that the much smaller mintages of Edward the Confessor's reign seem not to have modified either the ranking of the mints or the regional patterns of circulations noticeably, it may be that the scale of the currency before 1042 was far in excess of what was needed for normal purposes of exchange, and that many of the coins functioned mainly as a store of wealth.

Q.7. Where did all the silver come from?

Silver in the eleventh century was more valuable, gramme for gramme, than gold today, in what it would buy. It was carefully recycled. The regular recoinages of the eleventh century re-used the same national stock of silver time after time. Coinage, of course, had to be of silver, with an intrinsic value, and the possession of the necessary stock was a constraint on how many coins could be made.

A million Anglo-Saxon or Norman pennies required between a tonne and 1.5 tonnes of silver. They could easily have been produced, we may be sure, from a hundred dies. The Reform type, introduced by Eadgar in *c*.973 and continued by Edward the Martyr and by Æthelred II until *c*.979, is estimated to have been struck from a thousand dies. The Hand types (Types 2A and B) which followed used an estimated three thousand dies, and the Crux type, four thousand. From a peak of four and a half thousand in Cnut's Quatrefoil type, the quantities sank under Edward the Confessor to five hundred or even fewer.

Lincoln-based estimates using the Scandinavian sample

Type	*Dies*				
1	1,031	5	1,217	11	1,224
2A	2,055	6	4,152	12	601
2B	1,200	7	4,652	13	512
3	4,072	8	2,239	14	477
4	1,828	9	1,438	15	705
		10	868	16	193

It seems evident from these figures that recycling is not the whole story. The English currency was not a closed system. Even when we remind ourselves, as we should, that the average output of a die may have varied considerably from type to type, it is beyond reasonable doubt that large amounts of silver were being added to the coinage system up until *c*.1020, and that there were severe losses thereafter.

By putting questions to the Scandinavian finds (in the same way that we are here putting questions to the English finds) we can discover that millions of Anglo-Saxon pennies were exported to the Northern Lands. Paradoxically, the outflows from England, whether as Danegeld or as a trading deficit, seem to have been at their greatest in the decades 980-1020, just when the English stock of currency was nevertheless expanding. How was it replenished and increased?

We should consider three general hypotheses. First, that the English stock of silver was only partly invested in coinage, and that plate, church treasure, etc. could be down-loaded into the money supply if the choice was pressing. As a comment on that, one may add that we have estimated differences, from type to type, of the order of magnitude of ten tonnes. Secondly, that new silver was added to the currency stock by mining. The same comment applies; and one might expect corollaries, if the hypothesis were correct, of busy mints in the vicinity of the Mendips or the Peak District. That does not happen. Thirdly, that England had a balance-of-payments surplus in its trade with the Low Countries or the lower Rhinelands. Foreign coins flowing into England are largely invisible to us, because they were compulsorily reminted. The corollary of busy minting at London and the east coast ports is met by the statistics—although it has to be admitted that the share taken by the east-coast ports does not increase and decrease in the way that the model might lead one to expect. Four per cent of our single finds are foreign coins, which somehow escaped the net, either because they were lost soon after they were brought ashore, or in a district where there was no nearby mint, or at a time of confusion. If these single finds are random in respect of being foreign, i.e. their owners did not examine them and choose to lose them preferentially (and they are made of valuable silver) they imply a considerable population of foreign coins at large. Their evidence is carefully examined below (Q.33), leading to the conclusion that the figure of four per cent gives a much exaggerated impression.

The three general hypotheses are not mutually exclusive. Each may have made a contribution to the balance-sheet as we observe it, —and in different proportions at different dates. One's judgement is that inflows of foreign coin are by far the major contributor throughout.

The prolific Rammelsberg silver mines in the Harz mountains of Germany which first attracted mention just before 970 were boosting the Empire's stock of silver at exactly the time when the English stock of silver, too, was growing. Whether England benefitted, and if so by what transfer mechanisms, are intriguing questions. There may, for example, have been a thriving export trade in English wool. If so (and it is pure conjecture) one would have to say in the long perspective that it was a demand-led trade, led by the availability of plentiful silver on the Continent.

Scientific analysis of the metal contents of the coins might help to demonstrate the sources of the silver. Of trace elements and minor constituents of the alloy, gold is the most reliable, because it survived the recycling processes, including cupellation, in almost exactly the same ratio to silver. The measurement of gold contents shows that there seem to have been substantial changes in the composition of the stock of coinage metal in southern England at a date soon after Eadgar's reform. Connecting this with the German evidence is not simple. Analytical work on the Otto-Adelheid pfennigs has revealed many complexities. Any correlation with Rammelsberg will remain problematic until more work has been done on the German coins. In particular, a systematic programme of lead-isotope analysis of both English and German coins both before and after 973 is needed.

Meanwhile, a programme of analyses of minor constituents by Metcalf and Northover has shown that the recycling of the English coinage every few years by type changes did not result in progressive and thorough homogenization (as might have been expected), at least until the 1050s.

Q.8. How are the single finds distributed through the period c.973—1086? Are there any sudden peaks, or longer-term trends?

Between *c.*973 and 1086 there were 31 or 32 successive coin types, from every one of which there are some single finds. With 627 attributable finds, the number from each type is frequently less than 20, and is too low to be free from the uncertainties of statistical variation. We are constrained, in trying to interpret the variations decade by decade, by margins of uncertainty which may exceed the variation. In these circumstances, it is difficult to know what one should be looking for, until one has begun to find it. One needs a model against which to try to fit the statistics. But what pattern should one expect? Might there have been an equal number of accidental losses each year, subject only to statistical variability? (In order to test that hypothesis, the figures should be processed so that coin types which are thought to have had a validity period of six years can be compared on level terms with those issued for only two or three). Or might the pattern of losses have matched the curve of mint-output?, —or the scale of the currency?, —or good and bad harvests?, —or general levels of prosperity? What should one be looking for?

On an annualized basis the long-term trend seems to be fairly steady. The Crux and Long Cross types, it is true, are well above the trend-line, but the massive mint-output in Last Small Cross and Quatrefoil is not reflected in the numbers of single finds, nor is the decline after *c.*1020. Thus the broad pattern tends to rule out the hypothesis that the numbers of stray losses are proportional to the scale of the currency.

Certain types fall below expectation (on the hypothesis of a steady loss-rate), among which one may note Æthelred II's Second Hand and Helmet types and William I's Canopy and Sword types.

Of the types which seem to be over-represented, Cnut's Short Cross is the most remarkable, with 42 pennies plus 12 fractions. An inspection of the list shows that these 54 coins are widely scattered, with no unusual regional concentration to boost the statistics. The proportion of finds from the well-represented urban sites of London, Lincoln, and York is in line with the proportion over the whole period. In short, there is no obvious explanation.

The numbers of finds of each type (pennies plus fractions) are as follows. The percentages show fractions as a proportion of whole coins, and are placed in parentheses where the number of fractions is so small as to make the percentage figure statistically unreliable.

		%
1. Reform	24 + 10	42
2A. First Hand	20 + 9	45
2B. Second Hand	12 + 3	(25)
3. Crux	33 + 8	25
4. Long Cross	40 + 7	18
5. Helmet	14 + 0	(0)
6. Last Small Cross	20 + 2	(10)
7. Quatrefoil	18 + 4	22
8. Pointed Helmet	18 + 2	(11)
9. Short Cross	42 + 12	29
10. Jewel Cross	16 + 5	31
11. Fleur-de-lis	8 + 3	(38)
12. Arm and Sceptre	6 + 4	66
13. Pacx	9 + 4	44
14. Radiate/Small Cross	5 + 1	(20)
15. Trefoil-Quadrilateral	14 + 2	(14)
16. Short Cross (Small Flan)	20 + 3	(15)
17. Expanding Cross	29 + 8	28
18. Helmet	18 + 3	(17)
19. Sovereign	13 + 0	(0)
20. Hammer Cross	11 + 5	45
21. Facing Bust	11 + 8	73
22. Pyramids	11 + 5	45
23. Pax	6 + 3	(50)
24. Profile/Cross Fleury	9 + 0	(0)
25. Bonnet	12 + 0	(0)
26. Canopy	2 + 1	(50)
27. Two Sceptres	8 + 1	(12)
28. Two Stars	13 + 2	(15)
29. Sword	4 + 2	(50)
30. Profile/Cross + Trefoil	18 + 5	28
31. Paxs	14 + 2	(14)

Q.9. Were stray losses more or fewer in troubled times?

Occasionally one can notice a cluster of coin-hoards all concealed at much the same date, at a time of invasion or warfare. Most of the hoards that were buried in the ground, year by year, were safely recovered by their owners. Those that were permanently lost through some unknown accident or death were doubtless a tiny minority.

Stray losses behave in accordance with a completely different set of rules. One imagines that they were most numerous in settled and prosperous times, because monetary transactions were correspondingly more numerous. In troubled times, buying and selling may have been hampered, and there may even have been fewer accidental losses.

That is what one would expect. Of course, single finds may not all be stray losses. One should therefore be willing to keep an open mind about the data-base of single finds, and test the question wherever opportunity offers.

There are six or seven examples where a pair of very similar coins have been found at the same place, and published as single finds. They may very well reflect a part or the whole of a small hoard, and if so they do not properly belong in the list. They will confuse our interpretation, but there are so few of them that overall it is not a practical problem.

Thus, there are three Profile/Cross Fleury coins from York, from the excavations at the Minster in 1970. All three are from the site of a Roman barracks, and from Phase 6D of the centurion's quarter. In other words, they certainly constitute or reflect a hoard.

The Norwich (Magdalen Street) excavations of 1987 yielded two coins of Edward the Confessor, both of the heavy phase of the Expanding Cross type. When their contexts are published, it should become clear whether (as seems probable) they belong together. Two coins of William I's Profile/Cross and Trefoils type were both found at East or West Bradenham, Norfolk, in October 1994. The type is a relatively plentiful one among our single finds, and the coins are of different mints, but again the chances seem high that they belong together. Similarly, two London coins of Æthelred's Long Cross type found at Hangleton, near Littlehampton, Sussex may reflect a mini-hoard. See also two coins found in the neighbourhood of Lewes in 1874, of Edward the Confessor and Harold II, and two Bonnet type coins of William I found in Wallingford before 1894. From the view-point of the monetary historian, mini-hoards have their special interest. They may be under-appreciated just because the circumstances of finding leave room for doubt. And they may, of course, originally have been larger than two or three coins, witness the story of the Alfriston hoard, found in instalments. When the owner of a garden was shown some coins that were found there in 1843, he remembered that two others had been found in the same garden in 1830. By sieving all the garden soil he eventually recovered about sixty coins (see Q.37).

The obvious test-case à propos troubled times is the harrying of the north by William I. In 1068 and again in 1069 there were risings against the Normans, in and around the city of York, and in Northumbria beyond Tees. They were followed by Swein Estridsson's attempted invasion, with a base in Yorkshire. William's reprisals amounted to a deliberate attempt to ruin the population of northern England. Domesday Book shows that many districts were still derelict, seventeen years later. It is because the reprisals were so extreme that the harrying of the north is a good test-case for the monetary historian. Yorkshire bore the brunt of the harrying, which extended however to Cheshire, Shropshire, Staffordshire, and Derbyshire.

How, if at all, do the single finds reflect these events? Are the first two types of William I, which were issued during the years *c.*1066—1070, particularly plentiful as single finds in Yorkshire (or elsewhere in the counties which were laid waste by William)? The three Profile/Cross Fleury coins from York Minster, mentioned above, are certainly a hoard, and should not be considered as single finds, even though they were published as such. And hoards, as we have already said, behave in accordance with a completely different set of rules. From *c.*1068/9 there are four more York hoards, from High Ousegate, 1704, Baile Hill, 1802, Jubbergate 1845, and Bishophill, 1882, as well as the Minster hoard of 1970. There is a single find of a Bonnet type penny from Wentbridge, in the West Riding.

As there are at least 14 single finds of Profile/Cross Fleury and Bonnet coins from the rest of England, it seems safe to answer our question by saying that the harrying of the North did not cause an unusually large number of stray losses. It deserves to be considered whether the last types of Edward the Confessor were still in circulation in Yorkshire, and should be counted as potential losses from the years 1066-70, but as the single finds include so very few current coins, and as the hoards mentioned above are solidly of William's first two types, the possibility can safely be disregarded.

For the whole of William's reign, the numbers of single finds from York itself and from the rest of Yorkshire are below-average (in relation to the totals for *c.*973—1066) compared with the rest of England.

Q.10 How evenly are the stray losses distributed through England? How accurately is their pattern likely to reflect the situation at the time?

Metal detectorists, like other people, are encouraged by success. If a field produces two or three Anglo-Saxon pennies, they will persist in searching in that field. The resulting distribution-pattern of finds, viewed on a wider scale, will be uneven because of this enthusiasm factor. More broadly again, some counties have been better served than others, and there are some regions where the soil conditions or the topography are less favourable towards the recovery of single finds.

Archaeologists, in pointing out the above irregularities, have sometimes allowed themselves to imagine that they had raised an insuperable objection to the analysis of single finds as a random sample. The concentration of finds in the east and south-east of the country, and their scarcity in the west country and the west midlands has been used as an argument, they say, that an inter-regional money economy was driven by trade across the Channel and across the North Sea: might not that conclusion be unsafe?

The random principle can be rescued to some extent. There has been plenty of searching activity in the south-west and the west midlands, which has led to the recovery of large numbers of Roman and late medieval or modern coins, but virtually no Anglo-Saxon coins. The absence of the latter is to that extent a particularity of the evidence.

The distribution of single finds over the country as a whole (Map 1) will not be perfectly even, and there may be some bias in favour of the east and the south-east, but as evidence that the use of coinage fanned out from the Channel and North Sea coasts, and dwindled westwards, there is no risk that the conclusion could be overturned.

Far greater uncertainty attaches to the probable unevenness of single finds, in terms of coins per hectare, between town and country. This problem is addressed by Q.11.

Not only do single finds thin out westwards, a pattern which may be generated by various factors, ancient and modern, but there is also an interesting tendency for a higher proportion of the find-places in more westerly regions to be towns.

There is a method of analysis which is immune to the ambiguities of topographical variation in the recovery rate of eleventh-century coins. Regression analysis (Q.17 below) relies on the proportions, e.g. of coins from different mints, locally. Its conclusions are framed in terms of regional differences in those proportions. But it still does not directly address the question under discussion.

For a possible way round the difficulty, see the discussion of Q.12.

Q.11. If, at any given moment, the stock of currency was concentrated in the towns, would the evidence of stray finds allow us to detect the imbalance?

We really have no way of judging, from empirical evidence, whether the balance of the currency between town and country was 30:70 or 70:30.

Detailed die-studies cannot help, since of the thousands of coins struck from any particular die, some will have ended up in the town, and some in the country.

If there are any corollaries or implications of the balance (e.g. 30:70 or 70:30) it is difficult to see how they might be detected in the pattern of stray losses.

Where we have a good assemblage of excavation coins from a town—whether a shire town or a big port—large enough to judge which mints are most plentifully represented, we may be able to compare the mint-composition of that sample with what is found round about, in the town's shire or in its hinterland. The town's own mint may supply anything from a quarter to three-quarters of the coins circulating in the town. That tends to prove (particularly when the proportion was small) that there was a brisk interchange of currency *between towns*. The mint-composition of coins from the countryside seems usually to be close to what is found in the nearby town, and that in turn tends to prove that *town and country were integrated*, in their monetary circulation. But so far as one can see, either of these situations could equally well be consonant with either a 70:30 or a 30:70 distribution.

It would be thought-provoking if one could say that in a particular town, 40 per cent of the coins were locally minted, but that in the surrounding region the corresponding figure was, as it might be, 30 per cent or 50 per cent. To be sure of the figures, to within plus or minus 2 or 3 per cent, much larger samples would be needed than are currently available.

There is an intriguing clue in the composition of some of the hoards. At Winchester, for example, single finds from the excavations show that only about one-fifth of the coins circulating in the city were minted there; yet it is possible for a hoard to be over-weight in Winchester coins. If a merchant had visited a moneyer in Winchester and had come away with a batch of new coins, all by that moneyer, which he had then buried together with what other coins he possessed, the position would be understandable. But if the Winchester coins are by more than one moneyer, they will tend to suggest that there was an 'inner circle' of merchants visiting Winchester, who each perhaps called on the services of a different moneyer—and then did business with each other (Q.35). The mingling of coins by different Winchester moneyers might then be revealed by a hoard such as that from Stockbridge Down (Part 3, section 22). Winchester is a good starting point from which to consider this argument because of the single finds from the excavations which can be used as a yardstick.

There is a much larger hoard which is similarly weighted, with Chester coins, which provides statistically more secure evidence; but we have no direct evidence to set alongside it from a good-sized assemblage of single finds of the general composition of the currency in Chester. The details are discussed further in Q.36.

Q.12. Is the regional distribution of the stock of currency likely to distort our assessment of relative mint-output (Q.3—4)?

If we divide the country into eastern and western halves by an imaginary north-south line running immediately to the east of Southampton (leaving Winchester in the eastern half of the country, but Southampton in the west) and northwards roughly through Newcastle-upon-Tyne, there are far fewer single finds from the western half—117 mint-attributable English pennies against 471 from the eastern half. London is still the top mint among the western finds, with 16 per cent (against 23 per cent over-all). The top ten mints nationally take 56 per cent in the West (against 68 per cent). Superficially, therefore, it appears that there was a westwards drift of currency from the places where it was minted (the big east-coast mints) towards the regions where it was needed: minting was not matched to regional needs, probably because foreign silver was compulsorily reminted, mostly at the port of entry. (Today, money is moved about the country, and matched to the convenience of the public, by the clearing banks.) That is superficially the situation, but the figures, as we shall see, are to some extent misleading.

Because there are so many fewer finds from the west, and because more than half of those found there had entered the region from the east, one may wonder whether the mints in the western half of England, and perhaps especially the small western mints, are not under-represented in the samples as a whole—and possibly even more so in the Scandinavian sample, since it was eastern England which looked across the sea towards Scandinavia.

One could in theory check the results for the over-all sample against a corpus of dies for one or more small westerly mints, in order to see whether the survival-rate per die was out of line. But that procedure is very unsafe because average die-output may well have been lower at small westerly mints, and also because the margins of statistical uncertainty attaching to the output of small mints are unacceptable. If one assumed that average die-output was the same when in fact it was significantly lower, one would be led to the false conclusion that coins from western mints were under-represented, e.g. in the Scandinavian sample.

The broad composition of the currency, in terms of mints of origin, is quite different in east and west. In the west, 39 per cent of the single finds are from western mints, while 61 per cent have crossed the imaginary line to enter the western half of the country. In the east, on the other hand, 91 per cent of the finds are from eastern mints, and only 9 per cent are western.

If there were a persistent imbalance, visible as a westwards drift of currency, one imagines that money would have tended to accumulate in the west, and that the share of the national total taken by the western mints would have increased type by type. That does not happen, at least not as a longer-term trend.

There were no fewer than 45 mints in the western half of the country as defined,but they produced only a sixth to a quarter of the national output (Q.6). The variations are not large, as may be judged from the list by types:

	%		%
Reform	21	Short Cross	13
First Hand	26	Jewel Cross	19
Second Hand	24	Fleur-de-lis	18
Crux	19	Arm and Sceptre	23
Long Cross	24	Pacx	14
Helmet	18	Radiate	15
Last Small Cross	15	Trefoil Quad.	14
Quatrefoil	23	Short Cross	17
Helmet	17	Paxs	*c*.28

How could the bullion have been spirited back to the east, leaving no traces in the pattern of finds? Could local taxation have been followed by the secure transporting of treasure back to the east? From what we know in general about taxation and royal expenditure, it is hard to imagine that this could provide the necessary explanation. Could the western regions have been spending money overseas, importing goods at the price of a persistent balance-of-trade regional deficit? Again, that makes no obvious sense as a model of the regional economy.

If it is not possible to envisage invisible counter-flows on a sufficient scale, perhaps we should assume, at least as a working hypothesis, a rough balance.

On that assumption, the best available answer to the question under discussion is that the appearance of westwards drift may after all be misleading. It is crystal-clear that millions of coins crossed the line. But is it clear that more crossed in a westerly direction? The figures rehearsed above are proportions. Perhaps we should try to accept that 61 per cent, converted into actual numbers of coins, could be roughly equal to 9 per cent, namely x coins. That could be the case if the currency in the eastern half of the country were sufficiently larger than that in the west—specifically 6.8 times as large (Fig. 1).

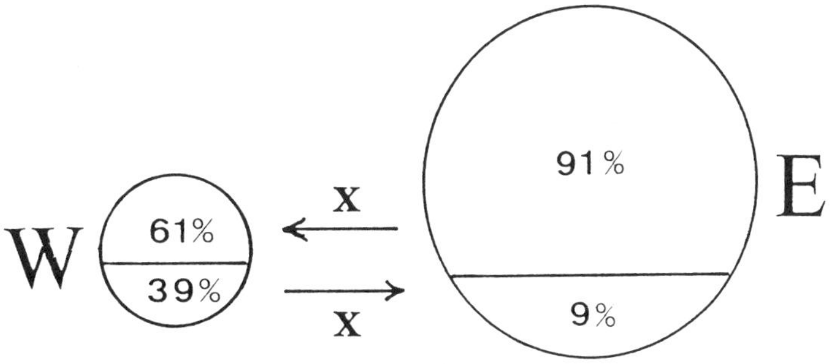

FIG. 1. A steady-state model of currency transfers between the eastern and western halves of England.

In our sample of single finds it is already five times as large; perhaps the recovery rate of casual losses has been sufficiently higher in the east to make up the difference.

Let us therefore think of a model in which the currency in the eastern half of the country was proportional in its volume to 10x, while that in the west was proportional to 1.6x (i.e. 100 over 61). A total of x coins from eastern mints dominate the western finds, but x coins from western mints are almost lost to view among the much more numerous eastern finds.

The situation on the ground will have been more complicated, because coins moved to and fro during the validity-period, possibly crossing our imaginary line several times before they were lost. The sample of stray finds represents an average of the east-west ratios as they were at *n* successive moments during the validity period. The figures in our model are for that reason at best approximate.

It is a natural conjecture that the Scandinavian sample might show a bias towards mints in the eastern half of England. In fact, the proportion of coins from western mints is marginally higher than among the English single finds—18.6 per cent against 15.0 per cent. One cannot exclude the possibility of a small degree of bias arising because coins of scarce mints were retained selectively in the Stockholm and Copenhagen systematic collections—or to speak more precisely, because coins of major mints were retained slightly less assiduously.

To summarize, we have so far built a model around the proposition that coins from the big eastern mints, and especially London, were carried westwards and north-westwards, often over long distances, and yet did not accumulate in the west, to judge from the share taken by the westerly mints at successive recoinages. To make the system balance, all that one needs to postulate is that the stock of currency in the western half of the country was far smaller than that in the east. But the model describes a closed system, whereas the reality was otherwise.

Relative mint output is (at least in principle) a matter of fact, practically free from the uncertainties of hypothesis. It is also a matter of fact, and roughly measurable, that millions of coins were lost to the English monetary system by outflows to Scandinavia, and that up until the 1030s the losses were somehow replaced or even more than replaced. If we postulate a healthy balance-of-payments surplus from foreign trade, we presumably need to look to the near continent as its source, and to envisage a triangular flow of bullion—outwards to Scandinavia, replenished inwards from the lower Rhinelands (as the only obvious region with a large silver supply to spend), and ultimately from Harz silver.

The inflows help to explain the activity of the east-coast mints. The outflows, by contrast, could have been partly collected through geld or tribute, and partly derive from the free play of trade. If tribute were levied on a hidal basis, it would potentially bear much more heavily on the correspondingly smaller stock of currency in the western half of the country. There is absolutely no reason to imagine that it had to be paid in coins of the local mint. But if money was taken out of the currency stock by taxation, in the western half of the country, it would allow us to envisage a westwards drift of currency in spite of the persistently small output of the western mints, and to interpret the single finds accordingly. In a steady-state model the scale of the westwards drift would be roughly equivalent to the scale of taxation on the region.

One can think of corollaries. If coins from the small western mints seem not to move eastwards, it may be mainly a matter of scale, but also (if there was some westwards drift) because they tended not to swim against the tide. In order to test whether such coins behaved differently merely because they were struck in small places, one would do well to compare them with coins from small eastern mints (see Q.16).

Another corollary might be that, through the payment of danegeld and tributes, coins from the small western mints may be relatively somewhat more plentiful in the Scandinavian sample than among the single finds from eastern England. Here we run into statistical imprecision, because the numbers among the English finds are so small.

Q.13. Do the coins of the first validity-period (c.973—c.979) show signs that Eadgar's reform required a settling-in period?

Eadgar's reform involved much more than the outward appearance of the coins. His preceding issue had been of somewhat debased alloy; the new type, as well as bearing his portrait and the name of the mint-place and the moneyer, was of exceptionally pure silver. Whereas the pre-reform coinages are relatively scarce as finds in southern England, from *c.*973 the number of mints in the south, and the volume of minting, seem to have been growing quite rapidly. There is an even more dramatic rise, type by type, in the numbers of coins found in Scandinavia, and a corresponding decline in hoards of English coins from Ireland and Scotland.

The regional patterns of minting of the Reform type under Eadgar (*c.*973-5) were significantly different from the corresponding patterns under Edward the Martyr (975-8), and indeed different from anything that happened subsequently. The reform was introduced, in other words, over a two- or three-year period.

The sample—of existing specimens of Eadgar's reform coins (*c.*973-5)—is too small for confidence: just over 300 coins from 200 pairs of dies, thus, very roughly, specimens from two-thirds of the dies that were ever used. Within that over-all assessment, however, certain mints are more fully known than others, in particular those that are well represented in the Chester and Oakham hoards. If we take the sample of *c.*200 (reverse) dies at face value, as a reasonable approximation, the leading mints, with percentages of the national output (this assumes that the average output of a die was comparable at the larger mints, but it probably understates the share of the national output taken by the top ten mints) were as follows: Winchester (13%), York (12%), Stamford (*c.*8%), London (6.5%), Northampton (5%), Canterbury (4%), Wilton (4%), Chester (*c.*4%), Oxford (3.5%), Ipswich (3.5%). The standard Scandinavian sample from which the Lincoln-based estimates are derived contains a paltry 68 specimens, too few to be statistically reliable except as regards broad groupings. The same ten mints take an identical 54 per cent of the total. The most conspicuous difference from the list of the top ten mints throughout the eleventh century (Q.3) is the poor showing of London, which was normally the premier mint of England by a long way. This is quite puzzling, and should attract the curiosity of general historians. Since one is reluctant to believe that the commercial importance of London was dramatically transformed inside fifteen years, it may be that there was some local prejudice, or reluctance of a social or political character, which had to be overcome (by evidence of the reform's success?).

The ranking of the mints in the Reform type under Eadgar shows other anomalies. Lincoln does not quite make it into the top ten. Thetford and Norwich are absent.

An analysis of the styles of die-cutting, i.e. of the work of the various die-cutting centres, makes the picture more secure. Winchester supplies at least 38 mints, and in most cases with all their dies. York (A) was the only other active centre. London, Canterbury, Stamford, Chester, Northampton, and Derby began their die-cutting work only later in the reform type. Norwich made a modest contribution at the beginning of the reform. Lincoln's contribution was minimal. In a word, the reform was originally planned and implemented from Winchester, with support on a very minor scale from York and elsewhere.

The list of Eadgar's mints, outside the top ten, includes a few that are conspicuously over-represented, such as Lympne. A number of mints which produced coins for Eadgar seem then to have been idle for the rest of the Reform type, presumably because of lack of demand for the moneyers' services.

There is, on the other hand, a considerable range of mints which very probably were inactive for the first two or three years, and only began to implement the reform under Edward Martyr. These include, for example, the minor Lincolnshire mints (and Lincoln itself increased its activity considerably under Edward). Where only one or two specimens from a mint have survived, a coin of Eadgar, of course, may yet surface.

So much for the minting-arrangements in *c.*973-5. What about the ways in which the Reform coins circulated in England? The dates of loss of the single finds cannot be judged precisely, but all or virtually all Reform coins will have been lost before *c.*980.

The Reform type, uniquely, was issued in the names of three successive kings. The numbers of single finds of each are: Eadgar, 9, Edward Martyr, 17, Æthelred II, 7.

The numbers of English single finds of the reform type now stand at 24, plus 10 fractions, which is not far behind the high totals recorded for Hand, Crux, and Long Cross.

The proportion from the western and eastern halves of the country, at 6:21, is close to the long-term average, and the general distribution of the finds (Map 3) is unexceptional. The distance that coins have travelled from their mints of origin appears to be no less than usual. The list of finds includes, for example, a Derby coin from Norfolk, a Wilton coin from Sussex, and a Lincoln coin from Herefordshire. On any simple test, therefore, the Reform type seems to have behaved in use in very much the same way as subsequent types.

There are three coins of Lympne in the sample, one found in London and two from Essex. From Lympne an old Roman road ran straight due north to

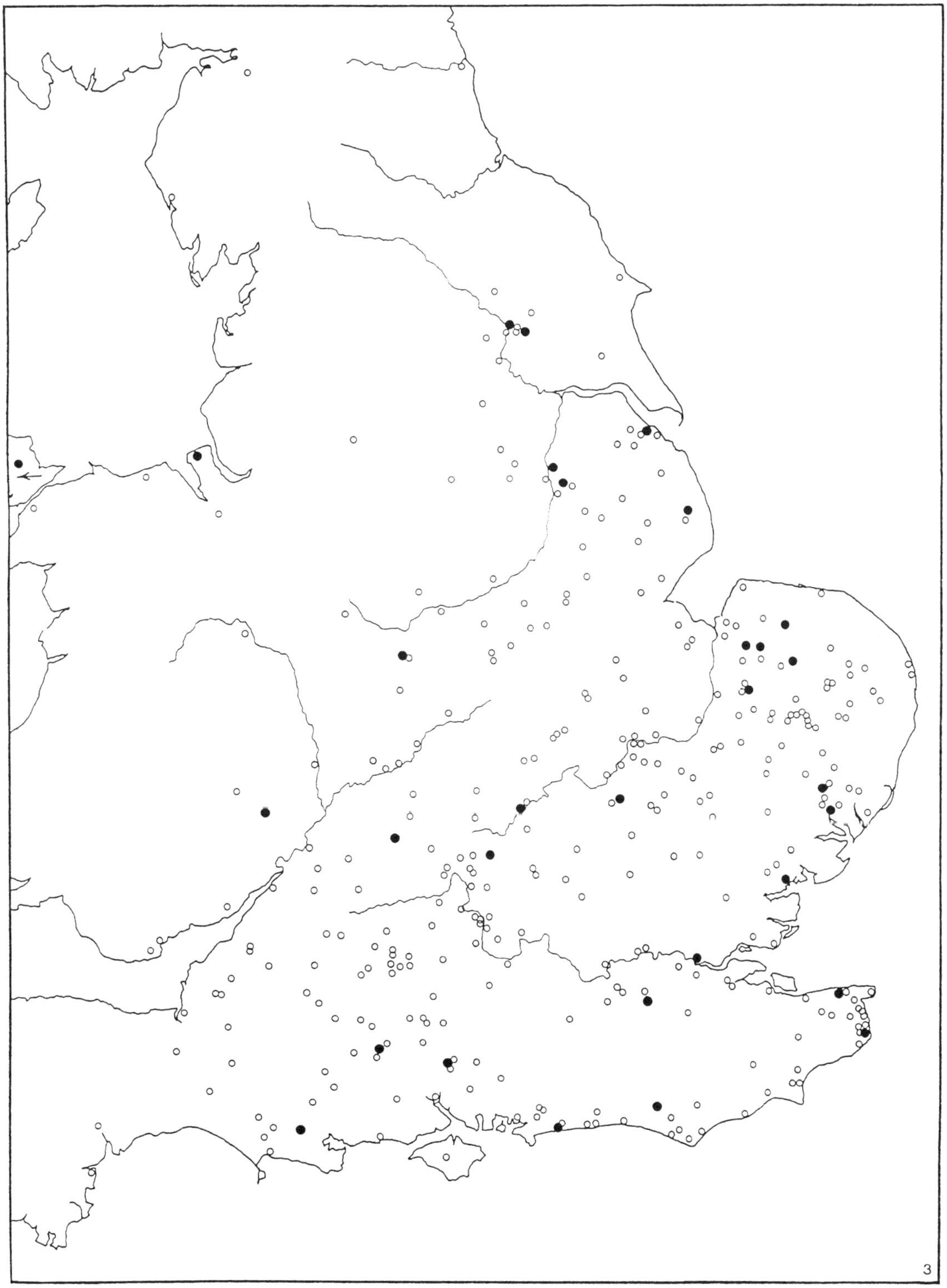

MAP 3. Coins of the Reform type, *c.*973–*c.*979.

Canterbury. Lympne minted an estimated 5 per cent of the Reform type, the only type in which its share exceeded one per cent. Its activity is suggestive of cross-Channel trade in the few years immediately following the reform, which subsequently dried up or shifted to other ports of entry. There were two coins of Lympne in the Fécamp hoard, and one of Southampton, all of Edward.

One should stoutly resist the temptation to make a trend out of a blip, but the absence of any finds of the Reform type from London, or Lincoln, coupled with a wide dispersal of coins minted in those two places, is intriguing.

London's share of the national output in the (Scandinavian) sample is estimated at only 7 per cent (on the basis of 8 coins!), jumping to 30 per cent in the Hand types and 26 per cent (shared with Southwark) in Crux.

The top mints in the Reform type as a whole are Winchester (13 per cent), York (9 per cent), and London (7 per cent), followed by Lincoln, Canterbury, and Lympne, equal fourth.

Q.14. What does the distance travelled by individual coins before they were lost tell us about the uses of coinage?

If farmers travelled ten or fifteen miles to their local market-town (with its mint) to buy and sell produce, *and if that were the sole use of coinage*, the resulting pattern of stray losses would consist simply of coins from the local mint. However numerous the transactions, the end-result would be geographically the same.

The pattern we observe is very different. Half the finds or more are not from their local mint, and some of the coins have been carried over long distances before being lost. *As well as* for local trade, therefore, it seems that coins were being used in other ways. Those other uses may have included trade conducted over a distance, and perhaps also the redistribution of coins through taxation. If money taxes were collected and transported to a central or regional treasury, and from there spent in different places, that process might generate a pattern of dispersion closer to what we observe, although not, perhaps, very quickly. It might take several years. It seems to be an inescapable conclusion that there were a great many inter-regional monetary transactions, whether unilateral or bilateral, especially in southern and central England.

There is little in the written evidence that could be used to verify that conclusion, which is of such radical interest for the study of the late Anglo-Saxon state that other methods of verification deserve to be found, if possible. There is a mass of evidence, in the directions and distances in which coins moved outwards from particular mints. Above all, the dominance of London coins throughout so much of southern England, and the matching dominance of Lincoln and York coins throughout Lincolnshire and Yorkshire respectively, point to the commercial character of long-distance movement of money.

The relative importance of local and long-distance transactions is more difficult to measure from the single finds. It might seem at first glance that one could compare the totals of coins of the local mint, and of other mints lost in the region. But that would indicate merely a rough minimum for the level of local transactions, because coins from more distant mints, once arrived, could perform that function too.

Q.15. Did the tendency for coins to become geographically dispersed increase or decrease over the period c. 973—1086?

The initial issues in a six-year validity period will have had a life of, let us say, six years before they were re-minted into the next type. Later issues during the validity period will have been recoined after only, perhaps, two or three years. Allowing for some bias towards minting early in the type, and perhaps also some delay in reminting, the average life-time of a coin in the period *c.*973—*c.*1020 may have been four to five years. As casual losses were presumably steady year by year, the lifetime of a single find before it was lost may on average have been closer to two or two and a half years.

The effect of the shorter validity-periods from *c.*1036 may have been partly offset by a greater tendency for coins to remain in use into subsequent validity periods. The net result may have been much the same average life-time, or (more probably) it may have been shorter.

We can assess and compare the geographical dispersal of coinage by measuring how far each recorded single find had travelled from its mint of origin. The results could be presented as an average distance for each type as a whole, or, better, in some graphic form which preserves and uses all the detail.

A coin that was lost fifty miles from its mint of origin may before that have been carried on a dozen journeys. It may have travelled a hundred miles away, and then returned closer to base. And there may have been a great many transactions within the mint-town itself, which leave no visible mark upon the distribution-pattern—especially if the recovery rate was lower in the town than in the countryside.

In each locality, whether near or far from the mint of origin, the coins lost should reflect the currency of that locality in the sense that they were random losses in respect of their mint-place. The implication that there were massive inter-regional transfers of money, visible after an average two-and-a half years' circulation or even less, is so surprising that we may neglect to press the enquiry.

We should be asking, however, whether there was a steady state and (crucially) whether it would have been reached in more or less than two and a half years. If more, considerable uncertainties arise in comparing the dispersion of coins from six-year validity periods with others from shorter periods. To that extent, the question under discussion may be difficult to answer accurately. It is taken up again in Q.24.

Q.16. Did the coins struck at small mints behave differently from those from large mints?

It has sometimes been noticed that hoards found near a provincial town contain a higher representation of coins of the local mint than would have been expected from the general character of the assemblage of single finds. If there is a conflict of evidence (which remains to be proved) should one believe the hoards or the single finds? Or is the conflict only apparent? There may be regional differences, e.g. in the face of westwards drift (discussed under Q.12) which are being misinterpreted as having been caused by the smallness of the mint.

Small mints produce small samples of single finds, which may tend to understate the distances over which the coins were carried, although they should in due course build up to produce a distribution-pattern directly comparable with the patterns for large mints. Progress might be made, therefore, by grouping small mints to produce a composite histogram of distances travelled.

In order to form a rough impression, let us look at a sample of small mints in the west (from which we have 19 single finds in total) and a sample in the east (18 finds). The western mints chosen for this exercise are Barnstaple, Bridport, Bristol, Christchurch, Cricklade, Lydford, Malmesbury, Tamworth, Warwick, and Worcester. The eastern mints are Bedford, Bury St Edmunds, Colchester, Derby, Guildford, Huntingdon, Hythe, and Maldon.

The list of finds from these places quickly dispels any notion of a predominantly local use of coins in places with small mints, different from the behaviour of the coins of large mints. The two recorded finds of Barnstaple mint coins are from Chichester and from near Oxford. The only Bridport coin is from Leicestershire. The only Christchurch coin is from Hertfordshire. Among 19 finds, 5 are very local. Half-a-dozen are from eastern England. The only curiosity in the list is that the two coins from the Lydford mint (struck from locally-mined silver?) are from the excavations at Mawgan Porth, in north Cornwall, and St. Lythans in south Wales—both regions where English coins scarcely penetrated.

Coins from the small eastern mints behave in the same way. Four or five are fairly local, but we see a Guildford coin found in Plymouth, a Bedford coin from Jarrow, both Huntingdon coins found in Yorkshire, and a Derby coin from Castle Acre in Norfolk.

The answer to our question is firmly in the negative. If hoards show signs of behaving otherwise, then one should explore possible explanations which apply specifically to hoards.

Q.17. What can regression analysis of the single finds tell us about the diffusion of the currency?

A more sophisticated approach to describing the geographical dispersion of the single finds makes use of the technique of regression analysis. For each mint, one draws a series of concentric circles around it (at a convenient interval, e.g. 25 km), and counts up all the mint-identifiable single finds within each zone. The coins of the mint in question can be expressed as a percentage of that total. The percentages are then directly comparable: it does not matter whether the totals are larger or smaller, except that smaller numbers will be subject to wider margins of random variation. Because of the small numbers it is probably appropriate to smooth the results by adding half the percentage value of each adjacent zone and then dividing by two, and that is what has been done. In effect we are looking at overlapping 50-km zones. One can then draw a graph of the percentages against distance from the mint, zone by zone. The graph will have a shape which characterizes the behaviour of the coins of that mint. For example, the percentage may remain much the same over long distances, suggesting that coins were being carried on long journeys in the course of inter-regional trade; or the graph may quickly tail off, suggesting a more restricted local circulation. A study of ninth-century single finds along these lines showed rather clearly that London and Canterbury coins were carried over long distances, whereas Winchester coins and East Anglian coins both had a more limited circulation. It seemed that the thrust of monetary circulation in the ninth century was from the south-east and from London up the Thames valley and into the midlands. To either side of this region were the kingdoms of Wessex and East Anglia, which were out of the main stream.

In the eleventh century, there is less of a contrast between mints with a long-distance function, and those with a more limited area of influence. London still shows a more prolonged profile, as may be judged from the slope of its histogram (Fig. 2a). The vertical axis is logarithmic, in order to make the angle of slope directly comparable. The percentage plotted as zone 0 is the unsmoothed figure for zone 1; and the broken line is the mint's estimated share of the national output. London's share is, of course, greater than that of any other mint, and that is reflected in the values of the logarithmic scale. Zone 8 takes in single finds up to 200 km from the point of origin.

It has to be concluded that most of the histograms in Fig.2 are basically quite similar in shape, even though the percentage values may be very different. Every mint had a zone of maximum influence in its immediately adjoining area, and every mint shows a steady decline for at least the first 75 km. This presumably reflects its regional function, and the increasing 'competition' with coins of other mints. There is no obvious sign of political or fiscal influences, e.g. in a discontinuity at the shire boundary, or in a steady percentage of coins redistributed from a central treasury, e.g. Winchester. The coins of all mints were able to pass freely anywhere in England, and the resulting pattern as illuminated by regression analysis seems to imply an essentially 'natural' mingling. The bumps or irregularities in several of the histograms are scarcely worth analysing at present, as they may well reflect mere statistical chance when there are only one to three coins from the mint in question, in an outer zone. Even if the numbers were larger, the task of analysing the interaction of competing mints would be complex. Information relating to the first three zones is for practical purposes the most interesting. Similarly, it is not worth analysing the small mints by this method until a larger data-base has accumulated.

One may supplement the regression analysis by noting that London coins were carried all over southern England. Winchester coins, on the other hand, tended to stay south of the Thames corridor (Map 4), and Thetford and Norwich coins stayed north of it (Map 5), mainly in East Anglia. The broad regional pattern of monetary circulation in the eleventh century thus seems to echo that of the ninth century, except that Canterbury's role has declined. The two northern regions of (essentially) Lincolnshire and Yorkshire have, by the eleventh century, been incorporated into the southern coinage system, but in terms of circulation they remain substantially separate (Lincoln, Map 6 and Fig.2f, York, Map 7 and Fig.2g).

The broad picture, then, is that the country can be divided into seven zones of monetary circulation, namely 1, the Thames valley and the Midlands, dominated by London, 2, East Anglia, 3, Wessex, 4, the South-West, 5, Kent and the Channel coasts, 6, Lincolnshire, 7, Yorkshire.

In each zone the circulation was substantially localized, except that London coins penetrated freely into zones 2, 3, and 4. In the south-central quadrant, for example, approximating to Wessex, London coins amount to *c.*35 per cent, whereas in Winchester itself they are only 3 out of 15, or 20 per cent. The South-West, namely Somerset, Devon, and Cornwall, is significantly more isolated, with less penetration by London coins.

That is the regional framework for English monetary history. Doubtless it has implications for our understanding of the dominant uses of coinage, and for the influence of the money economy on the political process.

Q.18. At any given moment, what proportion of the currency was to be found in each of the monetary zones?

There is no way round the problem that the average output of a die may have varied from mint to mint and from time to time. If one assumes that average die-output was a constant, one can calculate rough-and-ready answers for those zones where the issues of the local mint stayed largely within the zone, from the

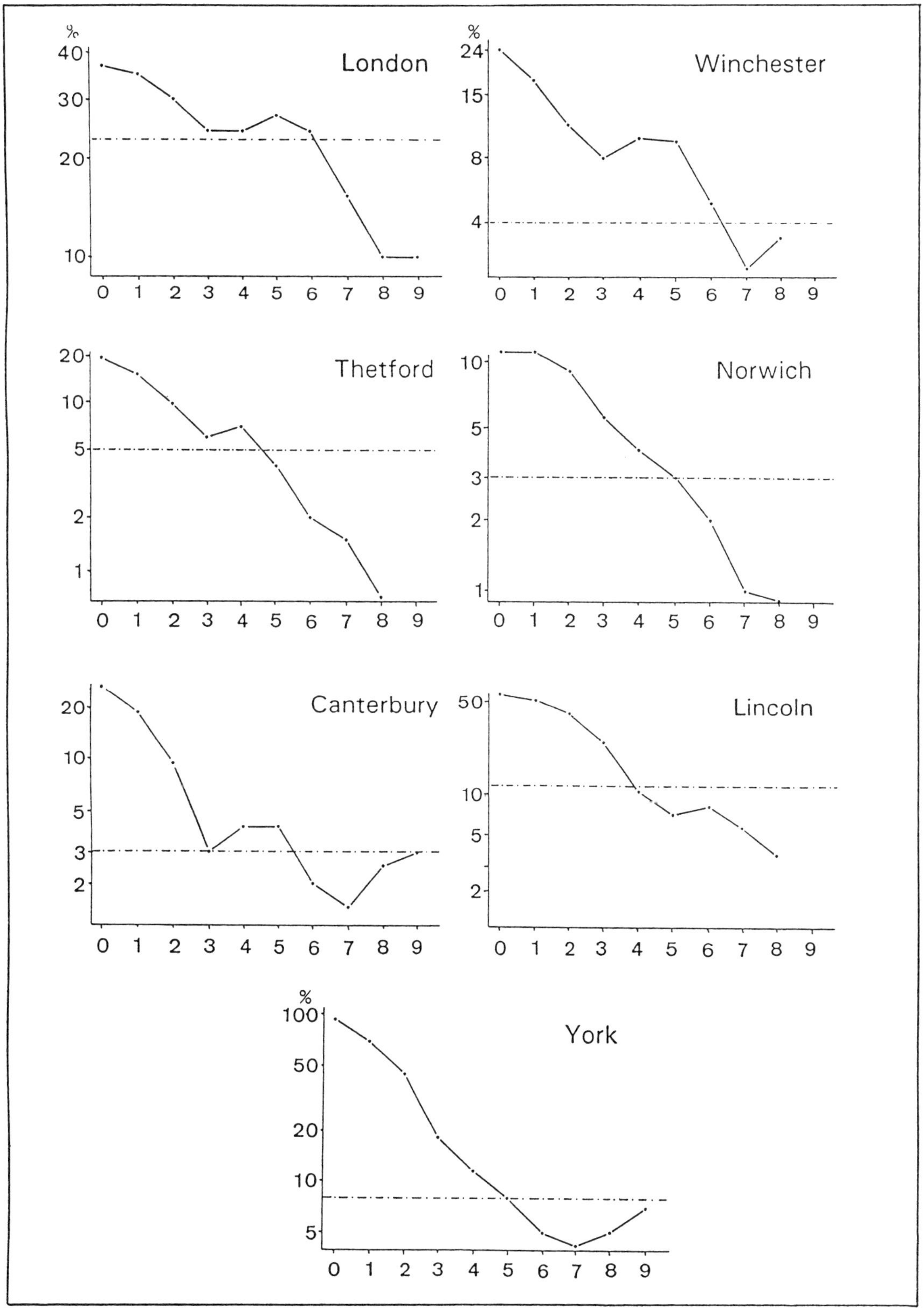

FIG. 2. Regression profiles for coins minted in seven active mints, namely a) London, b) Winchester, c) Thetford, d) Norwich, e) Canterbury, f) Lincoln, and g) York.

proportion that those local issues formed out of all the single finds from the zone. Thus, Winchester minted 4 per cent of the national currency, and Winchester coins make up 16 out of 105 single finds from south of the Thames and west of Chichester. As there are another 11 finds of Winchester coins outside the zone, one might argue (not very precisely) that those found within the zone represent 4 times 16/(16+11) or 2.37 per cent of the national output; and that because Winchester coins represent only 16/105 of those found within the zone, the total currency within the zone will amount to 2.37 x 105/16, or 15.5 per cent of the national total. By the same argument, one may say that Lincoln minted 12 per cent of the national output, and that Lincoln coins make up 35 out of the 85 finds from Lincolnshire and Leicestershire. As there are a similar number of finds of Lincoln coins from further afield, it would seem that half of 12 per cent, i.e. 6 per cent, multiplied by 85/35, indicates about 15 per cent of the national currency in Lincolnshire. Obviously, if one followed this procedure for all the regions of England, the results ought to approximate in total to 100 per cent.

The figures are subject to so many kinds of imprecision that they are not of much practical use. The best one can say about them is that they seem to add up to something not too far removed from 100 per cent, and can be adjusted or fudged *pro-rata* with a reasonably clear conscience. Their main interest is probably as part of a rebuttal to historians purveying the unfounded idea that the levels of monetization were significantly higher in the former Danelaw.

Q.19. Why were coins minted where they were minted, and in such varying quantities from place to place?

Moneyers worked only within the security of a borough. The risk of violence and of the theft of their bullion, and (even worse) of their dies, was obvious enough. Conversely, the king had every reason to discourage hole-and-corner operations which might well have led to fraud. It seems that any borough was entitled to a moneyer or moneyers, and the great majority of known boroughs were the seat of moneyers at some time or other, the name of the town appearing on the coins. In many cases, however, the number of coins known from a borough is minimal, and it is safe to say that there were long periods when no coins were minted there.

Neverthless, we can say that the pattern of minting is superimposed on the pattern of boroughs, and is in that sense determined by it. Where boroughs are few and far between (York, Lincoln, Stamford, Norwich, and Chester) so are mints. The relative quantities of coins minted in each town will have depended on the interaction of various causes, but among those causes we may surely list the size and character and prosperity of the town. Once again, therefore, we may say that the pattern of minting is determined, in part at least, simply by the existing pattern of towns.

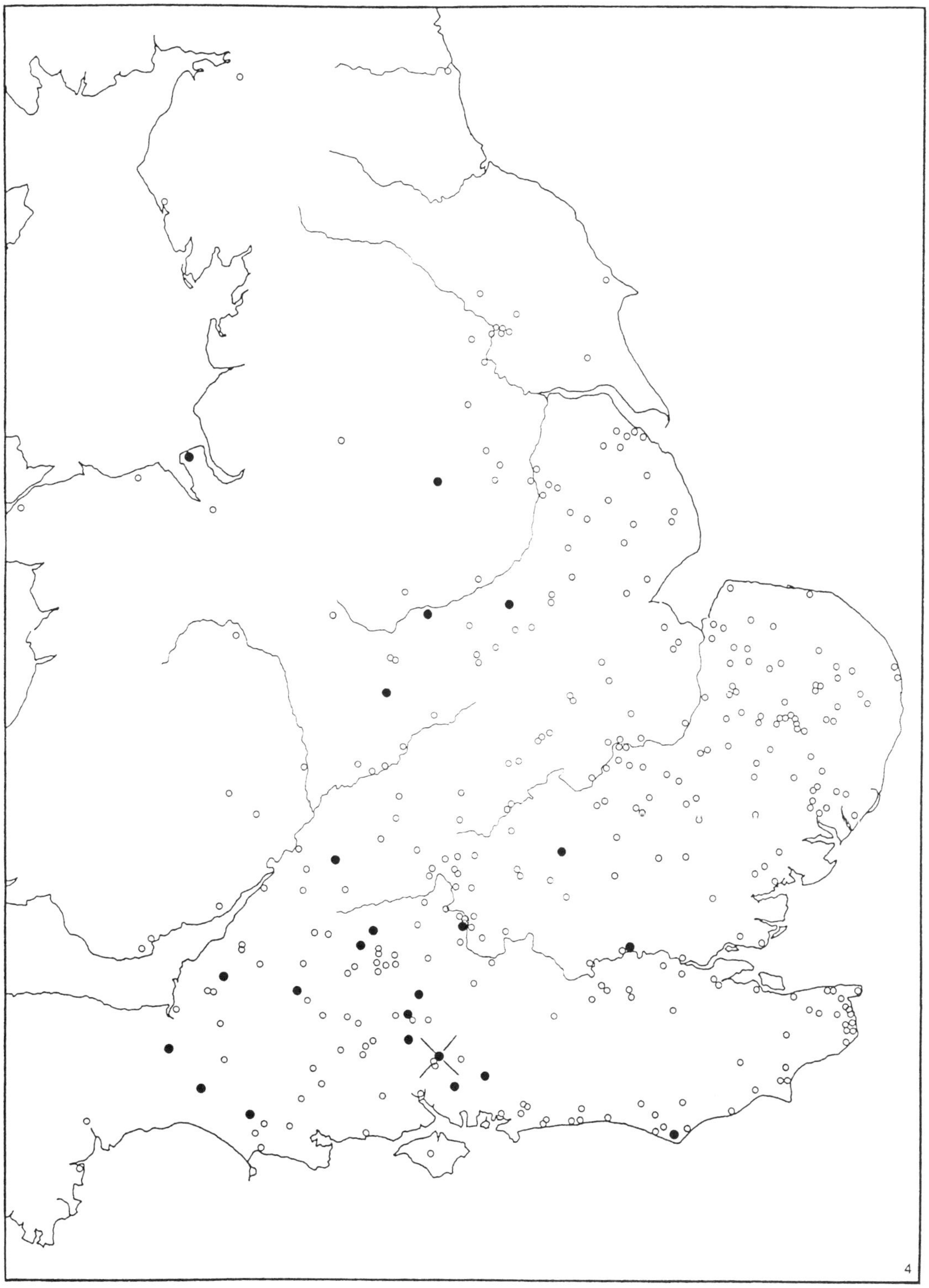

MAP 4. Coins minted in Winchester.

Why did so many small towns, throughout the eleventh century, retain the right to a moneyer's services, when it must have become abundantly clear that demand was minimal, and was not about to rise? The one-type hoards which are characteristic of the period from *c.*973 until at least 1040 have been taken as evidence that, with each type-change, recoinage was compulsory. As a necessary provision of good government, if recoinage was compulsory, moneyers were appointed for every town, so that hardly anyone (it has been argued) should have to make more than a day's journey in order to change their money. This somewhat romantic view of the governance of eleventh-century England has been much discussed and repeated. Its inner logic depends on the length of the period of grace (for which the interval from Michaelmas to Martinmas has been suggested, on the flimsiest of evidence) and on the general velocity of circulation, which may well have allowed people to come to private arrangements for changing their old coins without the trouble of visiting a moneyer. There will certainly have been a charge levied, and there may have been little or no point in paying that charge on coin that was about to be exported—since once they had left England, coins would lose most of their over-valuation. Some people might have found it marginally worth-while to keep obsolete coin with a view to its being exported, in the same way that nowadays one may keep a small amount of foreign currency for one's next visit, rather than sell it to the bank and pay commission. That hypothesis raises many questions in the analysis of the Scandinavian evidence, with which we are not concerned here. As regards England it is worth saying that there seems to be no way of verifying the evidence of the hoards indicating thorough recoinages, except by pointing out that some at least of the known hoards are likely to have been concealed in emergency, and to have comprised whatever money was to hand. But hoards can be surprisingly selective, and one cannot easily disprove the suggestion that some older coins continued in daily use (and therefore contributed to accidental losses) but were carefully excluded from hoards (see Q.37).

At all events, if periodic recoinages had been the sole reason for minting, the volume of output of each mint might have been expected to reflect the prosperity (and monetization) of the local region. The paucity of coins from, say, Hereford—in rich farming country—might be explained away, and the tiny output of mints in the home counties such as Guildford and Reading, and to a lesser extent Aylesbury, Buckingham, and Newport, might be attributed to the pull of London. But the dominating importance of the east-coast mints requires a quite different way of understanding the context of minting, in the needs of busy towns with merchant and craft communities, and in the recycling of foreign silver.

Attempts have been made to distinguish between these two broad reasons for minting. Where the coins of a validity-period can be dated more precisely within the period, by variations in their weight-standards (which at many mints, considered individually, are demonstrably chronological, more or less), one might

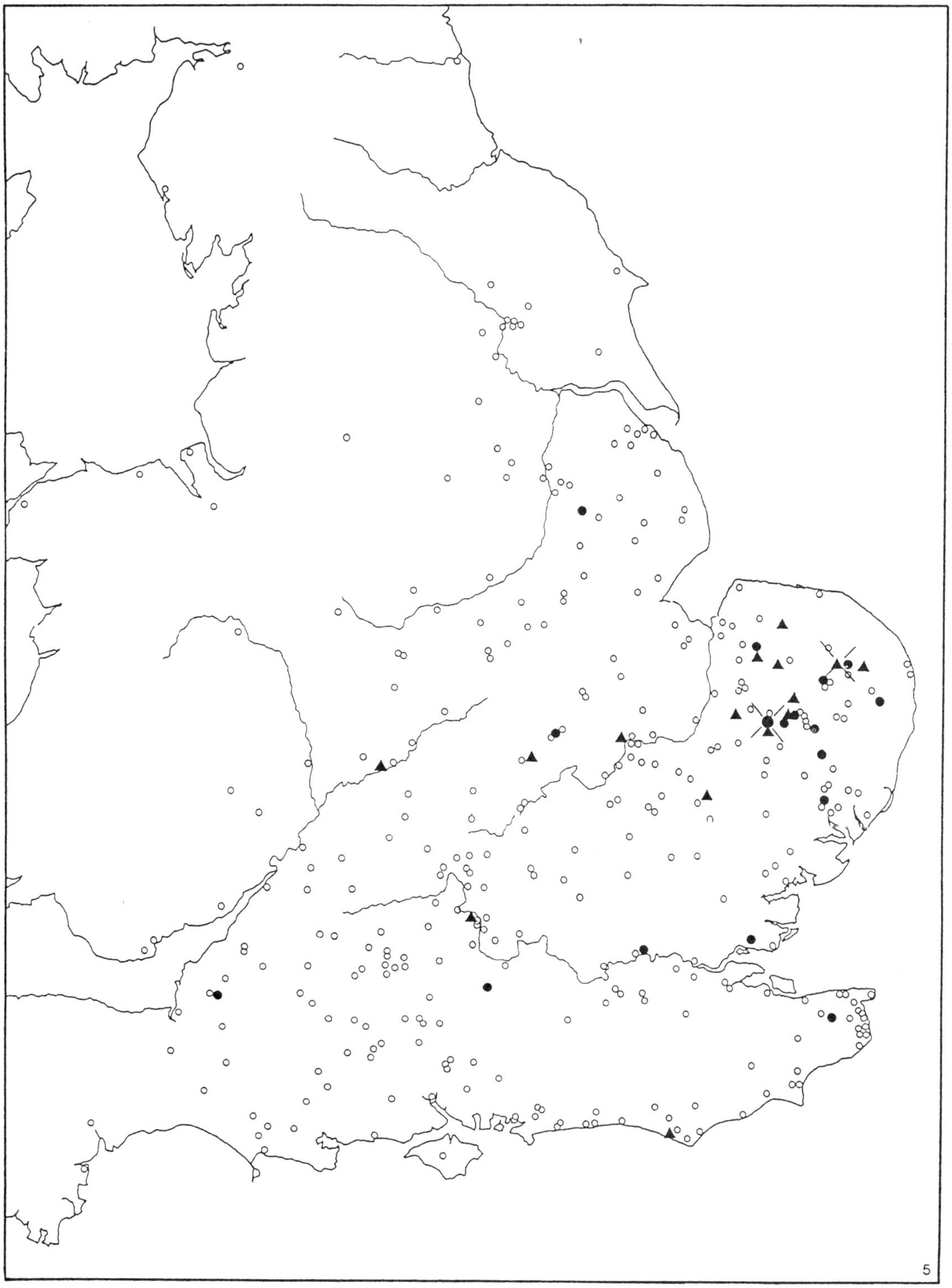

MAP 5. Coins minted in Thetford and Norwich.
(Norwich coins are shown by triangles.)

hope to separate out, roughly at least, the coins belonging to the initial recoinage, from those struck in order to recycle foreign silver, which presumably entered the country more steadily year by year. One might then have expected to see a contrast in the proportions between the ports and the 'shire' mints, early in the type and late in the type. It has to be said that studies along these lines have not yielded convincing results: the contrast, if any, is certainly not clear-cut nor is it repeated type by type. The concurrent minting of coins on different weight-standards may be a significant factor in this puzzling situation.

Coins of a uniform design were minted at all the mint-towns throughout the country, and merchants may well have been at liberty to take their silver to be recycled at which ever mint they chose. If they had no urgent need for cash they may not have needed to visit a moneyer at their port of entry, and even if there was a regulation obliging them to do so it would presumably have been difficult to enforce.

In some cases, e.g. Intermediate Small Cross, it is demonstrable that different weight-standards were in use at different mints concurrently. Presumably, therefore, a merchant might receive more or fewer coins for a given weight of silver, depending on where he took it to be minted. The subject of weight-standards is complex and its interpretation is full of ambiguities (see Q.21).

There are, then, no clear-cut answers to this question. If the mint of a particular small town was inactive or almost so, it does not imply that the townsfolk were managing their affairs by barter. They may have been using the coins of other mints. The way to judge the general level of the money economy in a region is from the single finds—their quantity, and the mints represented among them.

Just how open the question is may be judged from a radical re-statement of the evidence by Lord Stewartby, who argues from the Wedmore, Welbourn, and Walbrook hoards, of extended age-structure, and from various similar hoards from after 1050, that re-minting at each type-change was not compulsory, and that there may have been certain official purposes, in particular the payment of taxes and fines, for which only the current type could be used, but that otherwise older types continued to be acceptable. (But surely the coins were not required to be of the local mint?) He points out that, north of the Thames, there was normally just one mint in each shire, in the shire-town, and he leans towards the idea of minting to fit in with administrative requirements. (If that had been an important reason for minting, one would expect it to be reflected in the single finds: see Q.22). The numerous small mints of the West Country have perhaps unduly influenced our ideas, and (because they worked intermittently) even there it was by no means usually the case that most people were within 15 miles of a mint. Public convenience was hardly a consideration.

Today vast sums of money change hands daily in the City of London, whereas a well-to-do village may not have enough trade to keep the village shop viable. If

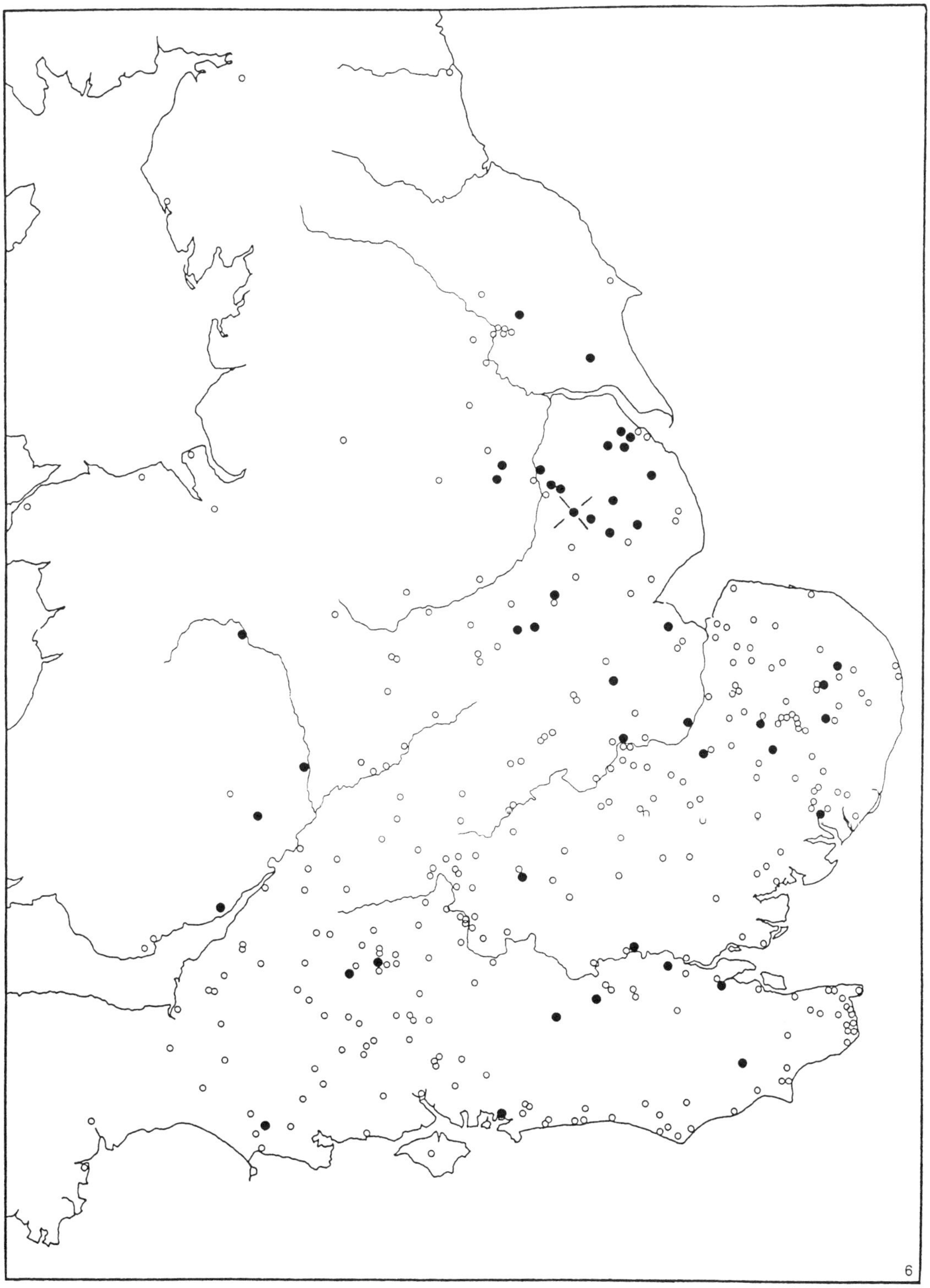

MAP 6. Coins minted in Lincoln.

in the eleventh century there was a hundred-fold or even a five hundred-fold difference between the quantities of coinage minted in London and in a small town in the south-west, we should be surprised not at how the small town managed, but at the wealth of London.

Q.20. Can one detect any blips in the statistics of estimated mint-output, which might suggest that particular mints were, briefly, minting for special reasons, and can such reasons be identifed from the written sources?

The exact ranking order of the mints varies from type to type, while remaining generally consistent. No historical significance can be attached to small variations, because they may be merely statistical in character.

The stability of ranking which is the keynote from *c.*980 to *c.*1050 suggests that the dominant reason or reasons for striking coin at the larger mints lay in the more settled aspects of political or economic life. If particular events affecting a borough or a region had loomed larger among the reasons for minting there would be more conspicuous irregularities in the ranking orders.

In 1044 and again in 1045, Edward was in command of the fleet at Sandwich. In 1049 in alliance with the emperor he blockaded Flanders from Sandwich. The Sandwich mint is unrecorded until 1042, and is active precisely in the four types minted between 1042 and *c.* 1050. It worked on a very small scale thereafter, perhaps intermittently, but specimens are not included in the Scandinavian sample. The mint revived somewhat under William I.

There seems, then, to have been a specific local reason for the establishment of the Sandwich mint. And in the Short Cross type (*c.*1048—50) the one and only moneyer, Leofwine, uses at least seven reverse dies instead of the normal two, possibly in the expectation of a special need connected with the blockade of Flanders. But Sandwich is, so far as one can see, a rare exception which proves the rule. And one should keep matters in perspective: its output is estimated at only 0.65 per cent of the national total in the Pacx type (*c.*1042-4) and *c.*0.5 per cent in the following three types.

Blips in the performance of small mints, as in the case of Sandwich, show up. There may have been special reasons for minting, from time to time, at larger mints, where the evidence is submerged by the greater output. It is small mints which can best provide test-cases.

As a negative example, Winchcombe in the northern Cotswolds became for a time the shire town of Winchcombeshire, as the result of an administrative reform in *c.*1007 or earlier which was revoked *c.*1017. The mint of Winchcombe was active from *c.*991 until 1086, rarely using more than four reverse dies in each type. In Last Small Cross, which certainly falls within the period of enhanced status of the place, there are no coins in the Scandinavian sample. Rather than

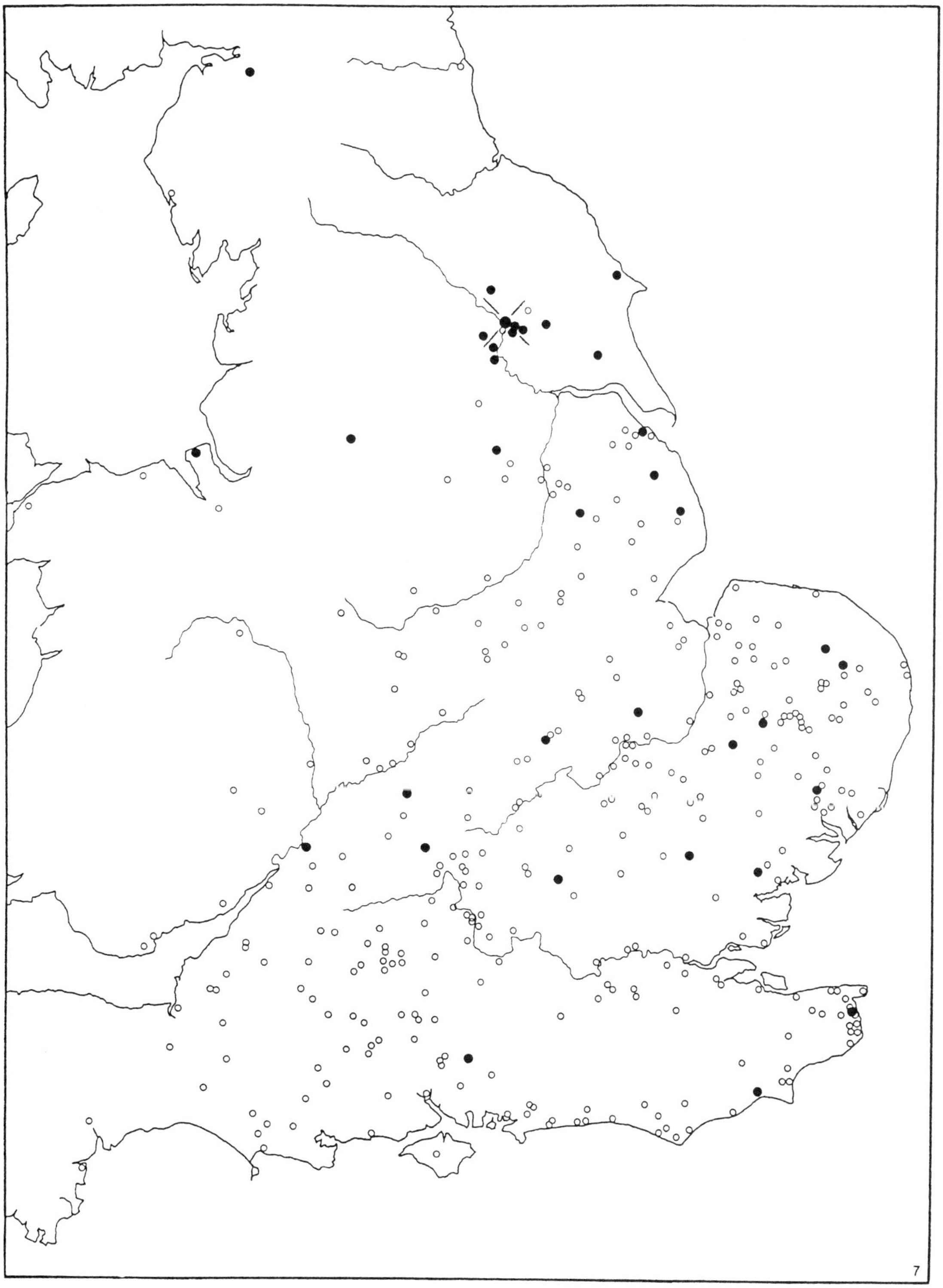

MAP 7. Coins minted in York.

showing a burst of activity in the years when it is known to have been a shire town, it seems that the mint hardly worked at all. See Part 4, section 9 (South Mercia).

Q. 21. *Where a type was struck on more than one weight-standard, were the heavier and lighter coins used differently in England?*

During the reigns of Æthelred and Cnut each successive coin type was struck on a variety of weight standards. The differences in weight are not trivial, e.g. between averages of 1.65g and 1.425g in the Crux type. Multiple weight-standards continue to be the norm after 1035, but the averages are closer together, and therefore tend to blur in our statistics. Moreover, when fewer specimens survive (from the mid-century onwards) it becomes difficult or impossible to determine, mint by mint, where the modal or peak values lie exactly. What is certain is that the patterns which the detailed evidence reveals are not due to indifference or incompetence on the part of the moneyers. At many mints we can see that they achieved close control over the weights of the flans. At Chichester in Edward the Confessor's Facing Bust type, for example, we see a tight normal distribution where more than 97 per cent of the recorded specimens lie within a range of only 0.1g around a modal value of c.1.12g. (Fig.3a). At York in the same type the histogram straggles from 0.7g to 1.4g, with

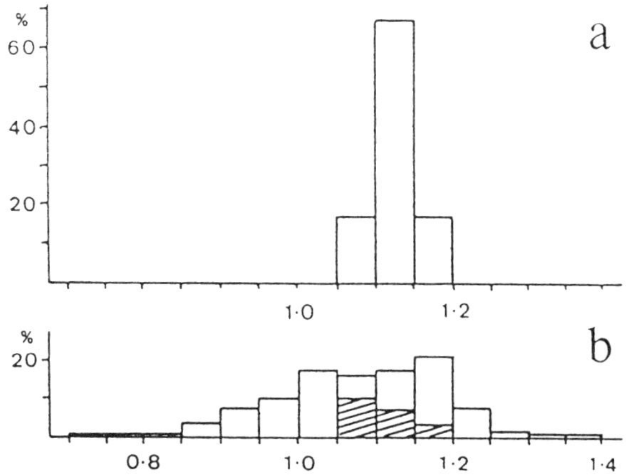

FIG. 3. An example of histograms generated by a) coins on a single weight-standard and b) coins on more than one weight-standard (Facing Bust, Chichester and York mints, 18 and 239 specimens respectively). For explanation of the shaded area, see text.

two peaks, at approximately 1.02g and 1.17g (Fig.3b). One can imagine two overlapping normal distributions. If the coins in the two steps between the peak steps are shared out advantageously (the shaded area hypothetically completes the lower distribution), the York pattern can be interpreted convincingly as a double, overlapping distribution with normal characteristics. The York moneyers were not hopelessly clumsy or careless in comparison with their colleagues down in

Chichester. It is just that the pattern of their activity, which we have to disinter from the data, was more complicated. All the material needs to be examined carefully in this way, mint by mint and type by type. The examination reveals that the administrative decisions that were taken about the weights of the coins were extremely various.

The general governmental purposes behind this remarkable system have defied convincing explanation. Earlier attempts have taken their starting-point from a supposed theoretical weight of the penny at 16 to the ounce, i.e. 1.82g, based on the Tower ounce. In practice the coins always weighed less than that maximum, often very much less. The difference was treated as an over-valuation, and Petersson (1969) developed a theory about minting policy which took account of the maximum practicable over-valuation. Various systems can be developed from the basic concept, because we have no information about what actually happened. Lyon, in 1976, wrote (critically) about a system whereby the weight of a type was progressively lowered during its validity-period, by increasing the minting-charge. He saw the rationale for lighter coins in a need for more coins, and connected the increase in weight mid-way through Expanding Cross with the abolition of the heregeld. Coins were often lighter in the Danelaw. Lyon recognized that the system was open to exploitation unless transactions were officially supervised 'to prevent Gresham's Law from operating'.

All these arguments are water under the bridge, on two counts. First, the facts are far more complicated and contradictory than was appreciated, in that individual mints operated on very different weight-standards concurrently, and did not necessarily conform to a progressive decline during each validity-period. Secondly, if minting charges varied by substantial amounts, there was no way of preventing people from consulting their own interests, and taking bullion wherever it could be minted most advantageously. If the weights on offer at different mints varied by as much as 15 or 20 per cent, and if a penny was worth something like a £20 note today, one did not need to place a very large order with a moneyer to justify the expenses of travel. We need to look again, therefore, at the simple questions, 'Who profited?' and 'Who bore the cost?' Let us go over the arguments again, keeping the options as open as possible.

It seems virtually certain that, within England, for most people and for many purposes a penny was a penny, whatever its weight. Otherwise—and this is a point on which one should insist—what would the point have been in adjusting the weight-standards?

It also seems virtually certain, even if the working-out of the idea is puzzling, that customers cannot have been given a choice. Otherwise, why would anyone bringing, say, half a pound of bullion to a moneyer opt to receive 120 pennies for it rather than 150 if each could be spent as a penny? There is the further conundrum how moneyers were persuaded to keep to the rules. If a single weight-standard had been universal in any particular year, policing it would not have been too difficult. But that was not the case.

However the weight-standards were determined, it would appear at first glance that the tax (if one cares to think of it as a tax) was paid at the point of exchange. Why, then, were coins heavier at the beginning of a validity-period? After a year or two, it seems that in general the average weight declined: did customers receive more coins for their pound of silver, while still paying a tax of, say, five per cent, or did they pay a higher proportion in mint-charges, and receive the same number of pennies as they would have done at the beginning, and of the same face-value in England, but lighter in weight? In the context of compulsory recoinage, that would probably have resulted (taking the validity period as a whole) in the merchant community supplying more silver, and therefore more profit, to the exchequer than the agricultural interest. But if a penny was a penny, the merchant who brought silver to the mint did not suffer at that point.

Indeed, one can envisage that he might have benefitted. A law of King Eadgar (III Eadgar 8.2) decrees that a wey of wool shall be sold for 120 pence, and that no-one shall sell it at a cheaper rate. After *c*.973 the effectiveness of this monopolistic law depended on the value of the penny. If it was variable, the law may in some sense have been subverted. A merchant engaged in the wool trade who sold his wool on the continent and brought foreign coin back to England to be reminted, to buy some more wool, might, it seems, receive 120 pence for a certain weight of silver, or he might receive 150. In so far as a penny was a penny, this would have made a considerable difference to the profitability of his venture.

Did the law permit the seller to seek a higher price than the floor price of 120 pence? Was the payment to be by tale, or was it, in fact by weight (half a pound)? The sting may be in the tail. 'If anyone sells it at a cheaper rate, either openly or secretly, both he who sells it and he who buys it shall pay 60 shillings to the king'. This does not strike one as clever drafting. Since both parties were liable to a severe financial punishment (equivalent to about 6 weys of wool, whatever a wey was) both had good reason to keep their business to themselves. Who could inform on how much money had changed hands?

Did the market price of wool remain the same, decade after decade? We do not know. Only written sources could tell us about prices, and virtually nothing that is helpful survives. A penny was still called a penny, but was its purchasing power the same under Edward the Confessor as it had been in the time of Æthelred II?

Thus the evidence for monetary history is lop-sided, and seriously defective. Systematic information about prices, from which to construct long-running indices (such as have been made for England and for Scotland from the high middle ages up to modern times) simply does not exist, and never will. All that one can hope to do in response to that deficiency is to interpret the numismatic evidence in an open-minded or in an ambulatory way, reviewing a range of hypotheses: that inflation was negligible; or that the value of a penny was steadily eroded over a hundred years; or that there were phases of sharp inflation.

When English money was taken abroad, it automatically lost most or all of its overvaluation, and would be judged on its intrinsic value, i.e. by purity and weight. This sounds like the party game of 'pass the parcel': the rapid circulation of coins in England resulted in a mixture of heavy and light pieces, each worth a penny. At the moment when one needed to make a payment overseas, a light penny was suddenly worth less than a heavy one.

Two corollaries: first, if the monetary outflows were on balance towards Scandinavia whereas inflows were from the near Continent, there was a political dimension to the system: potentially at least, it favoured English exports to the Continent, and was to that extent bullionist. It may also have been perceived as a tax bearing most heavily on luxury imports. Secondly, the situation sounds like an invitation to cull the currency, and to export the heavy coins. Danegeld, on the other hand, could have been collected locally at face value, and paid over by the authorities by weight. That would have been politically sensible, to avoid endless bickering and ill-will at the local level. If the English coins reaching the Northern Lands are liable to have been a mixture, chosen or not chosen according to their weight, that opens up a large and speculative field of research into the Scandinavian evidence. It should not affect the English evidence, however, except in so far as the currency left behind in England may have been a distorted sample, weight-wise, of what had originally been minted.

It is surprisingly difficult to find ways of exploring the idea of the export of culled, heavier coins. One might hope to compare histograms of Scandinavian and English material. Up to *c.*1050 the former is abundant, the latter hardly to be found. After *c.*1050 the situation is reversed, but equally unhelpful. Because of variation of weight-standards from mint to mint, comparisons should be restricted to one mint at a time. London is an obvious choice. Our general idea of multiple standards at eastern mints derives very largely from the Scandinavian evidence, and so we know before we start, that at least culling was not practised effectively.

If one looks at national averages for all mints, there is a clear picture of progressively declining weight-standards during each type, with a return to a higher standard at the beginning of the next type, which in Æthelred's reign is often anticipated by the striking, right at the end of a type, of heavy coins appropriate to the awaited new type. This pattern seems to imply either that weight-standards were managed according to how much of the validity-period, of foreseen length, had elapsed, or that obsolete dies were in use early in the next type.

In the Hand types, First Hand averages 1.51g, and Second Hand averages 1.31g. But at the very end of the type, there is a return to an exceptionally high average weight, of 1.59g in Benediction Hand. Similarly, the Crux type decreases in weight progressively, but Intermediate Small Cross reverts to a very high average weight, which is quickly abandoned at most mints and replaced by the very low weights of Transitional Crux.

Evidently there was some degree of national, i.e. royal, control over weight-standards. How were instructions conveyed when the standard was to be lowered or raised? Presumably writs were sent to all the sheriffs, who would pass on the instructions to the moneyers of their shire, either at a meeting of the *burh* court, or individually. This would have to have happened every couple of years or even every year, and it would obviously have been administratively convenient to all concerned if it happened at a regular date, such as Michaelmas (as Michael Dolley liked to believe).

It is tempting to a modern mind to read into this situation an intention on the part of those in authority to deal fairly with the customers who called on the moneyer's services, or perhaps to encourage inflows of silver to the mints by offering incentives. The customer who, four years into a six-year validity-period, brings his silver to be minted will be taxed again in only two years' time. Arguments of this kind have various built-in assumptions, e.g. that those in authority cared for the interests of ordinary people, in the way that modern politicians care for voters; or that a penny had a fixed value whatever its weight. Also, the model is more plausible for six-year than for two-year validity-periods.

The national average pattern conceals astonishing complexities. Different mints operated on very different weight-standards concurrently. Petersson has made an analysis of no fewer than 44,350 weights of coins according to mint and type, and has shown that different regions of England tended to strike heavier or lighter coins characteristically. Thus Winchester, for example, type by type seems to maintain the initial heavy standard when mints elsewhere moved to a lower standard. There is a theoretical difficulty with the evidence here, to be sure that Winchester (and other places similarly) did not mint all their coins early in the validity-period, and then close down.

The high average weight of Benediction Hand is by no means uniform at all mints. Because its duration was so short, it is certain that different standards were in use concurrently (as they were, similarly, in Intermediate Small Cross). Many mints operated at 1.62—1.67g, but Thetford coins average 1.40g, Stamford, 1.38g, and Tamworth and Guildford even lower.

Similarly, Small Crux is on different standards at different mints—and even at the same mint, presumably within a fairly short period.

Petersson's own analysis of his data (1990) takes as its premiss that the choice of weight-standard was made on a shire basis: where a shire had more than one mint, they acted in concert. There are exceptions to this generalization, which make it debateable. That should not be allowed to confuse the issue. It remains true that England was governed on a shire basis, and it is also true that different mints operated on different weight-standards. Many shires, in any case, had only one mint. The shires which should offer a test case for Petersson's hypothesis are nearly all south of the Thames. They include Devonshire (with mints at Exeter, Totnes, Barnstaple, and Lydford), Dorset (mints at Dorchester, Shaftesbury, Wareham, and Bridport), Somerset (Bath, Ilchester, Watchet, etc.), Hampshire (Winchester, Salisbury, and Southampton), Wiltshire (Wilton, Malmesbury, Cricklade, etc.), and in the south-east, Kent (Canterbury, Rochester, Dover, etc.) and Sussex (Lewes, Hastings, Chichester, etc.). In order to compare the weight-standards at the various mints in a shire, samples are needed large enough (even for the smaller mints in question) to generate reliable histograms showing the modal values clearly. Long Cross, Quatrefoil, and Pointed Helmet are the most prolific types as regards sample size, and in practice the case rests on them.

North of the Thames, one active mint per shire was usual, except in Norfolk (Norwich and Thetford) and Lincolnshire (Lincoln and Stamford, but during much of the eleventh century Kesteven may not have been united with Lindsey, and in any case the Stamford moneyers apparently always worked south of the river, in Northamptonshire). For shires with only one mint-place, the question is inappropriate: one can only make the assumption that administrative arrangements were similar to those in shires with several mints.

Petersson in 1969 created histograms for the weights of each type as a whole. Several of them show more than one peak, quite dramatically. If one creates and compares histograms separately for each of the active mint-places, using the data published by Petersson in 1990, further complexities emerge. The higher standard was not the same at all mints; there may be three standards rather than two; and so on. A strong peak or modal value in the histogram may 'swamp' or obscure another quite distinct standard, against which relatively few coins were minted. That difficulty lies in the nature of histograms. It can sometimes be overcome by patiently dissecting the evidence for one mint, moneyer by moneyer—as has been done, for example, for the mint of Watchet, or for Colchester in the Crux type. Petersson assessed the evidence of his 44,350 weights by shire and by type in only a summary fashion. The data he published provide a starting-point for new research on each and every mint, but one has to recognize that as one focusses in onto a smaller and smaller segment of the evidence, there comes a point where it blurs, and ceases to show statistical differences adequately. That is all the more so when the histograms are flattish. Even with such a very large data-base, there are detailed questions for which it is insufficient.

The patterns are complex and vary slightly from type to type, but Chester, like Winchester, tends to keep to a single high weight standard, as do the mints of Gloucestershire, Wiltshire, and Hampshire. Somerset and Dorset provide exceptions to the rules, but even so it is broadly the case that high weight levels were maintained in the western half of England, while reducing weight-standards, and lower weights generally, are characteristic of the eastern half of the country, including the Danelaw. London, Thetford, Norwich, Stamford, Lincoln, and York employ multiple weight standards.

If the east-west divide is the key perspective of the evidence, there is also the question of the balance between shire and national control. Decisions were in some sense being taken at two administrative levels. This is nowhere clearer than in the Expanding Cross type, where there was a directive from the centre to introduce new coins on a dramatically higher standard, but where the directive was interpreted with slight differences of weight-standard from mint to mint. The details are discussed more fully in part 3, section 17 below. The general question is this: was there full compliance with the central directive, modified only by local custom and practice, or was a degree of tolerance built into the directive?

The administrative decisions which lay behind weight variation remain deeply enigmatic. The evidence is inescapably statistical in character, because the starting-point is the identification of 'peaks' or modal values in histograms—which all too often are based on an insufficient number of specimens to define the parameters securely. Because the enigma of what was intended and what was achieved by weight-variation is so central to the late Anglo-Saxon currency, the test-case of the first validity-period is discussed more fully in an Excursus, below.

How might all these astonishing complexities be reflected in the English find-evidence? If a penny was everywhere a penny, or nowhere a penny, then perhaps hardly at all. *Parturient montes, nascetur ridiculus mus.* If users could without risk accept coins by weight, and expect to pass them on by weight, the number of coins they received will not have mattered. Conversely, if users could without risk accept coins at face value, and expect to pass them on at face value, the weight of each penny will have been a matter of indifference to them. It is the interaction of the two systems that creates the possibility of advantage or disadvantage. One could test this proposition on the ground by mapping the single finds from the high-weight shires, etc., to see whether there was any sort of contrast in the weights of the single finds, which would imply that only heavy coins were acceptable in the high-weight areas, and so on. But it seems a superfluous exercise, when one remembers how pervasive London coins were in the western half of the country, and how relatively small the combined mint-output was in the west.

A trawl through the single finds shows that there is no dramatic difference in the *currency* between east and west, as regards weight-distribution. If we look at all the coin-types of Æthelred and Cnut together, excluding finds of which the weight is not recorded, and excluding halfpennies and so on, the proportion of finds weighing 1.20g and over is about half in the east and north, but about 70 per cent (based on a rather small sample) in counties where in general high weight-standards were maintained.

The significance of metrology, for the monetary historian and the general historian, will lie at the point of minting, where someone (the merchant? —the moneyer? —the king?) will potentially have derived greater or less profits according to the weight-standard, in so far as the coins could be spent at face value. Surely the decision was not the customer's, nor the moneyer's, or all the coins would have been light. And surely the customer did not have the choice of receiving significantly more coins for his pound of silver, or those customers for whom a penny was a penny would have flocked to those mint-places which were operating on light standards, or would have sent their agents there, and the distortion would be easily visible in the statistics of our samples. Perhaps one was only entitled to the lower weight-standard on foreign silver. One imagines that administrative arrangements were required, whereby an instruction from the sheriff either announced that from such and such a date, a certain number of coins were to be cut from a pound of bullion, —or that the rate was so much for one category of customer or one category of bullion, and less for another category—or some combination of both these systems. We simply do not know how the weights were managed. We just have not got quite enough pieces of firm information from which to infer the outlines of the complex system into which they fit. At the time of Domesday and *tempore regis Edwardi* a simple procedure was in force, whereby the moneyer paid a standard fee for his die, and presumably recouped his outlay as best he could. Even so, it is difficult to see how the moneyers could have been left to select their own weight-standard.

And what exactly was the intention, in raising the weight-standard in Benediction Hand and Intermediate Small Cross? Who profited? Who bore the cost? Who was willing or needed to take bullion to be minted in the dying days of a validity-period on those terms? Or is that a mirage?

Lyon remarked that the initial weight-standard of Hand, as of First Small Cross, was *c.*25gr. and the average weight of the surviving coins of the various types with a Hand design taken together was *c.*22.25gr, as it had been for First Small Cross. That might be thought a strong argument, he said, for all the Hand types being part of a single issue. The argument is difficult to follow. Are we to suppose, from the identity of initial and average weights, that when the time for a type change was drawing close, the authorities increased the weight-standard in order to raise the average weight? How would they have known when they had done enough? Indeed, how would they have known what in practice the average weight was, if each shire was operating as it saw fit?

There is a further dimension to the problem of high weight-standards late in the validity-period. In Subsidiary Long Cross, which is generally on the lowest standard, there are some very heavy coins from London. Were these produced for a similar reason to that which inspired Benediction Hand? One should emphasize that there were relatively extremely few such coins, and also that they could not be recognized at a glance (unless the reverses were marked with two pellets).

Petersson has shown us, beyond any reasonable doubt, that weight-standards were determined at a local level; and that must mean at the level of the shire, for that is how England was governed. But then at times national policy was asserted and overrode local policy. The profits of minting doubtless belonged theoretically to the king, even if they were not nicely calculated and even if subsidiarity (e.g. the earl's third-penny) became an entrenched procedure. There was a widespread but not universal practice of progressively reducing weight-standards *on average*, but whether as an incentive or as a form of deferred taxation it will not necessarily have borne upon the merchants who took silver to the mints in the later stages of the validity-period. Indeed they may have been the main beneficiaries. Everyone was taxed at the beginning of a new type, both by a commission charge to the moneyer, and also if lighter coins (or a mixture of coins that was on average lighter) were exchanged for fewer, heavier coins. Thereafter, the rules of 'pass the parcel' operated, and the cost of the lighter coins, in so far as they were of fixed face value, will have fallen in the first instance on anyone seeking to export money, e.g. to Scandinavia (perhaps for luxury goods such as furs?). No doubt such merchants, selling to the well-to-do, found it necessary to pass their costs on. A modern chancellor of the exchequer might well be green with envy of the ingenuity that evolved such a politically blame-proof system of taxation.

It was adapted to the triangular balance-of-payments situation discussed under Q.12. When the outflows to Scandinavia dwindled, a simpler pattern of weight-standards accompanied the shorter validity-periods of Edward the Confessor's reign. Short Cross, minted *c.*1048-50, has an exceptionally low average weight, and seems to be on the three standards of *c.*1.125g, 0.94g, and 0.78g, a considerable percentage difference. The next type, Expanding Cross, is remarkable in that a light standard (*c.*1.12g) was followed by a far heavier standard (*c.*1.67g). This dramatic change, mid-way through the type, has commonly been associated with the abolition of the heregeld in 1051. It has seemed obvious that a relationship exists here, but (as Petersson prudently says) 'how this is conditioned, we do not know'. The *Chronicle* states only that in the thirty-ninth year from its origin the heregeld (which paid for the standing army and which had been an oppressive tax) was abolished. The heregeld was a general land tax, levied almost certainly on the basis of a cadastral codex of some sort; it was not collected through the charges on minting coinage. There was thus no automatic effect on the weight of the coinage. The big increase in the weight of Expanding Cross looks, therefore, more like a political gesture. A new interpretation is proposed in Part 3, section 17 below.

Intuitively one would like to think that the lighter weight-standards are connected with foreign trade. One looks, for example, at Exeter, where lighter standards are prominent, in contrast with many other mints in the western half of the country. The truth, however, may be counter-intuitive. The general idea that heavy coins reflect the agricultural interest and lighter coins the merchant's interest is no more than a suggestion. When one tries to work out all the corollaries and implications, it is by no means self-validating. It does not self-evidently rule out other hypotheses. What if, for example, all private customers received heavy coins, while tolls and taxes taken to be reminted by the king's officers were struck at a preferential rate? That would stand the scheme that has been suggested on its head, more or less. It should serve to show how hypothetical our ideas about weight-variation are, in that it cannot easily be dismissed. Either scheme would fit equally well with the triangular balance-of-payments situation, because the rules of 'pass the parcel' would still apply, and the costs (other than the general tax on everyone who held coin at the time of a recoinage) would fall, so far as one can see, on the exporters engaged in luxury trade.

The contexts of the uses of coinage by the very rich and the ordinarily poor were quite different. Eleventh-century wills frequently speak of tens of pounds of pence (e.g. *tyn pund peneta*, or *tyn pund penaga*), or alternatively pence in large numbers, e.g. a thousand pence. At the other extreme we read of a bequest of a hundred pence to Ely to feed a hundred poor people on a particular day. Just occasionally the wills refer to pounds by tale (*twelf pund be getale*). It is debateable whether pounds not so specified were paid by weight, but that is the natural reading of the evidence. Domesday Book distinguishes between four methods of payment, namely by tale (*ad numerum*), by weight (*ad pensum*, *ad pondus*), in assayed or blanched coins (*blancas*, *candidas*, etc.), and *ad numerum de xx in ora*. Sally Harvey has argued that the payment of 20 coins by tale to discharge a debt of 16 pence (an ora) was a device which the king imposed to compensate himself for any possible loss of revenue from under-weight coins. One can easily envisage that, from the time of Eadgar's reform onwards, those high in the power-structure would have devised methods of payment which ensured that they were not the losers. Such people may have made up only a small proportion of those who handled coinage. Merchants and traders were no doubt aware of the finer points; for ordinary people, light-weight pennies may have been just one more illustration of the fact that life was not scrupulously fair. Annoyance at having to accept under-weight coins may possibly be reflected obliquely in the insistence of the law-codes (e.g. IV Æthelred, 6 and 7) against false coins or base coins, since these seem to have been a very minor problem, if we can judge by the find-evidence.

IV Æthelred 9 imposes a legal responsibility on moneyers to see that their coins are pure and 'of the proper weight', with severe penalties for failure to comply.

But what 'of the proper weight' meant, in the context of multiple weight-standards, is hard to envisage. The same chapter goes on to say that those in authority in towns (*ipsi qui portos custodiunt*) shall ensure that all weights are marked according to the weight by which my money is received (officially? —or perhaps 'taken back'?) (*ad pondus quo pecunia mea recipitur*). Each weight is to be marked in such a way that 15 oras make a pound (*signetur ita, cur xv ore libram faciant*). This seems to offer further evidence of the practice of payments calculated by weight, for official purposes. It could even be taken to imply that at a recoinage, old coin would be taken in at a valuation determined by its weight.

The social gulf between great land-owning lords (who administered justice locally, in many cases) and ordinary people may have made the operation of an ambiguous system of monetary valuation less a source of friction than it would be in modern times, when everyone can understand small percentage differences in a sophisticated way.

That there was in the modern economist's sense a market, and that it was partly regulated by government intervention, is clear. On the one hand, Eadgar's law (mentioned above) controlled the floor price of what was probably a major export commodity. On the other hand, agricultural prices fluctuated (as is well documented for the later middle ages) with the success of the harvest, and so on: in 1040, as the *Chronicle* records, the price of a sester of wheat rose to 55 pence 'or even higher'.

Unfortunately we have no satisfactory way of measuring how large this agriculture-related sector of the money economy was, in relation to the uses of coinage for the payment of gelds and other taxes.

The baffling problems of weight-variation lie at the heart of the late Anglo-Saxon currency. We need to be very clear, not just about the boundaries between fact and theory, but also about the pitfalls of fact versus generalizations of the facts. The first two years, or thereabouts, after Eadgar launched his reform can offer us salutary lessons, and we turn next to look at the metrology of the Reform type in rather more detail.

Excursus. The enigma of weight-variation: the evidence of the Reform/First Small Cross type.

Because the coins of the first validity-period following Eadgar's reform were struck successively in the names of Eadgar, Edward Martyr, and Æthelred, their evidence for varying weight-standards within three successive phases of the type is particularly secure. This is the only type for which we have such secure evidence. The mean average weights for all coins of the three successive varieties are 1.53, 1.38, and 1.32g. These figures are almost meaningless. There are so many individual mints for which the corresponding three averages are approximately constant, or which progressively go up instead of down, and there is so much variation between one mint and another, that the idea of an orderly reduction by stages, imposed nation-wide by royal decree, is ludicrously at variance with the facts. Already in the first months of the reformed coinage, each mint-place was doing its own thing. At Gloucester, coins were struck on a standard of *c.*1.62g, but also at little more than 1.0g. At Chester, some coins weigh in excess of 1.75g, while most weigh 1.45—1.60g. At Derby there seems to be a standard of *c.*1.21g, and from Northampton all the surviving coins weigh less than 1.45g, with some as low as *c.*1.15g. At Lympne the coins are unexpectedly light, seemingly with a weight-standard of *c.*1.35g. At the major mints from which numerous coins survive, and where the evidence begins to be statistically sufficient, it is clear that coins in Eadgar's name were struck on more than one weight-standard: histograms show more than one peak. At York, for example, the peaks are at *c.*1.65g and *c.*1.45g. Something similar is true at Lincoln. Stamford, London, and Winchester yield long, straggling histograms without clearly identifiable subsidiary peaks, but which undoubtedly include coins intended to be on different standards. The mean average for a mint, even, may have very little real meaning: at London, where the mean is 1.56g, the main peak is at *c.*1.65g.

If they are based on fewer than forty or fifty coins, complex histograms can easily be erratic for statistical reasons, and may be misleading if taken at face value. There are only five mints for Eadgar, from which we have the weights of as many as a dozen reform coins, and at the other end of the scale there are fifteen mints from which we only have one weight or two.

Nevertheless we can see that the idea of weight-variation was present from the very moment of the reform. It did not evolve, pragmatically or otherwise, during the first validity-period. However one looks at it, there is an element of manipulation or even deception in the issuing of coins which look alike but contain different quantities of precious metal, —*if* they are to change hands at the same face value. They may not have done so for some purposes (e.g. large transactions) but for many others it is inconceivable that they should not.

Under Edward Martyr various mints can be seen striking coins on heavier standards than some of the coins they had struck under Eadgar.

From what has been said so far, it will be seen that the question whether a reduction in weight-standard coincided with the accession of Edward, and again with the accession of Æthelred, is simplistic, but even if it were a legitimate question it could not be answered accurately from sprawling histograms based on too few specimens.

Thus the general hypothesis of progressive, staged weight-reductions is by no means self-evidently correct, even if there is an over-all tendency for weights to decline. By calculating three general averages (1.53g, 1.38g, 1.32g) and then forgetting about the disparate detail from which those averages derive, one may invent a hypothesis about royal intentions for the sophisticated management of a national currency in response to national needs and international pressures, when such intentions may never have been formulated. It may be that in each shire, men were able to do whatever they decided as regards the weight of the penny (though not as regards its design or its fineness).

The hypothesis of three successive averages has been generalized, and has been assumed to apply to the different weight-standards found similarly in later types throughout the reigns of Æthelred and Cnut. There is plenty of hoard-evidence which supports the assumption that heavy coins belong early in each type, and lighter coins later. No doubt that is broadly true; but it is *broadly* true of the Reform/First Small Cross type. Where a precise chronology is available, namely in that first validity-period after the reform (and nowhere else), it can be seen to be nothing like the whole truth.

Again, it seems to be broadly true that die-linked coins show tighter parameters of weight than the coins of their mint in general. Light coins are quite often by other, and relatively inactive, moneyers. That seems to support a broadly chronological interpretation. But Eadgar's coins, and those of the first validity-period generally, demonstrate that at many individual mints, different weight-standards were in use concurrently, or certainly within the same 'phase' of the validity-period.

There is also a certain amount of scattered information from hoards which terminate with just a few coins of a particular type, the bulk of the hoard consisting of the preceding type or types. If those few coins belong very early in the validity-period, they demonstrate, quite often, that light coins were already being struck. English evidence of this kind seems relatively secure, but where the hoards are Scandinavian, their age-structure and dates of concealment may be more problematic.

It may well be that in later validity-periods the chronological pattern of the weight-standards became much simpler, and that the general averages conceal fewer divergences. One point at which the evidence can be tested, to some extent, is the Long Cross type, where the ethnic evidently becomes progressively shorter during the validity-period (ANGLOX, ANGLO, ANGL, etc.). On the hypothesis that these forms were successive, the detailed evidence is that the earliest issues were exclusively heavy, and the late issues almost all light. In Long Cross, therefore, it is reasonably clear that weight standards decline progressively and quite tidily. The political or monetary purposes of the decline remain just as problematic, however, and the analysis of the ethnic is a blunt instrument for solving the problem. The evidence is set out in more detail in Part 3.

The detailed facts about the Reform type might be thought to be equally capable of supporting an altogether different general hypothesis. For example, the weight of the coins might have been related to the standing of the customer or the category of silver he brought to be minted. A merchant would receive one kind of coins in return for his silver, while bullion brought to the moneyer on behalf of the king or the ealdorman or the sheriff would be minted at a different weight standard. That hypothesis is driven by the wide variation from mint to mint, and indeed within almost every mint from which there is sufficient evidence, within a very short time of Eadgar's reform. Administrative arrangements may have settled down differently within a decade or two, but that cannot be closely demonstrated. It is difficult to point to any mint other than Exeter which clearly exemplifies the idea of three successive standards in the Reform/First Small Cross type. Other mints might conform, if we had enough evidence to judge, but where there are just two or three specimens of each variety, who is to say what the weight of the next specimen to turn up will be?

One can try to test the hypothesis by asking why some shires struck predominantly light coins. Are the seven surviving coins of Eadgar from Northampton enough to allow us to ask what was so unusual about Northamptonshire? Why are the coins of Lympne markedly lighter than those of nearby Canterbury?

Conversely, at London, where one might have expected the needs of the merchant community to predominate, Eadgar's coins, which seem to be on three standards, are mostly heavy.

Q.22. Is there any evidence from stray finds that coinage was used to an important extent in the governance of the shires, or that it reflects the needs of taxation or of royally-controlled expenditure?

Nowadays householders pay a local tax, on a scale dependant on the value of their house. It may be typically between one and three per cent of gross earnings. The links between the council tax and regional patterns of monetary circulation are tenuous, to say the least. In prosperous regions the total receipts are larger, but the percentage remains similar, and small. Eleventh-century England was governed on a shire basis, and it is perfectly clear that the minting of coinage was controlled on a shire basis, even if we do not fully understand the mechanisms or the reasons (see Q.21). The collection of taxes was also no doubt delegated to a shire level. National danegelds will have been apportioned out in various ways, and are likely to have involved a land tax levied on a hidal basis. It seems clear that that was true of the heregeld. Increasingly through Æthelred's reign danegeld was a heavy imposition; and heregeld was remembered as onerous. But council taxes are generally thought of as onerous. It is to some extent a matter of perception, which needs to be corrected by percentage figures. If a hide yielded an income of a pound a year, then a 2s geld was a 10 per cent levy. A geld of 6s was indeed a 'mickle geld'. If the percentages were in fact fairly small in relation to the scale of the currency and in the context of the various uses of money, any effect that the governance of the shires had on monetary circulation may have been submerged by other influences.

Domesday Book was by no means England's first cadastral codex. It is high-profile because it has survived. But there were earlier codices of the same kind: the heregeld was almost certainly levied on a hidal basis (and a shire basis), and danegeld too. In the old debate on what the hide was, one can argue that it was not just a certain acreage of land, but a taxable unit of land. Edward the Elder's recovery of control over the Danelaw (which until then had not paid tax to the royal fisc) was followed by the hidation of reconquered shires. Indeed, one might even argue that the bureaucracy of taxation, together with the administration of justice, became the *raison d'être* of shire governance.

Taxation, then, in cash or kind, was to a significant extent organized on a shire basis. But was this reflected in the coinage? —either in the minting of coinage, or in the circulation of the currency? Obviously there was no requirement that tax should be paid specifically in the coins minted in one's own shire. The only mechanism one can imagine which might create a link between local tax and local minting would be if money had to be paid over very early in a new validity-period, in the new coins. Equally obviously, the currency of a shire was not ring-fenced to exclude coins minted in other shires. If there was a strong local flavour to the currency of the shire, it may have arisen naturally, that is to say without political intervention, either because inter-shire transactions were at a very low level, or because the demands of taxation dominated the uses of money.

Thus there are two propositions that we can test empirically. First, we can enquire whether there was mint-activity in every shire, and in every validity-period. We see that of the 32 shires (15 Danelaw shires, 8 more which were under Mercian law, and 9 under West Saxon law), there were several where the mint-output was persistently under one per cent of the national total (Warwick, Stafford, often Hereford, often Shrewsbury), and plenty of others where it was sometimes under one per cent (e.g. Cambridge, Huntingdon, Bedford, Northampton). One could argue that at most a third of the national output might (*might*) be connected with taxation at the shire level. London accounts for a quarter, and the east-coast ports account for a quarter.

Secondly, one can measure empirically, in each shire, the proportion of the single finds that are coins minted in that shire. If coins had been minted locally *primarily* to pay taxes, and if much of the money collected was spent locally by the sheriff or the earl as the king's representative, one would expect to see that pattern reflected in the single finds. In the extreme case, the finds from within the boundaries of each shire should be of coins minted in the shire. In the east, and anywhere near the east-coast ports, one would not expect to see such a pattern, but perhaps in the west, in Hampshire, Dorset, Devon, Somerset, Gloucestershire,

Warwickshire, and Staffordshire, a fiscal context for monetary circulation would dominate the picture? Not so.

The special case of Winchcombeshire, which existed certainly from *c.*1007 to *c.*1017, has been mentioned above (Q.20). In Hampshire, with its mints of Winchester and Southampton, and with a large sample of finds, only 3 out of 14 finds from Winchester itself are of the local mint, and elsewhere in the shire, about the same proportion, 5 out of 16. From Dorset only one out of half-a-dozen attributable coins is locally minted, from Somerset 2 out of 13, and so on.

Proportions like these give absolutely no encouragement to think that monetary circulation was confined within shire boundaries by the processes of local government. Of course, the coins of a mint tend to be more plentiful nearer to their place or origin, and regression analysis (Q.17) quantifies that statement usefully; but there is no shred of evidence to support the idea that shire boundaries coincide with discontinuities in circulation.

Q.23. Did Swein's brief rule in England leave any traces in the coinage? —and did Cnut's conquest of England lead to any changes in the patterns of monetary circulation?

In 1013 King Swein of Denmark (Svend Tveskæg) invaded England, and established himself at Gainsborough, on the River Trent. He was accepted as king by the leading men of Northumbria, Lindsey, the Five Boroughs, and the Eastern Danelaw. When he marched south, Oxford and Winchester swiftly surrendered to him. Only London held out; but at the end of 1013 Æthelred left England. If Swein had not died on 3 February 1014 at Gainsborough, his right to the kingdom would quickly have become unchallengeable. There are no English coins with the name and portrait of Swein, although he had struck imitations of English pence in Denmark, admittedly on a small scale. How soon would he have turned his attention to the work of the English mints, if he had lived? Perhaps London was the key. From Gainsborough there are site-finds (fully reported? —it is odd that they are all fractions) but none of them is dateable to 1013-14. Needless to say, there are no stray finds of Danish coins.

Encouraged by Swein's success, Cnut soon returned to the offensive, and with better personal fortune. A very large tribute was levied on the conquered English before a peace treaty was agreed, but thereafter the coinage system which had been in place for forty years continued much as before. Coins were minted in the same towns and in much the same relative quantities, and in the time of Cnut they remained in use for validity-periods of much the same length. The proportion of finds from the eastern and western halves of the country is not significantly different from the longer-term average. The volume of mint-output remained at the levels seen under Æthelred II. The quantities of coins found in Scandinavia remained at their earlier levels. The numbers of English single finds from each validity-period remain similar. By every obvious criterion, it was 'business as usual'.

There is just a small suspicion that relatively fewer of the stray losses had travelled long distances from their mints of origin. That might be either because long-distance trade had been to some extent disrupted, or because local exchanges had increased in volume. But the change is in any case so small that one hesitates to say that it is significant.

Q.24. If we did not know that there had been a foreign conquest of England in 1066, could we deduce from the coins that something of the sort had happened?

William's name replaced that of Harold on the coins, but there was no abrupt change in the English coinage system coinciding with the Norman Conquest. Periodic type-changes continued as before, with short validity-periods similar to those of the Confessor's reign. Weight-standards still varied from shire to shire, and multiple standards at the same mint are still found, e.g. at York. The moneyers' names continued to be predominantly Anglo-Saxon in much the same mixture as before. Indeed, many of the same men continued in office, with no obvious acceleration in the rate of turnover.

There were one or two significant changes in the ranking of the mints. Winchester, in particular, achieved greater importance. York declined; Lincoln declined. Norwich took priority over Thetford. Wessex gained a locational advantage as the region closest to Wiliam's territories across the Channel.

The coins continued to circulate over the same area in William's reign (Map 8), although perhaps a little less widely than for the previous ninety to a hundred years. The five major sites of London, Thetford, Lincoln, York, and Winchester account for 37 per cent of the single finds, compared with 26 per cent for the period *c.*973–1086 over all. Finds from the western half of the country account for 13 per cent, as against 20 per cent over all—a difference which one hesitates to interpret too firmly. The proportion of coins from eastern mints among the western finds should be a better indicator, discounting some of the uncertainties. There are three eastern coins among only 8 identifiable finds, or 38 per cent, cf. 37 per cent over all. The numbers are too small to be clear-cut. Two of the three eastern coins are from London, while the third is a Nottingham coin found in Oxfordshire.

It remains difficult, however, to know whether one can safely make a straight comparison between the dispersion of currency achieved in the earlier six-year validity-periods, and the post-Conquest two-year periods (discussed under Q.15). The exact length of the validity-periods, six years or seven years or whatever, does not affect this issue.

Among only eight western finds of which the mints are identifiable, three are

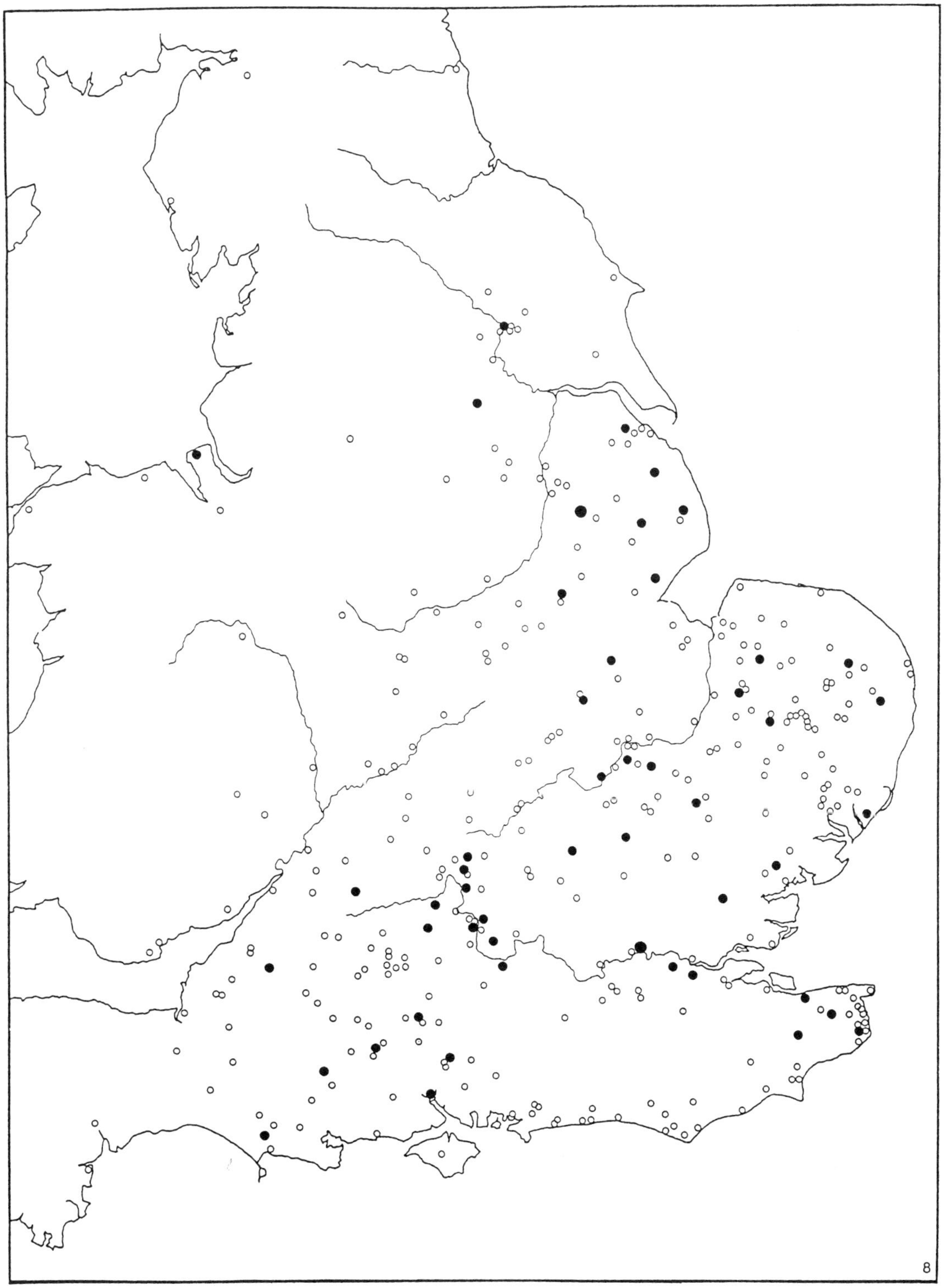

MAP 8. Coins of William I.

Wareham coins, found at Dorchester, Old Sarum, and Cirencester. They hint at journeys to and from Normandy. Again, the numbers are tiny, but it is intriguing that Wareham, which in Anglo-Saxon times had never exceeded one per cent of the national output, should colour the currency of the west so noticeably. Since Wareham's Norman hey-day is unlikely to have amounted to much, the finds suggest that the scale of the currency in Wessex may have been modest, outside Winchester itself.

One's judgement is that there may have been a geographical contraction of the currency under William I, in comparison with the period from *c.*973 onwards. But it by no means follows that the changes were brought about by the Norman Conquest. It seems more plausible that the major cause was economic, visible in the dwindling of outflows of English money to Scandinavia, and the decline in mint-output, from *c.*1040 onwards. Presumably exports of goods declined too. The rule of Norman kings may have reinforced these tendencies, by re-orientating England's overseas contacts towards the near continent.

The obvious question to ask next is whether the tendencies noticeable after 1066 were already to be seen from *c.*1040 onwards (when the decline in outflows to Scandinavia becomes apparent, and estimated mint-output, type by type, also declines). This step in the argument circumvents the uncertainties arising from comparing long and short validity-periods. If the answer turns out to be that the tendencies were already present before 1066, then we may judge that the Norman Conquest made no immediate mark on the coinage system, and little enough on monetary circulation.

Q.25. Was the fall in mint-output during Edward the Confessor's reign accompanied by any changes in the patterns of monetary circulation in England?

Estimated totals of dies, type by type, fell from their high point of over 4,000, at the end of Æthelred's reign and the beginning of Cnut's, to only about 500 at the beginning of the Confessor's reign. That represents a very significant decline in mint output. It was accompanied by a decline that was almost as sharp, in the numbers of coins in the Scandinavian sample. Whether those numbers reflect the reduced outflows from England, or whether they result partly from the growth of re-minting Anglo-Saxon silver in Denmark, is a topic for discussion. The die-estimates, however, are independent of that uncertainty.

Even though the size of the English currency had been diminished in the years *c.*1000—*c.*1020 by large outflows, it seem very safe to say that under Edward the Confessor there was a dramatic reduction in the size of the currency. The reduction may or may not have hindered the money economy of England, depending whether the country had previously been over-supplied with coin. There could, in principle, have been far more than was necessary to keep the

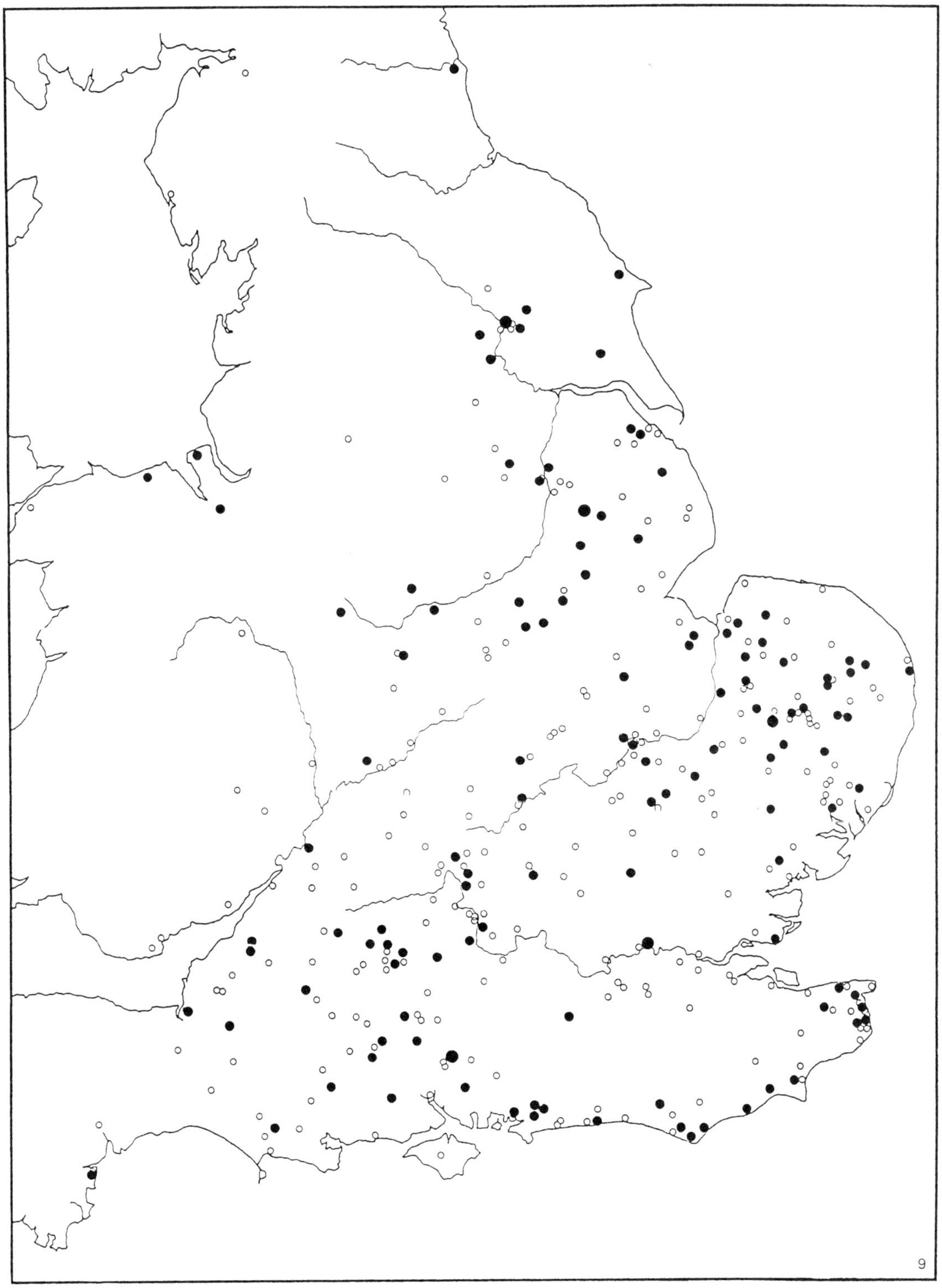

MAP 9. Coins of Edward the Confessor and Harold II.

wheels turning. The surplus will have lain unused or little-used, in 'reservoirs' of wealth.

First impressions are that the pattern of single finds of Edward the Confessor and Harold II (Map 9) looks no different from the general map. There are, however, only 28 finds from the western half of the country, or 15 per cent (compared with 26 per cent over all), of which half are from eastern mints. We can look at the relativities in another way, by saying that there are 28 western finds of coins of Edward the Confessor, but only 11 for William I, from periods of 24 and 20 years respectively.

There are differences, then, in the patterns of circulation between the years 1042-66 and 1066-86, but their significance for monetary affairs is quite difficult to assess. It seems that there was a trend throughout, and therefore that the Conquest as such had only a minor effect on monetary circulation.

Q.26. Were pennies cut up into halves and quarters by private individuals as required, or by the mints?

Round halfpennies from the period *c.*973—1086 are virtually unknown: there is one, of the Sovereign/Martlets type, from the Chester mint. Normally, pennies were cut up into halves and quarters to provide the smaller denominations.

The availability of coins of lower value than the silver penny is suggestive of a money economy better adapted to small, everyday transactions. The evidence of finds of cut halves and quarters therefore merits close attention. At any given date up to the 1030s, there were millions of cut fractions in use. The single finds may overstate the case, but the ratio of fractions to whole pence strongly suggests that, type by type, the numbers ran into six figures. In considering the numismatic evidence, we should keep the scale of the operation in mind. Cutting a penny in half was not an occasional expedient, done in order to make an exact payment.

After the end of the long validity-periods, when the size of each new issue was less, the proportion of fractions seems to have remained much the same.

Many questions spring to mind, and most of them can be tested against the coins. Was the use of fractions, for example, concentrated in the main commercial centres? The map of find-spots (Map 10) shows how widely dispersed through England the fractions became. They have been found away from the towns in much the same way as the pennies. It is difficult, however, to judge the relative importance of fractions from town and country, because so much depends on the skill of the individual detectorist or excavator.

And did people make their own fractions, as they needed them, or were they made in the mints and issued in the exchanges? Both procedures may, of course, have co-existed. It has commonly been suggested that fractions tend to be light, probably because coins at the light end of the range were selected to be cut up.

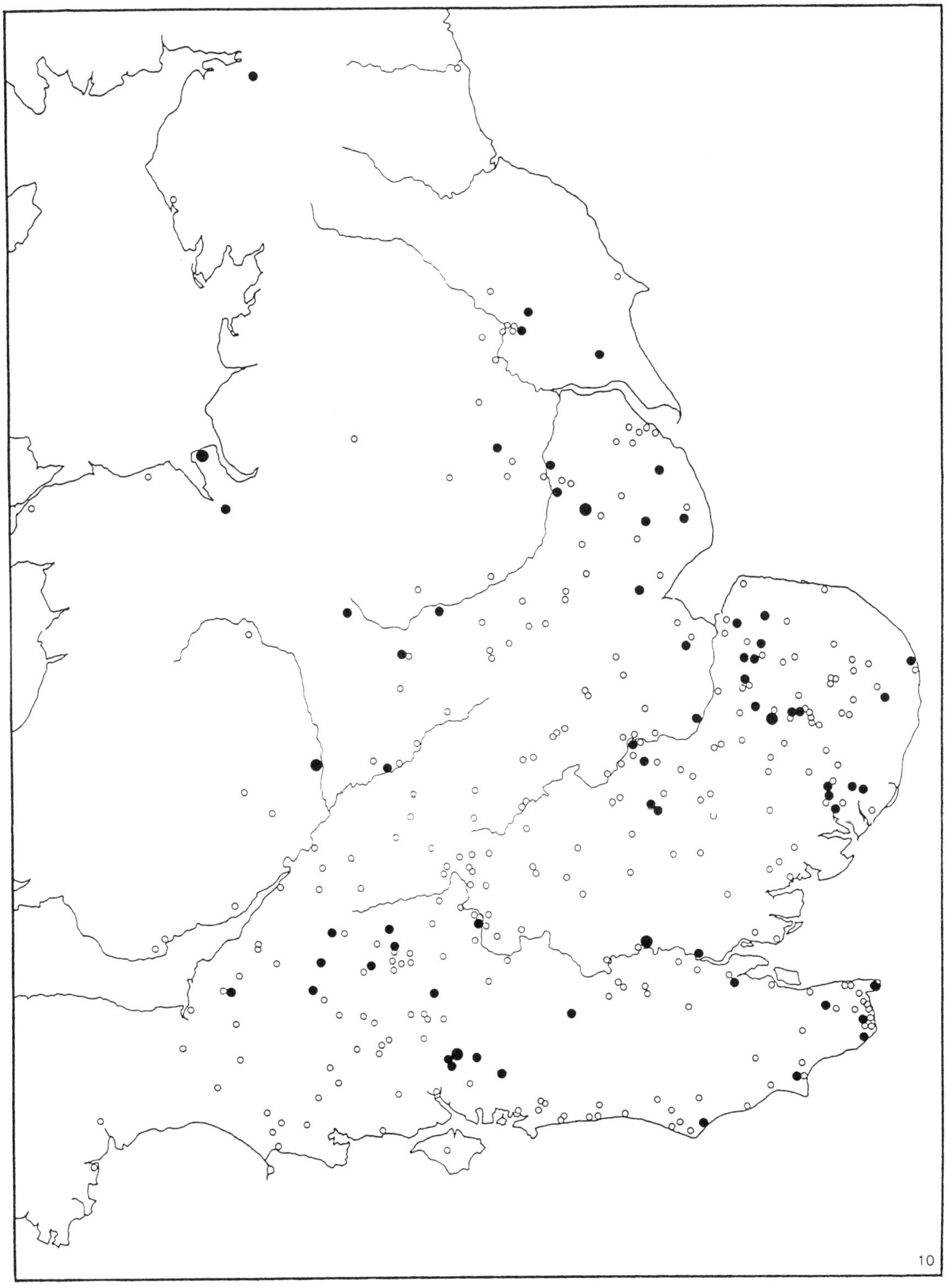

MAP 10. Cut halves and quarters.

That could have happened either privately or at the mint. If coins were checked after striking but before issue to remove any that fell outside the tolerated variation in weight, it would have been thrifty to cut the light coins up. They were, in effect, slightly deficient in intrinsic value, but the users did not care *de minimis*. Such coins would pass from hand to hand at their face value, where large payments might be checked to see that they gave full value. The claim that fractions tend to be light deserves, however, to be examined critically, and that is attempted below, using the Thwaite hoard as an example.

Halfpennies are usually cut neatly, with what looks like a chisel cut administered with a heavy blow. Where the reverse design of the coin has a clear horizontal and/or vertical axis the cut is usually carefully positioned one way or the other. By implication the coin was placed reverse side up to be cut; and often one can see from the angle of the sheared edge that that was so. Where the reverse design was, for example, a small cross, the cut is usually made diagonally. This neatness and regularity tend to show that the coins were cut in the mint, although of course private individuals may have supplemented the official stock.

If coins were cut while in use, one might expect them to be a random sample of the currency. There are three possibilities of disproving that hypothesis: if the ranking of the mints, among the fractions, is atypical; if the numbers type by type fail to match the sample as a whole; and if the proportion of specimens from early and late within particular types fail to match the sample.

A neat argument, if one had sufficient evidence, which would go far towards proving that coins were normally cut in the mint, before issue, would be by showing that the coins of certain towns are very rarely cut—or indeed that the proportion of fractions is significantly higher or lower at some mint-places. An acceptable random sample is difficult to put together, because of the rather high proportion of specimens from which the mint-name is missing. For what it is worth, the top ten mints among the fractions (where 93 mint-identifiable specimens are from 35 mints) match the top ten listed under Q.3 as closely as could be expected, allowing for statistical imprecision. They are: London, 23% (cf. 23%), Lincoln, 14% (cf. 12%), Thetford, 9% (cf.5%), York, 8% (cf. 8%), Winchester 6% (cf.4%), Canterbury, 5%, Norwich, 3%, and Stamford, Chester, Wallingford, and Hastings among half-a-dozen mints each taking 2%. This correspondence could have been achieved in two ways, either by randomly cutting coins drawn from circulation, or by each mint cutting roughly the same proportion of its output. One has to say that the former is easier to envisage. Cut fractions are known from even the smallest mints, such as Cricklade and Winchcombe.

A comparable argument would enquire whether variation in the number or the proportion of fractions from type to type offered evidence that they were cut in the mint: see Q.28.

A detailed examination and record of a large number of cut halves, with details of the dies, the weights, and the appearance of the sheared edge, would almost certainly yield valuable ideas. For such a project the coins need not be provenanced. Scandinavian hoards would serve very well. But for questions about how the fractions were used in England, English single finds and hoards are the necessary basis.

Because of differential loss of weight by leaching, etc., the evidence of a single hoard is particularly valuable. We can turn to the Thwaite hoard of 1832, which contained unusually large numbers of halves and quarters. The two diagrams, for the two most plentiful types in the hoard, Trefoil-Quadrilateral (Fig.4) and Short Cross (Fig.5), each show the weights of the three denominations in a way that makes direct comparison easy. The scale (in grains) for pence is doubled for halfpence, so that a 6-grain halfpenny falls vertically below a 12-grain penny. It is doubled again to give comparability with a 3-grain farthing. One can see immediately that, if the weight of a penny can be anything from 10 grains to 17 grains, the question whether a fraction tends to be under-weight could only be answered on a statistical basis. The spread of weights along the lower scales should be concentrated towards the lower, or left-hand end, in comparison with the penny scale, if there were indeed a systematic tendency for fractions to be on the light side.

The example chosen is from the 1040s, when average weights were settling into a narrower range(!). It is evident that the same general argument applies even more strongly to the period *c.*973—1035. That might lead us on to the potentially interesting question whether fractions were produced continuously through a validity-period, or mainly at the beginning, or mainly for a certain class of customer.

From the Thwaite hoard there is, in a word, no evidence that fractions tend to be lighter.

Up until the 1030s there were normally at least a million cut fractions in England, and thereafter, *pro rata*, hundreds of thousands. Cutting a penny in half was not an occasional expedient, as when neither party to a transaction can put their hand on anything smaller than a note (much less a chisel). It was provision made on a large scale; a million chisel cuts, neatly done.

Q.27. Was the cutting done during the validity-period of the type, or subsequently?

One imagines that less care was taken to have cut fractions reminted when the type was changed, and that they might have continued to be acceptable. The mints would doubtless have been reluctant to take them in, except by weight. But were obsolete pennies cut up? In so far as the cutting was done in the mint, one would assume that current coins, either drawn from stock as required (or

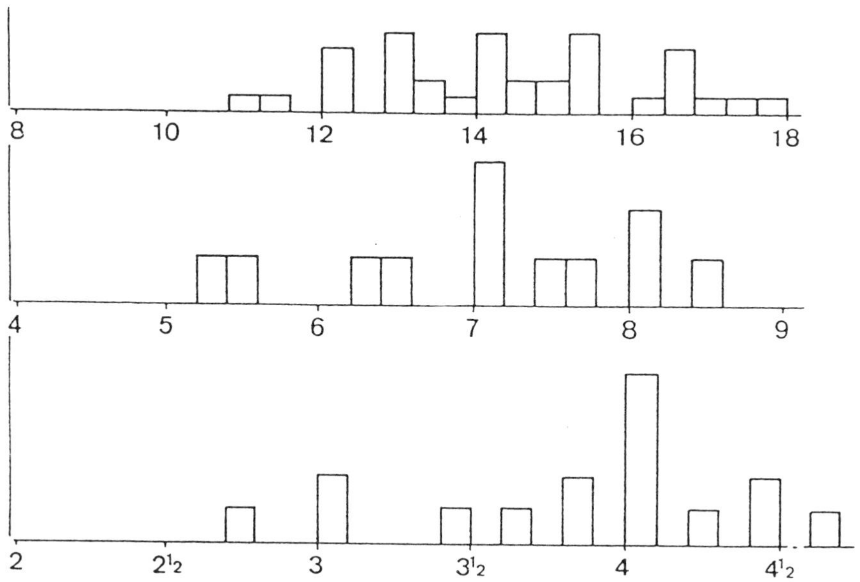

FIG. 4. A comparison of the weights of pennies, halfpennies, and farthings in the Thwaite hoard: Trefoil-Quadrilateral type (36, 12, and 16 specimens respectively). Weights in grains.

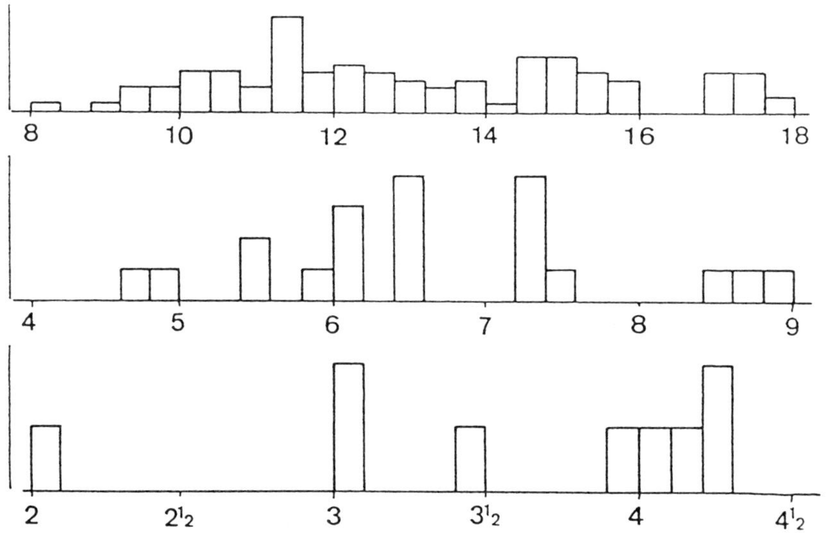

FIG. 5. The same: Short Cross type (96, 20, and 9 specimens respectively). Weights in grains.

requested?), culled before issue, were cut. One could hope to prove at least that the current type was already being cut up, from the evidence of one-type hoards, —which might also show that old fractions remained in use (even if the absence of old fractions does not altogether prove the converse). The Scandinavian evidence can safely be brought in to help to establish that the current type was already being cut up: there is a presumption that most of the halves found in the Northern Lands were already cut when they arrived. Single finds are, of course, quite useless for dating.

Where English one-type hoards include fractions, they are of the current type. As an example one may mention the London (Chelsea Reach) hoard of Second Hand pennies, with one cut half in a total of 14. The Shaftesbury hoard of 92 Long Cross coins included one that had been partially sheared, apparently from the obverse: it may be an example of a private attempt to cut a coin. The List Hoard, from the Frisian island of Sylt, includes a large parcel of Long Cross coins which had very recently left England. Among 580 English coins there were numerous cut halves and quarters, but unfortunately the report does not distinguish clearly between cut halves and broken halves. The Denge Marsh hoard of 1739, heavily coloured by coins of Harold II of the nearby Romney mint, included 'many halves and quarters'. Some of these may be studied in the Ashmolean, ex Knight (1795). His specimens include cut halves of Romney, (?) Dover, (?) Hastings, and, very interestingly, two die-duplicates of Winchester. (They are another small pointer to cutting in the mint.) Knight also had a Canterbury farthing of William I's first type, and a Canterbury halfpenny of his second type. As early reports mention coins of William, these coins may be thought to be from Denge Marsh too. Thus, it was not a one-type hoard. The Beauworth hoard is less ambiguous. Alongside 6,439 pennies of Williams I's Paxs type, it contained 18 cut halfpennies of the same.

Q.28. Within the find-evidence as a whole, are cut halfpennies and cut farthings random in their chronological distribution?

The numbers of single finds of whole coins plus fractions are set out, type by type, in the answer to Q.8: Reform type, 24 + 10, First Hand, 20 + 9, and so on. In all, there are 124 fractions, of which 25 are farthings. Farthings are such tiny objects that they are difficult to find by metal detector. Many of those on our list are from controlled archaeological excavations—where special care was exercised. In various excavations in Thetford, for example, ten whole coins (or fragments) have been found, and ten cut halves or quarters. The ratio of farthings to halfpennies in the list as a whole probably understates the case (even though excavations tend to be on urban sites). One suspects that farthings found by detectorists may have been under-reported unless they were mint-attributable. It is the general experience in excavating medieval sites, e.g. Byzantine Corinth, that the small denominations have a much higher loss rate. If halfpennies genuinely exceeded farthings as stray *losses*, one would conclude that they have exceeded them even more while in use. Striking a numerical balance between these conflicting arguments is not possible.

If we assume that the fractions were lost, essentially, during their validity-period, how should we assess the trend of the totals, type by type? Should we test them against the hypothesis that they are proportional to the finds of whole coins of the same type? Or might it be more appropriate to test them against the expectation that there was a steady demand for them, type by type? The numbers are, unfortunately, often too small to be statistically reliable. The high proportion in the Reform type, and similarly in First Hand is well attested. One wonders whether it reflects a change in the purchasing power of the penny, following the abolition of Eadgar's debased pre-reform coins. Cnut's Short Cross type stands out as having an unusually high number (but not proportion) of fractions. The figures remain high in the second half of Edward the Confessor's reign.

Expanding Cross provides an interesting test-case, where the great majority of the fractions are of the heavy issue. (But there is a preponderance of the heavy issue among the whole coins too.)

It will be sensible for the time being to keep to the broader conclusions. Thirty-seven fractions from the reign of Æthelred II, but only 13 of William I, indicates a decline.

If, as seems to have been the case, fractions were mostly cut in the mints, the quantities cut may have been determined as a matter of policy, or of instructions issued to the moneyers. In that case, it may be worth looking at those types with exceptionally high or exceptionally low proportions of fractions. There is only one in Æthelred's Helmet type and very few in Last Small Cross—and only one in Cnut's Pointed Helmet type.

Until 1066 about a fifth of the finds are fractions, but thereafter fewer.

Q.29. Do the mint-places of the fractions show, within statistical limits, the same proportions as the pennies?

If it is accepted that pennies were cut by the moneyers before issue, the mint-places of the recorded specimens take on considerable interest. We can then say straight away that the practice was very widespread. It was not confined to the east-coast ports. It was not confined to the larger mints.

When a coin is cut in half, one is lucky if the half that is found includes, on the reverse, the name of the mint. The moneyer's name may give the answer if it is an unusual name, or if the die can be matched. It seems perfectly safe to say that the fractions which can be securely attributed to their mints will be random in the sample of stray *losses* (although legible coins are perhaps more likely to be reported properly), and that the attributable finds are a random sample in respect of their mints. With farthings, of course, one is very lucky to be able to attribute them to their mint.

Among 93 attributable coins, the 'top ten' mints (as listed in Q.3) take 75 per cent. The difference from the figure of 68 per cent over all is just sufficient to be intriguing. There could be several contributing factors. The remaining 23 coins are almost all singletons, and include mints as far afield as Cricklade, Hereford, and Ilchester. One could extend the list of mints known to have produced fractions by drawing on unprovenanced material. There is no reason to suspect that there were any systematic exclusions.

So far as one can judge, most if not all mints issued a certain proportion of their output as fractions. Moneyers may have been required to supply fractions upon request, by royal instruction, but whether or not that was the case, the evidence is that the need for smaller denominations was widespread.

Q.30. Did fractions circulate as freely over distances as the pennies?

The same sample of 93 attributable specimens shows perhaps a slight tendency to a more localized use of the fractions (essentially, the halfpennies). From London, for example, four out of six fractions were minted in London, and at Lincoln three out of four. But at Thetford, only one coin out of seven is local, while at Winchester the three finds are from London, Maldon, and Salisbury. At Meols, the three are from Chester, London, and York. At Wallingford, two are from Cricklade and Winchester.

Sixteen out of 93 attributable finds are from the western half of the country, a slightly smaller proportion than for the sample as a whole (17 per cent, cf. 20 per cent). In the regional survey (Part 4), it is noted that there are very few cut fractions from the most westerly shires (Worcestershire, Gloucestershire, Herefordshire, Devon, and Cornwall), although this appearance may be exaggerated, because there are few finds at all. The general distribution of fractions (Map 10) shows that their use was widespread and was not confined to the larger towns. Fractions are known from the mints in the westerly shires.

What is remarkable is that the Reform type, *c.*973–*c.*979, should show a more vigorous circulation than later issues. Of seven listed fractions, five had been carried far from their places of issue: from Lympne (a coin of Eadgar) to Aveley in Essex, from York to Coddenham in Suffolk, from York to Meols, from Stamford to near Winchester, and from Torksey in Lincolnshire to Tamworth.

Fractions were acceptable as part of large payments, as the hoards show us. The proportion of fractions in the hoards seems hardly enough, however, to account for their dispersion among the single finds: there may have been some selective exclusion of them from hoards, which conceals from us the extent to which they were carried about.

London fractions in particular seem to have been carried far and wide, having been found for example at Caister-on-Sea, Cheddar, Ely, Royston, Stafford, Thetford, Winchester, and York.

Q.31. What were gold pennies for?

One of Edward the Confessor's first acts as king was to confiscate from his mother 'an indescribable number of things of gold and silver' —because, says the chronicler, she had been too tight-fisted with him. Wills provide ample confirmation that the very rich owned quantities of gold, as well as silver. Their treasures were closely guarded, and rarely suffered loss. Thus, objects of gold are almost a blank in the archaeological record of the eleventh century, and this may seem surprising by comparison with the thousands upon thousands of valuable silver pennies that were lost or concealed and never recovered.

Gold pennies, struck from regular dies, are excessively rare. Because there are so few of them from which to distil an idea of their human context, there is not much that can safely be said about them, except that they perhaps give us a glimpse of that archaeologically hidden sector, the treasures of the very rich. One can look at the mint-places of the gold pennies, and at how far they had travelled from their place of origin, and at their weight. That is about all.

From Hellingly, in Sussex, there is a gold penny of Æthelred's Helmet type, of the Lewes mint (*BMC* 1). It weighs 3.34g. Hellingly is a village near Hailsham, about 12 miles east of Lewes.

From Worcester, there is another gold penny, of Edward the Confessor's Expanding Cross type, minted at Warwick. It was found in 1824 by a workman clearing away the remains of the old church of St. Clement's.

There are other, excessively rare gold pennies from the eighth century onwards, including for example a continental equivalent in the form of a Carolingian gold denarius of Charles the Bald, minted at Chartres, perhaps in some way because of the special veneration of the Virgin's cloak there.

One imagines that such objects may have been struck specially for the king or for some other wealthy person to be used as a pious gift to a church or for some similar purpose.

The gold in them may eventually have been put to other purposes, such as the gilding of precious artefacts. Some may have had an after-life as coin-like objects, but obviously they will not have passed from hand to hand like everyday silver pennies.

Their loss-rate is accordingly likely to have been very low. Anglo-Saxon wills occasionally mention gold mancuses.

Q.32. Do coins which have been turned into brooches or jewellery show any signs of being anomalous in their chronology, mint of origin, or place of loss?

Nummular brooches were fashionable from Carolingian times, if not before. Some are made from real coins, while others merely imitate a coin design. Coins which have been adapted for ornamental use by the addition of a fastener (and, often, by gilding) may have had a much longer life than they would have done as ordinary coins. They had ceased to be coins, and probably have little that is useful to tell us about monetary affairs, but a few finds may be mentioned as examples.

There are three brooches made from Expanding Cross coins, and found at Alfriston (Sussex), Trowbridge (Wilts), and Walpole St Peter (Norfolk). In all three, the reverse of the coin is used as the face of the brooch. There is also another Expanding Cross coin, pierced and gilded, found at Aldbourne (Wilts). This little cluster attracts curiosity. One could speculate on various possible explanations, depending whether the coin was chosen to be made into a brooch during its validity-period. The political context of the Expanding Cross type is discussed in Part 3, Section 17.

Otherwise, too few brooches have been recorded for any patterns to emerge, except perhaps for a concentration after *c.*1060. There is no reason to assume that coins were selected to be made into brooches at the place where they were minted.

A case in point is a Swedish copy of Æthelred's Long Cross type, minted at Sigtuna. The brooch fittings seem to be of English workmanship. The coin was found at Old Romney in 1992. The obverse was used as the face of the brooch, which was not gilt. Another example where the portrait formed the face of the brooch came from Aldbourne, Wilts—a Helmet coin of Æthelred.

From the Chichester excavations there is a Bonnet coin of William I, of the Oxford mint, converted into a gilt brooch. From London (Billingsgate spoil) a William I penny of the Profile/Cross Fleury type, minted in London, uses the reverse as the face of the brooch. From Edington in Wiltshire, a coin of Edward the Confessor's Pyramids type, minted at Salisbury, was found as a gilt brooch. A coin of Harthacnut, from the convent of Nonbury near Worcester, was found in 1987.

Q.33. Were foreign coins permitted to circulate in England? Is the regional and topographical occurrence of foreign coins significantly different from that of English coins?

Out of 685 single finds, 27 or 4 per cent are foreign coins. It is possible that they have had a somewhat higher-than-average reporting rate, but many of them are excavation coins. Unless they had a significantly higher loss-rate than English coins, that is to say unless they were sometimes thrown away, there will have been at any particular moment many thousands of foreign coins, or even tens of thousands, in use in England. Nevertheless, the answer to the first part of the question is that foreign coins were not normally permitted to circulate. The English coinage was not such a closed system that only 4 per cent of foreign coins reached English shores, as measured against the size of the national currency. Most of the foreign coins were melted down and, we may feel sure, it was compulsory to change them for English coins.

A few coins (our 4 per cent) escaped this rule, presumably in one of two ways. Either they had been brought ashore by someone who had had no opportunity to call on a moneyer, or they were lost at some moment when the system had temporarily broken down. A study of ninth-century single finds has shown clearly that Carolingian coins were concentrated in England's southern coastlands, and often in places which were at a considerable distance from a mint. The same conditions no longer obtained in the eleventh century, when there were far more mints.

If there are any clues to what happened in the eleventh century, they will lie in the types of foreign coin which occur as stray losses, and their regional and topographical distribution (Map 11).

The 27 recorded finds include two categories which appear regularly, namely billon deniers from Normandy, and Norwegian coins of Olaf Kyrre. The Norman coins have been reported from Alfriston, East Sussex; the South Downs in West Sussex; Netherton, Hants; and the Winchester excavations—a classic south-coast distribution. There is also one from Billingsgate spoil in London. These coins are very difficult to date precisely, and there is always an unknown interval between the dates of minting and loss. One could not prove that they were lost before 1066. There is also a hoard from Southampton, consisting of a rouleau of 22 coins. Their date and mint-place are somewhat uncertain. They may have been struck at Saint-Ouen de Rouen or at Fécamp, and they may date from the 1030s—i.e. soon after the closure of the Southampton mint. One wonders whether they may not be connected with Edward's brief invasion of 1036. Another Norman coin recorded as a single find from Manchester may in fact be a stray from the Halton Moor hoard.

The coins of Olaf Kyrre have been found at Lincoln in 1977, as a stray find in the gardens of the Usher Gallery; at Thetford in 1964, in top-soil in an area then under cultivation; at the London Billingsgate site in 1984-5; and again at or, rather, near Lincoln in 1986 (together with a fragment, apparently part of a cut half, of an Expanding Cross coin of Edward the Confessor, of the Thetford mint).

They form another classic distribution-pattern, focussed on the east-coast ports.

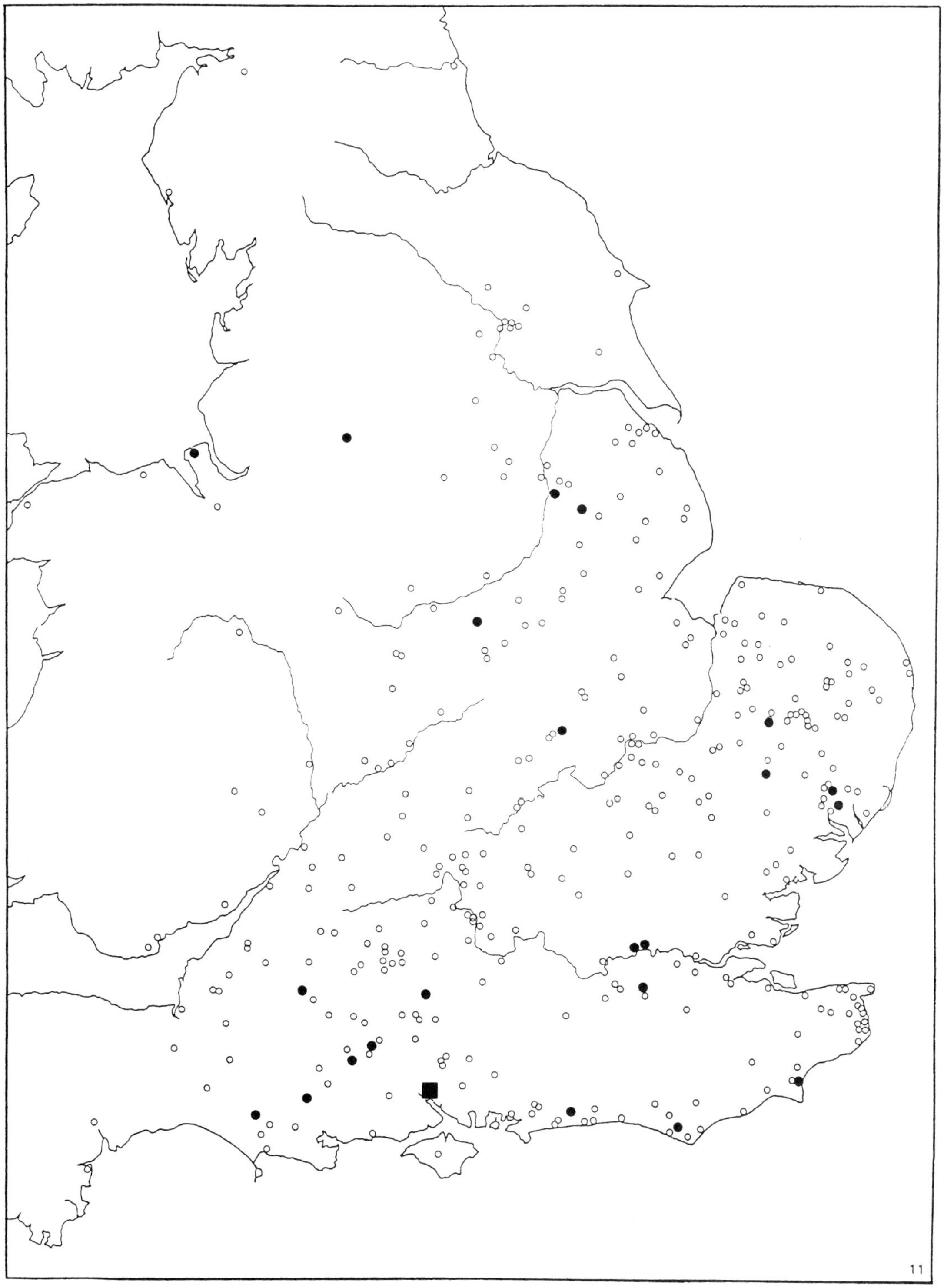

MAP 11. Foreign coins.

One may add a Danish coin of King Magnus (1042-7), excavated at Lincoln at West Parade in 1971. It is broken into fragments and battered, and its date of loss is therefore difficult to assess. The 1986 find is dated to *c.*1070-80. Coins of Olaf will necessarily be later than 1067.

It is natural enough that the Danelaw ports should have had close contacts with Scandinavia. Until at least *c.*1050, however, the monetary flows were strongly outwards. Peck-marked English coins of the eleventh century are very rarely found in England.

Hiberno-Norse coins are surprisingly almost unknown in England (suggesting that they reached Scandinavia without passing through the English currency, and that those in the List hoard, for example, were never disembarked in England), but Meols is an obvious place to find one: its identification is only tentative. There were two, of late date (Phase V) from Trowbridge, both originally from the back-fill of a grave. A cut half-penny has been found at Torksey, near Lincoln.

London (from where we have a large sample of single finds, from several different sites) is remarkably free of foreign coins. The earliest is from the first half of the eleventh century. Professor Berghaus suggested an attribution to the area of modern Belgium. Then there are coins of Olaf Kyrre and of Normandy already mentioned, which may well both have been lost after 1086, as may a Netherlandish imitation of a Duisburg coin of the Emperor Henry IV, minted in the 1080s or 1090s, and found in the Seal House excavation of 1974. There is also a Byzantine silver coin of 1059-67 found on the Thames Exchange site. Thus, foreign coins may account for as much as 7 or 8 per cent of the London finds, although one would not wish to insist on the randomness of the sample.

What is intriguing, however, is that at nearby Westminster (where the re-founding of the abbey was a major project of Edward the Confessor) the corresponding proportion should be 100 per cent. A German coin probably of Henry III, 1039-56, was excavated in pre-Norman footings at the Abbey, and in another excavation close to the Abbey an imitation of a coin of Conrad II, again of the Duisburg mint, was found. The imitation is unlikely to be German, but may be from the Low Countries. A score of two out of two may easily be overturned by future discoveries, but the evidence as it stands suggests that one should be alert for local or topographical variations in the pattern of finds.

Other German coins have been found at Blandford Forum, Bury St Edmunds, and Stanford-on-Soar, and a north Italian coin at Hemingstone. There is not much to be said about them, nor about a couple of French feudal coins, found at South Croydon, and at Tuddenham, except that their dates of loss are difficult to judge.

There is, finally, an Islamic dirham from Spain, minted in 999/1000, from the abbey ruins at Cerne Abbas.

Many of the foreign coins certainly, and other probably, are late losses, from *c.*1050 or even from 1066 onwards. It follows that the proportion of foreign coins in circulation in the period *c.*973—1050 was well below four per cent. A figure between one and two per cent over-all would be nearer the mark for the first half of the eleventh century, although the proportion will have been higher locally in the places where foreign coins are characteristically found, namely the southern coastlands, and the major ports.

Q.34. What do the single finds of foreign coins reveal about the destination of England's overseas trade?

A net deficit in England's balance-of-payments account with Scandinavia was reflected in the physical transfer of millions of English silver pennies to the Northern Lands. There, they soon became peck-marked. As peck-marked coins are extremely unusual among English finds (although the users would not have cared about the peck-marks, if indeed they noticed them) it is safe to say that very few coins returned from Scandinavia to England. One was found in the Bailgate at Lincoln in 1891; and a Scandinavian imitation of a Long Cross penny was found at Old Romney in 1992. In a deficit situation, then, the English single finds give no hint that there was any trade in that direction.

Throughout the reigns of Æthelred II and Cnut, the outflows of millions of English coins to Scandinavia were fully replaced or more than replaced by inflows which, so far as one can see, can only reflect a net surplus in England's balance-of-payments account with the near Continent. These millions of German and other coins are to an astonishing extent invisible in the English find-material. The reason can only be that the policy of compulsory reminting was extremely effective. One should remember that even one silver coin had a considerable purchasing power: eleventh-century coins were not of trifling value, like most modern coins. And after all, how often is one offered a 20-Deutschmark note in payment, in England? In the context of compulsory reminting, then, even a balance-of-payments surplus leaves no obvious evidence of the destinations of England's overseas trade.

Such few foreign coins as there are among the single finds should be interpreted accordingly. The presence of Norman coins after 1066 (and the absence of coins from Picardy or Brittany) should be seen in light of the political link between the two states. The occurrence of coins of Olaf Kyrre in or near the east-coast ports is more difficult to explain, but it may be that some special explanation is called for.

What do the single finds of foreign coins reveal about trade? —surprisingly little.

Q.35. Do hoards point to the same conclusions as single finds?

Hoards were not necessarily put together in the place, or even in the region, where they were concealed. Some hoards such as those from Castor, or Harewood, for example, will have belonged to travellers; and the risks, for a traveller, of losing his money may, although small, have been relatively much greater than for a stay-at-home.

The Shaftesbury hoard, to cite another example, of 92 Long Cross pennies concealed in a wooden or leather coffer cramped with iron bands, and buried on the outskirts of the town, a little way outside the defences, included 28 coins of York and 13 of Lincoln. Since the single finds from Wessex include extremely few coins from the mints of York and Lincoln, and certainly nothing like 45 per cent, we can say without hesitation that the hoard was not put together in Wessex. *One unhesitatingly prefers the single finds as evidence of the composition of the regional currency.*

To achieve the degree of inter-regional transfers of coinage which the single finds exemplify, thousands of sums of money such as the Shaftesbury hoard would have to have been carried about the country, in order to add up to the necessary volume of coinage, region by region. If the Shaftesbury hoard was unusual for Wessex, the York and Lincoln coins will have disappeared into the currency there, making up let us say less than one per cent. Among a hundred single finds, therefore, drawn from that currency randomly in respect of their mint-place, York and Lincoln would probably not occur at all, for purely statistical reasons.

In the circumstances sketched above, there is no reason to think of a conflict of evidence between hoards and single finds. It would be nearer the mark to say that they are complementary. The hoards, or those of them that can be characterized as traveller's hoards, reveal an intermediate stage in the process of diffusion, whereas the single finds reflect the end result more randomly. More precisely, the single finds are likely to reflect an average of the regional currency as it was at n moments (e.g. each year, or each six months) in the validity period. By the end of the validity period the diffusion will have been significantly greater than that indicated by the sample of single finds of that type (unless a steady state was achieved remarkably quickly).

There are hoards which deviate from our expectations in the other direction, i.e. with a higher proportion of coins of the local mint than is recorded among the single finds. Again the latter should be our yardstick. If only 3 out of the 14 attributable coins from the Winchester excavations are of the local mint, whereas a hoard from Winchester itself or from nearby has well in excess of that proportion of 21 per cent, we should unhesitatingly look for an explanation compatible with the evidence of the single finds. The six coins of the Stockbridge

Down find were all of Winchester, three being die-duplicates by the moneyer Anderboda and a fourth coin also his, while two were by Leofing. This raises puzzling questions, and all the more so in so far as the moneyers in Winchester are known to have worked independently of each other, on their own premises. Although customers will all the time have been visiting moneyers, and presumably receiving a batch of coins all by that moneyer, and indeed probably die-duplicates, it is quite difficult to envisage how a mixture of coins of different moneyers could be overweight in, e.g., Winchester coins. If there were several merchants or traders in the city who each had had occasion to obtain new coins from one or another moneyer, and who then did business with each other, the result might be achieved. Exactly the same phenomenon is identified in Q.36 with regard to Chester, and discussed in light of the Bryn Maelgwyn hoard.

The excess of die-duplicates in the Finnish material (and in Russia, and in Norway) points similarly to an 'inner circle' of merchants, through whose hands newly-minted money passed, and who bought and sold among themselves, creating a sector of the English currency which was less homogenized than what was to be found in the countryside at large—because it was 'closer to source'.

One possible route of reconciliation between hoards and single finds is to note that the figure of 21 per cent is a long-term average referring to the period *c.*973—1086. There seems to have been a tendency towards more localized circulation towards the end of the eleventh century (Q.24, 25), which might explain some of the hoards from East Anglia which raise this question.

Let us work our way through an example for which there are facts a-plenty: the Oakham hoard of 1749, for which a large sample has been reconstituted by Blunt and Lyon. The hoard was concealed at about the end of the first validity-period, *c.*979, and contained Small Cross coins of Eadgar, Edward Martyr, and Æthelred II. The local mint of Stamford, about 10 miles from Oakham, is the most plentifully represented, with 43 coins out of the sample of 189. Lincoln and York follow, with 34 and 21 respectively, thus 98 coins or 52 per cent of the parcel from those three northern mints. Our question is whether that is compatible with the single finds—of which we have 27 from the first validity-period, or 26 identifiable by mint. Three are of Stamford, two of Lincoln, and five of York: in all 10, or 38 per cent. If we look only at the single finds from the midlands and the north-east, which should correspond better with the regional currency within which the Oakham hoard was formed, we pay a price, namely that the numbers become much too small to be statistically reliable. Among only 11 finds from the northern half of the country (including Norfolk, Staffordshire, and Cheshire), the three mints in question account for 64 per cent. Thus, on a broad view there is no incompatibility. If we had a large enough body of excavated single finds from Stamford itself, it might well match or exceed the 23 per cent in the hoard.

Wells, in his study of the Stamford mint in 1938, claimed that under Edward

Martyr Stamford, 'from being an obscure mint with a very limited output sprang to the front with a greatly increased number of moneyers and its output increased to such an extent as apparently nearly to equal the combined output of all the other mints in England'. This bungling remark showed a poor grasp of methodology, and Blunt and Lyon were right to comment that 'there could hardly be a better example of the misinterpretation of evidence based on surviving specimens of one mint through failure to recognize the distorting effect that a single hoard can have'. Hoards behave differently from single finds.

The Lincoln-based sample (Q.6) shows Stamford taking 8 per cent of the national output in the Reform type, and that is probably the most reliable estimate for Stamford that is available to us.

The Reform type is especially useful as a test case because it includes the coins of three kings. In the Oakham sample the Stamford coins of Eadgar, Edward, and Æthelred are 5 plus 36 plus 2, = 43. That seems to bear out Wells's contention; but we now know of 8 moneyers under Edward, of whom 6 continue under Edward together with 8 new names, and 8 work under Æthelred (none of them new names). Of course, the output of individual moneyers varied considerably.

The Lincoln-based estimate suggests that Stamford's output was equivalent to that of 78 reverse dies. Jonsson's die-corpus shows 17 plus 43 plus 15, = 75 reverse dies. If Eadgar's coins are under-represented in Oakham, it may be through wastage, including export to Scandinavia. The under-representation of Æthelred's coins is more intriguing. Jonsson records specimens as ex-Oakham, by the moneyers Ælfwald, Grim, and Ogea. There may be a couple more moneyers, in coins that have lost their provenances.

The weighting of Oakham with coins of Stamford, Lincoln, and York can best be judged by the representation-rate per reverse die in Jonsson's corpus (although this is not ideal: one should be using die-estimates). For Stamford, 43 coins from 75 known dies gives 0.57, while for Lincoln the corresponding ratio is 0.70, and for York 0.27.

In the end, it seems that the Oakham hoard lies within the orbit of the Stamford mint, but that there is no obvious reason to think that it is a sum of money that had recently left Stamford.

The results of regression analysis (Q.17) give a general idea of what to expect in the way of falling proportions of coins of the local mint, as distance increases. It is only in a few cases that we are fortunate enough to have a good and varied sample of single finds from a large town—London, Thetford, Lincoln, York (Q.5). The proportions of coins of the local mint in each of these places are *c*.40 per cent, *c*.25 per cent, *c*.45 per cent, and *c*.80 per cent respectively. One may discern relative isolation and regional dominance of the mint as the main factors influencing these proportions, and guess that Stamford would be in the range

30—50 per cent, if information were available.

Q.36. What does the clustering of die-linked coins in hoards imply?

If the output of each die were equal or nearly so, there would be a clear statistical expectation that in a random sample the proportion of pairs (of coins from the same die) would far exceed that of triplets, and the proportion of triplets would far exceed that of groups of four. What we commonly find, in hoards of sufficient size, is that multiples greatly exceed expectation in comparison with pairs. This phenomenon of 'clustering' of coins from the same die will have arisen in two ways. First, die-output was far from equal, and multiples may simply point to heavily-used dies. Secondly, however, we must suppose that when a customer took silver to a moneyer, he would usually receive his money back in the form of new coins all from the same dies, or at most from a couple of different dies. After all, a reverse die may well have produced ten thousand coins before it was discarded, while most individual transactions with a moneyer will have involved at most a few hundred coins. In the course of making and receiving payments, the many duplicates will gradually have been dispersed into the currency at large, but little clusters might persist through many transactions, of coins that had stayed together ever since leaving the mint. In the same way today one sometimes receives a payment in bank-notes which includes some notes with consecutive numbers. What is perhaps surprising is that one very rarely meets with a hoard which contains long strings of duplicates. There could be no more dramatic testimony to the liveliness of the eleventh-century money economy, especially for the period of regular and thorough recoinages, when coins had at most about six years to become dispersed.

The little Titchmarsh hoard of 9 Fleur-de-lis coins, found beside the River Nene in Northamptonshire, included five die-duplicate coins by the moneyer Svartr of York, which obviously had stayed together. They were mixed with coins of London and nearby Huntingdon.

Two coins of William I's Two Sceptres type found at Cranwich, Norfolk, in November 1993 and October 1994, on the same site, are both by the moneyer Godwine of Northampton (a good eighty miles away), and are from the same dies. Although they have been listed below as single finds, there need be little doubt that they are a mini-hoard scattered by the plough, or in some such way. The odds against their having reached the site independently are astronomical.

Much the same argument applies to two coins of William I's Profile/Cross and Trefoils type, both found at East Bradenham, Norfolk, in October 1994, and similarly two coins of the London mint, from Æthelred's Long Cross type, found at Hangleton, near Littlehampton, Sussex.

Perhaps the nicest example of clustering is offered by the St. Martins-le-Grand hoard, of the Last Small Cross validity period. Out of 55 coins, 37 are of the London mint, and of these no fewer than 23 are die-duplicates by the moneyer Leofred. From the Scandinavian random sample one can see that Leofred was far from being a prolific moneyer. There were over 60 London moneyers of the Last Small Cross type, and a good two dozen of them struck on a greater scale than Leofred. The other 14 London coins in the hoard are by eleven moneyers.

There are astonishingly few English hoards of the period *c.*973—1086 that have been fully published and illustrated. The Bryn Maelgwyn hoard, from near Llandudno, illustrates an extreme case where there are many multiples partly because the number of specimens is high in relation to the total number of dies used. The hoard included no fewer than 171 Quatrefoil coins of the Chester mint, a relatively large total when set against the Lincoln-based estimate of 242 dies used at Chester for that type. The estimate is 'Lincoln-based' (see Q.6) and subject to margins of statistical error, but it rests on the substantial number of 151 Chester coins in the Scandinavian sample. Now, if the 171 coins from Bryn Maelgwyn had been an entirely random sample in respect of their die-varieties, the expected number of die-duplicates can be derived from the familiar formula

$$\frac{\text{non-singletons}}{\text{sample}} = \frac{\text{known dies}}{\text{all dies}}$$

The Bryn Maelgwyn coins are by 17 of the 28 known moneyers. Some moneyers were represented by only one or two coins, others by 16 or 17 or more. The coins comprise 18 singletons, 9 pairs (= 18 coins), 3 triplets, 2 groups of 5, 2 groups of 6, one of 7, one of 8, one of 9, 3 of 10, one of 13, one of 15, and one of 22. There are only 44 Chester reverse dies represented. An estimate based solely on the hoard would be

$$\frac{153}{171} = \frac{44}{x}$$

$$\text{therefore } x = 49$$

In order for x to become 242, the value 44 would have to become something like 125 (giving roughly 46 x 2 non-singletons) to balance the equation. In other words the Chester element in the Bryn Maelgwyn hoard is strongly affected by clustering. As 17 moneyers are involved, this again raises the problem discussed *à propos* Winchester in Q.35, and suggests that merchants did business with each other within the town.

Q.37. How long did coins remain in circulation?

'*Quando moneta renovatur*', explains the Domesday Book, 'when the coinage is renewed', certain charges are levied. It was a main plank of Eadgar's reform that it ushered in a period (of over 160 years) during which the English coinage was frequently renewed, normally (it seems) at regular or approximately regular intervals. The design of the coins was changed after roughly six years or after three or two years, in such a way that every man could see at a glance whether a penny was of the current type. (Closer inspection might be needed to see whether a halfpenny or a farthing was of the current type.)

One-type hoards are our evidence for asserting that the English currency from *c.*973 until 1083 and beyond was in fact regularly renewed, by a thorough recoinage of the existing monetary stock every few years. *Renovatio* has been seen as the supreme characteristic and distinction of the late Anglo-Saxon coinage, and as a political achievement which is remarkable in the eleventh century. Many corollaries flow from this view of the currency: first, that if coins only remained in use for a short time of known duration, their geographical dispersion (Q.14, 15) was necessarily rapid.

This paradigm has held the field for thirty years and more and, as is the way with paragidms, it has tended to enforce a particular view-point, and has been difficult to challenge, even though students have become to some extent dissatisfied with it.

Stewart has drawn attention to certain hoards which conflict with the general view of thorough periodic recoinage, and he has suggested that payment in current coin was compulsory only for certain types of payment, in particular payments to the king. The Wedmore hoard of 1853 contained types from Æthelred II to Edward the Confessor. The Milton Street hoard of 1843 included issues from Quatrefoil through to Edward's Helmet type. And the Walbrook (London) hoard contained a long range of types, with many coins said to be in very worn condition. There are various other hoards buried after 1050 which contained several types.

There is, then, a conflict of evidence, which needs to be taken seriously. If Stewart's case has substance, there are implications for the changing size of the currency, and also for the velocity of circulation as shown by the single finds, on the assumption that they were lost during their validity-period. In effect he is claiming that the great majority of the hoards from before *c.*1050 are misleading as evidence for the age-structure of the currency, in that they were put together selectively, and very carefully exclude older coins. Yet those coins were still in existence to be hoarded after *c.*1050. That is not implausible in terms of human behaviour. The single finds cannot be used to controvert the case, because their exact date of loss is unknowable.

How thoroughly was the coinage renewed, and did the coins of the old design lose a part of their face value when the type was changed? There was no doubt a period of grace to allow time for the practical necessities of re-minting millions of coins. But did some private individuals retain old coins as a matter of choice, rather than pay the charges levied on re-minting, because they calculated that it would be to their financial advantage to do so? If they planned to spend the money abroad, there might be no relative disadvantage in old coins, since old or new would be assessed on the same basis in a foreign mint, according to their intrinsic value. Or if they expected to retain their savings for longer than the current validity-period, they would do better to wait, and have their old money recoined into the next type, or the one after that, whenever it was needed, and thereby incur only one set of charges. But could these old coins be used meanwhile for ordinary transactions, or were they out of play—still in existence and still in private hands, but not part of the normal currency? (One merchant might accept payment from another merchant in old coins at an agreed discount, either with a view to export or as capital, but that is a special case. Such sums could still be considered as part of the money supply, but not M0, not the normal currency.)

The basic, common-sense position is that the design of the coins was regularly changed because the coinage was regularly renewed; but from the 1040s onwards there are many multi-type hoards. They seem to show that old coins remained available, often over five or six validity-periods. Alongside these multi-type hoards from *c.*1040–1086 there are the usual single-type hoards, occurring quite regularly both before and after the Norman Conquest. Which are we to believe? Can we believe both, or somehow strike a balance?

Things are not always what they seem. A multi-type hoard does not necessarily imply a multi-type currency. It may be a savings hoard, accumulated progressively type by type. Conversely, a single-type hoard does not necessarily imply a single-type currency. It might be selective, carefully excluding coins not of the current type even though they were freely available, in the same way that hoards commonly exclude halfpennies even though they were freely available. Only hoards can tell us about the age-structure of the currency—which might, of course, have varied from one region of England to another. Single finds are completely useless as evidence in that respect; and how we interpret the single finds will be influenced not a little by whether we believe they were all or nearly all lost during their validity-period.

If the age-structure of the hoards offers us evidence which is not only conflicting but also seriously ambiguous, how can we proceed with any conviction? There is one argument, about multi-type hoards, which escapes the ambiguity, as follows: the coins of different mints became diffused in circulation so rapidly that we might expect to see an increase in the degree of diffusion over the span of one validity-period. If a hoard is very much over-weight in the local mint for the validity-period in which it was concealed, and equally over-weight for the same mint for the previous type and the one before that, it is safe to say that it was not all withdrawn from a multi-type currency on one occasion. It is definitely a savings hoard put together gradually over the years, and it does not prove that there was a multi-type currency or even an alternative stock of old coins with an extended age-profile, other than the hoard itself and any others like it. There are

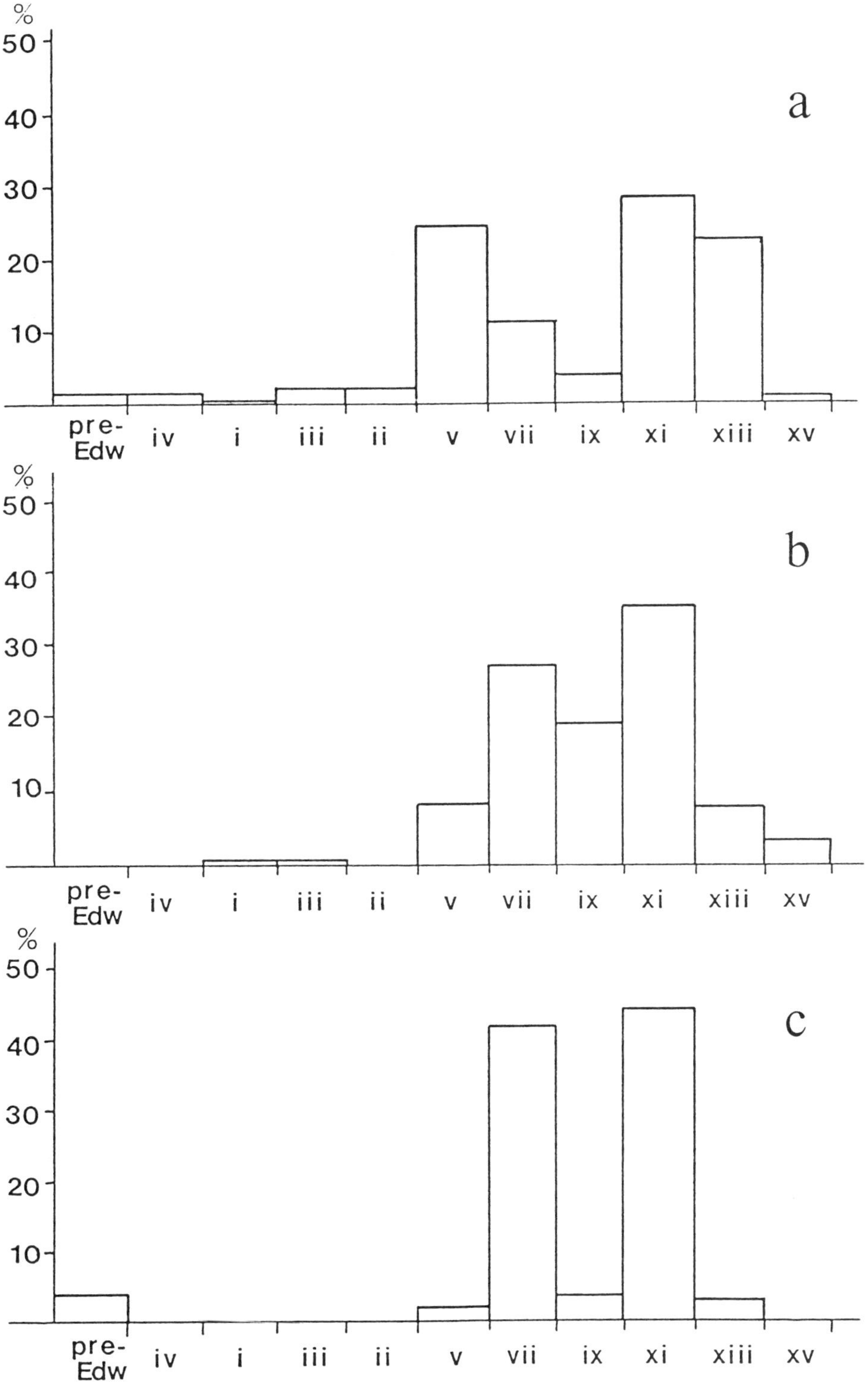

FIG. 6. An example of incompatible age-structures in multi-type hoards (on the hypothesis of a multi-type currency). Hoards from a) London (Queen Victoria Street), b) Chancton, and c) London (Gracechurch Street). (After Burrows.)

enough hoards which are clearly of this character, such as Sedlescombe, and York (Bishophill I), to establish the case. And it does not follow that hoards which are of more varied composition, not over-weight with a single mint all through their age-structure, are not savings hoards.

Even if a multi-type hoard does not betray itself by a persistently local flavour, its age-structure may be quite implausible when set against the hypothesis of a currency in which successive types remained in circulation. Were that hypothesis correct, one might expect a gradual dwindling of older types through wastage. More significant, one might expect that most of the relevant hoards would show a consistent profile. In fact, they are lumpy each in its own way. The owners had made savings when they could, irregularly in relation to the types, and the age-profiles are thoroughly incompatible. This can be studied from Oliver Burrows' histograms in Fig.6 (where a tendency may be noted for the Sovereign/Eagles type to be under-hoarded).

We can also proceed more generally by analysing the hoards in as wide a context as possible. Multi-type hoards tend to be large, although this is not always true. Single-type hoards are rarely very large, and are often small. It seems to be the case that large multi-type hoards tend to be from major commercial centres such as London and York.

The fact that there are many multi-type hoards from the years around 1066 should be judged circumspectly. It may be simply that there are a lot of hoards from those years, for obvious reasons. What would be significant would be if the *proportion* of multi-type hoards (against single-type hoards) were higher in those years, and it is doubtful whether the evidence allows us to say so, in comparison with the reign of Edward the Confessor, for example.

If it is true that the outflows of English money to Scandinavia dwindled dramatically from early in the reign of the Confessor (with a matching decline in the inflows from the near Continent), merchants who had previously found a ready outlet for obsolete coin may have had no obvious recourse, and may have had to change their habits. Although speculative, that seems a better general explanation than one which postulates dramatic social changes in the surplus wealth of the merchant class in England, before and after *c.*1040.

One should be very reluctant, therefore, to postulate a multi-type currency in England, even if it became common after *c.*1040 for obsolete coins to be hoarded. If, here and there, an individual kept a treasure, large or small, of old coins, it does not necessarily follow that numerous other people did the same, and it certainly does not prove that old coins remained in general circulation (and that most single-type hoards, therefore, were selective). The apparent conflict of evidence should probably be resolved (as we saw also with the conflict between hoards and single finds as regards the regional composition of the currency, in Q.35) by taking the view that some of the later hoards certainly, and others probably, reflect a special case in the uses of coinage. The volume of currency locked up in medium- or long-term savings hoards may have been small in relation to the volume of currency in more active use.

Q.38. Given that the uses of coinage were necessarily various and interlocking, can we strike any sort of balance between the public and private sectors of the monetary economy?

There is an obvious contrast between the eastern and western halves of the country: there was much less money in the west, even though the land was good, and farming, so far as we can judge, was prosperous. The Domesday Survey gives a measure of agricultural wealth. If taxation had been on a hidal basis, it would have been heavier in relation to the money supply in the west. Much taxation, however, was neither hidal nor *per capita* on the rural population. Total taxation included a large element of tax on merchants in the form of tolls, for example, on imports and exports. (To this day, one branch of the administration of tax is known as the *Inland* Revenue.) In the eastern half of eleventh-century England, there was more money, but more tax was paid, perhaps correspondingly.

The regional distribution of minting, and the patterns generated by the circulation of the coins of different mints, emphasize continuity, and are best explained on the assumption that inter-regional trade is the most visible factor in the uses of coinage.

Against that, there are intriguing differences from one mint to another in the weight-standards employed, particularly in the time of Æthelred II. Winchester, for example, may strike only coins on the heaviest standard. The hypothesis that that is somehow related to the requirements of a central treasury is attractive, but it should be kept in perspective.

The concept of public and private sectors is, of course, a modern one, but it provides a short-hand way of referring to the possibility that local taxation may mostly have been spent locally by the king's officers in the shire, without ever being transferred to a central treasury.

Taxation as a proportion of GNP (to use another modern idea) was normally modest by today's standards. Abnormal taxes, such as the payment of tribute after defeat in war, or of danegeld to deflect aggression, were painful necessities which were often imposed on a hidal basis (but London paid extra in 1018). Even in times of crisis—perhaps especially in times of crisis—it was politically necessary that justice should be seen to be done, at least roughly. And Domesday offers endless testimony to the king's willingness to listen to pleading on the subject of ability to pay.

There is otherwise little documentary evidence from the eleventh century, from which we could quantify GDP, levels of taxation, velocity of circulation, or any other economic measures, however approximately. The empirical evidence of the coins cannot be verified from independent sources, and its interpretation is and will remain a matter of judgement.

As new finds come to light, the increased quantity of numismatic evidence will gradually bring the patterns of monetary circulation into sharper focus. But it is difficult to see that any completely new arguments will become available. Unless variations and discrepancies in monetary circulation allow us to assess the balance between public and private uses of coinage, or between 'fiscal' and 'commercial' uses, nothing else will. The shape of the arguments about monetary circulation is already available to us through careful reflection, and is unlikely to change.

Q.39. Can we strike any sort of balance between the monetary and non-monetary sectors of the economy?

It is excessively difficult to reach any detailed estimates of the GDP of eleventh-century England, except by extrapolating from the view of people's ability to pay tax as recorded in the Domesday Survey. This relies on guesses about proportions of disposable income that could be taken from (mostly) farming people without driving them into the ground. In order to begin to form an idea about the scale of the currency in relation to the agricultural sector of the GDP, let us pluck some figures out of the air, and suppose that a prosperous farm allowed a family and their dependents to live comfortably. Cereal yields were infinitesimal compared with those of today, beasts were smaller, and hens laid eggs only in the spring. Let us say that the income of a prosperous farm was £20,000 in today's prices, and that a silver penny was like a £20 note: a thousand pennies. But most of the income may have been in kind, and enjoyed without any money having changed hands. A wey of wool brought in 120 pennies, or more. How many prosperous farming families were there in the eleventh century? Between a hundred and two hundred thousand?

The context of the eleventh-century coinage probably lay more in trade, however, than in agriculture. An Anglo-Saxon estate might, at least in principle, be economically almost self-sufficient and self-contained. The inter-regional transfers of money which are the most visible aspect of the uses of coinage tell us virtually nothing about the co-existence of an estate economy.

Of course there was a non-monetary sector. There still is today. Numismatics can in principle tell us little or nothing directly about it. The only available arguments are that the scale of the currency was so large that it could (not must) have serviced a money economy which touched the entire population; that coins were lost, and therefore used, in rural England very widely; that they circulated rapidly; and so on. Taken together, those arguments imply a strong and pervasive money economy.

The balance between the monetary and non-monetary sectors was different in the eastern and western halves of the country. In Wales, in north-western England, in the Borders, and in lowland Scotland there was hardly any monetary circulation. East Anglia and south-eastern England, by contrast, were heavily monetized. Exports to the Continent meant that an important part of English economic activity was geared to overseas trade. That, too, is an argument to suggest that ordinary farming folk were linked to the cash economy.

'Let me see', says Clown in *The Winter's Tale*, 'Every 'leven wether tods; every tod yields pound and odd shilling: fifteen hundred shorn, what comes the wool to?—I cannot do't without compters. Let me see; what am I to buy for our sheep-shearing feast?. . . What will this sister of mine do with rice?'

PART THREE

THE PERIODIC TYPES

AND THE HOARDS

Continuity and change, and the age-structure of the currency

1. Reform
2A. First Hand
2B. Second Hand
3. Crux
4. Long Cross
5. Helmet
6. Last Small Cross
7. Quatrefoil
8. Pointed Helmet
9. Short Cross
10. Jewel Cross
11. Fleur-de-lis
12. Arm and Sceptre
13. Pacx
14. Radiate/Small Cross
15. Trefoil-Quadrilateral
16. Short Cross (Small Flan)
17. Expanding Cross
18. Helmet
19. Sovereign
20. Hammer Cross
21. Facing Bust
22. Pyramids
23. Pax
24. Profile/Cross Fleury
25. Bonnet
26. Canopy
27. Two Sceptres
28. Two Stars
29. Sword
30. Profile/Cross and Trefoil
31. Paxs

For each type, a general discussion of its significance for monetary history is followed by information under six standard headings: a) English single finds, b) English hoards, c) Size of the issue, d) Evidence for dating, e) Weight-standards, f) Number of mint-places. Finally there is a list of bibliographical references (other than the obvious standard sources).

1. REFORM/FIRST SMALL CROSS

*c.*973—*c.*979

Hildebrand Types C2(Eadgar), A(Edward), A1(Æthelred).
BMC Types vi, i, and i (part).

Eadgar's Reform type was continued throughout the reign of Edward the Martyr (975-8), and into that of Æthelred II. Because the coins of this one validity-period fall into three chronological phases without any doubt or conjecture, their evidence for the spread of minting activity through the validity-period and for successive weight-standards is uniquely secure. We do not know, admittedly, how promptly the obverse dies were replaced after the death of a king; but in so far as the image and the reverse design were unchanged, and only the royal name was different, we may assume that as soon as the succession was known, any dies that were cut would be up-to-date. For the monetary historian the main practical point is that the weight-variation among coins in the name of Eadgar may be assumed to have occurred within roughly the first third of the validity-period. Eadgar died on 8 July 975, and Edward was martyred on 18 March 978, after a reign of two years and nine months. The duration of the other two issues is, however, not known, because the start and end-dates of the type (although much discussed) are inevitably conjectural.

The dies for Eadgar's reform coins are consistently of one style, and were doubtless produced centrally, to be distributed to their respective mints. Under Edward this policy of centralization was eroded, when Lincoln and York began cutting dies again, as they had done before the reform. By the beginning of Æthelred's reign there were at least six die-cutting centres.

The type has been intensively studied by Jonsson, who gives a thorough die-analysis arranged by mints, for a sample of *c.*350 coins of Eadgar, *c.*360 of Edward Martyr, and *c.*150 of Æthelred, in *The New Era*, 1987. A list giving the whereabouts of all known specimens is given in the same writer's *Viking-Age Hoards*, 1986. A few English single finds have been added to the canon since then, but otherwise there has been little new work. For chemical analyses, see Metcalf and Northover, in *BNJ* 1986, at pp. 52-3. Diffusion of the reformed coinage through England was rapid. see Q.13.

a) *English single finds. Eadgar:* Aveley (½), Colkirk (½), Deanshanger, Ipswich, Meols (½), Old Sarum, Pitt (¼), Shipdham, Stow-on-the-Wold.
Edward: Bere Regis, Biggleswade, Blackthorn, Caer Gybi, Castle Acre, Coddenham (1 + ½), Cranwich, East Walton, Felpham, Ipswich, Lewes, Reculver, Ringwould, Tamworth (½), Warlingham, West Mersea.
Æthelred: Alford, Dunnington (½), Gainsborough (¼), Grimsby (½), Much Marcle, Willingham, York.
The disproportion in numbers between the three issues (9, 17, 5), when compared with the numbers of known dies (*c.*200, 200, 100) is just sufficient to attract curiosity. Æthelred's coins might be expected to be

fewer because they had such a short period in currency, but conversely Eadgar's had longer. One wonders whether there was an initial tendency for the Reform coins to disappear into monetary reservoirs.

b) *English hoards.* Welwyn, Oakham (unless, as has been suggested, it terminates with First Hand coins), St. Austell, and (probably) Spettisbury Ring. The slightly later Chester (Pemberton's Parlour) hoard is a major source for the type in England: see under 2a, First Hand.
Welwyn (Great North Road), 1912. Just four coins, of which two are pre-reform, still in use in the time of Edward Martyr. One coin of the latter is of Winchester. See Dolley, 1969.
Oakham, Rutland, 1749. Some 300 coins, of which 189 (191) were listed by Blunt and Lyon (see Q. 35). Revised list by Jonsson, *The New Age*, pp. 233-5.
St. Austell. One Reform coin of the Winchester mint was included in a hoard of extended age-structure in the Rashleigh collection. Its credibility is discussed in Part 4, section 12. It seems to be similar to hoards from Ireland and Scotland terminating with coins of Eadgar, and is unlike English hoards which post-date the reform, except in so far as there was a delay in implementing it in some regions.
Spettisbury Ring, Dorset, *c.*1790. Three coins, of Eadgar (Totnes), Edward (Stamford), and Æthelred (type?). Ibid., p. 235.

c) *Size of the issue.* 1,031 equivalent reverse dies, based on the (rather small) Scandinavian sample. Jonsson, *The New Era*, pp. 114-18, records 788 specimens from 511 reverse dies, and arrives at an estimate of 919. He argues, in an excellent discussion, that this is likely to be an under-estimate, and that the true figure may have been between 1,500 and 2,000.

d) *Evidence for dating.* The exact dates and duration of the type have been discussed endlessly and inconclusively. Dolley suggested, in an article published in May 1973, that the unusually large number of moneyers working at Bath in Eadgar's 'Circumscription' type (*BMC* Type iii) may reflect the king's coronation in that city in May 973. In the Reform/First Small Cross type, only one of those moneyers is known to have continued to work. 'The need for largesse apart', Dolley writes, 'the ceremony would have. . . made heavy inroads into the royal resources, and against this background the creation of a special college of moneyers makes good sense.' Six moneyers are known in Type iii. The argument is formally circumstantial, because there are other mints with a fair number of moneyers in that type. Oxford, for example, has five, and Northampton has 11. What we can say is that if the coinage reform had preceded the coronation, more moneyers and more specimens might have been expected from Bath. The coronation thus seems to offer a *terminus ante quem non* for the reform.

Otherwise, the only facts in the case are the relative numbers of dies used with the names of Eadgar, Edward, and Æthelred respectively (fewer for Æthelred), but of course there is no reason to assume that the rate of production was uniform throughout the validity-period. It is hypothesis that the types were all introduced at the same season of the year (Michaelmas); that the validity-periods were all of the same length; that their duration was six years; or that periodic recoinage was envisaged from the moment of Eadgar's reform. The dates suggested should be viewed as approximate, to within a year or at most a couple of years. The Chester hoard of 1914, ending with a few coins of the First Hand type, may have been lost as a result of a Viking raid on Chester in 980. That suggests an end-date for the Small Cross type of 979. See Stewart, 'Coinage and recoinage', pp. 459-62 and 477-8.

e) *Weight standards.* For the country as a whole, Eadgar's coins have a mean weight of 1.53g, Edward's average 1.38g, and Æthelred's, 1.32g (Petersson, 1990, p. 347). These averages undoubtedly conceal numerous divergences and complexities, mint by mint. (See the Excursus following Q.21.) The sample is, unfortunately, rather small (508), and there are few mints where, for each or any of the three kings, the number of coins exceeds a dozen. No definitive assessment is possible, therefore, of the variation on a shire basis. Detailed work in correlating Petersson's mint-tables with the coins of individual moneyers may lead to some sharpening of the focus, but the tolerances seem to have been generally slack, making definition from small samples all the more difficult. In the eastern half of England, we see a falling weight-standard, but at London the modal values for the three reigns appear to have been *c.*1.64, *c.*1.51, and *c.*1.51g. At Lincoln, the best guess one can make is *c.*1.62, *c.*1.40, and *c.*1.36g. At Stamford there is reason to suspect two standards under Edward Martyr, of *c.*1,37 and *c.*1.28g. At Northampton it seems that the coins were on a low standard of *c.*1.40g from the very beginning.

In the westerly half of the country, Chester appears to maintain the same high standard throughout the validity-period, as was its wont in later types. For all other mints, one should examine the data (set out in Petersson, 1990), if only to persuade oneself that they are insufficient to sustain any generalization.

f) *Number of mint-places.* Some 40 mint-places are recorded under Eadgar, 35 under Edward, and 25 under Æthelred. The lists may well be incomplete. Remarkably few of the mint-places are newly established, so far as we can judge. Because not many coins were mint-signed in the period in between Athelstan and the reform, it is difficult to be certain whether a mint is new in *c.*973. The major quantitative change is the decline in output at Chester, which certainly precedes the ravaging of 980. Ipswich seems to be a new mint-place, and at Thetford minting may have begun only a short time before the reform. It is uncertain whether Cambridge falls into the same pattern of new developments in East Anglia. Various mints south of the Thames are so tiny that the presence or absence of one specimen changes our understanding. Thus Dorchester and Malmesbury are tiny mints and may be new (although it seems unlikely from the character of the places), while Guildford and Lydford may possibly be creations of the time of Edward the Martyr.

It seems to have been in his reign that a clutch of new mint-places were set up in Lincolnshire, namely Caistor, Horncastle, Torksey, and LV (Louth?). Their output was minimal, and they barely survived into the next validity-period, except for Torksey. For Grantham, see under First Hand. Although coins of Eadgar may still turn up, it seems likely that the Lincolnshire arrangements were a local initiative during the reign of Edward, and therefore that the reform of the coinage was still under political consideration at a shire level. The moneyers in question seem not to be Lincoln moneyers on temporary secondment.

For further discussion of the Reform type, see Q.13, and the Excursus following Q.21.

References.

R.H.M. Dolley, 'The Edgar millenary: a note on the Bath mint', *Seaby's Coin and Medal Bulletin* 1973, 156-9.

R.H.M. Dolley, 'Roger of Wendover's date for Eadgar's coinage reform', *BNJ* 49 (1979), 1-11.

K. Jonsson, *The New Era. The Reformation of the Late Anglo-Saxon Coinage*, Stockholm, 1987.

2A. FIRST HAND
*c.*979–*c.*985
Hildebrand Type B1.
BMC Type ii, var a; ii; iic; iib.

Within at most eighteen months of his consecration on 4 May 979, and very probably before the ravaging of the Wirral in 979/80, Æthelred replaced the rather basic coin design which he had inherited from his murdered half-brother Edward by an overtly religious reverse type showing the hand of God descending from heaven, flanked by the Greek letters *alpha* and *omega.* Many of the sources about the first half of Æthelred's reign are coloured by hindsight and are difficult to interpret, but the choice of coin-type is unequivocally an early act which reflects the thinking of the king's early days. The 'hand' type is political propaganda, claiming divine approbation of the young ruler. The coin type continued to be struck for about a decade, or perhaps even a little longer. It was modified by the addition of a pellet below *alpha* and *omega*, and a more elaborate 'cuff' (Second Hand), and then again by substituting a hand in the gesture of a trinitarian benediction, without the Greek letters.

The status and chronology of the First Hand, Second Hand, and Benediction Hand types have been much disputed, but their relative order as three successive phases is not in doubt. Dolley persisted in his original view that First Hand and Second Hand were each a six-year type, and that Second Hand demonetized First Hand (979-85, 985-91). Most other students have been unhappy with this thesis, in varying degrees, and some would see Hand as a single type (e.g. from a metrological point of view). The Chelsea Reach hoard, consisting exclusively of Second Hand coins, came to light late in Dolley's lifetime, and reinforced his convictions.

It is quite difficult to imagine satisfied customers who had just visited a moneyer to receive sixteen new coins for twenty old ones, or whatever, when Second Hand coins looked almost identical to First Hand.

There is an early variety of First Hand with left-facing bust (*BMC* ii) struck at Canterbury and Lympne, Chester, Hereford, and Shrewsbury. A variant with sceptre, known only from Ipswich, is apparently late. In general, many dies are of poor style.

The dies seem to have been cut at six centres, recognizable by their style. They are: East Anglia, Midlands A and B (Lincoln?), Northern A and B (York), North-western (Chester), Southern A and B (London?), and South-eastern (Canterbury). Dolley and Talvio (*BNJ* 1977) illustrate the styles, and indicate the proportion of dies from each centre, from a large sample. Obverse and reverse dies were used essentially one to one, but there is an unexplained curiosity at London, where it seems that style A used two reverses to each obverse, while the (lighter) coins of style B used two obverses to each reverse (!), with rather a lot of muling, which perhaps explains the apparent technical oddity. London cut half the national supply of dies, and East Anglia a quarter.

The coins have been very thoroughly studied by Jonsson, in *The New Era*, 1987, and in *Viking-Age Hoards*, 1986.

a) *English single finds*. Benson, Bredfield (½), Carlisle (½), Castle Rising, Crewkerne, Easingwold, Ecton, Eynsham (½), Glastonbury, Grimsby (½), Hemingford Grey, Hempnall, Horncastle (½), Ipswich (½), Lincoln (2 x ¼), Meols (2), Netherton, Nottinghamshire, Oxford, Ramsbury, Reculver, Sevenoaks, Wallingford (½), Worcester (½), Yapton, York (2). See Map 11.

The proportion of fractions among the single finds is again unusually high (see the statistics in the answer to Q.8), perhaps because the reform was still in process of taking effect, or because there was still some resistance to coins with a higher intrinsic value than the pre-reform coins. The mint-places of the fractions do not show any obvious correlation, however, with regions that were tardy in implementing the reform.

b) *English hoards*. The Oakham hoard (see Q.35) may have terminated with a few First Hand coins. Chester, soon after the Hand type was introduced, and Ipswich, later but before the introduction of Second Hand. See also the commentary on the Welbourn hoard, under 4, Long Cross, below.

Chester (Pemberton's Parlour, = 'near the cathedral'), 1914. More than the 133 coins, of Eadgar's Reform type (22), Edward (59), Æthelred (40), and First Hand (left-facing bust, 4; right-facing bust, 8) which are fully listed in Jonsson's *New Era*, pp. 231-3. The Chester mint accounts for seven Small Cross coins, or six per cent of that type, and five First Hand, or 42 per cent, against four and two per cent respectively in the Scandinavian sample. Acording to the pure doctrine of the sexennial cycle, the Chester hoard will have been concealed during the period of grace from Michaelmas to Martinmas, during which people had to change their money. Even though it is so overweight in the latest Chester coins, the hoard already contains First Hand coins from as far away as London, Winchester, Lincoln, and York. There can be no proof that it was not concealed somewhat after Martinmas 979. Indeed, there is a good probability that its non-recovery was connected with the ravaging of the Wirral in 979/80.

Ipswich (at the corner of Old Buttermarket and White Hart Lane), 1863. About 150 coins, of which only 75, all First Hand, can be listed. Left-facing bust (3), right-facing bust (72). The 75 include 23 coins of Ipswich (31 per cent) and 16 of London. See Dolley, 'The 1863 Ipswich hoard', *BNJ* 1964. The hoard's association with the ravaging of Ipswich by the Vikings in 991 requires special pleading, if First Hand is dated conventionally to *c.*979—*c.*985. In so far as the chronology is negotiable, most students would prefer Crux to begin earlier than 991. The Ipswich hoard seems to be from 985 at the very latest. See Dolley and Metcalf, 'The reform', pp. 154-5. See also the commentary on the Ipswich mint in section 5, East Anglia, below.

c) *Size of the issue*, The Lincoln-based estimate is 2,054 equivalent reverse dies. Taking into account the margins of statistical uncertainty, this may represent anything from a modest increase on the scale of the Reform type, to a doubling. See section 1.

d) *Evidence for dating*. At Rochester the moneyer Sidewine used an altered obverse die of First Hand, with sceptre added, to strike Second Hand coins (having previously used the same die without sceptre). No other case of an added sceptre has been discovered (although they may exist): there are a few dies that look as though they have been altered, but the unaltered state has not been found. What seems to have been an emergency arrangement has been tentatively connected by Dolley with the *Chronicle* record that in 986 the king laid waste the diocese of Rochester. The city had previously undergone a siege. This offers evidence, admittedly fragile, that Second Hand was introduced in

985 or 986. (Brand, in *NCirc* 1965, 182, and Dolley, ibid. 1967, 33f.).

The Iona hoard, mainly of pre-reform coins, contained three Second Hand coins (of Exeter and Winchester). Dolley sought to connect it with a known raid in 986. A six-year period for First Hand presupposes that it was intended to be replaced by Second Hand, *q.v.*

e) *Weight-standards.* First Hand averages 1.51g (Petersson, 1969, pp. 104-7). Petersson examines the metrology of all three Hand types as a single pattern (Second Hand is lower, at 1.31g, and Benediction Hand is very high, at 1.59g). The pattern as a whole shows regional resemblances with the Reform type. The same cautionary remarks apply (see above). Some mints show a very satisfactory histogram with a single peak, e.g. Canterbury at *c.*1.55g, Ipswich at *c.*1.60g, Norwich and Thetford both at *c.*1.63g, Chester at *c.*1.66g. Lincoln and Stamford, by contrast, yield very straggling histograms, which doubtless reflect more than one standard. The same is true of Exeter. London has a peak at *c.*1.54g, but there may be another, lower standard. At Winchester, similarly, a peak at *c.* 1.62g may not be the only one. At York there may well be more than one peak.

f) *Number of mint-places.* Some 52 are known, with Grantham as a recent discovery (Jonsson in *BNJ* 1987).

References.

Extensive information on the First Hand type will be found in Jonsson, *The New Era*, and id., *Viking-Age Hoards*.

J.C. Sadler, 'Some contemporary literary sources relating to the 1863 Ipswich Buttermarket hoard', *Seaby Coin and Medal Bulletin* 1981, 220-3.

2B. SECOND HAND

*c.*985—*c.*991 or earlier

Hildebrand Type B2. *BMC* Type ii d.

Second Hand is an anomalous variety, in that it is excessively rare or unknown at the two major northern mints of York and Lincoln. London accounts for a quite exceptional 42 per cent of the national output, and there was a strong production in the south-west. North of the Thames, other than in East Anglia, mint-output is weak. Lyon has argued from the relative rate of turnover of moneyers that the type had a distinctly shorter duration than six years. In contrast with First Hand, the dies are very uniform in style, and of 'metropolitan' quality. Jonsson suggests that they were cut in London.

The 42 per cent is not sufficiently explained by the inactive mints: 42 per cent of, say, 75 per cent would still be 32 per cent. The estimate, calculated from the Lincoln-based sample (Q.5) is of course dependent on the number of coins in the sample from the Northern Lands. One should ask, therefore, whether London coins of Second Hand type were over-represented there for reasons unknown—for example, an unrecorded local geld. One could, laboriously, get around the uncertainty through a study of die-duplication in the type, but it is hardly necessary. Already before 1000, Second Hand coins in the Northern Lands were submerged by the flood of arriving Crux coins. The Klockarebacken hoard (*CNS* 3.1.27) is a major source of information, with 104 Second Hand coins (against six Benediction Hand and 79 Crux coins). Of the 104, exactly half are of London. Only one pair and one reverse die-link are recorded among the 52, which are the work of some 25 moneyers. In short, there is no sign in Klockarebacken of special circumstances involving the export of London coins.

The English sample of single finds, which should in principle give a more reliable idea of

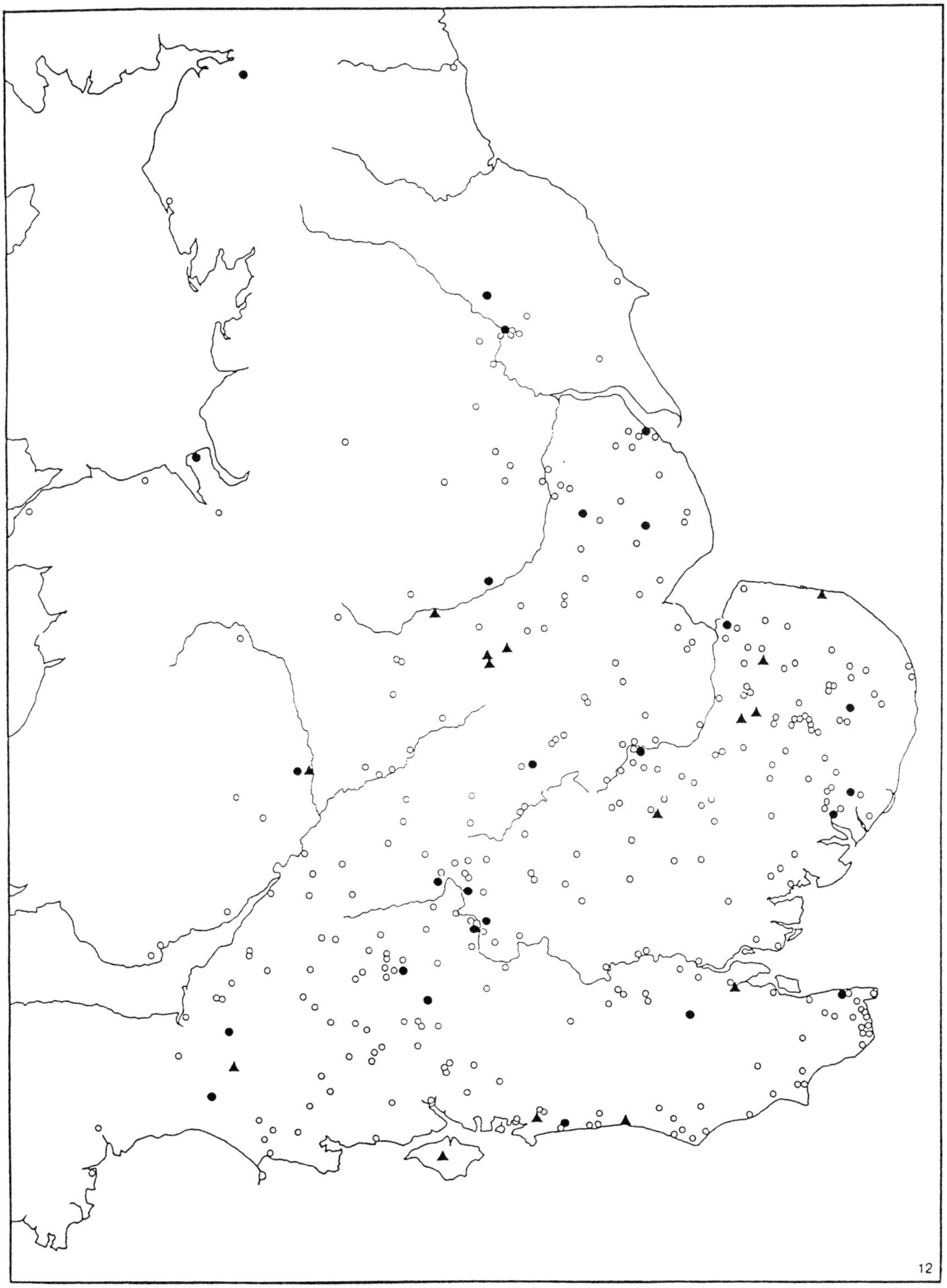

MAP 12. Coins of First Hand and Second Hand types.
(Second Hand coins are shown by triangles.)

the ranking of the mints than the Scandinavian sample, is still rather small. Of 14 mint-attributable finds, just half are of London. This is well within statistical limits in being in harmony with the Scandinavian figure.

It is by no means clear how the inactivity of the northerly mints should be interpreted. Were they in fact inactive, or did they continue to strike First Hand coins? The latter option is very difficult to envisage: it would involve either the continued supply of First Hand dies from a southern die-cutting centre, or the prolonged use of dies previously supplied. Excessive die-wear has not been observed among the York and Lincoln coins. On the other hand, if York and Lincoln were inactive, what happened to inflows of foreign silver? First, we should be clear about the facts. Plenty of mints are not recorded in Second Hand, but specimens may still turn up. What is significant is the ratio between First Hand and Second Hand. At Huntingdon it is 10:1, and at Northampton 10:0. It would be rash to say that Northampton was completely inactive in Second Hand. Similarly one should hesitate over Shrewsbury (8:0), where the neighbouring mint of Chester (17:2) suggests that Shrewsbury's inactivity may not have been absolute; and the same cautionary remark applies to Worcester (6:0). Lincoln is another matter, with 42:0, and York has 94:2. Derby is probably inactive, with 16:0, but the other Five Boroughs mints do nothing to build a harmonious regional picture: Leicester, 8:4, Nottingham, 2:0.

The *Chronicle* draws a veil over the events which led to the banishment of Ælfric Cild, the ealdorman of Mercia, in 985. Another dissident ealdorman, Thored of York, disappears from the sources, probably (Pauline Stafford suggests) through exile, in *c*.993. The evidence is too thin to allow us to reconstruct exactly what happened, although one may suspect that the young Æthelred's clumsy handling of the Danelaw brought his northern territories into disaffection or even revolt. His full personal rule probably began only from *c*.985. By *c*.993 there was not a single ealdorman left in England north of the Thames. Even if the exact dates of the Second Hand validity-period are uncertain, its political context in the north is reasonably clear.

Was a decision taken not to supply dies to York and Lincoln, as some kind of punishment, or because central control was ineffective? Might there even have been a naval blockade of the northern ports? (Cf. the ratio at Stamford, 42:8.) Some extra trade might have been diverted to London as a result, offering a possible explanation for the 42 per cent.

The resumption of activity at the northern mints is dated by a Second Hand/Crux mule at Lincoln, by Ubeinn, and by Benediction Hand/Crux mules at York, by Godric, Sunnulfr, and Wulfstan, and at Lincoln, by Kolgrimr. One may puzzle over the administrative arrangements and the exact chronology. The mules were, by definition, struck after the introduction of Crux, so were the obsolete obverse dies supplies at the same time as the new reverses, and from where? —and why? Are the mules actually from the moment of transition, or could they have been a later expedient? (Their weights constitute part of the evidence.)

Jonsson has published a corpus of the known specimens of Second Hand, and Petersson has analysed their weights. Stewart devotes a section to the problems which the type raises, in his 'Coinage and recoinage'.

a) *English single finds*. There are only about half as many single finds as for First Hand, in line with estimated output. There is no evidence that they penetrated the northerly parts of England correspondingly.
Brandon, Chichester, Ilchester, Isle of Wight, Lakenheath, Leicester, Repton (½), Rochester, Royston, Shoreham-by-Sea, South Croxton, Swaffham, Thurcaston, Weybourne, Worcester (½). Three finds from Leicestershire attract attention. See Map 12.

b) *English hoards.* London (Chelsea Reach), 1981. This hoard of 14 coins from nine different mint-towns was recovered in the mud on the north side of the Thames, nearer to Chelsea Bridge than to Battersea Bridge. All 14, including a cut half, are Second Hand coins, among them three of Stamford, two of Rochester, and only two of London. Fully published by Dolley in *Num. Meddelanden* 33 (1983). He saw the absence of First Hand coins as a vindication of his claim that Second Hand was a full sexennial type. The *Ecton* hoard of 1762 (Blackburn and Pagan no. 182) is at best a grave-find from which two coins are reported. Only one is shown to be a Hand coin. This has been transferred to the list of single finds.

c) *Size of the issue.* The Lincoln-based estimate is 1,200 equivalent reverse dies. If this were supplementary to the stock of silver tied up in First Hand, it would represent substantial net inflows from abroad already in the 980s.

d) *Evidence for dating.* There is little or none, except what may be extrapolated from the arguments about the Crux type (see below). The Watchet evidence seems to suggest that the Hand validity-period ended *c.*987.

e) *Weight-standards.* Second Hand is on average of much lower weight than First Hand—1.31g against 1.51g. There are exceptions. Chester, as usual, maintains a high standard. Winchester, and the other mints of Hampshire, Wiltshire, and Gloucestershire follow a high standard in Second Hand.

There is more than one weight-standard in both First and Second Hand in Dorset, Somerset, and Devon, and perhaps also in Herefordshire and Oxfordshire.

f) *Number of mint-places.* Jonsson records 39 mints, and envisages that a few more may turn up. See the comment at the beginning of this section.

References.

D. Whitelock, 'Dealings of the English kings with the North in the tenth and eleventh centuries', in P. Clemoes (editor), *Anglo-Saxons, Studies Presented to B. Dickins,* 1959, at pp. 78-80.

P. Stafford, 'Historical implications of the regional production of dies under Æthelred II', *BNJ* 48 (1978), 35-51.

P. Stafford, 'The reign of Æthelred II, a study in the limitations on royal policy and action', in *Ethelred the Unready. Papers from the Millenary Conference* (edited by D. Hill), Oxford, 1978, pp. 15-46.

I. Stewart, 'Coinage and recoinage after Edgar's reform', in *Studies in Late Anglo-Saxon Coinage in Memory of Bror Emil Hildebrand,* Stockholm, 1990, pp. 455-85.

2C. BENEDICTION HAND
*c.*991 or earlier
Hildebrand Type B3. *BMC* Type ii f.

This late, heavy variety is very scarce, being recorded in only *c.*140 specimens, plus some mules with the following Crux type. The portrait is bare-headed, except for an excessively scarce early transitional variety, with diadem. The type is restricted to southern mints, but Lincoln and York (which are not known to have struck Benediction Hand) struck mules. Canterbury, London, Winchester, and Rochester account for 65 per cent of the known specimens. These anomalies, and (perhaps) the existence of Second Hand/Crux mules, suggest that the Benediction Hand variety reflects a very brief phase of die-cutting, and perhaps that plans for a longer issue were cancelled.

a) *English single finds.* None. If *c.*2,500 known specimens of First and Second Hand are matched by 44 single finds, 140 Benediction Hand coins might be expected to yield 2 single finds *pro rata.* Their absence is not statistically significant.

b) *English hoards.* None, but see Isleworth

(Crux type).

c) *Size of issue.* Small. (The list of 140 specimens is not a die-corpus.)

d) *Evidence for dating.* The relative chronology is securely established by 2B/2C and 2C/2B mules and the 2C/Crux mules already mentioned. The absolute date remains speculative. If the type was aborted because of a crisis, the tribute of 991 offers a likely occasion. If, however, (as the heavy weight-standard very probably implies) the introduction of the Crux type was foreseen, that argument falls to the ground.

e) *Weight-standard.* Heavy (foreshadowing the introduction of Crux?), but half-a-dozen mints use Benediction Hand dies (when?) to strike coins on much lower standards.

f) *Number of mint-places.* Jonsson records 22 mints.

References.

R.H.M. Dolley and F.E. Jones, 'The transition between the "Hand of Providence" and "Crux" types of Æthelræd II', *Commentationes* 1 (1961), 173-86.

K. Jonsson and G. Van der Meer, 'Mints and moneyers *c.*973-1066', in *Studies in Late Anglo-Saxon Coinage*, 1990 lists Second Hand/Crux and Benediction Hand/Crux mules at pp. 120-1.

3. CRUX
c.991—c.997 or earlier
Hildebrand Type C. *BMC* Type iii.

The Crux type accumulated in Scandinavia in unprecedented quantities (1,295 coins in the sample, compared with 671 Hand coins), and its designs were imitated by the new royal coinages in Norway, Denmark, and Sweden, and in Dublin. The scale of the issue, too, was greater (an estimated 4,072 dies, compared with 3,254 for the combined Hand types). The Crux type has for a long time been associated with the first recorded national payments of Danegeld, of £10,000 in 991 and £16,000 in 994. To keep the quantities in perspective, we should remember that £16,000 is equal to less than 4 million pennies, while 4,072 dies would have been capable, if they were reasonably fully used, of striking 40 million coins. (Lawson, *Cnut*, p. 17 suggests that the true figure was £22,000, on the basis of a surviving treaty probably from 994.) The rich find-material from the Northern Lands raises many puzzling questions about the exact chronology of the Crux type (Metcalf, 'The fall and rise of the Danelaw connection'), and so do the events surrounding the Battle of Maldon (Metcalf and Lean, 'Post hoc, propter hoc'). Meanwhile, the Crux validity-period has its own chapter in the history of the English currency, including an abortive type-change, namely the Intermediate Small Cross type. That, and some late varieties, the Transitional Crux and Small Crux varieties, are discussed separately below.

There is also an excessively rare early Crux variant, with right-facing bust distinct from , if not unlike, that of Benediction Hand. It is known from the mints of Lydford, Exeter, Wilton, and Hertford. A dozen mules of Second Hand/Crux or Benediction Hand/Crux are also on record.

Even if the Danegeld payments were high-profile in the political discussion of the day, and if they made demands on individuals for extra taxation which were painful and resented, the loss of, say, six or seven million coins out of a mintage of up to 40 million will not have completely distorted or dominated the patterns of monetary circulation. There is what looks like a flurry of minting activity at a swathe of mints extending from Southwark through Hertford and Colchester to Cambridge and Thetford. At those four mints, however, it is clear that there was an earlier phase of Crux, when only a few moneyers were working there, and when they were striking heavy coins. This early phase accounts for nearly a third of the production for the type. So the flurry of mint-activity involving moneyers specially drafted in from London was certainly not right at the beginning of the Crux issue; and the mints in question had been created previously. There are two stages: an administrative reform of minting, which involved the creation of some new mints, and then—in the same vein?—a big increase in the complement of moneyers (a 'flurry'), although not necessarily a correspondingly large increase in output. It is not clear whether the same two stages apply also to Southwark, where London moneyers were much involved. Southwark first became

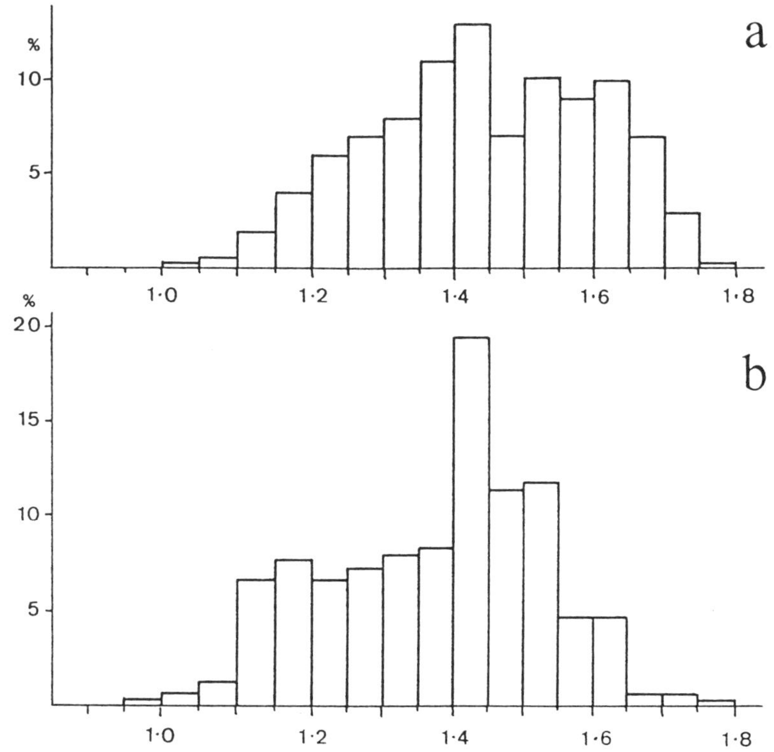

FIG. 7. Histograms of weights for Crux coins of the mints of a) London and b) Southwark (994 and 414 specimens respectively).

a mint-place at this time, and struck an amazing eight per cent of the national output in the Crux type as a whole, cf. less than one per cent thereafter. London still took 18 per cent against Southwark's eight. The idea that London moneyers moved to Southwark because access to London was prevented by the blockade by Olaf Tryggvason and Svend Tveskæg with 94 ships is not believable. London Bridge made London and Southwark equally accessible. Southwark, the southern bridgehead, was on a patch of firm ground surrounded by marshes (see Part 4, Map 8). The bridge was of strategic importance, in preventing the free passage of the Viking ships. (In a later raid, the Viking attackers would cut a channel through the marshes right around Southwark, in order to float their ships through it at high tide, precisely in order to circumvent London Bridge.) Up-stream from the bridge, there was no special risk in crossing the river by boat.

The figure of eight per cent was not accumulated overnight, nor even in a few months. Nineteen moneyers worked at Southwark. In short, one may doubt whether the attempt to decentralize minting from London was connected with the Viking attack on the city.

A comparison of the pattern of weights of the Crux coins from London and Southwark respectively is far from showing that activity at Southwark slotted into a brief phase within the validity-period. The histograms (Fig 7a, b) show a wide spread of weights at both boroughs, and it may well be thought that they raise more questions than they answer. An elaborate analysis of the weights of coins struck by particular moneyers might clarify the picture to some extent.

For what it is worth, the Klockarebacken

hoard (*CNS* 3.1.27) already contains Southwark coins, of which one weighs as little as 1.12g.

In the end, the question whether the geld of 991 was paid wholly, partly, or hardly at all in Crux pennies remains problematic. If the type began as early as *c.*989, it might be possible for the flurry of activity at mints in eastern England to be associated with the geld of 991 (about which Pauline Stafford remarks that there is no reason to suppose that it was other than local to East Anglia, Essex, and the south-east).

a) *English single finds.* Andover, Caerwent, Cambridge, Cheddar (½), Colchester, Dringhouses, East Meon (½), Ipswich, Lincoln (1 + ¼), Lincolnshire, Little Wittenham, London (1 + ¼), Longparish, Long Sutton, Meols, Norwich, Painswick, Portland, Rochester (2), Roydon, St. Mawgan, Stafford (¼), Thetford (5 + ½ + ¼), West Walton, Winchester (½), Winston.

b) *English hoards.* Isleworth, Bury St Edmunds 1873, Bury St Edmunds 1993, Thetford, Monmouth.

Isleworth, 1886. The hoard was concealed in a pot. The find-spot is fairly close to the River Thames, 'in the Twickenham Road'. The coins were corroded, fragile and difficult to read. The 28 whole specimens which were recovered were of First or Second Hand (2), Benediction Hand (5), and Crux (21). The survival of Hand coins when Crux coins of seven other mints had had time to reach London casts doubt on the thoroughness or promptness of the recoinage of *c.*991. At least half the surviving coins were of London. There was a Thames estuary flavour to the rest of the hoard (Canterbury, 3, Rochester, 2, Colchester, Maldon).

Bury St. Edmunds, 1873. Two Crux coins, bought in a silversmith's shop in 1873, probably reflect a small hoard from central East Anglia. The coins, of the London and Winchester mints, are noticeably heavy—1.60 and 1.64g respectively.

Bury St. Edmunds, 1993. A fused lump of at least eight coins, of which five are identifiable as Crux pennies (Cambridge, London, York). The lump weighed 10.32g. *NC* 1995, 333. If it were possible to demonstrate (which it is not) that this and the next hoard antedated the tribute of 991, they might lend point to Pauline Stafford's comment, above. Hoards fused by fire are unusual, but cf. Great Barton, below (Long Cross) and (?) Ipswich, above (Second Hand).

Thetford, 1993-4. A fused lump of Crux coins was recovered from spoil from the Thetford by-pass. It consisted of at least seven coins, of which one is clearly identifiable as a Crux penny, and two others could be. The lump weighs 9.49g. *NC* 1995, 333.

Monmouth, Gwent, 1991-2. A dozen Crux coins were found by metal detector on the Buckholt, a hill 2 km north of Monmouth, scattered over several square feet on a steep slope. They included two of Gloucester, two of Hereford, one of Ilchester, and others from further afield (London, 2, Southwark, 2, Oxford, Nottingham, ?York). (*BNJ* 1993, 84-5).

c) *Size of the issue.* A very large issue. The Lincoln-based estimate is 4,072 reverse dies.

d) *Evidence for dating.* The metrological evidence from a comparison of Southwark and London, as we have seen, offers no support for a dating to the siege of London. A close link between the ravaging of Watchet in 997, and the loss of a coin-die from there, which was subsequently used in a rusty state in Dublin, is impossible, because Watchet ceased minting quite early in the Crux validity-period. It is more likely that the link is with the raid which the *Chronicle* mentions under 987 or 988, although that would impose a very early start-date for Crux. Dolley's observation that the Crux coinage at Dublin (a brief or compact phase) includes imitations of Transitional Crux and therefore falls at the end of the English validity period cannot yield a close date on the back of the Watchet connection, as he envisaged.

Dolley's further suggestion that the introduction of Crux can be dated by the sharp increase in quantities of English coins in Scandinavia, and connected with the Danegeld of 991, is likewise far from secure. The Swedish finds suggest that there was a distinct delay in English coinage reaching Gotland. Depending upon where that delay was located (in England, or in Denmark/Skåne), one may go on to suggest that the tribute of 991 may have been paid partly or wholly in Hand coins. Because of the delay factor, the Swedish evidence would not preclude a start date for Crux before 991. Heavy Crux coins are noticeably few in Sweden.

Also, the accelerated trend of inflows to Scandinavia was not numerically as dramatic as claimed, and judging from the weight-standards of the Crux coins it did not occur as early as the beginning of the type. If there was indeed a connection between the upturn and the geld of 991, it might imply that Crux began *c.*989-90.

e) *Weight-standards.* The Crux type was struck on successive, declining weight-standards. The modal value was initially *c.*1.65g (including Benediction Hand/Crux mules). There is a later modal value of *c.*1.425g. Eventually Small Crux was struck at only *c.*1.32g. The middle phase may have been more complicated.

As usual there are variations on a shire basis. Winchester keeps to a single high standard, as do Chester, Oxford, and the Wiltshire mints. In the south-east, the weight-standards seem to be lower. At Lympne, for example, there is reasonably clear evidence of a modal value in the area of 1.52g or possibly 1.50g. There seem to be other local anomalies, which the evidence is statistically insufficient to establish with certainty.

f) *Number of mint-places.* Southwark is a major new mint-place, and Colchester (with 14 moneyers) is also new. Cambridge (11 moneyers) and Hertford (11 moneyers) are virtually new. Wallingford has 12 moneyers where previously it had three. These and similar changes may follow partly from the increased national mintage (an estimated 4,072 dies against the combined total of 3,254 for Hand) but that seems a very inadequate explanation. The total number of moneyers commissioned was somewhat greater than previously, and that is conspicuously the case at the mints which have been mentioned. At York the total rises from 32 to 43, and at Lincoln from 11 to 19. All the figures may be inflated by turn-over during the validity-period (whether Hand or Crux). It seems clear, however, that there was some general encouragement to take office as a moneyer, whether from the 'unseen hand' of expected profit, or from direct governmental initiative, involving some transfer of activity from London.

The large surviving sample means that the list of mint-places should be fairly complete, at 58, although there are still ten mints from which fewer than five specimens are recorded (Petersson, 1990, Table 4).

References.

D.M. Metcalf, 'The fall and rise of the Danelaw connection, the export of obsolete English coin to the Northern Lands, and the tributes of 991 and 994', in *Sigtuna Papers,* edited by K. Jonsson and B. Malmer, Stockholm, 1990, pp. 213-23.

D.M. Metcalf and W. Lean, 'The battle of Maldon and the minting of Crux pennies in Essex: *post hoc, propter hoc*?', in J. Cooper (editor), *The Battle of Maldon, Fiction and Fact,* 1993, pp. 205-24.

M. Carlin, *Medieval Southwark,* 1996.

(3.) INTERMEDIATE SMALL CROSS
*c.*996 or earlier
Hildebrand Type 'A2'. *BMC* Type i (part).

Late in the Crux validity-period there was a revival of the Small Cross design with which Eadgar's reform had been introduced. Dies were supplied to nine or ten mints in the west and south-west, perhaps from a die-cutting centre at Winchester—but the type was not struck there. Perhaps the strategy was to provide for the outlying mints first; and the project was cancelled before the die-cutters embarked on the next stage. Jonsson has published a corpus in *Viking-Age Hoards*. Only about 36 specimens exist, of which 17 or 18 are from the Wilton mint. The number of dies among these 17 or 18 is not recorded. Other mints are Barnstaple, Ilchester, Winchcombe, Malmesbury, Gloucester, Oxford, Worcester, and Warwick. Two specimens from York stand so far outside the pattern that they have been seen as Scandinavian imitations; but both Dolley and Veronica Butler, and Jonsson, defend them as official English coins. The story is complicated in that the York moneyer in question, Arnketill, then decamped to Scandinavia with a number of dies, where he produced 'mules the wrong way round' (Crux/ISC). His York colleague Asketill (a relation , even?) seems to have made a similar career move.

When the type-change was cancelled, the obverse dies were still used, with regular Crux reverses. There are far more of these Intermediate Small Cross /Crux mules than of the regular coins: 124 specimens are listed, half of them from Winchester, 22 from Exeter, 18 from London, and in ones or twos from other mints not on the original list, namely Hereford, Rochester, Southampton, Stamford, and Wareham. (Had a large batch of obverse dies been cut, as a separate task, for which the corresponding reverses were never made?) A few of the 124 are in fact Intermediate Small Cross/Transitional Crux mules (at Hereford and Winchester). Some of the mints which struck Intermediate Small Cross also struck the mules, namely Ilchester, Oxford, Wilton, and (notably) York.

It seems, then, that Intermediate Small Cross allows us a glimpse of the early administrative arrangements for a change of type, and the thrifty using up of obverse dies when it was cancelled. The cancellation presumably came within a couple of weeks or so, and Winchester was quicker off the mark than other die-cutting centres. The northern coins are crucial, as evidence that the planning envisaged that the new type would be introduced nation-wide.

The weight-standard of Intermediate Small Cross is of the highest, *c.*1.70g (cf. Benediction Hand), everywhere except at York (1.43, 1.44g). As Stewart remarks, the fact that the system then reverted to light-weight Crux coins is very damaging to Dolley's rigid hypothesis that each validity-period was of exactly six years. Could Intermediate Small Cross conceivably post-date Transitional Crux? The mules make it implausible, even if almost all of them are from mint-places which were probably die-cutting centres. It would involve the hypothesis that old reverse dies had been stored, and not destroyed, during the production period of Transitional Crux.

Moreover, the ISC/Crux mules, which can hardly be earlier than ISC itself, are on various weight-standards according to their mint, as Jonsson pointed out (*NC* 1977, 177-80)—although the lighter coins are not found at mints which strike the true ISC type.

There is virtually no English find evidence relating to this intriguing episode. Cancellation of the Intermediate Small Cross type was presumably prompted by some crisis.

(3.) SMALL CRUX AND TRANSITIONAL CRUX

c.995-7 or earlier

Hildebrand Type Ca; —. *BMC* Type iii.

Two very scarce varieties of Crux and a cluster of associated mules belong late in the validity-period. They are named Small Crux and Transitional Crux. Small Crux, or Hildebrand var. Ca, is know from a couple of hundred specimens—roughly one-twentieth as many as Crux itself. The Small Crux coins are, quite simply, from distinctly smaller dies, on smaller flans, and are lighter in weight, with rather plain, unseriffed letters, and various small differences of style from the regular Crux coins, e.g. a quiff of hair swept back from the forehead. Transitional Crux is more complicated to define, but at its most distinctive it shows a bust with curly hair, and omits the sceptre. On the reverse, the copulative uses a symbol resembling an omega in MΩO. Transitional Crux, too, is generally light, but at Winchester in particular it consists mostly of very heavy coins which presumably foreshadow the introduction of Long Cross, thus repeating the pattern of Benediction Hand. Only fifty or so specimens of Transitional Crux are recorded. It has been suggested that there are four versions of TC, namely without sceptre and with diadem, without either, with both, or with sceptre but without diadem. The exact status of the minor varieties is a delicate subject, because all the later variants seem to hybridize rather freely, with Crux and with Intermediate Small Cross. The hybrids may even be more plentiful than the varieties from which they derive (e.g. ISC/Crux, of which Jonsson lists 124 specimens). Considered as a whole, all these scarce coins reflect a period of administrative uncertainty in the last couple of years before Long Cross was introduced —or perhaps less than a couple of years. Not all mints strike the late variants or ISC. The latter, as we have seen, belongs essentially to Winchester and the south-west, whereas Small Crux is essentially the work of two die-cutting centres in London and Canterbury, and occurs mostly at eastern and Kentish mints.

Small Crux was, not surprisingly, struck at different weight-standards in different mints. The national mean average is 1.32g, but Exeter, for example, strikes at *c*.1.15g, and Cambridge at even less. Several mints, including London and Dover, apparently use multiple standards (Fig. 8, a-d). Very occasionally, what seems to be a genuine English Small Crux coin is found of very heavy weight, presumably prefiguring Long Cross (*SCBI Cop*. 341, Ipswich, 1.81g; ibid., 650, London, 1.77g).

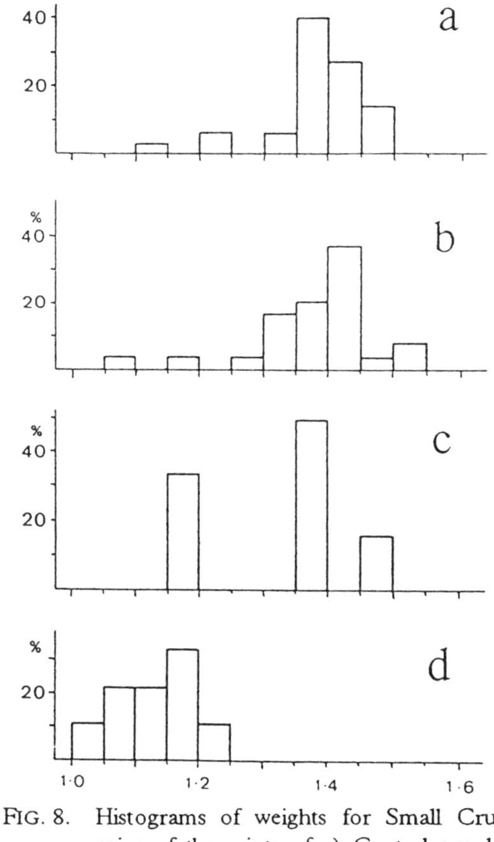

FIG. 8. Histograms of weights for Small Crux coins of the mints of a) Canterbury, b) London, c) Dover, and d) Exeter (No. of specimens, 29, 24, 6, and 9 respectively).

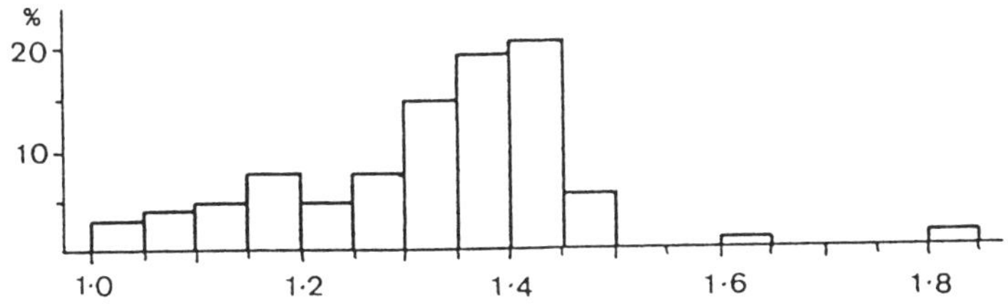

FIG. 9. Histogram of weights for Small Crux (all mints). After Petersson, Table 17.

The data-base of English single finds includes four of Small Crux, one of Transitional Crux, and none of Intermediate Small Cross, against 35 ordinary Crux coins. The proportion is somewhat over the odds, but still within the limits of statistical variation. It would only be necessary for one or at most two of the Small Crux coins to have been lost in particular circumstances connected with Viking raiding, to make the numerical pattern unremarkable.

What is possibly of more interest for English monetary history is how far the late Crux coins (given their short official life-time) had travelled from their mints of origin before they were lost. Only one was far from home: the Canterbury coin found at Tilshead/Shrewton. Otherwise, the distances from Oxford to nearby Wheatley, from Dover to Romney, and from London to north Essex are modest.

a) *English single finds*. Essex (north), Ipswich, New Romney, Tilshead, Wheatley.

b) *English hoards*. None. Given the proportions in which they were issued, the absence of late Crux coins in a hoard terminating with Crux would not offer good proof of an exact date of deposit unless there were upwards of 80 Crux pennies in it.

c) *Size of the issues*. One might make a rough guess, *pro rata*, of 250 dies.

d) *Evidence for dating*. Dolley noted the absence of Small Crux in the Glemminge hoard from Skåne, terminating with 196 Crux coins. Small Crux was also apparently lacking among 443 Crux coins in the Värpinge hoard, although this is not quite as certain. A late date for Small Crux is indicated.

The absence or virtual absence of mules between Small Crux and Intermediate Small Cross may be because there is so little overlap in the mints striking the two varieties. At Exeter, they seem to be on the same weight-standard. Which came first remains problematic.

e) *Weight-standards*. See above, and Fig. 8, for the weight-standards used at Canterbury, London, Dover, and Exeter. For most mints, there are too few specimens to yield a histogram. Petersson's Table 17 (of 1969) is clearly multi-modal (Fig. 9), with lower regional means in east Mercia as well as at Exeter.

f) *Number of mints. Small Crux*. London and Canterbury were responsible for half the total output, but the variety is known also from Bath, Cambridge, Colchester, Dover, Exeter, Hertford, Huntingdon, Ipswich, Lincoln, Rochester, and Southwark.

Transitional Crux. Fourteen mints are recorded, with Winchester in the lead. The list by no means corresponds with that for ISC: Aylesbury, Bath, Buckingham, Chichester, Dorchester, Exeter, London, Oxford, Shaftesbury, Totnes, Wallingford, Wareham, Wilton.

References.

I. Stewart, 'The Small Crux Issue of Æthelræd II', *BNJ* 28 (1958), 509-17

I. Stewart 'Notes on the Intermediate Small Cross and Transitional Crux types of Ethelred II', *BNJ* 37 (1968), 16-24.

4. LONG CROSS
c.997 (or earlier?)—1003
Hildebrand Type D. *BMC* Type iv a.

Æthelred's Long Cross type was introduced at a higher weight-standard than any previous type. At Norwich and Thetford, at Winchester and various westerly mints, the modal value was close to 1.72g. Elsewhere it was a little lower: at Wallingford, 1.70g and at Oxford 1.68g, at London 1.65g. These very heavy coins are conspicuous in the Scandinavian finds.

There is another clear peak in the general histogram, at *c.*1.40g.

Late in the validity-period there is a small, light variant, distinctive in style, and confined to London and a few easterly mints. Only seventy or so specimens are known. They show a clear peak at *c.*1.26g, but there is also a peak at *c.*1.62g, at London. One wonders whether the same general explanation applies to these heavy coins as to Benediction Hand and Intermediate Small Cross; but Helmet coins at London are hardly ever as heavy as that. The double peak (Fig. 10) offers some sort of guarantee that the subsidiary variety is English, and not a Scandinavian imitation, —as does the occurrence of a specimen in the Honey Lane hoard.

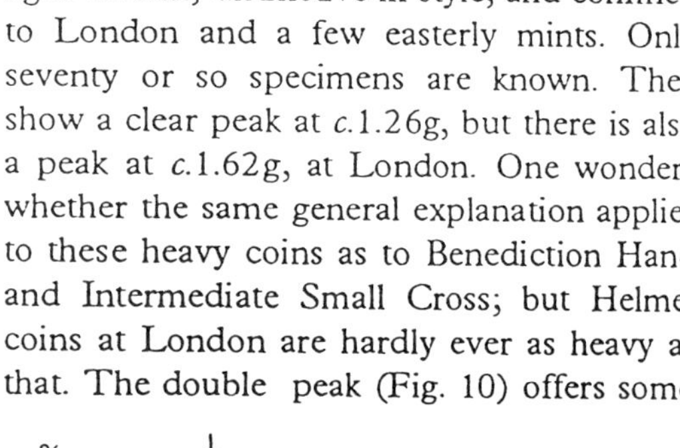

FIG. 10. Histogram of weights for Subsidiary Long Cross (64 specimens) Weights in grains and grammes.

Another late variant with pellets in two angles of the cross on the reverse includes a still higher proportion of heavy coins, with a peak at *c.*1.72g. The variant is confined to London, where most if not all of the same moneyers who strike Subsidiary Long Cross are involved. The two varieties are evidently very closely connected, but the coins with pellets deserve a full die-study to establish their stylistic consistency and to search for die links. The coins with pellets are conspicuous in the List hoard.

Hildebrand lists 11 varieties of the ethnic in the obverse legend, *Anglorum*. We may group these as ANGLOX, ANGLO, and ANGL, etc. Potentially the ethnic offers complicated but important evidence for the chronology of weight-standards within Long Cross. If we make the working hypothesis that the forms ANGLOX, ANGLO, and ANGL reflect successive phases of die-cutting, we may hope to acquire independent evidence as to whether different weight-standards were in use concurrently. One complication is that the argument will only be secure with reference to individual die-cutting centres, if then. Another is that imitations will blur the English patterns. There may also be an element of random variability if the die-cutter sometimes misjudged how much space he would have left at the end of the legend. We can, however, test the working hypothesis for a few selected

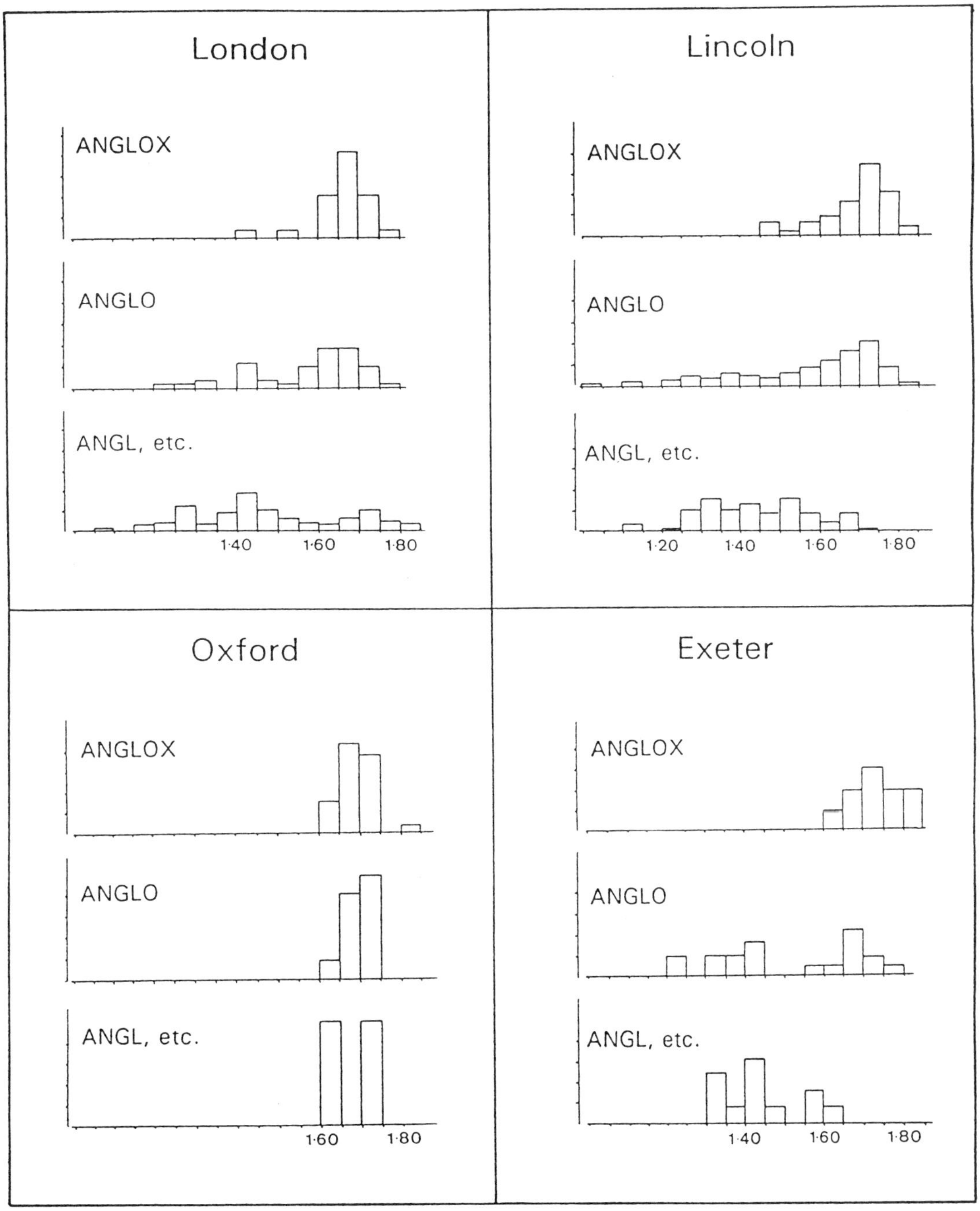

FIG. 11. Histograms of weights of Long Cross coins with longer and shorter ethnics, for the mints of a) London, b) Lincoln, c) Oxford, and d) Exeter.

mints. If it yields consistent patterns in spite of the procedural uncertainties, we may be disposed to accept the implications, at least in broad terms. Fig. 11 shows histograms for London, Lincoln, Oxford, and Exeter, in each case for ANGLOX, ANGLO, and ANGL. Each small histogram is on the same percentage scale, even though the relative proportions of the three varieties vary widely from mint to mint. Lincoln is very fully documented. It was obvious, when the histograms were being compiled, that anomalous weights were clustered on particular dies, and also that die-duplicates were more tightly grouped than the material as a whole.

Errors and omissions excepted, it seems clear that all the selected mints began work on a very high standard, and that during the initial phase (which may have been brief) all or virtually all the coins were heavy. Later in the validity-period, a progressively large share of the output was on lower standards. Even the coins reading ANGL, etc. still include a few heavy coins. The individual mints vary and Oxford, for example, continues to strike only heavy coins throughout the validity-period, although in dwindling quantities.

For the monetary historian, the next most rewarding step is to look at the composition of individual hoards in terms of the varieties with ANGLOX, ANGLO, and ANGL. The Shaftesbury hoard (or hoards?), for which a date of loss in 1002 is postulated, contains a small proportion of coins reading ANGL, etc.; all the London coins in the hoard have longer ethnics, although ANGL, etc. is the most plentiful London variety generally.

a) *English single finds*. Attlebridge, Aylesbury, Beverley (½), Blyth, Caister-on-Sea (½), Caistor-on-the-Wolds, Canterbury, Charlbury, Cheddar, Cheriton (2 + ¼), separate losses?), Church Hanborough, Cleethorpes, Compton (½), Congham, Great Wolford, Hangleton (2, separate losses?), Horncastle, Ickleton (lead ½), Ixworth, Kingston-on-Thames, Lincoln (2), London (½), Meols, Merton, Mildenhall, Sf, Mildenhall, W, Mundham, Nailsworth, Newchurch, North Curry, Oxborough (¼), Padstow, Rochester (½), Seaford, Rockland, Sheffield, Shoreham-by-Sea, Southill, Stonehenge, Sulgrave, Tiptree, Welford-on-Avon (¼), Whepstead, Winchester. There are three finds from the Sussex cost, but otherwise, these finds (Map 13) show no obvious divergence from the usual pattern, such as might reflect the harrying of the south and the south-west. (Note Padstow, not within the area of the map.)

b) *English hoards*. Shaftesbury remains the only substantial hoard adequately recorded from the validity period. Great Barton; Harting Beacon; London (Honey Lane Market); Welbourn; York (Micklegate); and possibly Cheriton and/or Hangleton..

Shaftesbury, *c.*1941. For a general introduction to the hoard, see Q.35. It was rescued in two parcels, fifteen years apart, and with some scattering of the contents (see Dolley in *NC* 1956). If St. Brice's Day is a likely hypothesis (see below), one may ask whether there could not, without too much coincidence, have been two hoards, especially as Parcel A contained 11 coins of London, and Parcel S only one. Moreover, Parcel S contains six coins of the Chester mint, (22 per cent of the parcel), of which five are by the same moneyer, who is not generally prolific. Parcel A contains only two Chester coins (three per cent). The idea that there should have been two hoards from Shaftesbury is surprising, but a plausible historical context is to hand. What stretches credibility is that both should have a northern flavour. We should probably try to believe that all the coins are from a single discovery, giving some weight to the Winchcombe die-duplicates. There may have been substantially fewer die-duplicates than claimed by Dolley, who did not have a photographic record of all the coins.

Great Barton, *c.* 1857. A fused lump of silver with the weight of about 50 pennies, found a

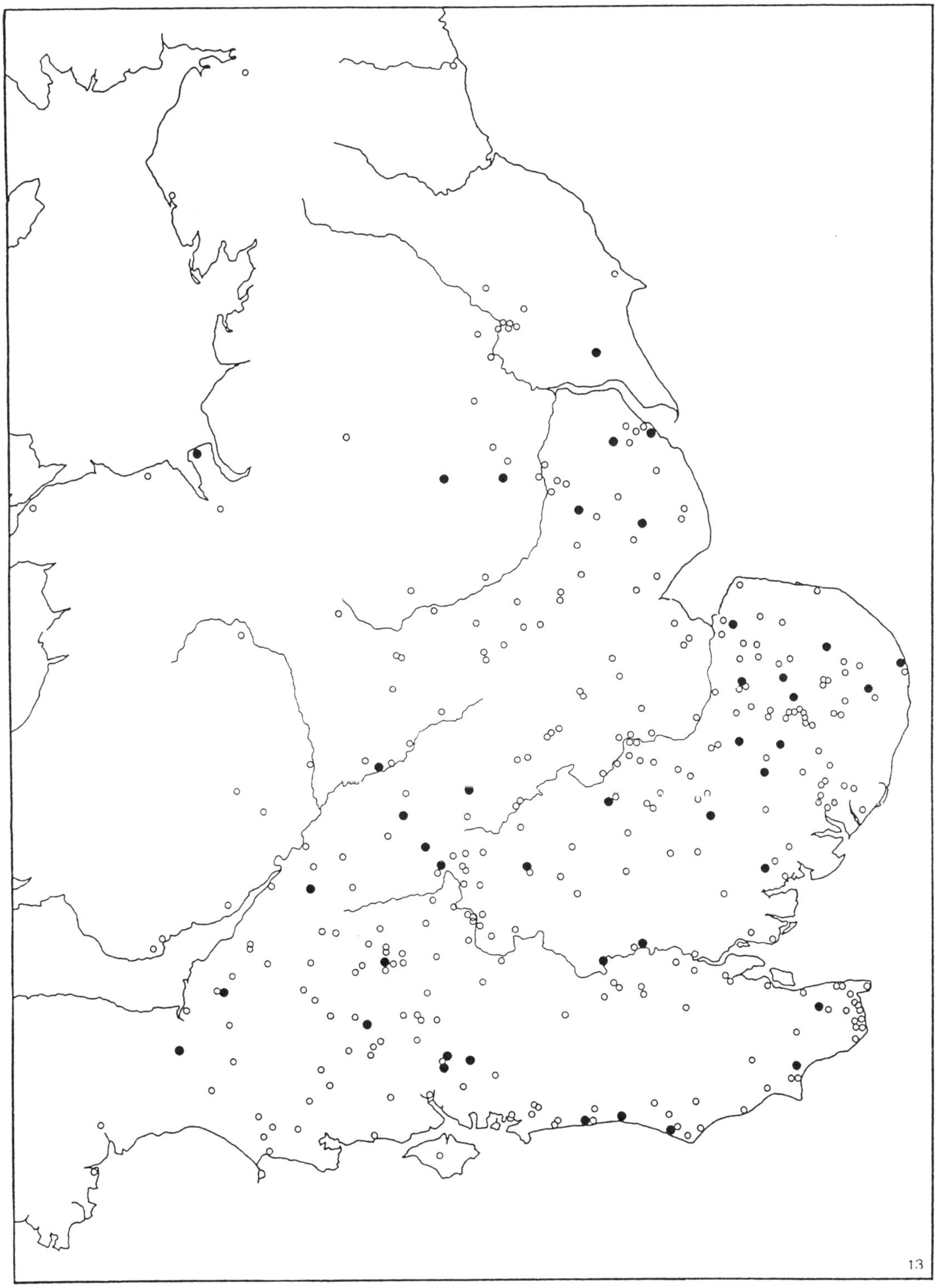

MAP 13. Coins of Long Cross type.

couple of miles NE of Bury St Edmunds, was evidently a hoard of coins which had almost melted in a fire. All those of which traces remained were Long Cross coins, and two or three on which a mint-signature could still be made out seemed to be of Thetford. It is likely, then, that the hoard was a one-type hoard of East Anglian flavour, but the evidence as to its composition is slender.

Harting Beacon, 1892 (near South Harting, 4 miles from Midhurst). Five pennies of Æthelred II found immediately beneath the turf by an idiot boy digging for flints. They were 'of the common type'. The inclusion of a London coin by Godman confirms that Long Cross, not Crux, was meant. Four coins of London and one of Colchester make it likely that this is a traveller's hoard. Having regard to low cunning, one wonders whether there may not have been more than five coins.

London (Honey Lane Market), 1837. Found to the north of the western end of Cheapside. Eight coins, listed by Roach Smith, are of London (4), Bedford, Exeter, Stamford, and Wallingford. The hoard may thus reflect the currency of London. As it included one example of the (rare) Subsidiary Long Cross variety, of the Bedford mint, weighing 1.30g, it probably falls very late in the validity-period.

Welbourn, Lincs., 1980-2. A problematic hoard, found scattered over a stretch of 250 yards when a deep trench was dug mechanically. Eight pennies and one cut half were found by various detectorists. Disclosure was far from candid and complete, and the hoard may well have been twice as large. The coins were of three if not four types. They have been accepted as a multi-type hoard. Four and the cut half are First Hand, and these may certainly be accepted as belonging together. There were also one Crux coin, one Long Cross, and one Small Cross (First or Last?). Whether any or all of these were associated with the First Hand coins is somewhat conjectural.

York (Micklegate), 1882. Five coins are recorded, of which 3 are of York and 2 of Lincoln.

Cheriton, 1993. Three metal-detector finds from the same site, listed as single finds, may reflect a small hoard. They are of London (1.11g), York (1.44g), and a cut farthing of uncertain mint.

Hangleton, 1987. Two coins, both of London, and weighing 1.38 and 1.35g, are possibly a mini-hoard. The weights suggest a date in the latter part of the validity-period.

c) *Size of the issue.* The Lincoln-based estimate is only 1,824—much less than for the Crux type.

d) *Evidence for dating.* There can be little doubt that the sack of Wilton in 1003 caused the cessation of minting there for the rest of Æthelred's reign, and the migration of the Wilton moneyers to nearby Salisbury (i.e. the iron-age hill-fort of Old Sarum, not before then a mint-place). Three of the four Wilton Long Cross moneyers are found striking the Helmet type there. Thus it is certain that the issue of the Helmet type had not begun at the date of the sack. Moreover it is clear that Wilton was still striking Long Cross coins fairly late in the type, from the short ethnic of *Copenhagen* 1317 (Lyon, 1966). One's only hesitation is whether there could have been a delay before the three moneyers were able to begin work at Salisbury (allowing Long Cross to continue at other mints until, say, 1004?).

The argument from the sack of Wilton seems secure, but one should criticize it for being a little naïve. After all, the *Chronicle* entry which mentions the sack begins by reporting the utter destruction of Exeter. Yet Exeter strikes Helmet coins. Salisbury, too, was attacked. One might add that Norwich and Thetford were 'burned and utterly destroyed' in 1004, yet they too strike Helmet coins.

Whether Long Cross had begun six years before the sack, in 997, or some time before that, is a more open question, if one accepts the possibility that not all validity-periods were necessarily of exactly six years' duration.

There is an unusual number of English hoards from the Long Cross period. It has been suggested that several of them may have been lost as a result of the massacres of 1002, when, according to the *Chronicle*, Æthelred ordered all the Danish men in England to be killed on St. Brice's day, 13 November. No such slaughter could have been carried out in the Danelaw, and it is uncertain how widespread it was elsewhere, although it is well recorded at Oxford. In fact, the number of hoards from southern England is hardly unusual enough to call for any special explanation.

The St. Brice's day hypothesis is again just a little romantic, in that the internal chronology of the Long Cross type is imprecise in real time, and the hoard-evidence is in any case sketchy in the extreme, from this point of view. The *Chronicle* speaks of extensive ravaging in the south of England, offering plenty of other occasions for the loss of hoards. In 997 the Vikings sailed up the Severn estuary, and harried Cornwall, Wales, and Devon. (Note a single find from Padstow.) They then sailed into the Tamar estuary (i.e. Plymouth) and did much damage in and around Lydford and Tavistock. In 998 they ranged all over Dorset, and commandeered supplies from Hampshire and Sussex. In 999 they attacked Rochester and ravaged the whole of west Kent. In 1001 Exeter and its whole district was attacked.

e) *Weight-standards*. There are two clear peaks in the general histogram, at *c.*1.70g and *c.*1.40g. Shires which keep to a single high standard are Berkshire (Wallingford), Cheshire, Dorset (all four mints), Gloucestershire, Hampshire, (?) Northamptonshire, Oxfordshire, Shropshire, Staffordshire, Warwickshire, Wiltshire (four mints), and Worcestershire. Somerset shows irregularities.

f) *Number of mint-places*. Petersson records 62 mint-places, from a sample of 5,906 specimens. Mints not recorded in the preceding Crux type are Axbridge and Bruton (singletons), Warminster (8 coins), and Romney (17 coins)—this last clearly a newly established mint. Warminster is very probably also new. Subsidiary Long Cross is recorded from Colchester, Exeter, Hunstanton, Lincoln, London, and Romney.

5. HELMET

*c.*1003—1009

Hildebrand Type E, *BMC* Type viii.

The Helmet type, which can be thought of as a modified version of the Long Cross design, seems to be metrologically a continuation of Long Cross, lacking an introductory high weight-standard at those mints which used two or more standards in Long Cross. Thus there are analogies with the problematic First and Second Hand. There are no English hoards, but the Penrice hoard from south Wales, consisting solely of Helmet coins, has been seen as evidence that Helmet was a proper, demonetizing type, which replaced Long Cross by *renovatio*, (*pacè* Brand, 1967). It was struck at 52 mints, with very much the same regional distribution of mint-output as in Long Cross, and no anomalies to speak of in the ranking of the larger or the medium-sized mints.

The tribute of 1007 will have absorbed a significant proportion of the issue, if the geld was collected in Helmet pennies. One wonders whether the tribute dominates the Scandinavian sample (from which our ranking of the mints is derived), and conversely whether what was left behind in England might have showed a different ranking. If the suggested dates for the validity-period are correct, however, the English stray losses are likely to be predominantly from the period before the tribute was collected. Of a dozen mint-attributable finds, four are London coins.

a) *English single finds.* Bovingdon, Brandon, Ewell, Exeter, Gloucester, Hellingly (gold penny), Higham, London, London (Agnus Dei), North Lopham, Polstead, Ringstead, St. Lythans, Tring.

b) *The Penrice hoard*, 1830 (or 1825?). Originally about 30 coins, all of the Helmet type, of which 11 can be listed. These have a strong south-westerly flavour: Barnstaple, Bath, Cricklade, Exeter, 'Geothaburh', together with London, Lincoln (2), Canterbury, and Winchester (2).

c) *Size of the issue.* The Lincoln-based estimate is 1,217 reverse dies. The small size of the Scandinavian sample and the small number of English single finds make one wonder whether the average output per die was lower than usual.

d) *Evidence for dating.* The relative scarcity of Oxford and Wallingford coins of the Last Small Cross type has led to the suggestion (Lyon , 1966) that the burning of Oxford (and Wallingford?) by the Danes in the winter of 1009/10 caused such severe damage as to prevent the reopening of either mint for several years. That the coins in question are heavy should no longer be seen as a conclusive argument. The estimated percentage at each mint in Last Small Cross is well below its medium-term contribution to the national total.

e) *Weight-standards.* The histogram for Helmet is unusually compact for a substantive type, with a peak at just over 1.4g, i.e. heavy coins are absent. Negative skewness suggests other, lower standards. These may be detected or suspected in the easterly shires as usual. Norwich provides a clear example. So, more intriguingly, do Exeter (*c.*1.42 and *c.*1.15g) and Winchester (*c.*1.47 and *c.*1.28g).

f) *Number of mint-places.* There are 52 on record, from a relatively small sample.

(5). AGNUS DEI
*c.*1009
Hildebrand Type G. *BMC* Type x.

A coin type uniquely lacking the royal portrait, with religious designs of exceptional artistic execution, was introduced at about the end of the validity-period of the Helmet type. It has generally been assumed that it was intended as the next substantive type, but that (like Intermediate Small Cross) it was cancelled at an early stage in the preparations. Dolley was thus inclined to date it to a period of about 3 months in the late summer or early autumn of 1009. There is an Agnus Dei/Last Small Cross mule, which tends to suggest that Agnus Dei was immediately replaced by Last Small Cross, or even (according to Stewartby, below) that it interrupted the Last Small Cross issue. It is most certainly not to be dated to the millennium, as was once thought.

Only a dozen specimens are known, including a cut farthing. The mule is a cut half. Moreover, the dozen include three pairs of die-duplicates, in each case found quite separately. Six non-singletons among a dozen coins, from nine dies, would imply that there were only ever about 18 dies.

Dolley (1971) recognized the hands of three die-cutters, based probably at three centres (London, Winchester, and Chester??), and he attributed the coins of the different mints as follows: Hand A: Derby, Malmesbury, Northampton, and Stafford. B: Leicester, Nottingham, and Stamford. C: Hereford. The mint of Salisbury can now be added to the list. One may well hesitate over the validity of these three stylistic groups, defined from such a small sample, and even more over identifying their die-cutting centre or centres—except to note that the list of mints has a very different regional flavour from Intermediate Small Cross. Kluge, who illustrates almost all the known specimens conveniently on a single plate, points out that they tend to be from medium-sized or smaller mints. The suggestion, again, is that the die-cutting centres prioritized their work, and cut dies for outlying places first—presumably to allow time for dispatch.

It is remarkable enough that such an impressive new coin type should have been cut up to provide a farthing, and even more so if it was done (so soon) in the mint.

Lawson has suggested that the new design was prompted by a national council held at Enham (in Hampshire) probably in 1008, at Pentecost. The name Enham apparently means 'the place of lambs'. The Holy Dove is appropriate to Pentecost. Altogether the type seems to be penitential and intercessory. If the date suggested for Enham is correct, however, there are difficulties in associating the Agnus Dei type closely with the council, because the Helmet type was apparently still being issued until the autumn of 1009.

Some specimens are very heavy (Malmesbury, 2.40g, Hereford, 2.21g), simply because they are looped. The weight of the coins themselves was probably quite closely controlled at the normal maximum (e.g. 1.82 to 1.75g). Both Derby coins, however, weigh appreciably less (1.64 and 1.59g). Although several specimens were either looped or pierced for use as adornment because of their special design, it seems clear that the type was intended to circulate and did circulate.

Stewartby's assessment (1990, p. 477) is that, if not a new substantive type which was cancelled, Agnus Dei may have been 'a special issue with religious significance struck on a particular occasion during the currency of Last Small Cross type and never intended to be a full-scale issue. . . It is by no means so evident that Agnus Dei was an abortive recoinage type'. The idea of a 'special issue' of a commemorative or medallic nature, such as we are familiar with in the 1990s, is probably anachronistic, but it has to be said that the quality of the die-engraving is well above average, and that the absence of the royal portrait is curious. The type was struck widely throughout Mercia but not in Wessex—except that Salisbury is close to Enham.

There is a nummular brooch from excavations at Sulgrave, showing the Lamb of God.

The Agnus Dei design found favour in Denmark, where it was copied intermittently over many years (both obverse and reverse, associated as in the English type). A Lund copy (Hauberg 6) was sold by an English dealer, who gave to understand that it was a stray find from East Anglia.

References.

B. Kluge, 'Das älteste Exemplar von Agnus Dei-Typ', *Studies in Late Anglo-Saxon Coinage*, Stockholm, 1990, pp. 137-56.

J.S. Jensen, *Tusindtallets Danske Mønter*, Copenhagen 1995, p. 58, no. 2, and see p. 141.

M.K. Lawson, *Cnut, The Danes in England in the Early Eleventh Century*, 1993, at pp. 58-61 (the Council of Enham).

B. Malmer, *The Anglo-Scandinavian Coinage, c.995—1020* (Commentationes, new series, 9), Stockholm, 1997, at pp. 430-1 and 546-7.

6. LAST SMALL CROSS
*c.*1009–Nov. 1016 or later (1017?)
(Hildebrand) Type A3. *BMC* Type i (part).

The validity-period of Last Small Cross, which was continued for more than six years, was a time of prolonged political crisis in England. The year 1012 (certainly within the validity-period) saw the payment of the largest-ever danegeld of £48,000, equivalent to 11.5 million coins. This would have been a substantial fraction of the whole issue, which (using a conventional multiplier of 10,000) may have been of the order of 30 million coins. The level of taxation was even higher than that implies, for in addition, Thorkell the Tall and his men, who were temporarily in King Æthelred's service, received £21,000 in 1014. The money to pay them very probably came from a new tax, institutionalized as the heregeld, which was levied from 1012 onwards. Meanwhile, the state was under the threat of conquest by the Danes. King Swein of Denmark attempted to conquer England in 1013, and was indeed accepted as king in the Danelaw, and received the submission of Oxford and Winchester (see Q.23). Swein died in February 1014, and his younger son Cnut succeeded to the allegiance of the host. But Æthelred, who had fled the country, returned in March-April to rally the English, and Cnut went back to Denmark. In the summer of 1015 the Danish assault was renewed, when Cnut again landed in England. Æthelred's eldest surviving son Edmund rebelled against his father and was accepted as lord of the Five Boroughs. In April 1016 Æthelred died, and Edmund was chosen in London to be king. But elsewhere Cnut was recognized. King Edmund ('Ironside') was defeated in the autumn, and England was partitioned, Wessex being allotted to Edmund, and everywhere north of the Thames to Cnut. In November 1016 Edmund died, and Cnut was accepted as the king of all England. While the country was still technically at war, Cnut levied a tribute or geld of no less than £72,000, plus a further £10,500 from London. The *Chronicle* says that this was paid in 1018, and it is debateable whether its numismatic repercussions should be sought in Last Small Cross or Quatrefoil. The problem is discussed further under Quatrefoil.

To what extent was the Danish conquest of England, and the turmoil of the years 1012-16, reflected in the English single finds and hoards? Was the currency so depleted by taxation that it showed unusual regional patterns of circulation? Did the siege of London prevent coins of the London mint from being widely dispersed through England? Did the partitioning of England along the line of the Thames restrict the movement of coin to north and south?

In general, the ranking of the mints shows few irregularities in Last Small Cross. London is completely normal, with a quarter of the national output. In the Five Boroughs, Lincoln is slightly more active than usual. In Wessex, Winchester is more active than usual. Otherwise, there is nothing of note.

This assessment of the ranking of the mints is, of course, entirely dependent on their frequency in Scandinavia. Bearing in mind the extremely heavy gelds, it is a pertinent question whether the coinage that was left in England showed significantly different proportions, as between the mints. One could also ask whether the activity of the mints after the geld of 1012 had been paid showed the same ranking order as before, but there is no reliable way of apportioning coins on different weight-standards, mint by mint, to before and after 1012.

The number of single finds in Last Small Cross is much lower than in Crux and Long Cross, and evidently is not swollen by forced losses or mini-hoards. Of hoards we have only one. In short, if we did not know that England had been in a state of civil war, we really could not have guessed it from the coins. Cf. Q. 23.

a) *English single finds.* Alderton, Alfriston, Bluntisham, Butcombe, (Cardiff), Chester, Coleshill, Great Mongeham, Irthlingborough, Lincoln, Little Mongeham, Llanstephan, London (4), Middle Harling, Peterborough, Silbury Hill (¼), Southill, South Lopham, Swindon (½).

b) *English hoards.* London (St. Martin-le-Grand), c.1870. Fifty-five (out of an original 60?) coins, all Last Small Cross. Two-thirds are of the London mint. Even if one excludes a group of 23 die-duplicates (discussed under Q.36), London coins still account for a quarter of the hoard. There is no particular regional flavour to the other mints, except perhaps for singletons from Barnstaple, Exeter, and Lydford. The styles of die-cutting suggest a date mid to late in the validity-period. The hoard is described and well discussed by Dolley in *BNJ* 29 (1959).

c) *Size of the issue.* The Lincoln-based estimate is 2,935 reverse dies. (In light of the very large danegeld one may add that the estimate is in principle, and as usual, in no way dependent on the size of the Scandinavian sample (1,774 coins) except as regards the margins of statistical error attaching to the sample—and with such a large sample they are acceptably small.)

d) *Evidence for dating.* The sack of Oxford in the winter of 1009/10 has been used as evidence that Last Small Cross was introduced at Michaelmas 1009, i.e. the Last Small Cross coins of Oxford (and Wallingford) make up a smaller share of the national output than usual, and were presumably minted in the short period between the introduction of the type, and the sack. That allows only four or five months; but the date of the type-change precisely at Michaelmas is conjectural.

The type was struck on more than one weight-standard, and the general historical questions raised in the preceding paragraphs deserve to be explored in more detail, in terms of the pattern of mint-output in each phase of the validity-period, etc., since the military and political circumstances were not constant throughout the validity-period. The large Scanian hoard *CNS* 3.4.59 terminates with just five Last Small Cross coins, which *prima facie* will be from the beginning of the validity-period. They are by no means of the heaviest: Ipswich, 1.29g, Lincoln, 1.30, 1.49, and 1.43g, and Winchester, 1.72g.

There are a few very rare Last Small Cross coins minted at Norwich by the moneyer Oswold, in the name of Cnut. The question obviously arises whether they are official issues. Fortunately there is a die-link to a normal coin, of which the dies are East Anglian in style. The obverse of the Cnut coin shows close stylistic affinities with a normal coin, also by a moneyer Oswold, at Nottingham (Lyon, 'Some problems', plate 12, d, e, and f). The three coins of Cnut could presumably have been minted at any time after April 1016, but perhaps in the autumn, after the defeat of Edmund Ironside and the partitioning of England. Whether Cnut stayed in Norwich is not known. All that it is necessary to suppose is that an enterprising East Anglian die-cutter had heard the name of the new king, and acted on it before receiving instructions for the new type.

e) *Weight-standards.* The general histogram for the type (Petersson, Fig. 6) shows peaks at c. 1.72g, *c.* 1.62g, *c.* 1.32g, and probably *c.*

1.12g. The numbers of coins on the heaviest standards are small.

The regional pattern of weight-standards on a shire basis can be studied from a satisfactorily large sample (4,251 coins). It seems complicated, with an apparent breakdown of shire uniformity. The general pattern of a single high standard in western parts of the country, contrasting with declining standards in the east, is considerably eroded. One can detect more than one weight standard at Chester, and in Devon, Dorset, Gloucestershire, Herefordshire, Shropshire, Somerset, Warwickshire, and Wiltshire.

Whether all this arises from the very large geld of 1012 is an obvious question to be asked. Because absolute dates cannot be assigned to individual coins, progress will be difficult. One could begin by correlating Dolley's nine die-cutting styles as represented in Hildebrand, mint by mint, with their weights (published in 1990 by Petersson). That should help to show whether the creation of regional die-cutting centres was a response to the urgent needs generated by the very large geld of 1012.

f) *Number of mints.* Some 60 mints struck the type, among which Bristol is new, as is the (temporary) mint of Cissbury. The Bruton, Crewkerne, and Ilchester mints are removed to Cadbury, which signs coins only in this type and into Quatrefoil.

Reference

C.S.S. Lyon, 'Some problems in interpreting Anglo-Saxon coinage', *Anglo-Saxon England* 5 (1976), 173-224.

CNUT
7. QUATREFOIL
c.1017—*c*.1023 or 1024
Hildebrand Type E. *BMC* Type viii.

On the coins introduced at the first *renovatio* of his reign, King Cnut is shown wearing a crown. One has to go back many years to find a precedent in the English coinage. Kingship had been transferred from the old English royal family, by conquest, and that fact is advertised by the coinage. It seems unlikely from a political view-point that the new design could have been introduced before Cnut's coronation.

Any further conclusions depend on whether (as now seems likely from the evidence of Danish coins copying the Last Small Cross type) Cnut had already struck coins at Lund on which he claimed the title *rex Dænorum*, as early as 1014-15, rather than in 1018. If the earlier chronology is possible, there is no insuperable obstacle to supposing that the heavy geld of 1018 could have been paid in Quatrefoil pennies. As this point is of considerable interest for English monetary history, the arguments are set out quite fully below. It is tempting to suppose that imperial aspirations were already in Cnut's mind (with the empire of Henry II as his near neighbour). He may even have seen Byzantine silver coins with the portrait of the emperor in a *clipeus*, and sought to copy it in the so-called Quatrefoil design—which will then have been not merely decorative.

Cnut's Quatrefoil type was probably the largest of all the sexennial types, struck from even more dies than Æthelred's Crux type. It accumulated in Scandinavia in much greater quantities than any other periodic type (although Cnut's Helmet type was not far behind). A careful correlation of style with weight suggests that, at the major mints, there were as many as five successive weight-standards, averaging roughly (and with some local variations) 1.4, 1.3, 1.2, 1.1, and 1.00g. Output was not divided equally between the standards. The top three standards account for roughly 30 per cent of the coins at the major mints, the fourth standard (*c*.1.1 or 1.05g) alone accounts for about 40 per cent, and the fifth (*c*.1.0 or 0.95g) for about 30 per cent. There are one or two heavier coins from the western half of England (Axbridge, Ilchester, South Petherton), but they are excessively scarce.

Dr Nightingale has suggested that Cnut introduced a new weight-standard shortly after his conquest. 'It appears from the weight of the coinage', she writes, 'that he reduced the English pound from fifteen to ten oras and struck the penny to a standard of 24 pence to the ora . . . A few years later, *c*.1026, he altered the weight of the ora in Denmark and in England' (*English Hist. Rev.* 1987, 561). Blackburn and Lyon's correlation of stylistic and metrological analysis puts a large question-mark against this reading of the evidence; and on a longer view, weight-variation within each validity-period certainly persisted.

The *Chronicle* states that a geld of £72,000, levied by Cnut before the peace agreement at Oxford, was paid in 1018, and that the citizens of London paid an additional £10,500. If these very large sums were paid in Quatrefoil pennies, they would have been equivalent to nearly half the entire issue, roughly estimated at £195,000 (assuming 10,000 coins per reverse die). The credibility of the *Chronicle*'s figures has been strongly debated by Lawson, Gillingham, and Metcalf. So far as the numismatic aspects of the evidence are concerned, the exact date of introduction of the Quatrefoil type is of interest. Even if it was in production when the geld was paid, it is not certain that payment was made wholly in Quatrefoil coins. Indeed, it is very difficult to suppose that that was so, because not enough Quatrefoil coins would have been minted by 1018—unless (improbably) the geld absorbed virtually every coin minted in the first year of the validity-period, or unless the weight-standards were not successive. In judging that question one should hesitate to assume that there were neat and tidy successive weight-standards, even if that was the general tendency. If the early Quatrefoil coins did disappear thoroughly, it might follow that the estimate of 4,655 reverse dies was an under-estimate.

More probably, much of the geld was paid in Last Small Cross coins; and the sudden heavy demand may also have drawn old money out of savings hoards—although that would only work if payment by weight was accepted. Another general question is whether the very heavy geld beggared the monetary system in England, leaving traces in, for example, a less vigorous or less far-ranging regional circulation. One might look to see whether single finds from the rest of the validity-period had travelled less far from their mints of origin than was normal.

Of course, if the geld was paid largely in old coins, it cannot be used as an explanation for the large scale of the Quatrefoil issue. That argument falls to the ground. It may be that much of the money that Cnut exacted did not leave England, and was soon recycled into Quatrefoil pennies, e.g. on the fourth weight-standard. The question is in any case acute, 'where did all the silver come from?'. The succeeding type, Pointed Helmet, is estimated at 2,233 dies, or less than half as many.

Given that almost all the arguments rehearsed so far are speculative, or debateable, one may turn with some interest and perhaps relief to the coins themselves. The issue is unusual in at least two respects. First, there were an exceptionally large number of die-cutting centres. Secondly, the patterns of mint-output show a dramatic surge of production at the smaller and medium-sized mints, far out of proportion to what happened at the large mints.

Nineteen die-cutting centres have been identified on grounds of style. Of these, eight were the usual major centres (London, Winchester, Lincoln, York, Chester, Gloucester, Exeter, and Thetford). Five minor centres seem to have been active from the beginning of the type (Lewes/Hastings, Chichester, Bath, Worcester, and Norwich), and six more seem to have opened during the course of the type, at Oxford, Taunton/Ilchester, Shrewsbury, Stamford, Bedford, and Northampton/Huntingdon. Such a plethora of die-cutting establishments cannot have been strictly necessary unless there was great urgency to strike coin. The number of dies cut by each centre varied, of course. Perhaps the witan took a decision which, in practical terms, was not required.

Secondly, the smaller mints increased their relative output dramatically, compared with what they had done in Last Small Cross. Their output then usually fell back again, just as dramatically, in Pointed Helmet. The increase in output, far above the national trend, was coupled with an unusually large complement of moneyers. We do not know exactly how men became moneyers—whether they applied to be appointed at their own discretion, or whether (as seems more likely in this case) there was a directive to increase the quota of moneyers in a town. All the developments that have been described are visible especially in the western half of the country, whereas in the south-east, the pattern is almost diametrically opposite.

If we look at estimated numbers of dies for Last Small Cross, Quatrefoil, and Pointed Helmet, we see at the major mints:

	LSC	Q	PH
London	702	1033	741
Lincoln	370	378	219
Winchester	291	298	98

At Southampton (so close to Winchester) and in the West Country, the proportions are utterly different:

	LSC	Q	PH
Southampton	5	35	0
Bristol	3	72	0
Ilchester	0	120	10
Taunton	2	29	0

In the midlands and at Chester the contrast is less dramatic:

	LSC	Q	PH
Bedford	13	37	19
Oxford	21	90	31
Gloucester	18	61	25
Chester	76	242	69

And in the south-east the trend may even be reversed:

	LSC	Q	PH
Canterbury	71	59	54
Dover	46	34	44

In the south-east and at the major mints one generally finds a relatively higher proportion of heavy coins. At Winchester, quite exceptionally, nearly two-thirds of the specimens weigh over 1.10g.

To summarize: Quatrefoil was very unusual in the demand for moneyers' services at the smaller mint-places (and in the numbers of moneyers who provided those services). The aberration shows up most dramatically in the south-west where Ilchester was briefly a more active mint than Exeter, but is found very widely through the western half of the country. In the eastern half, the major mints dominate the national trend, and the smaller mints generally show an intermediate pattern. In the south-east the pattern is more or less reversed.

We may now turn back to look at the arguments derived from the Scandinavian evidence in more detail. Because there are Danish coins in the name of Cnut, imitating the English Last Small Cross type, it seemed probable to scholars that the Last Small Cross type was current when Cnut became king of Denmark in 1018. The Danish coins could, admittedly, have copied an obsolete English type; but there are dies of English workmanship, made at Lincoln, which are absolutely identical in style with English coins. They read CNUT REX DÆNOR and would seem to have been commissioned from a Lincoln die-cutter. He or one of his colleagues subsequently provided Quatrefoil dies with the same legend, in exactly the same style as English dies. It is beyond reasonable doubt, therefore, that coins in the name of Cnut were being minted in Denmark before the Quatrefoil type was introduced in England. That is unlikely to mean that Quatrefoil was not introduced until 1018. Rather, it now seems that Cnut's Last Small Cross coins were struck as early as 1014/15, when he returned to Denmark following the death of Svend Tveskæg and, according to one source, contested the throne with his brother Harald. Hoard-evidence supports this view: there is a *rex Dænorum* (Short Cross) coin in the Slethei hoard from Norway, which terminates with 530 English Last Small Cross coins. The Everlöv hoard from Skåne also ends with Last Small Cross and includes 9 specimens of Cnut's early coinage. Die-chains have been constructed showing that Cnut's early Danish coins begin with a Small Cross phase.

Since the Danish evidence is by no means an insuperable obstacle to dating the introduction of Quatrefoil before 1018, one may judge the English evidence of abnormal levels of activity at provincial mints on its

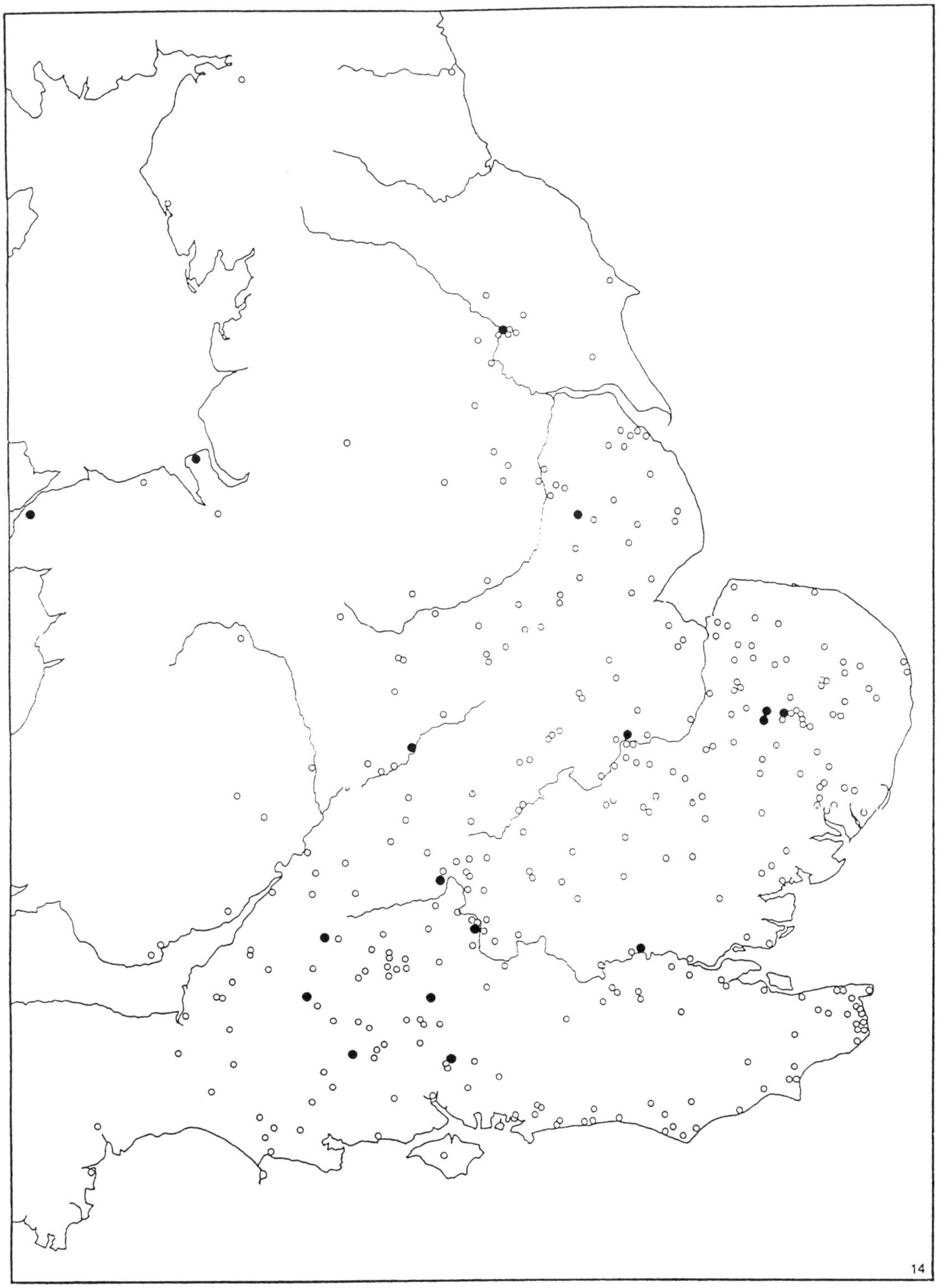

MAP 14. Coins of Quatrefoil type.

merits.

The only other type in which anything like so much money (in absolute terms) was minted in the western half of England was Crux, and it is in the west that the question is most acute: where did all the silver come from? Did ordinary people, after all, keep a nest-egg of obsolete coin? (See the comments on the Wedmore hoard, in Part 4, Section 12.)

a) *English (and Welsh) single finds.* Baverstock, Caernarfon, Croxton, Eynsham, Hungtingdon, Lincoln, London (4), Meols (2), Netherton (½), Stanton St.Quintin (½), Thetford, Trowbridge (½), Wallingford (½), Warwick, West Harling, Winchester, York. (See Map 14.)

b) *English (and Welsh) hoards.* Gloucester (Kingsholm); Pant-yr-Eglwys; for Barrowby and Bryn Maelgwyn, which are essentially Quatrefoil hoards, see also under Pointed Helmet (below); also for Drwsdangoed.

*Gloucester (Kingsholm), c.*1780. There is a run of some 110 Quatrefoil pennies in the British Museum with pedigrees taking them back to *c.*1780 (until when the type had been rare among English finds). This group is noticeably overweight in coins of Gloucester, Bath, Langport, Oxford, and Chester. It may well reflect a very large hoard found at or near the palace site of Kingsholm, *c.*1000 metres north of the centre of Gloucester. The evidence of the Kingsholm hoard (*BNJ* 29, 1958) for the monetary history of the period cannot be very firm, because the eighteenth-century collectors whose coins are now in the British Museum may have done their best to select from a range of mints, thus distorting the proportions in the sample. Conversely, the lightest coins in the run cannot individually be said with certainty to come from the hoard. It is clear that the heaviest coins are over-represented in the parcel, e.g. from the Bath mint, but whether this reflects an early date of concealment within the validity-period, or merely the westerly character of the hoard in some way, is as yet far from clear.

Pant-yr-Eglwys, 1981. Three Quatrefoil pennies and one imitation were found, partially melted, near Llandudno, close to the church-yard of (the eponymous) St. Tudno's, i.e. close to the sailing route between Chester and Ireland. Two of the three coins were of Chester, and the third of Hereford. The hoard may originally have been larger, but no more coins could be recovered. It might also date from the validity-period of Pointed helmet, like the nearby Bryn Maelgwyn hoard. (The Bryn Maelgwyn hoard, superbly published and analysed, is a source of great importance for the Quatrefoil type. See below.)

Bryn Maelgwyn, 1979. There are 171 coins of Chester, with very heavy die-duplication (discussed in Q.36), and 29 coins from other mints. Given the location of the hoard (beyond Chester), it is a reasonable assumption that 29 coins can be considered as a sample of what had reached the Chester area by the end of the validity-period. Mints from the western half of the country make a good showing: Shrewsbury (5), Warwick, Worcester (2), Gloucester (2), Hereford, Bath, Cricklade, and Exeter. There are two coins each from London, Lincoln, and Stamford, five from Winchester, and singletons from Leicester, Lewes, Oxford, and Salisbury. The major east-coast mints are thus noticeably under-represented.

c) *Size of the issue.* A massive total of 4,655 reverse dies has been estimated, and one cannot see any reason why the estimate should be seriously flawed or biassed. If a large proportion of the earliest coins were missing from the sample, the statistical procedure would tend to yield an under-estimate.

d) *Evidence for dating.* There were three substantive types in Cnut's reign (1016-35), which would allow an average of roughly six years for each type. The question has been asked, above, whether a crowned bust design could have been used before Cnut's coronation. The end-date of 1023/4 is purely a guess.

e) *Weight-standards.* Petersson's general histogram, with about 19 per cent of specimens in the central step, and a modal value of *c.*1.02g, is at first glance more or less normal. The suggestion that there were up to five successive weight-standards (see above) is therefore surprising. But weight-distributions for the individual mints (Petersson, 1990) make it perfectly clear that every mint for which there is sufficient material to judge employed several standards, —although they were not everywhere the same. Doubtless there was a tendency for the average weight to decline, but the assumption that weight-standards were successive needs to be considered carefully, to make sure that no circular argument is involved, and that the facts are sufficient to prove the case.

f) *Number of mint-places*, Some 72 mint-places are recorded, including some in the west country, and also in the south-east, that are either new, or reactivated after having stood idle for many years. They include Ilchester, with 9 moneyers (inactive in Last Small Cross), Axbridge, Bruton, Crewkerne, 'Eanbyri', Langport, and Petherton; Aylesbury, Buckingham, Guildford, Hythe, Lympne; and Peterborough.

Bristol (created in the previous validity-period) rises in importance, perhaps in response to a shift in trading patterns in the Irish Sea area.

References.

B. Malmer, *King Canute's Coinage in the Northern Countries* (Dorothea Coke Memorial Lecture in Northern Studies delivered at University College London, 30 May 1972), 1974.

M. Blackburn, 'Do Cnut the Great's first coins as king of Denmark date from before 1018?', *Sigtuna Papers* (Commentationes, new series, vol.6), Stockholm, 1990, pp. 55-68.

M. Blackburn and S. Lyon, 'Regional die-production in Cnut's *Quatrefoil* issue', in M.A.S. Blackburn (ed.), *Anglo-Saxon Monetary History*, Leicester, 1986, pp. 223-72 (with stylistic attributions of the Stockholm and Copenhagen systematic collections, and detailed metrological analysis by styles).

G.C. Boon, 'Bryn Maelgwyn', in *Welsh Hoards 1979-1981*, Cardiff, 1986, pp. 1-35.

M. Blackburn, 'English dies used in the Scandinavian imitative coinages', *Hikuin* 11 (1985), 101-24 gives enlarged illustrations, at p. 110, of the Danish dies commissioned from Lincoln.

J.S. Jensen and M. Blackburn, 'The oldest Lund coinage of Cnut', in *Tusindtallets Danske Mønter fra Den kongelige Mønt- og Medaillesamling*, Copenhagen, 1995, at p. 28. See also the Viborg coin at p.44.

M. Blackburn, review in *BNJ* 58 (1988), 167-9.

K. Jonsson, 'The coinage of Cnut', in *The Reign of Cnut, King of England, Denmark, and Norway*, 1994, pp. 193-230.

M.K. Lawson, 'The collection of Danegeld and Heregeld in the reigns of Aethelred II and Cnut', *English Historical Review* 99 (1984), 721-38.

J. Gillingham, '"The Most Precious Jewel in the English Crown": levels of Danegeld and heregeld in the early eleventh century', ibid. 104 (1989), 373-84.

M.K. Lawson, '"Those stories look true": levels of taxation in the reigns of Aethelred II and Cnut', ibid., 385-406.

J. Gillingham, 'Chronicles and coins as evidence for levels of tribute and taxation in late tenth- and early eleventh-century England', ibid. 105 (1990), 939-50.

M.K. Lawson, 'Danegeld and Heregeld once more', ibid., 951-61.

D.M.Metcalf, 'Can we believe the very large figure of £72,000 for the geld levied by Cnut in 1018?', *Studies in Late Anglo-Saxon Coinage*, Stockholm, 1990, pp. 165-76.

8. POINTED HELMET
*c.*1023-4—*c.*1029-30?
Hildebrand Type G; *BMC* Type xiv.

Whereas the two preceding validity-periods coincided with turbulent political and military events in England, with great impact on taxation, the Pointed Helmet type covers a relatively uneventful phase. It is still large, with an estimated 2,233 reverse dies. The Scandanavian sample is almost as large as for Quatrefoil. The ranking of the mints and the regional shares of mint-activity show no obvious irregularities except that London takes an unusually prominent role, minting a full third of the national output. (There is, however, no significant increase in the number of moneyers at London: from 67 in Quatrefoil to 72.) The reason is not apparent. Otherwise, the patterns return to normal, after the anomalies discussed under Quatrefoil.

The basic study of die-cutting styles was undertaken by Dolley and Ingold (*Commentationes 1*), and their scheme was reviewed critically by Lyon (*BNJ* 1960). There are two main styles, and two spellings of the king's title, REX and RECX. Lyon sees the Pointed Helmet type as transitional between Quatrefoil, with its proliferation of die-cutting centres, and Short Cross, in which die-cutting was essentially centralized. He envisages that the provincial die-cutting centres were closed down at some intermediate date in the Pointed Helmet validity-period.

The average weight of the type, at 1.02g, is particularly low, and the histogram which the coins generate over-all is more compact than anything previously seen since Eadgar's reform. Nevertheless it conceals variations. Many mints clearly strike on two standards. In the western half of the country (and at Oxford and Wallingford) these seem to be close to 1.12g and 1.02g. At Winchester the heavy standard is marginally higher: perhaps 1.15g and 1.02g. At London (which tends to dominate the pattern with its large share) and elsewhere in the eastern half of the country, all or most of the coins are on a standard of *c.*1.02g. Thus the perennial east/west pattern is maintained, even if the percentage difference between the two predominating standards has narrowed. There are rather few mints offering exceptions to the scheme described, but at Exeter there seems to have been a third, even lower standard of *c.* 0.87g. At Canterbury the lower standard seems to have been *c.*0.97g, and Dover may match that figure.

In the Bryn Maelgwyn hoard, concealed surely at the very beginning of the Pointed Helmet validity-period, the two coins of the type weigh 1.00g (Chester, where the standards are 1.12 and 1.02g) and 1.02g (Shrewsbury, where almost all the coins are around 1.12g). One should hesitate to assume, then, that the weight-standards were altogether successive.

a) *English single finds.* Bullington, Cerne Abbas, Colesbourne, Gastard (½), Lakenheath, London (1 + ½), Manchester, Meols, Milton, Norwich, Ramsey, Silchester, Stowmarket, Thetford (2), Trowbridge, Wellingborough (2, mini-hoard?), Winchester.
b) *English (and Welsh) hoards.* Bryn Maelgwyn and perhaps also Pant-yr-Eglwys

(see under Quatrefoil); Drwsdangoed; Barrowby; Halton Moor; Wellingborough.

Bryn Maelgwyn, 1979. From near Llandudno, reflecting the shipping route between Chester and Ireland. Two hundred Quatrefoil coins, predominantly of Chester, and with numerous die-identities (see Q. 36), plus 2 Dublin Quatrefoil copies. Two Pointed Helmet coins, of Chester and Shrewsbury (see above, and also under Quatrefoil).

Drwsdangoed, near Chwilog, Gwynedd, *c.*1850. No further details were published about a find of 18 coins of Cnut, in beautiful condition, under a carnedd. The find-spot is 4 miles NE of Pwllheli, and the hoard may, like the other Cnut hoards from NW Wales, reflect coastwise navigation. (*Arch. Cambr.* 2 Ser., 1, 1850, 334.)

Barrowby, 1872. The hoard is from a location a little to the west of Grantham, i.e. about 20 miles from Stamford, and all the recorded coins are of the Stamford mint. They are described by Sharp (*NC* 1880), who was a specialist on the Stamford mint. Dolley, in a full critical study of the hoard (*Seaby Bulletin* 1978, 343-5), suggests that only Stamford coins from a much larger hoard were offered to Sharp, because of his known interest, and that the two (worn) coins of Æthelred II, also from that mint, may not derive from the hoard. Thus, the regional composition of the hoard remains unknown. The coins were concealed in the shin-bone of an ox, broken (not sawn) at each end, and stopped with clay. They included 10 Quatrefoil coins and 2 of the Pointed Helmet type, in 'excellent and fresh condition'. They are by a range of moneyers (and perhaps even selected with that in view). The two Pointed Helmet coins weigh 0.90g and 0.86g, well below the modal value of 1.02g seen at Stamford. It is not clear whether the pronounced peak conceals a much smaller peak at a lower value, nor whether a correlation of style and moneyers' names could resolve the question.

Halton Moor, 1815. The treasure was found about 5 miles from Lancaster, in newly-enclosed land. A silver-gilt cup contained 860 coins, six pieces of stamped gold, and a gold torc. Four hundred of the coins were examined. It is an open question how random a sample they were, but our understanding of the hoard is unlikely to be distorted. Twenty-one were Norman deniers and 379 were Pointed Helmet coins of Cnut (cf. the single finds listed s.v. Manchester). All but a handful of these were of the York mint, the others being of Lincoln (4), London (4), Cambridge, Exeter, Leicester, Maldon, and Winchester. Most of the York moneyers recorded for the type are well represented.

Wellingborough. Two York coins may reflect a mini-hoard. Cf. Part 4, Section 6, Middle Danelaw, for the Titchmarsh and Castor hoards.

c) *Size of the issue.* The Lincoln-based estimate is 2,233 dies.

d) *Evidence for dating.* There is no obvious event which would account for the concealment of Bryn Maelgwyn and Barrowby early in the validity-period. See the general remarks, above.

e) *Weight-standards.* See above.

f) *Number of mint-places.* Steyning is a new mint, together with Milborne Port and 'Laewude'. The burst of activity at lesser mints in the preceding Quatrefoil type offers some sort of statistical guarantee that these three really are new. In all, 64 mints are known.

References. A thorough stylistic analysis of the type is given in R.H.M. Dolley and J. Ingold, 'Some thoughts on the engraving of the dies for the English coinage, *c.* 1025', *Commentationes* 1 (1961), 187-222, 6 plates. See also the review by C.S.S. Lyon in *BNJ* 30 (1960-1), 197-8.

9. SHORT CROSS

*c.*1029-30—November 1035/early 1036

Hildebrand Type H. *BMC* Type xvi.

The big east-coast mints (London, Thetford, Norwich, Stamford, Lincoln, York) as usual account for the lion's share of mint-output, with *c.*60 per cent. There are hints—no more—of a revival of trade at and out of these main centres: an exceptional number of stray losses for the validity-period as a whole; more single finds than usual from the urban centres; their coins carried over long distances. In quantitative terms, however, the estimated number of dies is down by a third on the Pointed Helmet type, and the Scandinavian sample is smaller by a similar proportion. The decline, in this and the types of the next decade, is shared out around the mints quite evenly, e.g. London maintains its traditional share, but not its volume, of output. What this tells us about the reasons for taking silver to the mints is far from clear.

The great majority of mints work to a single standard of *c.*1.12g (the heavier of the two general standards in the preceding type). London, Lincoln, and York work essentially on the same standard as the mints in the western half of the country. There are still a few local exceptions, which are quite enough to show that administration in the shires could still behave independently. At Stamford there are evidently two standards, of *c.*1.15g and *c.*1.00g. At London and Lincoln, negative skewness in the histograms suggests that there was a secondary standard, possibly at *c.*1.02g. For these two mints there are enough specimens to settle this question by re-drawing the histograms with smaller and/or different step-intervals, in order to define more exactly what is going on in the region 1.15—1.00g. At Hastings there are two standards, of which the lower one is clearly at *c.*1.02g. At Guildford, Hertford, Shaftesbury, and Warwick, something similar seems to be the case. At Derby, exceptionally, there seem to be two very low standards, of *c.*1.00g and *c.*0.77g.

There is an iconographically remarkable variety, known from one obverse die at the London mint, which shows Cnut holding a traditional Viking triangular banner in place of the usual lis-sceptre. An analogous variety at Winchester, iconographically less ambitious, shows the king holding a lance. Given Cnut's enthusiastic support of the church, it is puzzling to interpret these rare varieties. It seems that they are from a particular moment, towards 1035, and that nothing similar occurs in other types. One is inclined, therefore, to look for a political context, rather than the whim of an individual moneyer. No satisfactory explanation has yet been offered.

a) *English single finds.* There are more finds from this validity-period than from any other, and they include a good proportion of cut halves and quarters. Abingdon, Bishops Cannings, Boston (½), Bracon Ash, Bramford, Brandon (½), Bromeswell (½), Bullington, Caistor-on-the-Wolds, Carlisle, Cheddar, Claxby-by-Alford (½), Dover (½), Drigg, Ely (½), Essex (North), Gainsborough (½), Harborough Magna, Hereford, Kenninghall, Leatherhead (½), Lincoln (3), Little Horwood, London (5,including one ½), Meols (3), Normanby-by-Stow, Osbaldwick,

Osmington, Richborough, Riddlesworth, Rolvenden, St. Nicholas at Wade, St. Peters (½), Shipston on Stour, Stanford on Soar, Steyning, Takeley, Thetford (2 including one farthing), Wallingford (¼), West Walton, Woodmansterne, Worcester (2), Worth, York.

b) *English hoards.* Bottisham; Polstead.

Bottisham, Cambs., 1982. Three Short Cross coins, of London (2) and Stamford (*BNJ* 53, 1983, 177).

Polstead, Suffolk, 1980 x 1990. Four Short Cross coins from the same ploughed field, within an area *c.*20m wide. They are of Lincoln, Norwich, Wallingford, and a fragment from an unidentified mint (possibly London?) There is no positive reason to suppose that a Helmet coin of Æthelred II found nearby was associated.

c) *Size of the issue.* An estimated 1,439 reverse dies.

d) *Evidence for dating.* There are two Short Cross coins in the name of Harold (*BMC* 65 and *SCBI Stockholm,* 1), of London and Bristol which, if they are regular English coins, show that minting persisted after the death of Cnut. (There is also a Short Cross/Jewel Cross mule (*SCBI Stockholm* 2) which is in principle less informative.)

As to the start date of Short Cross, there is no evidence of substance.

e) *Weight-standards.* Different opinions have been expressed, but see now the comments above, in light of Petersson 1990.

The Börringe kloster hoard (*CNS* 3, 1, 8) ends with just eight coins of the Short Cross type, among which one may note three of Lincoln weighing 1.07, 1.04, and 1.03g.

f) *Number of mint-places.* Some 60 are known, of which about a quarter are recorded from extremely few specimens.

References. Special studies of the Short Cross type are lacking. The official English character of the variety with banner is demonstrated in M. Blackburn, 'A variety of Cnut's *Short Cross* coinage depicting a banner', *Festskrift till Lars O. Lagerqvist,* edited by U. Ehrensvärd *et al.,* Stockholm, 1989, pp. 39-43.

HAROLD I and HARTHACNUT
10. JEWEL CROSS
Early 1036—*c.*1038
Hildebrand: Harold I, Type A; Harthacnut Types A (left-facing) and Aa (right-facing); Cnut, Type K.
BMC, Harold, Type i; Harthacnut, Types i (left-facing) and i, var. a (right-facing); Cnut, Type xx.

Cnut's illness and untimely death in November 1035 deprived England of a very able ruler. He left two sons, by two wives: Harold 'Harefoot', the son of Ælfgifu of Northampton, and Harthacnut, the son of Emma of Normandy (the widow of Æthelred II). Harthacnut might well have succeeded to the English crown if he had been present in England in the months following his father's death; but he was unable to leave Denmark, where the political situation required him to remain. The succession was disputed, reopening old conflicts of loyalty, and setting the Mercians against the West Saxons. At a meeting of the witan early in 1036, at Oxford, Earl Leofric and the leading men north of the Thames, acting in concert with Cnut's lithsmen in London, elected Harold as regent of all England on behalf of himself and his half-brother Harthacnut. Earl Godwin and the men of Wessex opposed this decision without success, except that it was agreed that Queen Emma was to live in Winchester, and to retain a body of Harthacnut's housecarles, in order to maintain his interests in Wessex. In 1037 Harold was recognized as sole king, and Emma took refuge in Flanders.

When Harold died in March 1040 he was succeeded by Harthacnut, who arrived in England in June with a large fleet. He exacted a geld of £21,099 to pay off the 62 ships' crews, and a further £11,048 for the 32 ships which he retained in his service. He rapidly acquired the reputation of being vindictive, and not a good king. He died in June 1042, while drinking at a wedding-feast.

The six and a half years from the death of Cnut (November 1035) to the accession of Edward the Confessor (June 1042) saw three successive coin-types, which obviously had much shorter validity-periods than the six-year average duration of the types in the preceding sixty years. The three types are Jewel Cross, Fleur-de-lis, and Arm and Sceptre, in that order. They name Harold, Harthacnut, and 'Cnut' confusingly. The Fleur-de-lis type is in Harold's name only, and doubtless falls within his sole reign (1037-40) although arguably with a delay after Harthacnut's accession before it was replaced. The Arm-and-Sceptre type names Harthacnut or Cnut, but the latter seems to have been merely an abbreviated form referring to Harthacnut. In any case the type is to be dated to 1040-2. The Jewel Cross type is much more complicated. What follows is an attempt to describe the position, as established by Talvio's researches. He undertook a full-scale stylistic analysis of the type (in *Anglo-Saxon Monetary History,* 1986) and subsequently published a Sylloge volume of the large Stockholm collection. Talvio identified four stylistic varieties of obverse, which he linked with die-cutting centres at London, Winchester, and Lincoln. His variety R (right-facing bust, produced at Winchester for Harthacnut) seems to have been concurrent with L1 (left-facing), for which the dies were cut in two ateliers, namely London (National style A, cut for Harold, Harthacnut, and 'Cnut') and another, or possibly also London (National style B, only for Harold). L2, with a simpler diadem, is found only in the name of Harold: it is later and lighter. In L2, both styles A and B are continued. At Lincoln we find L1 followed by L2, both on a relatively modest scale.

Because a single atelier supplied southern mints with dies reading Harthacnut or Cnut, while at the same time supplying northern mints with dies reading Harold, it is clear that there was a formal agreement concerning the half-brothers' interests. The main uncertainty is whether L1B began at the same date as L1A, or only when Harold had gained complete control. Talvio makes the point that without an agreement between the two, a national recoinage would not have been practicable.

The numbers of known obverse dies in the different categories may be judged from the following figures:

	Harthacnut	*Cnut*	*Harold*
R	73	-	-
L1A	17	17	83
L1B	-	-	103
L1L	-	-	21
L2A	-	-	166
L2B	-	-	72
L2L	-	-	15
	90	17	460

By analogy with the (later) 'Cnut' coins in the Arm and Sceptre type, one may suppose that the name 'Cnut' simply refers to Harthacnut, but one should consider whether it is deliberately ambiguous. It occurs at London (6 dies), Bristol, Dover (2), Exeter, Lydford, Salisbury, Southwark (2), Wallingford, and Cambridge.

Harthacnut's coins with his name in full are nearly all from mints on or south of the Thames, with Gloucester as the most conspicuous exception—perhaps because Gloucestershire gave allegiance to him. But there are also Winchester-cut (right-facing) dies from Hertford, Lincoln, Stamford, and Warwick. The L1A dies for Harthacnut are exclusively southern, and the L1A dies reading Cnut are almost exclusively so.

The Jewel Cross type evidently persisted into the sole reign which began early in 1037. How much longer it lasted can only be guessed from the relative quantities of coins in the different stylistic groups (hampered by uncertainty about the start-date of L1B). It looks as though at least 253 out of 460, and perhaps more, of the dies are from the sole reign. That does not fit easily with hypotheses about an intensive recoinage at the beginning of the validity-period, followed by slacker working.

Harthacnut, as well as Harold, is called *rex* during the early period which the *Chronicle* describes as a regency (or perhaps one should say, Harold as well as Harthacnut is called *rex*).

For the Jewel Cross type as a whole, the ranking of the mints and the regional shares in the output of the type remain exactly normal, with not a discrepancy in sight. Winchester, for the type as a whole, shows no extra output such as could be connected with Emma's presence, and the number of moneyers there is much the same for Harthacnut and subsequently for Harold. In short, it seems that the name of the king on a Jewel Cross penny mattered to the user about as much as the Chief Cashier's signature on a Bank of England note today. Presumably the named king expected to take the profits, but whether Harthacnut received what was owed to him is unknown. If his dies were cut at Winchester, perhaps his mother was able to collect the fees. There could be no clearer demonstration, than from these statistics of mint-output, that the political and monetary aspects of coin-production responded to circumstances independently.

As to the ways in which coins were used, once they had been put into circulation, the evidence derives, as always, from the English single finds and hoards.

There is a sharp drop in the estimated size of the currency, and an even sharper drop in the numbers of single finds, but the latter is fully accounted for if one calculates *pro rata* for a validity-period of only two to three years. The rate of stray losses *per annum*, that is to say, was not at this point sensitive to the volume of the currency. One is encouraged to think that it reflects primarily the volume of transactions.

a) *English single-finds.* i) in the name of Harold: Alford, L, Canterbury, Croughton, O, East Harling, Nf, Ham, K, Horseheath, C, London (½), Louth, Repton, Db, Thetford (3), Wittering, Nth (½), Wroxeter, Sa.
ii) in the name of Harthacnut: East Harling, Nf (½), Ogbourne St. Andrew, W, Plymouth, West Rudham Nf, (½), West Walton, Nf (½), Winchester (2)

b) *English hoards.* None.

c) *Size of the issue.* An estimated 874 dies.

d) *Evidence for dating.* It is presumed that the type was introduced soon after the witenagemot at Oxford early in 1036, and continued for roughly a year after Harold gained sole power early in 1037.

e) *Weight-standards.* There are still some local variations, which bear a marked resemblance to those in the later part of Cnut's reign. At Winchester and in many western mints there is a single, well-defined standard of *c.*1.12g. London seems to work on the same single standard for Harthacnut, but on more than one standard (*c.*1.12 and ? *c.*1.02g) for Harold. Norwich and Thetford yield straggling histograms which reflect more than one standard. At Stamford, the modal values are *c.*1.12 and c.1.02g. At Lincoln there are two peaks, at *c.*1.09 and *c.*0.92, and at York a similar mode of *c.*1.09g is visible. As before, there are a few 'odd men out': Derby is very straggling and low; Dover strikes coins of low weight (but Canterbury has its main standard at *c.*1.12g, with another possibly below 1 gramme); Exeter shows multiple peaks; and Salisbury, curiously, uses a standard of *c.*1.07g.

Talvio has shown that at London L2 coins are distinctly lighter than L1 (1.01g against 1.08g). Likewise there is a decline at York (1.10g down to 1.08g), Lincoln (1.05g to 0.98g), and Stamford (1.07g to 1.00g). He sees this as generalized evidence for progressive weight-reduction during the validity-period, while recognizing that modal values cannot be deduced from mean averages. Winchester keeps to a single standard of *c.*1.12g throughout.

f) *Number of mint-places.* Sixty-one, often from a tiny number of specimens. The tally could increase as new material comes to light. (Again, that statement is not necessarily incompatible with the fact that the number of known dies is already close to the total of estimated reverse dies.)

References.
T. Talvio, 'Harold I and Harthacnut's *Jewel Cross* type reconsidered', in *Anglo-Saxon Monetary History*, Leicester, 1986, pp. 273-90;
id., *Anglo-Saxon Coins. Harold I and Harthacnut*, 1035-42 (SCBI, vol. 40, Stockholm, Part 4), 1991.

HAROLD I
11. FLEUR-DE-LIS
*c.*1038–*c.*1040
Hildebrand, Harold I, Type B. *BMC* Type v, var. c.

A sample of 873 Fleur-de-lis coins in Stockholm, meticulously catalogued by Talvio, provides an opportunity to conduct a check on the Lincoln-based estimate of the number of reverse dies used during the validity-period. The sample is thick with duplicate reverse (and obverse) dies, and should, so far as the arithmetic is concerned, give an estimate with quite small margins of statistical uncertainty. The probability that money left England for Scandinavia separately or to some extent separately from the three regions of Yorkshire, Lincolnshire, and the south of England, and the possibility that the balance as between those three regions may have varied puts a question-mark against the reliability of the over-all national estimate based on counting dies at the Lincoln mint only. The Lincoln-based estimate is 1,225 dies, and the Stockholm sylloge estimate (343 non-singletons, 615 recorded dies) is 1,565. As the systematic collection derives largely, in this type, from a single hoard, namely Äspinge, *t.p.q.* 1047, the estimate may in principle be somewhat depressed by clustering. The discrepancy between the two estimates could, in other words, really be somewhat wider. There are a few instances of multiple die-identities in the sample, e.g. from Stamford. The Lincoln die estimate depends on the number of coins in Mossop's sample, namely 156, and one should prefer the figure based on Talvio's work. As regards any possible north-south bias in the Scandinavian sample, the Lincoln mint takes 116 out of a national total of 1,225 estimated dies, or between 9 and 10 per cent, whereas on the Talvio-based estimates, the corresponding figures are 155 and 1,565, or very much the same. See further section 17c below.

Even if the Lincoln-based estimates are, by the years around 1040, becoming less reliable, it is reasonably clear that Fleur-de-lis corresponded with a sharp blip in mint-output, reminiscent of what happened in Quatrefoil, although less dramatic. For three successive types, the estimated numbers of 'equivalent reverse dies' are

Jewel Cross	868
Fleur-de-lis	1,224
Arm and sceptre	601

Many individual mints show the same pattern, which tends to be most remarkable at the second-order, 'shire' mint-towns. Thus we see:

Bedford	1	12	3
Hertford	1	17	1
Northampton	5	20	3
Wallingford	6	25	14
Dorchester	4	11	3
Wilton	2	8	3

The east-coast ports, with the partial exception of Lincoln, show signs of the same blip:

London	204	323	100
Thetford	25	43	24
Norwich	22	33	20
Stamford	45	64	38
York	89	108	47

From the statistics for these and other mints, it seems that the rate of mint-output increased temporarily. A historical context within the sole reign of Harold is not to hand. The heavy tax of *c.*£32,000 which Harthacnut imposed at the beginning of his reign would make excellent sense, taking into account the analogy of Quatrefoil, but it falls, at first sight, into the wrong validity-period. In order to bring the heavy tax and the (very) unusual pattern of mint-output into conjunction, one would have to say that Fleur-de-lis coins in Harold's name were still being struck in the early part of Harthacnut's reign. When one remembers that Harthacnut caused his half-brother's corpse to be disinterred and flung into a swamp, one is surprised that he should countenance the minting of coins which still named Harold. It might be sufficient, just, to suppose that the change of type was delayed until Michaelmas, and that the moneyers' response to the needs of the geld occurred between midsummer and September. But it is odd. Perhaps the change of type was made later than Michaelmas: we do not know. Perhaps Harthacnut did not regard the design of his coinage as being of much significance.

It is in principle very difficult to date most validity-periods from independent evidence. The problem was touched on in the discussion of the Reform type (section 1 above). The pattern of mint-output in Fleur-de-lis is so unusual, and rests on such a range of data (for many mints) that the case for association with a heavy geld seems a strong one, in spite of the difficulties in accommodating the chronology. At the very least, it deserves consideration.

If much of the mint-output fell at the end of the Fleur-de-lis validity-period, there is the further difficulty of explaining the quantities of coins reaching Scandinavia (unless they were obsolete when they were exported). We may note that the blip in mint output is not fully matched by the numbers of specimens in the Scandinavian sample for Types 10, 11, and 12 (832, 919, 535).

Whether the discrepancy between the two die-estimates could be explained by special circumstances is not clear.

Few active mints run counter to the trend, but one should mention Exeter, Hereford, and Shrewsbury. Perhaps the discrepancies reflect differences in the monetary affairs of different regions.

a) *English single finds*. Canterbury (½), Ely, Isleham, London, Oxborough (¼), Oxford, Sotwell, Southwick, Thetford (½), Winchester, York.

b) *English hoards*. *Titchmarsh*, Northants, 1979-82. Nine Fleur-de-lis coins found scattered over 20m of river bank beside the Nene comprised one from the nearby mint at Huntingdon, 3 of London, and 5 die-duplicates by the moneyer Svartr of York (*Coin Hoards* 7, pp. 375-8).

c) *Size of the issue*. See above.

d) *Evidence for dating*. Peter Seaby's paper on the sequence of Anglo-Saxon coin types, 1030-50, cleared away many confusions. For the type in question he listed Jewel Cross/Fleur-de-lis and Fleur-de-lis/Arm and Sceptre mules. The careers of moneyers, and the rate of turnover between types, are a valuable indication. Scandinavian hoards terminating with Fleur-de-lis are listed by Blackburn and Jonsson, 1981 (G.119-20, S.66, D.78-80, N.43, F.33, W.139).

e) *Weight-standards*. Over all, the pattern resembles that for Jewel Cross. Many western mints operate on a standard of *c.*1.12g; many eastern mints clearly use more than one standard, generally with *c.*1.12g as the higher and dominant standard. Thetford shows a strong proportion of lighter coins. Lincoln's heavy standard is lower than 1.12g, as it is at Derby and Nottingham. Canterbury and Dover tend to be low, and Salisbury is oddly low.

f) *Number of mint-places*. Many mints are represented by only one or two specimens. Other mints which operated on a very small scale may await discovery. The current tally of 55 is therefore not significantly different from the total for the preceding type.

The mint of Southwark seems to have been almost inactive during this one type.

References.

Talvio, *SCBI* 40 (see preceding section).

HARTHACNUT
12. ARM AND SCEPTRE
*c.*1040–1042
Hildebrand, Harthacnut Type B and Cnut, Type I, *BMC*, Harthacnut Type ii and Cnut Type xvii.

Following the death of his half-brother, Harthacnut returned to England, 'before midsummer'. He quickly imposed a heavy tribute, amounting apparently to *c.*£32,000. Reasons have been given in the preceding section to wonder whether exceptional quantities of Fleur-de-lis coins were not minted to pay the necessary geld. The difficulties in supposing that it was paid in Arm and Sceptre coins are a further argument tending to support that suggestion.

As the geld would have amounted to 7.7 million coins if paid in pounds by tale, and considerably more (one supposes) by weight, and as the estimated number of dies for the type is only 602 (6 million, using the conventional multiplier), the evidence is severely puzzling. Either Harthacnut recycled the money he received very rapidly, by disbursing it, or the conventional multiplier (10,000) is far too conservative at this period. If a lot of coins from early dies were taken out of circulation, that might tend to distort the die-estimation, yielding an under-estimate, but hardly by enough to resolve the conundrum.

Although Edward 'shared the kingdom' with Harthacnut, there is no question of a dual coinage.

Just over a third of the coins bear the name Harthacnut, while nearly two thirds name Cnut. Many mints strike both kinds, and there are even a few die-links. Talvio has suggested that the coins with the king's name written in full are generally earlier, and that the legend was shortened later in the type because it was inconveniently long. The coins reading Harthacnut tend to be heavier. If that conjecture were essentially correct, it would offer the monetary historian insights into the chronology of mint-activity, and from that, perhaps, into the reasons for minting. The picture is, however, probably complicated by regional variation, e.g. York and Canterbury mint only with the name Cnut.

Seaby was able to list 27 mints which used both legends, ten which are recorded only with the name of Harthacnut, and 16 only with the name of Cnut. They show no geographical separation. As coins continue to come to light, some smaller mints may need to be transferred to the joint list.

For the 'top ten' mint-places (for this type) the numbers of coins reading Harthacnut and Cnut respectively in the Stockholm sylloge are:

	'Harthacnut'	'Cnut'	Total
London	23	49	72
Lincoln	22	35	57
York	0	38	38
Winchester	6	28	34
Stamford	9	18	27
Thetford	4	16	20
Exeter	14	4	18
Chester	9	3	12
Oxford	10	2	12
Norwich	5	5	10
Dover	1	8	9

An east-west contrast in the ratios is visible, but Winchester is anomalous. Seaby's suggestion that minting at York and Canterbury was entirely in the archbishops' hands is interesting, but even if it is correct there is no obvious reason why the coins should therefore have read 'Cnut'.

The ranking of the mints for both varieties together shows few deviations from the normal pattern, although London's share of the total seems to be a little less than usual. Again, as observed in the commentary on the Jewel Cross type, political vicissitudes had virtually no effect on the regional patterns of coin production.

a) *English single finds.* Axbridge, Caerwent, Doncaster (½), Lincoln (½), London, Meols (½), Rochford, St. Neots, Stratford-upon-Avon, York (½).

b) *English hoards. Bowthorpe, Norfolk,* 1991. Three Arm and Sceptre coins of Harthacnut, all of the Norwich mint, were found apparently close together in a field about 5 km west of Norwich. Intensive searching of the area failed to find any more. (*BNJ* 1991, 125-6).

c) *Size of the issue.* The Lincoln-based estimate is 602 reverse dies.

d) *Evidence for dating.* There is little scope for uncertainty.

e) *Weight-standards.* The majority of mints seem to be operating on a uniform and single standard of *c.*1.12g. Lincoln maintains a higher standard, and apparently strikes a few coins at *c.*0.92g. Oxford uses two standards, of *c.*1.12g and *c.*1.02g. Winchester also uses a lower standard in addition to *c.*1.12g.

A correlation of the histograms for the major mints with the use of 'Harthacnut' or 'Cnut' makes it seem unlikely that there is a chronological decline in weight during the validity-period.

f) *Number of mint-places.* 52, from a small sample.

References.

Talvio, *SCBI* 40 (see Section 10 above).

EDWARD THE CONFESSOR
13. PACX
1042—*c.*1044
Hildebrand Type D: *BMC* Type iv.

The obverse of Edward's first coin-type is superficially similar to the design it replaced. The reverse has the letters PACX disposed around a voided cross. Keynes has drawn parallels with the ornamental chrismon seen in manuscripts, and points to an enjoyment of puzzles and double meanings (*Anglo-Saxon England*, 7).

In the regional distribution of minting one can detect a small decline in the west country, but the picture is essentially, as usual, one of continuity. The shorter validity-periods established from *c.*1036, and the accompanying weight-standards, were maintained. The numbers of stray losses are within normal limits, bearing in mind the shorter validity periods, and cut fractions retain a similar place in the currency, which however was smaller than ever.

a) *English single finds*. Great Wakering, Huntspill, Lincoln (1, ½, ½), Louth (2), Melton Mowbray, Meols (½), Minster-in-Thanet, Ogbourne St. George (½), Oxford, Repton.

b) *English hoards*. Wedmore, and (?) Thwaite.

Wedmore, Somerset, 1853. This hoard of some 200 coins, found in a pot in the (modern) churchyard, is the earliest major multi-type hoard. It is dated by just five coins of Edward's Pacx type (plus a transitional Arm and Sceptre coin essaying Edward's name). Two of the five are of the scarce variant reading PAXX, which are in all probability early issues within the type. The date of deposit will have been soon after the introduction of the PACX type. The velocity of monetary circulation was such that the six recent coins already included issues from Lincoln, London, Winchester, and Dorchester, as well as Bristol and Taunton.

The case for saying that Wedmore is a local (i.e. west-country) savings hoard rests on the proportion of coins from western mints type by type. Coins were set aside locally during their validity-period: if there had been a currency of extended age-structure from which most or all the hoard had been withdrawn in *c.* 1042-3, the older types should by then have become regionally more mixed, creating an age-profile of local colour within the hoard. The relative proportions, moreover, of the successive types might have been expected to be roughly in line with estimates of the scale of issue of the types, probably modified by wastage over time.

The quantities of each type are: Æthelred II, Helmet, 1. Cnut, Quatrefoil, 21, Helmet, 43, Short Cross, 64, Harthacnut/Harold, Jewel Cross, 7, Fleur-de-lis, 19, Arm and Sceptre, 20, Edward, Pacx, 5. Thus, Cnut's three types, and especially Short Cross, are over-represented in terms of the hypothesis of a currency hoard.

Among the Quatrefoil coins 13, or 62 per cent, are from mints in the western half of England, as compared with an estimated 21 per cent in the Scandinavian sample. In

Cnut's Helmet type 33 per cent are western, compared with 17 per cent, and in Short Cross 43 per cent compared with 13 per cent. Thus the westerly bias is strong even among the oldest coins in the hoard.

Thwaite, Suffolk, 1832. This hoard, which is more fully discussed in section 16, is known to have been concealed in two or more separately wrapped parcels. The Pacx coins from Thwaite have a strong Thetford flavour, quite unlike the other types, and it is possible (not certain) that they were set aside separately either during the Pacx validity-period or very soon after its end. See below under section 16.

c) *Size of the issue.* The Lincoln-based estimate is 511 dies.

d) *Evidence for dating.* The place of the Pacx type in the sequence of Edward's issues is shown both by mules (Seaby, *BNJ* 1955) and by the Wedmore hoard. The duration of the validity-period can only be guessed.

e) *Weight-standards.* The standard of *c.*1.12g is predominant, and the patterns are unchanged from the previous types. Stamford offers a particularly clear example of two standards, *c.*1.12g and *c.*0.97g.

f) *Number of mint-places.* Freeman records 53.

References. P. Seaby, 'The sequence of Anglo-Saxon coin types, 1030-50', *BNJ* 3rd ser., 8 (1955-7), 111-46. For Wedmore, R.H.M. Dolley and J.S. Strudwick, 'The provenances of the Anglo-Saxon coins... in the British Museum', ibid., 26-59.

14. RADIATE CROWN/SMALL CROSS

*c.*1044—*c.*1046

Hildebrand Type A. *BMC* Type i.

The spiked crown of Edward's second coin type is no doubt copied from a Roman antoninianus found by chance in the soil of England.

a) *English single finds.* Brampton, Chichester, Coningsby, Guildford (½), Ixworth, Wellingore.

b) *English hoards.* None, unless part of the Thwaite hoard (see section 16) was set aside at the beginning of the validity-period.

c) *Size of the issue.* The Lincoln-based estimate is 481 reverse dies. The size of the currency in this validity-period may however have been greater than that implies, if the preceding type was not fully recalled. See the discussion of the Thwaite hoard, under section 16.

d) *Evidence for dating.* Seaby lists mules between Types 13 and 14, and also 14 and 15.

e) *Weight-standards.* The traditional arrangements were continued, of a single heavy standard of *c.*1.12g in the west, and multiple standards in the east. London and Canterbury appear to have used mainly standards of *c.*1.12g and *c.*1.02g. Norwich offers a good example of a histogram with two separate peaks.

f) *Number of mint-places.* The total remains very similar: Freeman records 56. Reading was created in this type, but worked only for three or four years.

15. TREFOIL-QUADRILATERAL
*c.*1046—*c.*1048
Hildebrand Type C; *BMC* Type iii.

The trefoil-quadrilateral type bears a superficial resemblance to Æthelred's Helmet type. Like others of Edward's coinages, it awaits a thorough stylistic analysis.

a) *English single finds.* Bosham, East Dean, Fiskerton, Ipswich, London, New Romney (½), Northampton, Ogbourne St. George, Oxborough (fraction), Pulham Market, Salisbury, Swallow, Thrupp, Winterbourne Bassett, York.

b) *English hoards.* None.

c) *Size of the issue.* The Lincoln-based estimate is 697 reverse dies, representing an increase over the preceding types. As with them, however, the size of the currency in this validity-period may have been greater than the (conventional) estimate of 6.97 million, if the preceding types were not fully recalled. See the discussion of the Thwaite hoard, under section 16.

d) *Evidence for dating.* None.

e) *Weight standards.* Although the traditional weight-standard of *c.*1.12g remained in widespread use, there are signs of innovation. In particular, a lower standard well below 1.0g is in evidence at many mints. London seems to have operated on *c.*1.12g and *c.*0.97g, Lincoln on *c.*1.12g and *c.*0.82g. The low standards are not confined to mints with a history of eccentric behaviour, such as Hastings, Nottingham, Salisbury, or Southwark. At the other extreme, Exeter strikes unusually heavy coins, and Hertford, Leicester, and Reading exceed the 1.12g standard.

f) *Number of mint-places.* Freeman records 56. Bedwyn is a new mint, where the moneyer Cild was to work for a long time (in Trefoil-Quadrilateral, at more than one weight-standard). At Berkeley, similarly, a moneyer Eadgar began work in this type. The attribution of a Pacx coin to Berkeley is debateable. Its low weight is somewhat against it.

16. SHORT CROSS
*c.*1048—*c.*1050
Hildebrand Type B. *BMC* Type ii.

Edward's Short Cross coins are struck on exceptionally small flans, but maintain the normal weight-patterns. Their small size did not prevent their being cut to provide fractions. Single finds are noticeably plentiful. A good proportion of them have travelled a long way from their mint of origin, e.g. a Worcester coin found in Lincolnshire, a Chester coin found in Sussex, a Southwark coin found at Meols, and a York coin found at Gloucester.

a) *English single finds.* Aldworth, Amington (2), Ancaster, Bawtry (2), Boxgrove, Congham (½), Easingwold, Essex (North), Fulbourn (½), Gloucester, Higham, Lincoln, London, Meols, Norwich, Quidenham, Repton (¼), Sutton-on-the-Hill, Thetford, Welwyn, Wreningham.

b) *English hoards. Thwaite,* Sf, 1832. The coins were enclosed in 'thin lead cases' or 'packages'. One contained roughly five hundred coins, while another or others contained a smaller quantity, amounting to a further hundred or two hundred coins. It seems that the packages were found in close proximity, while removing the stump of an old pollard oak. (A tree that is regularly pollarded can live for many centuries.) The hoard was highly unusual in containing numerous halves and quarters. It is not recorded whether the large and smaller parcels were of similar composition, nor whether the fractions were wrapped up separately. The *Gentleman's Magazine* for 1832, p.355 claims that about 600 coins were in the possession of a Mr.Page of Woodbridge. A couple of hundred others were quickly in various hands. The British Museum acquired 180 specimens (including 66 fractions) plus a further 29 coins which came much later as a gift from the landowner, the Hon Mrs. R. Wilson, in 1877. In the same year she gave the Bodleian Library 12 specimens, including 2 halfpennies and 4 farthings, and a similar parcel to the Fitzwilliam Museum. There are two further coins in the Ashmolean, ex Chester.

The 223 coins surviving with provenances (which may to some small extent be weighted with scarce mints, selected at the British Museum) are of Edward the Confessor's first four types, as follows:

		Pence	*Halfpence*	*Farthings*	*Total*
Type iv	Pacx	6	7	1	14
Type i	Radiate	7	7	0	14
Type iii	Trefoil	39	12	15	66
Type ii	Short Cross	99	21	9	129
		151	47	25	223

Dolley and Strudwick list *BMC* 179 (Type vii) as being from Thwaite. One may venture to doubt whether that is correct: some misplacement or substitution may have occurred earlier in the century.

The interpretation of the hoard depends to some extent whether the coins tabulated above are a random sample, —in effect, on how selective the British Museum was in rejecting duplicate mint-moneyer combinations. As the museum took so many unattributable fractions, and so many London coins, and as the coins which remained with Mrs Wilson until 1877 are not appreciably different as a sample, one may hope to be reasonably safe in proceeding on the assumption the available coins as a whole do not deviate very far from being random.

We appear to have, then, a four-type hoard, withdrawn from currency during the Short Cross validity period, rather than a savings hoard. The declining numbers of the older types suggest that they had to a significant extent fallen out of circulation before the hoard was assembled. The proportion of fractions, type by type, is over half in Pacx and Radiate, declining to under a quarter. If one assumes that the proportion of each issue that was cut up tended to be fairly constant, that might suggest that the fractions of Edward's first three types were not rounded up and recoined when Short Cross was introduced, but were allowed to remain in use, at least in the district where the hoard was assembled. The original parcel in the British Museum and the 1877 material agree in respect of that conclusion. It tends to suggest that the hoard was put together at one time, and was not a savings hoard.

When we look at the mints represented in the hoard, type by type (percentages of mint-identifiable specimens), the picture is surprising. In Short Cross (the most recent type), London accounts for no less than three-quarters of the coins, whereas the local mints of East Anglia are entirely absent. The national average for London (estimated output) is 29 per cent, and the proportion of London coins in the currency of London itself (see Q.5) was 40 per cent long-term, although possibly rather higher in the time of Edward the Confessor (see QQ.24, 25). The figure of 75 per cent in Thwaite suggests strongly that the hoard originated in London, even if it was concealed in Suffolk. The absence of coins of Ipswich, Norwich, and Thetford (where the national average in Short Cross is 7 per cent) points to the same conclusion. One should not rely too implicitly on the statistics for the Thwaite hoard, because what we have is a sample of less than half, which may be selective in ways that are not now clear. But the gap between 75 per cent and 29 per cent is very large.

For the four successive types in the hoard, the percentages (with national or expected percentages in parentheses) are a follows

	(Coins)	*London*	*Ipswich,Norwich, Thetford*
Pacx	14	21 (26)	43 (8)
Radiate	11	64 (21)	9 (9)
Trefoil	59	63 (24)	0 (5)
Short Cross	87	75 (29)	0 (7)

The last three types look like a multi-type hoard of London origin, and on balance, perhaps a savings hoard. The Pacx coins, however, with 6 coins of the Thetford mint, out of 14, are almost certainly local. It is not unreasonable to recall the separate packages wrapped in lead sheets, and to wonder whether a smaller package was not earlier in date than the bulk of the hoard. For a human context, one thinks of the Paston family, later in the middle ages. Cf. the Gracechurch Street hoard, discussed in section 21 below.

The mint-places of the (later) fractions are as diverse as those of the pence. It is clear that fractions were carried freely, e.g. from Lincoln and York to London, in the 1040s.

The weights of the fractions from Thwaite are discussed more fully in Q.26.

c) *Size of the issue.* The Lincoln-based estimate is only 193 reverse dies, and there is no particular reason to suspect systematic error. If the figure is anywhere near correct, it makes an incomplete recoinage more understandable. It should also influence our judgement on the high proportion of Short Cross coins in Thwaite.

d) *Evidence for dating.* Abnormal activity at the Sandwich mint is plausibly connected with the blockade of Flanders in 1049 (Q.20).

e) *Weight-standards.* In the western half of the country the traditional standard of *c.*1.12g predominates (with light levels of activity) but in the east multiple standards over a wide range return with a vengeance. London mints at *c.*1.12, *c.*0.92, perhaps *c.*0.77, and apparently *c.*0.65g, with coins on the lower standards in great quantity. Canterbury behaves similarly. Various other eastern mints show long, straggling histograms —e.g. Hertford, Ipswich, Hastings, and Lewes. Sandwich (see above) mints at anything from over 1.20g to under 0.70g, but mostly at a low standard, apparently *c.*0.72g.

Lincoln and York, however, have most of their output at *c.*1.12g, with lower standards in only trifling quantities.

f) *Number of mint-places.* Freeman records 55 mints. The mint signing DYR or DERNT is linked to Ipswich and Norwich but, ironically, its occurrence in the Thwaite hoard should now be viewed as ambiguous evidence for an East Anglian attribution.

The creation of a mint at Bury St Edmunds, at which the moneyer Morcere worked for half-a-dozen types, has been connected with the royal grant of abbatial juridiction in west Suffolk in *c.*1044.

17. EXPANDING CROSS
*c.*1050–*c.*1053 or later
Hildebrand Type E. *BMC* Type v.

The Expanding Cross type was issued successively on two very different weight-standards, namely a light standard, followed by a dramatically heavier standard, of *c.*1.67g, on larger flans. The validity-period seems, for the first time, to have been three years rather than two, namely from 1050 to 1053. In 1051 the heregeld was abolished, and it was as a consequence of the lifting of that heavy and burdensome tax that the weight of the penny, which had for many years been no more than 1.12g/1.02g, could be increased by such a margin. Everyone repeats all this as fact. But where has the case been argued? What evidence is there, indeed what could there be, to establish independently the dates of the validity period? What evidence is there that the light and heavy coins were consecutive in that order? Our understanding of weight-standards is becoming substantially clearer since Petersson's work published in 1990. Expanding Cross needs to be reconsidered in light of that progress. And as we shall suggest, the assumed association of the heavy coins with the abolition of the heregeld turns a blind eye to the political crisis of 1051-2, and thereby fails to set the coinage convincingly into its historical context.

In purely monetary terms, it is not obvious how the abolition of the heregeld would translate into a political opportunity for heavier coins. If the money collected as heregeld was used for its stated purpose (but cf. modern parallels, such as the road tax,) most of it was probably spent again in England. In that case, it may have been a stimulus to the monetary sector of the economy and perhaps even a stimulus to growth. Ending the tax would presumably in the short term leave more money in people's pockets. The king might then have turned round and imposed a new tax, by ordering a weight-increase at the next recoinage, which would mean that people received only 7 new pence for 12 old ones. Such a tax would have fallen more heavily on the merchant class and the townsfolk than on the agricultural interest. But what was the political motive for introducing it?

Again, paying off his ships' crews in 1049-50 may not have made quite as great a difference to the national finances as has been represented. What Edward did was to privatize the navy, relying thereafter on the availability of vessels in what were to become the Cinque Ports, and making financial concessions to the citizens of those places. The tax benefits were felt most by the farming population.

The possibilities of circular argument are considerable. Connecting the new, heavy coins with the abolition of the heregeld is an intuitive leap, and a plausible one, but the regularity of the two-year cycle, and the change-over at this point to a three-year cycle, are very much hypothesis. The range of weight-standards in the preceding Short Cross type could well be spread over longer. What if the Expanding Cross type as a whole began after the abolition of heregeld? And what is the evidence, other than flan- and die-size, that light and heavy coins were successive?

Could they have been concurrent? Mules between the heavy coins and the preceding type are almost ruled out by the discrepancy in size. And dies could in any case be saved for a couple of years, and skip a type, as Pointed Helmet/Hammer Cross coins demonstrate. Hoard-evidence might in principle offer a clear answer, if for example there were a hoard terminating with Expanding Cross coins all of the light series. The English element in the Danish Bonderup hoard of 1854 ends with just two Expanding Cross coins, and is inconclusive. A Scandinavian hoard in which the English element terminated with a few heavy and a few light coins would, on the current chronology, automatically be dated to after 1051, whatever the exact terminal date of the German and Danish elements (if exactly dateable), since there is often a discrepancy in the t.p.q. of the English and continental component respectively. As proof that the heavy series was later, that would obviously be worth very little.

The turnover of moneyers might in principle offer persuasive arguments for chronology, particularly at the larger mints. Placing the light and heavy series in the wrong order might be expected to show up as a nonsense. The practical problem arises from the low survival-rate of the type. At London, for example, some 37 moneyers worked during Expanding Cross, of whom 26 struck other types both before and after, and another 5 are recorded only in Expanding Cross. The remaining 6 tend to be inactive moneyers (working mainly in earlier types), for whom new specimens, light or heavy, could still turn up.

Let us begin afresh, with an open mind on earlier hypotheses, and say that the heavy issue is heavier than anything that had been seen since Last Small Cross, at least on any scale. It may have been harking back even further. The experiment had no sequel: it was a reform which failed. Neverthless, during the one validity-period, heavy coins outnumbered light coins. Petersson records 426 heavy specimens, against 308 light specimens. Was there a delayed *renovatio* half-way through the validity-period?

In 1050 and 1051, England was in political crisis. The West Saxon earl, Godwine, and his party brought England to the very brink of civil war. Godwine's colleagues in the other earldoms saw clearly enough that conflict would merely revive the risk of foreign invasion and conquest, which had receded since the death of Magnus and since Harald Hardrada had made peace with England. Godwine was expelled in 1051, but in 1052 he returned, and was poised to destroy Edward by a naval battle in the Thames at London, when good sense prevailed. A great council was summoned outside London, at which the king capitulated. He 'took earl Godwine and his children back into his favour, and gave him back the whole of his earldom, and restored to him and all his supporters everything they had previously owned'. This was done 'without reservation... and the council ratified complete friendship between them, and made a promise of good laws for the whole nation'. Peace was made in mid-September, 1052. Edward's personal loss of prestige was inevitably considerable, even though the outcome was statesmanlike and wise, and thereafter he turned his thoughts to religion.

The decision to increase the weight of the penny may well have been taken at the council, as the monetary equivalent of a huge sigh of relief, and as a sign of hope for the future. It is difficult to identify a moment earlier in the 1050s when such a decision would have been made. The occurrence of no fewer than three brooches made from Expanding Cross coins offers an intriguing hint of political awareness. The heavy coins were minted in all parts of the country. A thorough stylistic analysis of the dies remains to be undertaken, but they seem to be uniform in style except in the north-east (where Lincoln, Stamford, Norwich, and York show distinctive styles). Elsewhere, the treatment of the bust is very similar, in large and small varieties (sketches in North, *English Hammered Coinage*, vol. 1).

The weight-standards, as usual, seem to vary somewhat from mint to mint. At York, for example, the peak for the heavy coins is at *c.*1.70—1.71g, whereas at Winchester it is at *c.*1.63g. At Lincoln it is *c.*1.67g, with a hint of an even higher standard at *c.*1.76—1.77g. At London and at Canterbury again it is *c.*1.67g.

In the task of assessing the balance between central and shire control of weight-standards, Expanding Cross provides a particularly useful test case. Because the heavy coins were such a dramatic novelty, and because they were introduced at all mints, it is obvious that there must have been a central directive. Because there are slight variations in the actual average weights from mint to mint, and because the histograms conform quite well (in most cases) to a normal distribution, it seems almost as obvious that at each mint-place the moneyers put the directive into effect according to their own understanding of its meaning.

The lower standard is, with few exceptions, the old higher standard of *c.*1.12g, both in the western half of England and in the east. London and Canterbury are the main exceptions, striking apparently at *c.*1.07g, with a hint of a much lower standard at *c.*0.87g. Thus, in the west, the traditional standard of *c.*1.12g was maintained, and a new, much higher standard was (then) introduced. In the east, where typically there had been two standards at *c.*1.12g and *c.*1.02g, the lower of these is abandoned, and the same much higher standard as in the west was introduced. Thus a new uniformity between east and west was created. Our understanding of the 1.12g standard in the east depends on whether we think that the opening phase of Expanding Cross would have been wholly or almost wholly on the single standard anyway. If not, we would have to say that reform was in the air before the heavy issue was devised, which might mean before the abolition of the heregeld. In Short Cross, as we have seen, London had minted a big proportion of its output at lower standards down to something like 0.65g. Something similar was true of many mints in the east. The light Expanding Cross coins thus offer a sharp contrast.

All mints from which sufficient specimens survive from which to judge, strike both light and heavy coins. There is, however, a marked difference in proportions between east and west. As ever, coinage in the west is heavier over-all. The specimens recorded by Petersson break down as follows:

	Light	Heavy
Western mints	43	99
Winchester	18	15
Midlands	9	27
South-eastern	56	23
Eastern and / north eastern	182	262
	308	426

Numbers of specimens are only a rough approximation to output statistics (which are not yet available), but fortunately the differences in proportions are substantial. In the west the ratio is in excess of two heavy coins to one light one. In the south-east it is at the opposite end of the scale—thanks mostly to the mints of Lewes and Hastings (31:6). Those two places seem to have been far more active (in the light series) than the Channel ports otherwise were. Sandwich seems not to have worked at all in Expanding Cross. From Dover, Petersson records only 4 specimens (3:1), Romney is inactive, and at Steyning the figures are 4:2. Thus it is clear that the new system of naval procurement did not translate into activity at the local mints.

In the main east-coast trading-places the pattern, it has to be said, is very confused, with 43:57 at London and 75:63 at York, but 36:67 at Lincoln.

Where did bullion come from, in the middle of a validity-period? If there was a revival in the western half of the country, is it an indication that a heavy penny was somehow advantageous to the agricultural interest? —and to Godwine and his party? The inner logic of the situation remains elusive, but the regional responses, in terms of mint-output of the heavy coins, should eventually provide us with valuable insights into the working of the system. For the present, one has to say that it all remains enigmatic.

To sum up, the detailed evidence leaves the relationship of the type to the heregeld still quite conjectural. The light series already shows distinct differences from the preceding type, with the virtual disappearance of the *c.*1.02g standard, at most eastern mints. It could be the case that it simply faded out for commercial reasons, but if an administrative decision was taken (at national level?) to abolish it, then we should have to say that reform of the coinage was already on the agenda before the heavy coins were introduced. The idea that light and heavy coins were issued concurrently seems altogether too radical, especially as there are so few single finds of the light series (see below).

At the end of the validity-period the heavy standard of *c.*1.67g was abandoned almost as abruptly as it had been introduced—again presumably by central direction—in favour of a standard of *c.*1.32g. This was higher than anything found during Edward's first four types, and may represent some sort of compromise, or backing-away from the level of *c.*1.67g which was presumably judged to be unworkable. Since it had been struck in considerable quantities, the advantages and disadvantages as perceived by the king and his council remain puzzling. Perhaps complaints from the merchant community were registered. Perhaps the royal finances were adversely affected. The death of Earl Godwine had changed the possibilities, in the king's favour. The main point about the heavy coins is that they represent an attempted reform which was put into effect vigorously throughout the country, but which was quickly cancelled. Nothing of the sort was tried again.

a) *English single finds*. Most unusually, there is clear water between the histograms for the heavy and light varieties, even when aggregated. Any specimen of 1.30g or above is almost certainly heavy. The single finds are identified as L or H, wherever possible.

Aldbourne (H), Alfriston (brooch), Elsfield, Godmanchester (½H), Halnaker, Holme Hale (H), Hunmanby (L), Lincoln (H), near Lincoln (L), London (L, ½H), Lower Waterston (H), Norwich (H, H, mini-hoard?), Papworth (½, H), Reculver, Southery (L), Stokeinteignhead (H), Stoke Mandeville (H), Swindon, Thetford (H,½H, ½H), Thetford, Tivetshall St Mary (L), Trowbridge (H, brooch), Upper Seagry (H), Walpole St Peter (H?, brooch), West Rudham (L), West Walton (½, L), Wetheringsett (¼, H), Winchester, near Winchester (½, H?). The preponderance of heavy coins (17 against 7 light coins, excluding the brooches) is intriguing. If the discrepancy is confirmed, it might be interpreted as reflecting a new impetus in monetary circulation. During the light phase, the monetary economy may have been faltering a little. There are hints of strain in the results from chemical analyses of the light coins, which suggest that a proportion of them (on very low weight-standards?) fell some way below the traditional fineness.

b) *English hoards*. None, unless the two coins from Norwich were found together.

c) *Size of the issue*. The Scandinavian sample shrinks from *c.*190-200 in the two preceding issues, to just 101 coins, of which Lincoln contributes 24. One hesitates to rely on a Lincoln-based estimate, for reasons that have been discussed in section 11 (Fleur-de-lis) above. And indeed the single finds, which offer a completely separate sample from which relative mint-output can in principle be estimated, give us a very different picture, admittedly based on only 26 mint-attributions. Of these, London takes 12, Lincoln 4, Thetford 2, and other mints one each

(Cambridge?, Canterbury, Ipswich, Malmesbury, Norwich, Stamford, Winchester, York).

d) *Evidence for dating*. It is not self-evident that the decision to strike very heavy coins was triggered by the abolition of the heregeld. A more plausible context is the great council at London at which Earl Godwine was reinstated, in September 1052. The validity-period must have continued for long enough for a considerable quantity of heavy coins to be minted. The best guess we can at present make about the light series is that their scarcity as single finds reflects the political crisis of 1051-2.

e) *Weight-standards*. See above.

f) *Number of mint-places*. Freeman lists 53.

Reference.

P.H. Robinson, 'Two medieval coin brooches from Wiltshire', *Wiltshire Archaeological Magazine* 83 (1990), 208-10.

18. POINTED HELMET

*c.*1053–*c.*1056

Hildebrand Type F. *BMC* Type vii.

With the Pointed Helmet type, a realistic image of the king was introduced. Edward, who had always been bearded, had until now been represented on his coinage as clean-shaven, in portraits modelled on Roman coins. Now he is shown bearded and wearing a helmet of contemporary design. The change in fashion is perhaps borrowed from German coins.

BMC lists as a variety (type vii, a) coins with an annulet added to the reverse, in one angle of the cross. Almost all York coins are of this variety, which is only occasionally found elsewhere, e.g. Lincoln, and Northampton (*BMC* 526). At York it almost certainly signifies that the profits had been assigned to the archbishop.

A scarce early variety with left-facing bust is recorded in two metropolitan styles, at a range of mints with no particular regional focus (Bath, Chester, Gloucester, Hereford, Leicester, Lewes, London, Northampton, Shaftesbury, Shrewsbury, Taunton, Warwick, and Worcester) and in a north-eastern style at Lincoln. One wonders whether the change to a right-facing bust (as an afterthought?) was considered useful as a way of drawing attention to the higher weight-standards of the new type.

Petersson was able to record the weights of 769 specimens of the Pointed Helmet type, but our Scandinavian sample includes only 38: the outflow from England to the Northern Lands had almost ceased. The statistical base from which one might hope to comment on continuity and change in English monetary history in the validity-period is thus of very little use.

The Milton Street hoard is a multi-type hoard, but whether the English currency at large had an extended age-structure is debateable. Single finds are reasonably plentiful, and include coins a long way from their mint of origin.

a) *English single finds.* Ashwellthorpe, Bassingbourn (½), Bishops Waltham, Brandon, Catterton, Gainsborough (½), Hose, Ixworth (3) (mini-hoard?), Littleborough, London, Louth, Meon Hill, Shepreth, Stoke Rochford (mini-hoard?), Surlingham, Thetford (½), West Ravendale, Winchester, Worthing.

b) *English hoards.* Ixworth, Milton Street. *Ixworth.* The auction sale of the coins of Joseph Warren of Ixworth, Sothebys 1869, included a lot (55) of seven coins of the Confessor, the last three stated to have been found at Ixworth, i.e. locally to Mr Warren. These were a Radiate/Small Cross coin of Hertford, a Pointed Helmet of Chester, and an early Pointed Helmet coin (head left) of Lincoln. They are very probably from a small hoard, and may have been retained from a larger number as being different varieties or, in the case of the Lincoln coin, a rarity. If the mints were typical of the whole, one would say a traveller's hoard.

Milton Street, Sussex, 1830/1843. The curious circumstances of finding are referred to in Q.37. Some 51 coins were described, out of (?)60. They ranged from Cnut's Quatrefoil

(4) and Short Cross (6) through Harold, Harthacnut, Pacx (5), Radiate (12), Expanding Cross (2), and Pointed Helmet (18). The age-structure is thus erratic, Cnut's Helmet type and Edward's Trefoil Quadrilateral and Short Cross types being under-represented. The mint-distribution sends a clear signal. Out of 51 coins, no fewer than six are of Hastings and six of Lewes, the two nearby mints, giving a combined proportion of 24 per cent (against an expectation, from the Lincoln-based sample, of 2-3 per cent). There are in addition three coins of Dover, one of Romsey, and one of Sandwich. The Sussex/Cinque Ports flavour of the hoard is thus quite strongly marked. London contributes 15 coins, or 29 per cent.

Moreover, out of 14 listed coins from before 1042, 4 are of Hastings and Lewes (29 per cent, against a similar 2-3 per cent expectation). The local character runs through the hoard, early and late. That strongly suggests that it is a savings hoard put together in Sussex over a period of time, rather than a sum of money withdrawn from circulation in *c.*1055. By that date, Cnut's coins (if they had indeed still been in circulation) would have become regionally more diffused, and the currency homogenized: single finds from the first half of Edward's reign generally reveal a brisk circulation.

c) *Size of the issue.* No reliable estimate has yet been made.

d) *Evidence for dating.* There is no specific evidence, and the three-year duration assigned to the validity-period is hypothetical.

e) *Weight-standards.* Pointed Helmet introduces a new phase of the late Anglo-Saxon coinage, during which a weight-standard of *c.*1.32g was widespread. This probably represents a compromise with the failed reform of Expanding Cross. Weights are now transposed to a level some 18 per cent higher than in the early part of Edward's reign, but we still see the familiar regional pattern of a basic east-west divide, with numerous westerly mints striking on a single standard of *c.*1.32g, while in the east straggling histograms reflecting multiple weight-standards are the norm. As usual, there are exceptions and irregularities. At Norwich and Ipswich and Southwark there seem to be two main standards of *c.*1.32g and *c.*1.17g. At London, the lower of these standards looks to be closer to 1.12g, and there may be a third standard, lower still. At Canterbury the lower standard looks to be closer to *c.*1.27g, but at Steyning and Lewes *c.*1.32g. Winchester works at *c.*1.32g, but Wilton at *c.*1.27g.

York, where the coins are again distinguished by an annulet (for the archbishop?) firmly maintains a standard of *c.*1.37g and Lincoln, following earlier form, also has a top standard of *c.*1.37g, but accompanied by another at *c.*1.22g. Shrewsbury, unusually for the west, uses 1.37g. Nearby Chester is even more eccentric. It occasionally mints at over 1.70g (a hangover from the preceding type?), and its normal standard is definitely below *c.*1.32g —apparently *c.*1.26g.

f) *Number of mint-places.* Freeman records 59 mints, with some reduction in the complements of moneyers in the larger centres.

19. SOVEREIGN / EAGLES
*c.*1056–*c.*1059
Hildebrand Type H. *BMC* Type ix.

The design of Edward's next type is extremely innovative. The obverse shows a full-length figure of the king enthroned. It is copied, apparently, from a Roman gold coin-type, and bears an unusually long legend, EADVVEARDVS REX ANGLORV, variously modified, but including the ethnic. The king holds a bird-topped sceptre, which is seen also on the Great Seal. It was probably intended as an eagle, as were the four birds in the angles of the cross on the reverse of the coins. A unique London coin, which is no doubt from early, experiemental dies, shows the king holding a globus surmounted by a bird rather than by the cross; in his other hand he holds an ordinary cross-sceptre. The Sovereign/Eagles coin type is probably the origin of the coat of arms bearing four heraldic 'martlets', anachronistically attributed to Edward.

Although the coins are so distinctive in their designs, it made not a whit of difference to the ways in which they functioned as money.

It may be no coincidence that the only recorded round halfpenny in the late Saxon series should be of the Sovereign/Eagles type. It is of the Chester mint. Now that so many single finds are on record, it seems safe to say that it was a *rara avis* indeed.

a) *English (and Welsh) single finds.* Castle Acre, Cholsey, Garthorpe, Great Mongeham, Higham, Lewes, Lincoln, Meols, Middle Harling, Rhuddlan, Stafford, York (2, mini-hoard?).

b) *English hoards.* Nottingham, 1789; Nottingham, 1786; York?

North of Nottingham, 1789, 'among some sand, which had been dug near the Forest', 'several' pennies of Edward, in good condition. Five that were illustrated are of the Pointed Helmet (4) and Sovereign/Eagles (1) types. The mint-places are Chester, Nottingham, Sandwich, and York (Pointed Helmet), and Wallingford. The hoard thus illustrates a lively transfer of coinage from region to region.

Nottingham (Barkergate), 1786. Some 20 coins, all apparently of the same type. One which was illustrated is a Sovereign/Eagles coin, of the Nottingham mint. An account published in 1789 mentions coins of Nottingham, Cambridge, and Shrewsbury.

c) *Size of the issue.* No reliable estimate can be offered.

d) *Evidence for dating.* None that is specific.

e) *Weight-standards.* As a whole, the pattern of weight-standards shows extreme similarity with that in the preceding type. In the western half of the country there are numerous mints where the weights are closely controlled at *c.*1.32g. They include Barnstaple, Bath, Bristol, Chester, Exeter, Hereford, and Wallingford. In the east straggling histograms point to multiple weight-standards, usually with not enough information to define the lower modal values well. Mints in this category include Bedford, Leicester, Lincoln, London, Northampton, Oxford, Stamford, and Thetford. York seems to have a high standard of *c.*1.37g. The same high average is clear at Winchester (while Wilton operates on *c.*1.27g with signs of still lower standards).

A *c.*1.27g standard is less clearly attested at Buckingham, Malmesbury (unexpectedly), and some minor mints.

In the east and south-east, the *c.*1.32g standard is in use at Cambridge, Chichester, (?)Dover, Lewes, Southwark, Steyning, and Wallingford.

f) *Number of mint-places.* Freeman records only 53.

References.

R.H.M. Dolley and F. Elmore Jones, 'A new suggestion concerning the so-called 'martlets' in the 'Arms of St. Edward', in Dolley (ed.), *Anglo-Saxon Coins,* 1961, pp. 215-26.

C.S.S. Lyon, 'A round halfpenny of Edward the Confessor', *BNJ* 34 (1965), 42-5.

20. HAMMER CROSS
*c.*1059–*c.*1062
Hildebrand Type G. *BMC* Type xi.

The obverse of the Hammer Cross type is somewhat similar to that of the Pointed Helmet, except that the king wears a crown. Mules with the Pointed Helmet type are recorded, and mules with the Sovereign type are relatively common.

a) *English single finds.* Brandon, Caistor-by-Norwich (mule), Canterbury (½), Gainsborough (¼), Glastonbury (mule), Great Yarmouth, Hastings, Jarrow (mule, ?plus one regular coin), Lewes (2), Lincoln (mule), London (Billingsgate, 2 x ½), Marham (¼), Rye, Sandwich. The Channel Ports region is conspicuous among the finds. It is intriguing that there should be as many as four mules in the list.

b) *English hoards. Mayfield*, Staffs., before 1844. The existence of a dozen Hammer Cross coins of the Stafford mint, which is otherwise a very scarce mint, has been very tentatively associated with a nebulous hoard from Mayfield.

c) *Size of the issue.* No reliable estimate can be offered.

d) *Evidence for dating.* The relative chronology is secure from mules. Absolute dates are merely extrapolated.

e) *Weight-standards.* The regional patterns of metrology are in close continuation from the Sovereign type, with a well-controlled standard of *c.*1.32g prevalent in the west, and clearly to be seen also at various other mints such as Dover and Lewes. In the east, straggling histograms betoken multiple standards.

There is some development, in that multiple standards are in evidence at certain western mints, notably Chester, Exeter, Shrewsbury, and Wallingford.

f) *Number of mint-places.* The total reaches a maximum of 63, which includes Aylesbury, Buckingham, Bury St. Edmunds, Hythe, Newport Pagnell, Stafford, and Sudbury. There is also a noticeable upturn in activity (or at least in survival, which may be erratic and due to hoards) at various western mints and, conspicuously, at Hastings.

21. FACING BUST/SMALL CROSS

*c.*1062—*c.*1065

Hildebrand Type Ac. *BMC* Type xiii.

The choice of a facing bust was highly unusual in the Anglo-Saxon coinage, the nearest precedent being the archiepiscopal issues of the early ninth century, where a deliberate differentiation was being made from the profile bust of the king. Edward's crown is shown with pendants curling outwards in an unnaturalistic way. This detail strengthens the case for seeing a German coin of the emperor Conrad, of the Duisburg mint, as the prototype.

The dominant weight-standard of *c.*1.32g, which had been applied for three validity-periods, was abandoned, with a return to smaller flans and much lower weight-standards. This was to prove only a temporary aberration, cancelled in the following type. In terms of national monetary policy, it is not clear whether the change should be viewed as fine tuning, or as an error of judgement. In spite of (or perhaps because of?) the small size of the coins, cut halfpennies and farthings are very plentiful.

a) *English single finds.* Bawsey (¼), Bromeswell (¼), Canterbury (½), Castle Acre (½), Chester (½), Hampshire, Idmiston, Ipswich, Kimpton, Lincoln (Flaxengate, 2, ?separately), Little Mongeham (½), London (All Hallows), London (Pudding Lane, ½), Stamford Bridge (½), Thetford, Westbury-on-Trym, York (2, separately).

b) *English hoards.* London (Gracechurch Street), London ('City'), Sedlescombe.

London (Gracechurch Street), mid-nineteenth century. A parcel of 56 coins in the Guildhall Museum is believed to represent this mid-nineteenth century hoard. It terminates with just two Facing Bust coins, both of Ipswich, but consists mainly of coins of earlier types, namely Expanding Cross (1), Pointed Helmet (24), Sovereign (2), Hammer Cross (27). The virtual exclusion of the Sovereign type is curious. The Hammer Cross coins are heavily of London (32 per cent) and the East Anglian mints (36 per cent)—'a fact' (as Dolley acutely observed) 'that may well attract the attention of students of London's trade'. Cf. the comment on the Thwaite hoard, in section 16 above, and cf. the City hoard below. London coins are much less conspicuous in the Pointed Helmet type (8 per cent), where East Anglian coins account for 50 per cent.

These proportions are most convincingly explained if the hoard was formed in East Anglia and then brought to London, where it was concealed. The two Facing Bust coins of Ipswich reinforce this hypothesis. As to whether the whole sum was withdrawn from circulation in the 1060s (with the implication of a multi-type currency), or whether it was a savings hoard, the evidence is contradictory. The erratic age-structure (see Q.37, and Fig.6) favours a savings hoard (since one cannot see why Sovereign/Eagles coins would have been discriminated against), but the greater penetration of London coins into East Anglia in the Pointed Helmet type points in the other direction. In the human context of an East Anglian merchant travelling to and fro to London it is, of course, not necessary that all the coins were withdrawn in one place. To that extent, the cynical may say, the percentages may mean whatever one wants them to mean. Conversely, however, one cannot prove that Gracechurch Street is not a savings hoard.

London ('City' or 'Walbrook' or 'Queen Victoria Street'), 1872. A very large hoard, reputedly containing as many as seven thousand coins, was found during excavation work in the City in 1872. The greatest secrecy was observed about the find-spot. Ernest Willett acquired about 2,800 of the coins from a Mr Baily of Gracechurch Street, deceased in 1876, when Willett gave a full and clear account of the coins he had been able to secure. They were of Æthelred II (4 coins), Cnut (19), Edward the Confessor (2,798), Harold II (1), and William I (5), with 2 foreign coins. Willett states that about 600 coins were illegible, being broken or corroded, and that he refused several pounds' weight of coins that were also broken and in bad condition. He was able to list 2,198 coins of the Confessor. These may be presumed to approximate to a random sample of the hoard as regards the mints, and probably also the types, represented. Sir John Evans in 1885 added an appendix to Willett's work, in which he reported that, of the remainder of the hoard, 'a considerable number' came into his hands. He gave a list of 580 legend-varieties, but regrettably not the quantities of coins. All he adds in that respect is that, of some of the scarcer types in Willett's list (Pacx, Radiate, and Short Cross) 'a larger proportion seems to have fallen to my share than did to Mr Willett's'. Evans had 5 specimens of Harold II, 4 mules belonging with Hammer Cross, and 3 coins of William I (Hawkins 233, 237, 237). We may guess from these few remarks that Evans acquired two or three thousand coins. His information cannot be exactly combined with Willett's (which is exemplary in its clarity). The earlier account is the better evidence for the monetary historian.

It can be supplemented by a parcel of a further 183 coins, which Burrows has convincingly shown to be from the hoard.

Willett's account, together with that of Burrows, reveals a very large multi-type hoard, in which the five types from Expanding Cross onwards made up *c.*93 per cent. Its age-structure, within the main body of material, was somewhat erratic, Sovereign/Eagles in particular being poorly represented.

	W.	B.	Total
Æthelred, Last Small Cross	4		4
Cnut, Helmet	1		1
Short Cross	18		18
Edward, Pacx	27	4	31
Radiate	4	1	5
Trefoil-Quadrilateral	47	4	51
Short Cross	50	3	53
Expanding Cross	553	57	610
Pointed Helmet	238	19	257
Sovereign/Eagles	94	4	98
Hammer Cross	649*	52	701
Facing Bust	503	30	533
Pyramids	2	3	5
Pax	1		1
William, Bonnet (Type ii)	2		2
Two Sceptres (Type iv)	2		2

* Including 4 mules

Blackburn and Pagan suggest a date of deposit of *c.*1066. Dolley suggests that the Norman coins belong to a separate hoard, concealed *c.*1075. The virtual absence of Pyramids coins, set against more than five hundred of the preceding Facing Bust type, suggests that this is, in effect, a hoard put together in that validity period. Whether the few Pyramids (? and Pax) coins belong to the same hoard is debateable. The Facing Bust coins are heavily London/East Anglian in flavour (see the Table), as are the preceding Hammer Cross coins. The Pyramids coins (including a further 8 specimens which fell to Evans) on the other hand are not. Looking further back, Expanding Cross and Pointed Helmet are East Anglian in flavour, but Sovereign/Eagles, curiously, is not:

No simple message emerges from the Table, about the character of the hoard. One's best guess will be that it belonged to a London-based merchant with trading connections to various regions, particularly East Anglia, but perhaps also Lincolnshire and Wessex. The 24 per cent of London coins in Expanding Cross might be used to argue that the hoard is a savings hoard, but really there is no clear message.

	London	Thetford	Ipswich	Cambridge	Norwich	Colchester	5 E. Anglian mints	Lincoln	Winchester
Expanding Cross	23	8	2	0	5	2	17	18	6
Pointed Helmet	11	9	7	3	17	6	42	6	6
Sovereign/Eagles	10	1	1	0	1	0	3	4	21
Hammer Cross	16	12	3	1	9	2	27	5	4
Facing Bust	25	13	1	6	4	3	36	5	4
Pyramids (13 sp.)	8	0	0	0	8	0	8	0	23

Sedlescombe. Sussex, 24 August 1876. The hoard was found buried in the middle of a field, between two and three miles east of Battle Abbey. The coins, which were thickly coated with brown corrosion products, were at first thought to be worthless, and were used by the village children as playthings. Raper, a few years later, published a list of 1,136 coins which he had succeeded in examining, and he conjectured that there may originally have been between two and three thousand. The question arises whether the listed coins are a random sample. Their corrosion helps the case. When they were cleared it could be seen that many were considerably worn, while many were fresh. Dolley, in publishing a parcel of 32 coins apparently from the hoard speaks of the 'pristine brightness of the individual pennies', which showed that they 'had changed hands no more than once or twice'. He does not comment whether this was equally true of the oldest coins in the parcel, nor does he consider whether the 32 coins may have been selected for quality. It is difficult to know exactly what to think about these various statements. The list of 1,136 coins includes specimens of four periodic types, with a very heavy emphasis on Hastings (and without any subsidiary presence of coins from the other Channel ports, even, until the final type). The numbers of coins, and the percentage of Hastings in each type are:

Pointed Helmet 121 (Hastings 30%)
Sovereign/Eagles 112 (Hastings 48%)
Hammer Cross 706 (Hastings 64%)
Facing Bust 183 (Hastings 78%, Romney 19%).

If the coins which Raper succeeded in seeing are in any degree selective, one imagines that purchasers may have wished to acquire at least one specimen of as many different mints as possible, and that the statistics may somewhat understate the predominance of Hastings coins. The hoard was obviously put together in Hastings or its immediate vicinity. The very high proportions of Hastings coins (from a mint which is estimated to have produced 0.5 per cent of the national output in this period) suggest that the owner of the treasure had regularly over a decade or more had occasion to obtain sums of new money from the Hastings mint, since it is difficult to believe that the currency of the town generally was so isolated from the monetary circulation of the south-east as to be dominated by the local mint to such an extent, and yet at the same time to include coins from forty other mint-places. So, in spite of the 'pristine freshness' of the coins, the hoard does not look like a savings hoard built up over the validity-periods from a one-type currency; and yet it does not look like a sum of money withdrawn from circulation in Hastings in *c.* 1064. Indeed one would go so far as to say that it cannot be. Perhaps the owner had a reserve of capital which he dipped into but did not deplete. Coins of the Lewes mint, in the four successive types, run at 2.5%, 5%, 5%, and 0.5%.

The suggestion that the hoard was lost at the time of the nearby Battle of Hastings is plausible, provided one distinguishes between the date when it was put into the ground (*c.*1064) and the occasion which caused its owner to fail to recover it. We are invited to believe that he added no new money to this large capital sum, for about two years.

The theory, expressed by Dolley in 1960, that the hoard was 'almost certainly part of the bullion reserve of the Hastings mint at the time of the Norman invasion' seems ill-considered, since there is no reason to think that moneyers held bullion reserves, at least not in their capacity as moneyers.

c) *Size of the issue.* No reliable estimate can be offered.

d) *Evidence for dating.* There are mules with both the preceding and the following types.

e) *Weight-standards.* The Facing Bust type reverts to the standards of Short Cross (1048-50), namely *c.*1.12g in the western half of the country, and multiple standards in the east. London and Canterbury appear to work predominantly on *c.*1.12g and *c.*1.02g. Various East Anglian and Danelaw mints show the usual straggling histograms. York seems to employ standards of *c.*1.17g and *c.*1.02g (see Q.21). There are as usual various inconsistencies among the Channel ports.

At Wallingford the old standard of *c.*1.32g seems to have survived (briefly?); and there is the odd heavy coin from Shrewsbury, and from Thetford.

f) *Number of mint-places.* Freeman records 53.

Reference. T. Talvio, 'The designs of Edward the Confessor's coins', in *Studies in Late Anglo-Saxon Coinage,* ed. K. Johnsson, Stockholm, 1990, pp. 487-99.

22. PYRAMIDS
*c.*1065–6
Hildebrand Type I. *BMC* Type xv.

Edward's last type returns to the *c.*1.32g standard, again with a right-facing bust. It is documented by enough single finds to put a small question-mark against the received chronology, and also by three interesting hoards which terminate with Pyramids coins (two of which are single-type hoards).

a) *English single finds.* Boxgrove, Bury St Edmunds, Cawood, Eastbourne (½), Keelby, Little Mongeham, London (Billingsgate, ½), London (Thames excavation, ½), Melton Mowbray, Middle Harling (¼), Monkton Up Wimborne, Soham, Thetford (½), Welford, Winchester, Wixford.

b) *English hoards.* Stockbridge Down, Harewood, York (Bishophill).

Stockbridge Down, Hants., 1935-6. Six Pyramids pennies accidentally buried with a corpse. (see Q.2 and Q.35). They are all of the Winchester mint, by two moneyers, and include 3 from the same dies.

Harewood, Yorks, 1895. Forty to fifty Pyramids pennies, of which 34 survive intact, together with fragments. The hoard was found when a tree blew down 'close to the gate leading to the west end of the church at Harewood' (in Wharfedale, about half-way between Leeds and Harrogate). The hoard was heavily weighted with coins of the Northampton mint. The undoubted explanation for this anomaly is to be found in the *Chronicle* s.a. 1065, which describes how Morcar, with the men Yorkshire and Northumberland, marched south as far as Northampton and waited there for a reply to his demands, sent to King Edward. While their envoy was away, 'the northerners did much damage around Northampton: not only did they slay men and burn houses and corn, but carried off all the livestock . . . They took many hundreds of captives . . . so that that shire and the other neighbouring shires were for many years the poorer'.

The absence of York coins in the Harewood hoard is conspicuous. It consists of coins of Northampton (16), 'London' (4), Warwick (3), Bedford, Oxford, Tamworth, and singletons from further afield. Of the Northampton coins, five share a reverse die and four of these are also from the same obverse; there is another pair of duplicate coins and another reverse link. The three Warwick coins are duplicates. Three of the 'London' coins (which use the Northampton privy-mark of a trefoil substituted for a pellet in one quarter of the reverse) are from the same reverse and only two obverses. The degree of duplication in the hoard seems to be well above expectation, but an estimate of the size of the Pyramids issue as a whole is needed before one could support the suggestion (taking account also of the Warwick duplicates) that the sum of money had belonged to a merchant. 'A south midlands hoard with a Yorkshire find-spot'.

York, Bishophill I, 1882. Four to six hundred coins in an earthenware cup, found during redevelopment of the Bishophill area (in the south-western quadrant of the walled city), of which 387 can be listed, including five cut halfpennies. The hoard is remarkable in that it was composed almost exclusively of coins of the York mint, the exceptions numbering only a dozen. The types were as follows:

Radiate	1	
Expanding Cross	2	
Pointed Helmet	36	
Sovereign/Eagles	67	(includes Leicester, 2, Lincoln 4, Stamford, 1 and 1 York mule)
Hammer Cross	91	(includes Nottingham, 1, and 2 York mules)
Facing Bust	134	
Pyramids	56	
	387	

Could this hoard reflect the currency of York during the Pyramids type, or is it a savings hoard? And can it be true that the currency of York (in either case) was composed so exclusively of coins minted in York? The single finds from York are very heavily of the York mint, although not quite to the tune of 97 or 98 per cent. But one cannot judge, from the available quantity of evidence, whether the monetary isolation of the city increased during the years *c.*1053-66. The coins of other mints are from the earlier part of the hoard (but not in Pointed Helmet). Future discoveries may enable us to reach a more definite decision on the character of the Bishophill hoard. One's present guess is that, like the Sedlescombe hoard (section 21), it reflects the savings of someone with frequent access to the mint, i.e. that it is a merchant's hoard. It would be special pleading to date it any later than the Pyramids validity period, although (again as with Sedlescombe) one should leave open the small possibility that the date of deposition and the 'date of loss' were separated by a year or two.

c) *Size of the issue.* No good evidence is available.

d) *Evidence for dating.* Pyramids is conventionally given a short validity-period, arising out of a doctrinaire view of the regularity of the system. A significantly shorter period might have been expected to be reflected in fewer stray losses, which is not obviously the case. It has even been argued, however, that Harold's coins counted with the Pyramids type as a single issue. The volume of losses is more difficult to assess if there was a multi-type currency.

e) *Weight-standards.* Although there are, for most mints, far too few weights from which to construct an informative histogram, it is perfectly clear that Pyramids restored the metrological patterns of Hammer Cross. The notional standards of *c.*1.32g and *c.*1.22g are still to be seen, e.g. at Chester, or at Chichester and Lewes. In the east a standard of *c.*1.27 is widely used, but the histograms are often straggling. York operates on an exceptionally high standard (or standards?), apparently *c.*1.40g, while Winchester goes to the opposite extreme, with a standard, apparently, at *c.*1.17g.

f) *Number of mint-places.* Freeman records 50 mints.

Reference.

R.H.M. Dolley, 'The mythical Norman element in the 1882 Bishophill (York) find of Anglo-Saxon coins', *Yorkshire Philosophical Society Annual Report*, 1971, 88-102 ably reconstructs the hoard of 1065.

HAROLD II
23. PAX
1066
Hildebrand Type A.

Earl Harold Godwinson, the brother-in-law of the Confessor, and since 1053 very much his right-hand man, succeeded him as Harold II on 6 January and died on 14 October 1066. All his coins will have been struck within that period. They break with tradition by using a left-facing bust. The image of the king, inspired presumably by some Roman coin, shows a long neck, with truncation, undraped. Harold wears a crown very similar to that on Edward's coins. The reverse type, with the word PAX in a panel across the field, is presumably political in inspiration.

The short duration sharpens the conclusions of a stylistic analysis of the type, as regards die-cutting; and the availability of hoards concealed at the time of the Conquest or shortly thereafter gives an unusually good opportunity to assess the velocity of circulation of the currency in the final months of the old English state.

Records of no fewer than five hoards from Sussex, far above statistical expectation, point very strongly towards the Norman Conquest as the occasion for the non-recovery of most if not all of them. There are various possible explanations. Individuals slain at the Battle of Hastings may have concealed their money before setting out to war (but this would not necessarily lead to an emphasis on hoards in east Sussex). After the Norman victory there may have been some indiscriminate savagery in the county. In that case, Sussex hoards concealed in haste are likely to be unselective, containing whatever coin-types were to hand at the time.

a) *English and Welsh single finds.* Axford, Barham (½), Beverley (½), Bristol, Lewes, Peterborough, St Davids, Sudbury, Thetford (½). The Peterborough find was minted at London, and the Sudbury find at Wallingford. The Axford, Bristol, and Lewes finds are of local coins. There is no hint of single finds which were lost in the face of the Norman occupation, e.g. in the south-east.

b) *English hoards.* Chancton Farm, Ashdown Forest, Offham, Arundel Castle, Oving, Castor, London (Walbrook).

Chancton Farm, Sussex, 1866. Found while ploughing, about one mile north of Chanctonbury Ring hill fort, and three miles from Storrington. About 1,720 coins came to the attention of the British Museum, but others were dispersed locally, and were said to have been sold in Shoreham, Brighton, and London. The coins had been concealed in a pot. Barclay Head was able to publish an enumeration of some 1,694 coins of Edward the Confessor and Harold II, of the following types:

Radiate/Small Cross	4	
Trefoil-Quadrilateral	1	
Short Cross	0	
Expanding Cross	133	
Pointed Helmet	430	(incl. one mule and 4 with bust left)
Sovereign/Eagles	303	
Hammer Cross	578	
Facing Bust	138	
Pyramids	54	(incl. one full-face)
Pax	58	
	1694	(1699)

He then gives a list of legend varieties, after

the style of Hildebrand. From this list it is unfortunately impossible to obtain more than a general impression of the number of coins of each mint, type by type. Of the 578 Hammer Cross coins which Vaux and Barclay Head examined, he lists 137 variant legends, from 41 mints and 96 different moneyers. The British Museum retained nearly 700 coins from the hoard, but again they do not tell us accurately about its make-up in terms of the proportions from each mint, because they were selected as legend varieties. Only the 58 coins of Harold II were listed in full. They were of Lewes (36, or 62 per cent), Steyning (16, or 28 per cent), London (4), Northampton (1) and Wilton (1). Among 54 Pyramids coins in the hoard there are already 19 mints (and 35 moneyers) represented, from as far afield as, e.g. Cricklade, Exeter, Lincoln, Stamford, Warwick, and York. It seems that the hoard may have been narrowly focussed only in the latest type.

Ashdown Forest , 1822. A hoard of Saxon coins which included at least one specimen of Harold II is probably the same as was found 'on the northern slopes of Camp Hill, between Nutley and Crowborough, and near Duddleswell'.

Offham, Sussex, 1796. A small quantity of coins, 'chiefly of Edward and Harold'.

Arundel Castle, Sussex, before 1899. Publication is promised by Hugh Pagan.

Oving, Sussex, 1789. A pot containing more than two hundred coins of Edward and Harold, and a large silver brooch. Oving is near Chichester. (*NC* 1957, 198).

Castor, Northants, June 1759. About five hundred coins, of which John White bought some and had a plate engraved, entitled 'Saxon coins found in June 1759'. The eight coins illustrated are one each of seven of Edward's types, and one of Harold II. There is a curious absence of the Sovereign/Eagles and Hammer Cross types, which is echoed in the holdings of two eighteenth-century collectors, Hodsoll and Hunter—who between them had just over a hundred coins of Edward, many of which may have come from Castor. The illustrated coins are mostly of the York mint (Radiate, Short Cross, Expanding Cross, Pointed Helmet, Facing Bust, Pyramids). The exceptions were Trefoil Quadrilateral (Lincoln), and Harold II (Oxford). John White might have chosen to illustrate York coins for devious reasons of his own; but the character of the hoard, and in particular the paucity of Lincoln coins in it, can be argued from the Hodsoll collection, which contained specimens (not necessarily all from Castor) of the following mints:

Radiate. York (6), Lincoln.
Trefoil-Quadrilateral. York (4), Lincoln, London, Thetford.
Short Cross. York (5), Wilton.
Expanding Cross. York (5), London.
Pointed Helmet. York (6), Chester, Maldon.
Sovereign/Eagles. York, Chester, Winchester.
Hammer Cross. York.
Facing Bust. York (4).
Pyramids. York (5), Gloucester.
Harold II. York (3), Lincoln, London (2), Nottingham, Stamford.

It seems safe to say that the Castor hoard was put together in Yorkshire, and carried south to be concealed in Northamptonshire. (Thus it is just the opposite of the Harewood hoard.) It is a multi-type hoard which may have been made up of roughly four-fifths York coins in type after type—like the Bishophill hoard.

c) *Size of the issue.* Pagan has counted 258 reverse dies in a sample of 512 coins which could be checked. For some regions the sample is doubtless virtually complete, while for others it certainly is not. Of London, for example, there are 50 different reverse dies among 69 coins—which might mean 38 non-singletons, and an estimate of roughly 90 dies. The national total may have been somewhere between 350 and 400 reverse dies, yielding a conventional estimate of 3½–4 million coins. This is at the lower end of the range found in the Confessor's reign. The top ten mints show one major change, namely Wilton in second place, or perhaps second equal with York.

Norwich and Wallingford edge their way up the league table a little. Wilton's unusual activity was terminated abruptly at the Conquest, with the dismissal of Harold's moneyers.

d) *Evidence for dating.* Not applicable.

e) *Weight standards.* The familiar patterns are continued, with various mints using a standard of *c.*1.32g, Wilton clearly on *c.*1.27g, York on *c.*1.37g, and Steyning and Lewes apparently on *c.*1.37g. London seems to mint at *c.*1.37g and *c.*1.27g, and Lincoln perhaps does similarly. Good evidence of multiple weight-standards at particular mints would be of some theoretical interest as showing that standards were in use concurrently or virtually so (because the reign was so short). The evidence is still insufficient simply because the number of specimens from most mints is so small.

f) *Number of mint-places.* Pagan records 146 moneyers working at 48 towns.

References

H.E. Pagan, 'The Castor hoard of mid-eleventh century pence', *BNJ* 54 (1984), 289-90.

H.E. Pagan, 'The coinage of Harold II', in *Studies in Late Anglo-Saxon Coinage* (edited by K. Jonsson), Stockholm, 1990, pp. 177-205.

WILLIAM I
24. PROFILE/CROSS FLEURY
October 1066—*c.*1068
BMC Type i. Hawkins 233.

To an illiterate user the obverse of William's first type, with its left-facing bust, would have looked almost identical with Harold's coins, although the bust is now draped. The reverse adopts an ornamental cruciform design.

BMC records some formal varieties within the type, and notes that certain specimens are of unusually rough workmanship as regards their dies. Winchester coins of this type are mostly rough, and their legends blundered. In the late Anglo-Saxon series that would be taken as pointing to a separate die-cutting centre. A thorough stylistic analysis of the type will call for as many specimens as can be assembled.

The organization of the English coinage suffered no immediate change as a result of the Norman Conquest. The same system of periodic type-changes (at intervals of about two years) was maintained, at a similar range of mint-places, and with a similar ranking of the mints. Many moneyers continue in office. Single finds of coins continue in similar quantities as in the time of King Edward, although with rather fewer cut fractions. Single-type hoards still occur, implying periodical renewal of the currency, alongside multi-type hoards, as in the reign of Edward the Confessor.

The weights of William I's coins continued to be regulated on a shire basis, with different weight-standards at different mints. The number of specimens published with weights, type by type, is usually insufficient as a basis for the sort of analysis that can be undertaken with the late Anglo-Saxon types. Specifically, straggling histograms are usually (not always) difficult to interpret. Winchester throughout the reign operates on a single standard, tightly adjusted, which allows us to say that William's early types there are on a standard of *c.*1.27g, and his later ones, *c.*1.37g. The change was introduced with the fourth issue of the reign, Two Sceptres (and not, as has been stated, the sixth). Local regulation persisted after the weight-increase.

a) *English single finds*. Benson, Foxcotte, London (one and a brooch), Norwich, Reading, York (3, but these are certainly a mini-hoard). No fractions are as yet recorded.

b) *English hoards*. Rotherham, Soberton, Norwich, Denge Marsh, York.

Rotherham, Yorks, 1939. The exact find-spot in modern Rotherham is known, but the hoard was partially dispersed before official intervention. Thirty-two coins were recovered, out of a total believed to have been 43.

Thirty coins were of Harold II and two of William's first type. Harold's coins were of Lincoln (12, including 2 pairs plus an obverse link involving 3 different moneyers), London (5), York (2), and ten other mints. The two coins of William are from Derby and York respectively. Since neither town fell into William's hands until early 1068, it is arguably the case that they did not mint for William before that, and that 1068 is accordingly the *t.p.q.* The hoard is plausibly connected with the harrying of the north. It is in effect a one-type hoard, which appears to demonstrate that Pax involved a recoinage—and therefore that the big multi-type hoards demand special explanations.

Soberton, Hants., 1850/1. Found in a field near Wickham Lodge, i.e. nearer to the village of Wickham than to Soberton. Wickham lies about half-way between Winchester and Portsmouth, in the Meon valley. The hoard comprised two massive gold ear-rings and 259 pennies. Of these, 78 were of Edward the Confessor (Pyramids, 77 specimens), 159 were of Harold II, and 22 were of William's Profile/Cross Fleury type. The exact proportions of coins of different mints cannot now be reconstructed. London, Wilton, and Winchester seem to have been well represented. Pagan suggests that the British Museum purchased only 7 Winchester coins of Harold II (out of a considerable number?) because the residue were die-duplicates by the moneyer Anderbode.

The British Museum acquired 16 Profile/Cross Fleury coins out of the 22 reported. Of the 16, 12 were of Winchester (with only one reverse die-link), and the others were of Exeter, Gloucester, Norwich, and Wareham. Thus it seems virtually certain that the latest type in the hoard was dominated by Winchester issues.

Norwich. (Garlands departmental store, London Road), March 1972. Nine complete coins and four fragments (from two or three coins?), all of the Profile/Cross Fleury type, are from the mints of Norwich (5, including two pairs, by two moneyers, plus a fragment certainly from the same obverse die as one pair), Thetford (3), and Cambridge (1). Thus, a small one-type hoard found within the city where over half the coins in it were minted. (*BNJ* 1973, 142f., and *SCBI East Anglia* 1348-57.)

Denge Marsh, Kent, June 1739. A carpenter of Lydd, while digging a post-hole on Denge Marsh, a mile and a half from Dungeness lighthouse, found a hoard of several hundred pennies, halfpennies, and farthings, chiefly of the Pax and Profile/Cross Fleury types, among which a high proportion of coins of the Romney mint, by the (sole) moneyer Wulfmær. There are various early accounts which do not tally exactly in detail (*NC* 1957, 186-90), but we can be reasonably sure that the hoard belongs to the Profile/Cross Fleury validity-period, because Romney coins with old pedigrees are plentiful in that type, but are not recorded in the succeeding Bonnet type (*SCBI Cumulative Indexes*, 1-20, 21-40). Coins of other mints were probably present (Canterbury, Hastings), but it is not possible to say in exactly what proportions. Nor can one be specific about the numbers of cut coins. In general it seem that the percentage of Romney coins vastly exceeded the mint's share of the national total, cf. the Sedlescombe hoard (section 21 above), where coins of

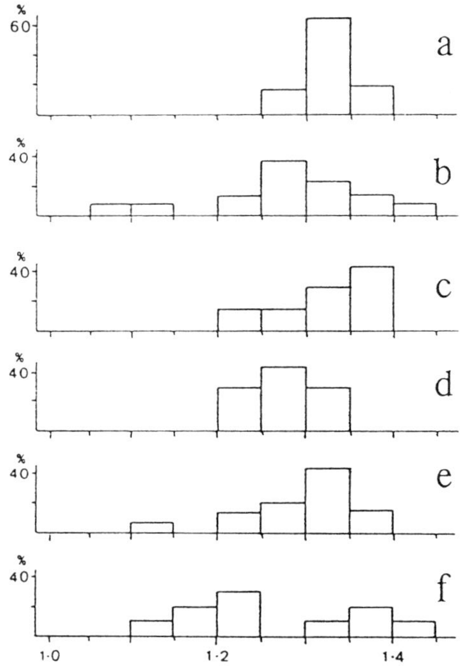

FIG. 12. Histograms of weights for Profile/Cross Fleury coins of the mints of a) Winchester, b) London, c) Canterbury, d) Hastings, e) Romney, and f) York. (No. of specimens, 20, 17, 7, 7, 14, and 10 respectively.)

Hastings were similarly overwhelming.

York (Minster), 1970-1. A small single-type hoard, with coins of Derby, Huntingdon, and York.

c) *Size of the issue.* No exact information, but one would suppose similar to, or smaller than, the later types of Edward.

d) *Evidence for dating.* See the comments on the Rotherham hoard.

e) *Weight-standards.* It is generally difficult to assemble sufficient evidence to obtain statistically clear answers. Winchester produces a very compact histogram (Fig.12), obviously on a single standard at *c.*1.27 or 1.28g (in spite of the rough workmanship of the dies). Canterbury strikes heavier coins, undoubtedly, and York shows a straggling histogram which we need not hesitate to interpret as reflecting more than one standard. At London the median value is close to *c.*1.27g, and one might argue that a single standard was intended, but was less accurately executed than at Winchester. More evidence from London could, however, reveal a continuity with mint-practices before 1066.

f) *Number of mint-places.* North records 36 places.

Reference. D.M. Metcalf, 'The taxation of moneyers under Edward the Confessor and in 1086', in J.C. Holt (editor), *Domesday Studies. Papers Read at the Novocentenary Conference*, 1987, pp. 279-93. (See footnotes 12 and 32 on the weight-increase.)

25. BONNET
c.1068—*c*.1070
BMC Type ii. Hawkins 234.

On the so-called 'Bonnet' type, William is shown full-face, wearing a large crown with two pendants or pendilia at each side.

a) *English single finds*. Alderton, Dorset, Lincoln (St. Mary's), Longworth, Market Deeping, Meols, Norwich, Oundle (i/ii mule), Wallingford (2, probably a mini-hoard), Wentbridge, York? No fractions have as yet been recorded.

b) *English hoards*. Oulton, Bierley, Bramham Moor, Middleham, York (Bail Hill), York (Jubbergate), York (High Ousegate), York (Bishophill II), (?) Beetham, and (?) Wallingford. See also Corringham (section 26) and St Mary Hill (section 27). Many of these hoards are plausibly associated with the harrying of the North.

Oulton, Staffs., 1795. Oulton lies in the upper valley of the River Trent, a few miles south of Stoke-on-Trent. The hoard was found 'in Mr Shelley's garden', and comprised a gold ring, a lump (ingot?) of gold, and a large number of coins (? a thousand or more). It was a multi-type hoard running from Expanding Cross to Pyramids, with relatively few of William's Bonnet type. Although coins of Harold and of William's first type are not known to have been present, it seems reasonably safe to say that this was a single hoard. Only a small sample of coins can be traced to the hoard, and they may well not be random. Our impression of a high proportion of coins of Chester and Shrewsbury and (towards the end of the hoard) of the very scarce local mint of Stafford may not be numerically secure. So far as the evidence goes, however (*BNJ* 1979), it suggests that these three north-western mints may have been relatively well represented.

Bierley. R. Thoresby, *Ducatus Leodiensis* (1715), p. 60 gives no useful details.

Bramham Moor. Ditto.

Middleham. A letter of 1848 from William Boyne tells how he bought 'three fine Conqueror pennies found in the neighbourhood of the late owner at Middleham...' From the description it is clear that the coins were of the Bonnet type, two being of York and the third of MAINT (cf. *BMC* 130 and *SCBI Yorks* 1161, die-linked to Thetford). These may reflect part or all of a small one-type hoard from Wensleydale.

York (Baile Hill), 1802. Baile Hill is on the right bank of the Ouse, just within the southern line of the walls, and overlooking the platform of Bishophill. The hoard was said to contain about a hundred coins, of which only three can now be identified. They are Bonnet coins, two of York and one of Norwich.

York (Jubbergate), 1845. Jubbergate lies at the centre of the city. The hoard, of some 600 coins of William I, has been reconstructed by Elizabeth Pirie (*YPS*, 1972), who was able to list 190 specimens. These comprised one Profile/Cross Fleury coin and 189 of the Bonnet type (including one mule). They probably approximate to a random sample so far as their mints are concerned, with hints that selections were made of as full a range of mints as possible. York and London may therefore be somewhat under-represented. This one-type hoard reflects a high velocity of circulation, with coins from all over England, namely York, 91 (48%. These include 30 coins of the moneyer Autholfr and 28 or more of Thorr), London, 34 (18%. These include 11 by Ælfsi), Lincoln, 14 (7%), Thetford, 9, and coins from 16 other mints, with a north midlands flavour (Derby, 2, Nottingham, 2, Leicester, 4, Tamworth, 4). There are only 5 coins from south of the Thames.

York (High Ousegate), 1704. Found within about 150 yards of the preceding hoard, and containing *c.* 250 coins of Williams's first two types, probably with a preponderance of Bonnet coins.

York (Bishophill II), 1882. In 1882 a wide area round Baile Hill and Bishophill was redeveloped, following the demolition of the old County Gaol, and more than one hoard was found. XRF analysis has shown that the patinas associated with Bishophill I (section 22 above) and Bishophill II are chemically different (Pirie, 1972). Elizabeth Pirie has reconstructed a list of 47 coins (5 Profile/Cross Fleury and 42 Bonnet pennies). Missing specimens, probably of the Bonnet type, might take the total to between 50 and 60. The Profile coins are of York, 4, and Lincoln, 1. The Bonnet coins are of York, 14 (33%), London, 9 (21%), Lincoln, 6 (14%), Thetford, 5, and half-a-dozen other mints. Almost a one-type hoard, and not dissimilar to Jubbergate. Cf. also the proportion in Corringham (section 26). (Pirie, 1972.)

Beetham, Cumbria, 1834. A hoard from the churchyard included a coin of Edward, and two of William, undescribed, among a larger number. The find-spot, close to Morecambe Bay, lies outside the usual range of the English currency. The date of the hoard remains vague.

Wallingford, 1987. Two Bonnet coins of William I, both of the Wallingford mint, may well reflect a mini-hoard.

c) *Size of the issue*. No exact information.

d) *Evidence for dating*. A two-year validity-period or thereabouts is to be assumed.

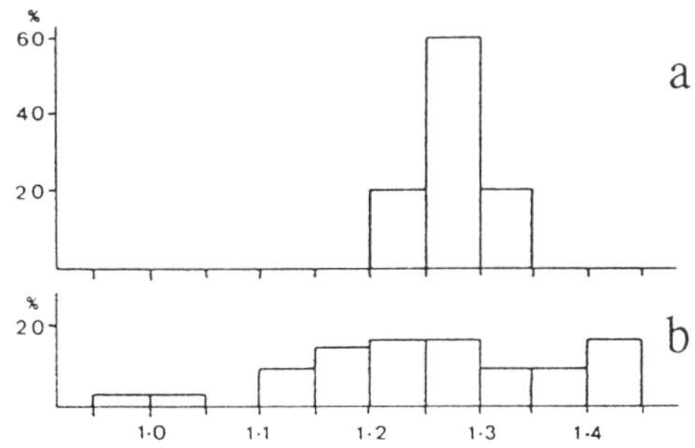

FIG. 13. Histograms of weights for Bonnet coins of the mints of a) Winchester and b) York.

e) *Weight-standards*. It seems reasonably clear that Winchester follows the same standard of *c.*1.27g as in the preceding type. York (from which a large sample survives) offers an extreme contrast (Fig.13).

f) *Number of mint-places*. North records 44 places.

26. CANOPY
*c.*1070 –*c.*1072
BMC Type iii. Hawkins 236.

A crowned, facing bust of the king (without pendilia) is framed in a porch or archway of two composite columns with an architrave between. The reverse design is composed from a central lozenge or knot, with four fleurs.

a) *English single finds* are extremely few: Grantham, London (Noble Street) (½), Winchester.

b) *English hoards.* Corringham, Grantham (near), Whitchurch.
Corringham (near Gainsborough), Lincs., 1994. A multi-type hoard of 100 coins, of the following types: Pyramids (46), Pax (30), Profile/Cross Fleury (12), Bonnet (11), Canopy (1). The proportion of Lincoln coins rises, from 35 per cent of the Pyramid type, and 37% of Pax, to 58% of Profile and 45% of Bonnet. The single Canopy coin is of Lincoln. York, which is the second mint overall, falls off even before the harrying of the North—48%, 23%, 8%, 9%. Otherwise, there are singletons from various mints, among which one may note Derby and Nottingham. As the proportion of coins from mints other than Lincoln and York is lowest in the older types, one may suspect that the hoard's character is that of a savings hoard. (*NC* 1995).

Near Grantham, Lincs., 1735 ('Cotesworth', (?) = Colsterworth). Coins of William, described originally as 'Peter's pence' (by a clergyman). The Canopy type is merely an inspired guess.

Whitchurch, Oxon., 1902 or earlier. A multi-type hoard, with relatively many coins of the Facing Bust and (?) Pyramids types, and coins of William's first three types. It seems that there was a strong representation of the (local) Wallingford mint, perhaps already from the Facing Bust type onwards, and if so one may suspect a familiar type of local savings hoard.

c) *Size of the issue.* No exact information.

d) *Evidence for dating.* None that is specific.

e) *Weight-standards.* On the basis of only a small sample, it nevertheless seems clear that Winchester continued to mint at *c.*1.27g (and not yet at *c.*1.37g).

f) *Number of mint-places.* North records 37 places.

27. TWO SCEPTRES
*c.*1072–*c.*1074 or later
BMC Type iv. Hawkins 237.

The Two Sceptres type is on a new, heavier weight-standard at Winchester. It sets the pattern for the succeeding types.

The obverse shows a crowned, facing bust of the king, holding two sceptres, which are carefully distinguished. The one in the king's right hand is a cross-sceptre, whereas the one in his left hand has a cross pommée. This may have constitutional significance.

The dies used at Lincoln, Stamford, and York are of rough workmanship and resemble each other.

a) *English single finds.* Cranwich (2, presumably a hoard), Darenth, Hammersmith, Lincoln (1 + ½), Norwich, Rockland, Seasalter.

b) *English hoards.* Beddington Park, Malmesbury, London (St. Mary Hill), Cranwich.

Beddington Park (between Croydon and Sutton), Surrey, 1978. A small one-type hoard with 3 pennies and one cut halfpenny. The mints are Thetford (2) and Canterbury, and (for the halfpenny) London.

Malmesbury, Glos., 1828. An essentially one-type hoard, said to have been found under a large foundation-stone of an eleventh-century chapel in the Burnivale. 'Many' pennies were found, out of which a dozen were listed, all of the Two Sceptres type, except for one Bonnet penny (of Exeter?). The current coins were of Canterbury, (?)Cricklade, Exeter, Hereford, Lincoln, London (3), Malmesbury, Oxford, and Winchester. It is not clear whether these were selected to reflect a range of mints.

London (St. Mary at Hill), E.C.3, 1774. Found while digging foundations on the east side of Love Lane (between Eastcheap and Lower Thames Street). A selective but very precise description of the hoard was made by the Revd. Dr Griffith. It comprised a sapphire and pearl brooch, and many coins, of which three to four hundred were carefully examined, out of a total that was probably much larger. There is no reason to doubt that the sample was random. There were many halves and quarters. The hoard was contained in a pot, with a smaller pot or crucible upside-down inside it. There were ten coin types in quantity, of Edward, Harold, and William. The quantities of each type were not specified, but the coins of Edward were considerably above half, and of six types. Of William, it is clear that there were four substantive types.

Griffith adopted a sampling technique, by recording in detail only three types (which particularly interested him), namely Sovereign/Eagles, Pax, and Canopy. Of these he described 27, 31, and 16 mint/moneyer varieties. He noted with surprise that there were no duplicates: thus, the number of specimens of those three types was the same or virtually the same as the number of varieties. That was the case also, he noted, for the other three types of William. Thus we can sample the proportion of London mint coins throughout the age-structure of the hoard, and can know whether there was any regional bias in the other mints represented. The list of mints was:

Sovereign/Eagles, 16 mints. London (6), Wilton (5), Lincoln (2), York (2), Cambridge, Canterbury, Colchester, Derby, Hastings, Hereford, Horndon, Oxford, Salisbury, Stamford, Sudbury, Thetford.

Pax, 22 mints. London (5), Thetford (2), Winchester (2), York (2), Bedford, Canterbury, Chichester, Colchester, Exeter, Hastings, Hereford, Huntingdon, Lincoln, Northampton, Norwich, Nottingham, Oxford, Southampton, Stamford, Wallingford, Warwick, Wilton.

Canopy, 9 mints. London (5), Canterbury (3), Thetford (2), Exeter, Lewes, Oxford, Stamford, Wareham, York.
(*Archaeologia* 4, 1786, 356.)

Cranwich, Norfolk, 1994. Two coins of the Northampton mint, both by Godwine, and indeed die-duplicates. They came from the same site, and although one was found nearly a year later than the other, they are almost certainly a little hoard.

c) *Size of the issue*. No exact information.

d) *Evidence for dating*. Dolley suggests a *t.p.q.* of 1075 for the St. Mary Hill hoard, connecting it with the revolt of Roger and Waltheof. That might be reason to date the end of the validity-period a little later than has been conventional.

e) *Weight-standards*. A provisional survey shows that Winchester minted on a well-defined standard of *c.*1.36g, whereas York coins yield a straggling histogram with lower values (Fig. 14).

f) *Number of mint-places*. North records 40.

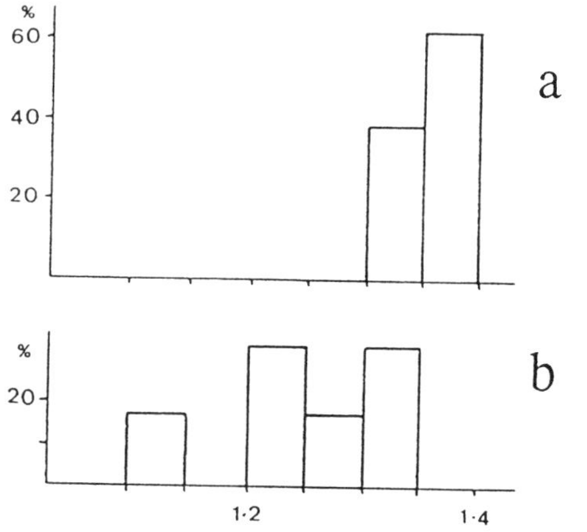

FIG. 14. Histograms of weights for Two Sceptres coins of a) Winchester and b) York (8 and 6 specimens respectively).

28. TWO STARS

*c.*1074–*c.*1077

BMC Type v. Hawkins 238.

William's crowned, facing bust is flanked by two stars. *BMC* lists various minor varieties.

Several small mints in the south-west and in the south, which had apparently been inactive in the first half of the reign, reappear and in some cases resume regular production. There may possibly have been some central directive or encouragement, following on from the introduction of a heavier weight-standard in the preceding type.

a) *English single finds.* Checkendon, Chelmsford, Hadstock, Horncastle, London (Milk Street), London (Thames Exchange), Meols (½, ¼), Saltford, Sparsholt, Thetford (Fulmerston Road), Woodeaton, Wye, Yelling, York (Clifford Street).

b) *English hoards. Scaldwell,* near Northampton, 1914. A substantial one-type hoard containing 260 pennies and halfpennies, all except one of the Two Stars type. There were at least 60 coins of Northampton by the moneyer Sæwine, and at least 50 London coins. There was also a high proportion of Stamford coins. The rest of the hoard reflected 36 further mints, demonstrating a lively circulation.

c) *Size of the issue.* No exact information.

d) *Evidence for dating.* None.

e) *Weight-standards.* There is clear evidence of a weight-standard of *c.*1.37g at Lincoln and at Winchester. At London the average weight of the penny is *c.*1.30g (Fig.15).

f) *Number of mints.* North records 55 mints. These include Shaftesbury, Barnstaple, Bridport, and Launceston, which had been inactive earlier in the reign. Dorchester, beginning again in Type iv, may be part of the same pattern. Further to the east, Pevensey and Romney work in Type v.

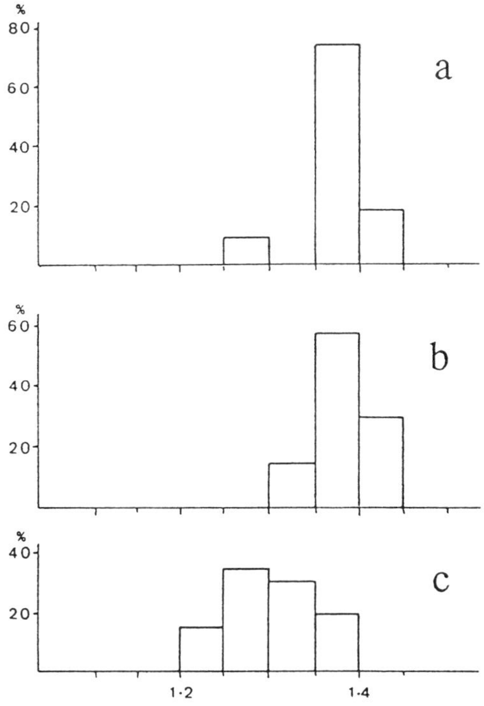

FIG. 15. Histograms of weights for Two Stars coins at a) Winchester, b) Lincoln, and c) London (11, 21, and 26 specimens respectively).

29. SWORD
*c.*1077—*c.*1080
BMC Type vi. Hawkins 243.

The king is shown, crowned and full-face, shouldering a naked sword.

A scarce variety has a cross added in the field right.

a) *English single finds.* Knapwell, London (Thames Exchange), Old Sarum, Winchester (1 + ½), near Winchester (½).

b) *English hoards. York (Monkgate),* 1851. The hoard was found close outside the walls to the north-east, when the new County Hospital was being built. It contained 75 pennies, among them the Two Sceptres type (1), Two Stars (42), and Sword (30). The York mint accounted for 18 out of 42, or 43 per cent, and 14 out of 30, or 47 per cent. There were 5 Sword coins of Lincoln. Southerly mints were quite well represented.

c) *Size of the issue.* No exact information.

d) *Evidence for dating.* None.

e) *Weight-standards.* The evidence is perfectly clear that weight-standards still varied from mint to mint (Fig.16). At Winchester, the standard is *c.*1.37—1.38g.

f) *Number of mints.* North records 36 mints.

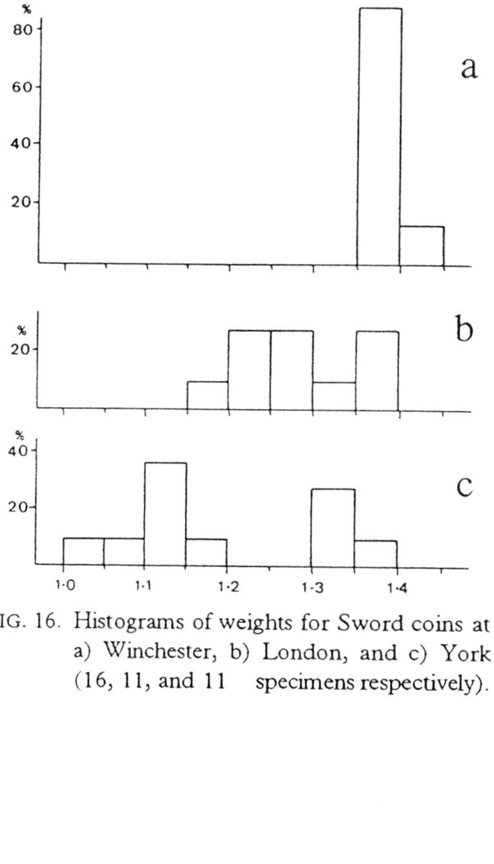

FIG. 16. Histograms of weights for Sword coins at a) Winchester, b) London, and c) York (16, 11, and 11 specimens respectively).

30. PROFILE/CROSS AND TREFOILS
*c.*1080—*c.*1083
BMC Type vii. Hawkins 239.

The design marks a return, after more than a decade, to a profile type, but now right-facing.

a) *English single finds.* There is a sharp increase in the numbers of single finds.

Bekesbourne, Boston, Cheriton (½), Cirencester, Donington (½), Dorchester, East Bradenham (2, possibly a hoard), Essex (North), Keelby, Kirby Cane (¼), London (Thames Exchange) (2), London (Thames Waterfront), Louth, Methwold Hythe, Middleton Stoney, Ripple, Southampton, Swaffham (¼), Thetford (Fulmerston Rd.), Weston, Winchester (½). Of these, 8 are London coins, widely dispersed.

b) *English hoards. Bradenham* (East or West?), 1994. Two coins, possibly a mini-hoard, of the London and Thetford mints.

c) *Size of the issue.* No exact information.

d) *Evidence for dating.* None.

e) *Weight-standards.* The contrast between Winchester and London is repeated, as in the preceding types.

f) *Number of mints.* North records 40-42 mints.

31. PAXS

*c.*1083—*c.*1086

BMC Type viii. Hawkins 241, 242.

William's Paxs type, which is so plentiful today because of the wide dispersal of specimens from the very large Beauworth hoard, is estimated to have been struck from roughly 880 reverse dies. Paxs coins were, so far as we can judge, current at the time of the 'heavy and severe' tax levied by William in 1084, at the rate of 6 shillings per hide. They were probably a larger issue than those immediately preceding, but it is difficult to judge, because there is insufficient evidence to assess the scale of William's earlier issues at all accurately. We may note, however, that Paxs coins are more plentiful in Scandinavian finds than his earlier types.

The novel aspect of the type is that, for the first time for over a hundred years, the great majority of the coins are on a single weight-standard, at all mints. This should be viewed as a radical reform. Its intention may have lain within the context of firmer government, of which the Domesday survey is the clearest sign. The end of the Profile/Cross and Trefoils validity-period was the end of an era, and this book might logically have taken *c.*1083 as its limit.

If we compare the ranking of the mints in the Paxs type with what it had been before the Conquest, we see that Winchester stands first, with an estimated 15 per cent of the national output, followed by London (*c.*11 per cent), Canterbury (*c.*10 per cent), Southwark (*c.*7 per cent), Norwich (*c.*6 per cent), Bristol (*c.*5 per cent), and Salisbury (*c.*4 per cent). Even allowing for some imprecision in the estimates, it is clear that there was a dramatic increase in Winchester's importance. It is interesting that Salisbury (Old Sarum) also more than doubles its share. A level of activity at Southwark not seen since the Crux type is presumably to be ascribed to administrative or political rather than economic changes. (In 1066 William had burned Southwark to the ground. Minting resumed in the Bonnet type, 1068-70, but was thin and sporadic until late in the reign.) Canterbury's share is substantially increased. Lincoln is much diminished, and so, of course, is York. These shifts taken together seem to point to a government centralized more at Winchester, and to a severing of contacts between the Danelaw and the trading partners of that region across the North Sea.

The question has been raised whether the increased scale of minting in Paxs was because of the need to pay the heavy geld of 1084. A levy of six shillings per hide, in relation to an estimated total mintage of 880 dies, say roughly £36,000 at 10,000 coins per die, would indeed involve a substantial proportion of the currency if the king gathered it all in and kept it in his coffers. One must wonder, therefore, whether the tax clawed reserves of obsolete coin out of ordinary people's savings, as may have happened in 1018. On the earlier occasion the corresponding figures were very much higher, at about a pound a hide (£72,000), and 47 million pence (approaching £200,000).

On balance, it seems more plausible that the Paxs type was a larger issue than usual, mainly because it represented a reform of the coinage, and it may in that sense have been of a piece with the Domesday Survey.

a) *English single finds.* (?) Alford, Bekesbourne, Bexley, Dunstable, Lincoln (Bishop's palace), Lincoln (near) (2) London (Billingsgate) (2, both of Canterbury), London (London Bridge), London (1854), Oxford, Roxton, Seasalter, Thetford (Fulmerston Rd, ½), Thetford (Redcastle Furze, ½). A high proportion of these have travelled well away from their mint of origin.

b) *English hoards.* York (Jubbergate), Beauworth.

York (Jubbergate/Peterlane), 1847. Probably fewer than 30 pennies and cut halfpennies, of which eight can be listed, all of the Paxs type: Dover, Lincoln (½), London, Southwark (½), Steyning, Wallingford, York (2). Like the single finds, this hoard shows Paxs coins circulating very vigorously.

Beauworth, Hants, 1833. A leaden box contained upwards of 8,000 coins (of which 6,468 can be listed plus 18 halves). Andrew conjectured that it was one of the donations of six marks of gold (i.e. 8,640 pence) which William II distributed to monasteries in 1087 for his father's soul. Technically it is a multi-type hoard, but the coins of Types v, vi, and vii amount to only *c.*1.3 per cent of the total. Hawkins lists only mint/moneyer varieties for these earlier types, and so the totals derived from his information may be slightly on the low side. The earlier types have a Wessex flavour. For the Two Stars type, for example, we have coins from the following mints: Bedford, Canterbury, Chichester (2), Cricklade, Dorchester, Ilchester, Lewes, Lincoln, London (5), Shaftesbury, Taunton, Thetford (3), and Winchester (6).

The Paxs type, which made up the great bulk of the hoard, included specimens from 65 mints, of which the most plentiful were Winchester (26 per cent), London (12 per cent), Southwark (8 per cent), Canterbury (4 per cent), Wallingford (4 per cent), Chichester (3 per cent), and Bristol (3 per cent). A comparison of the quantities with die-estimates for the various mints suggests that their representation-rate in the hoard varies greatly, either because of the under-use of many dies, or because the money entering the royal treasury at Winchester was not a random sample of mint-output.

c) *Size of the issue.* The large number of surviving specimens makes possible a rough estimate of the number of dies (which suffers in reliability through being derived so largely from a single hoard). The regional figures, with margins of statistical uncertainty (as presented in *BNJ* 1981, pp. 84-5) are as follows:

Hampshire Basin	122 - 201
West Country	32 - 53
Channel Ports	110 - 230
London and Southwark	78 - 198
Home Counties	30 - 54
Easter Danelaw	74 - 130
Five Boroughs	23 - 39
Western mints	83 - 190
York	5 +
Total	550 -1100
'Best guess'	600 - 880

d) *Evidence for dating.* It is debateable whether the Paxs validity-period could be moved a little later than the conventional dating to the triennium 1083-6. If the choice of reverse design referred to the oath-taking at Salisbury in 1086, that would necessarily be the case. It would then be difficult to associate the type with the six-shilling tax of 1084. A start-date of 1086, however, seems very improbable. In spite of its large volume, the three-year duration of the type is no more than hypothesis. It could have overrun into the early reign of William II, but one's guess is that there would have been a type-change as soon as conveniently possible.

e) *Weight-standards.* The evidence, presented in a diagram for selected mints (Fig.17), is perfectly clear that the Paxs type was overwhelmingly on a single standard of *c.*1.37 - 1.38g, even if the modal value varied marginally from mint to mint.

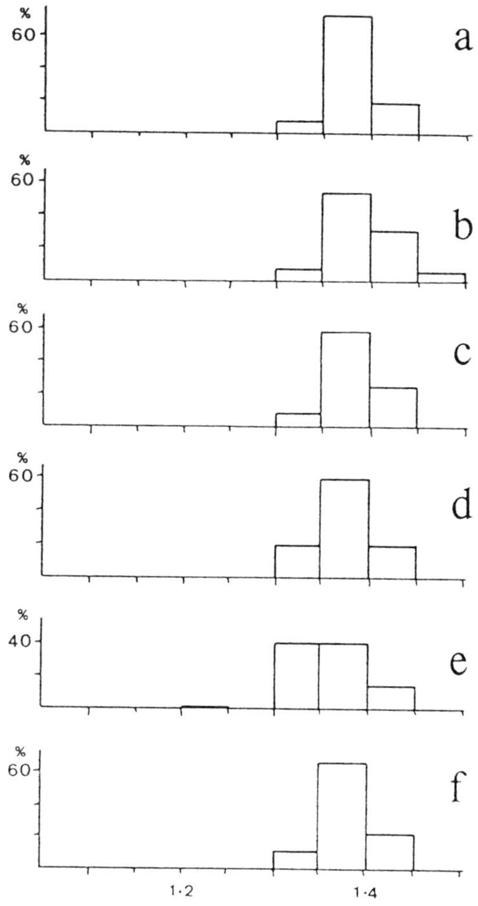

FIG. 17. Histograms of weights for Paxs coins at a) Winchester, b) London, c) Canterbury, d) Exeter, e) Norwich, and f) York (97, 70, 55, 27, 25, and 9 specimens respectively).

The long obverse legend ending REX I seems to have more than its share of coins weighing under 1.30g, possibly reflecting an initial hesitancy.

f) *Number of mint-places.* North records 66, some of which are known from very few specimens, in spite of the large total of coins surviving from Beauworth. The implication is that we may not know of all the mint-type combinations from earlier in William's reign.

References

D.M. Metcalf, 'Notes on the PAXS type of William I', *Yorkshire Numismatist* 1 (1986-7), 13-26.

D.M. Metcalf, 'Large danegelds in relation to war and kingship. Their implications for monetary history, and some numismatic evidence', in S.C. Hawkes (editor), *Weapons and Warfare in Anglo-Saxon England*, Oxford, 1989, pp. 179-89, at pp. 186-7.

J.C. Holt, '1086', in *Domesday Studies*, (ed. Holt), pp. 41-64.

PART FOUR

THE REGIONS

AND THE MINT-PLACES

Regional characteristics
of mint-activity and monetary circulation

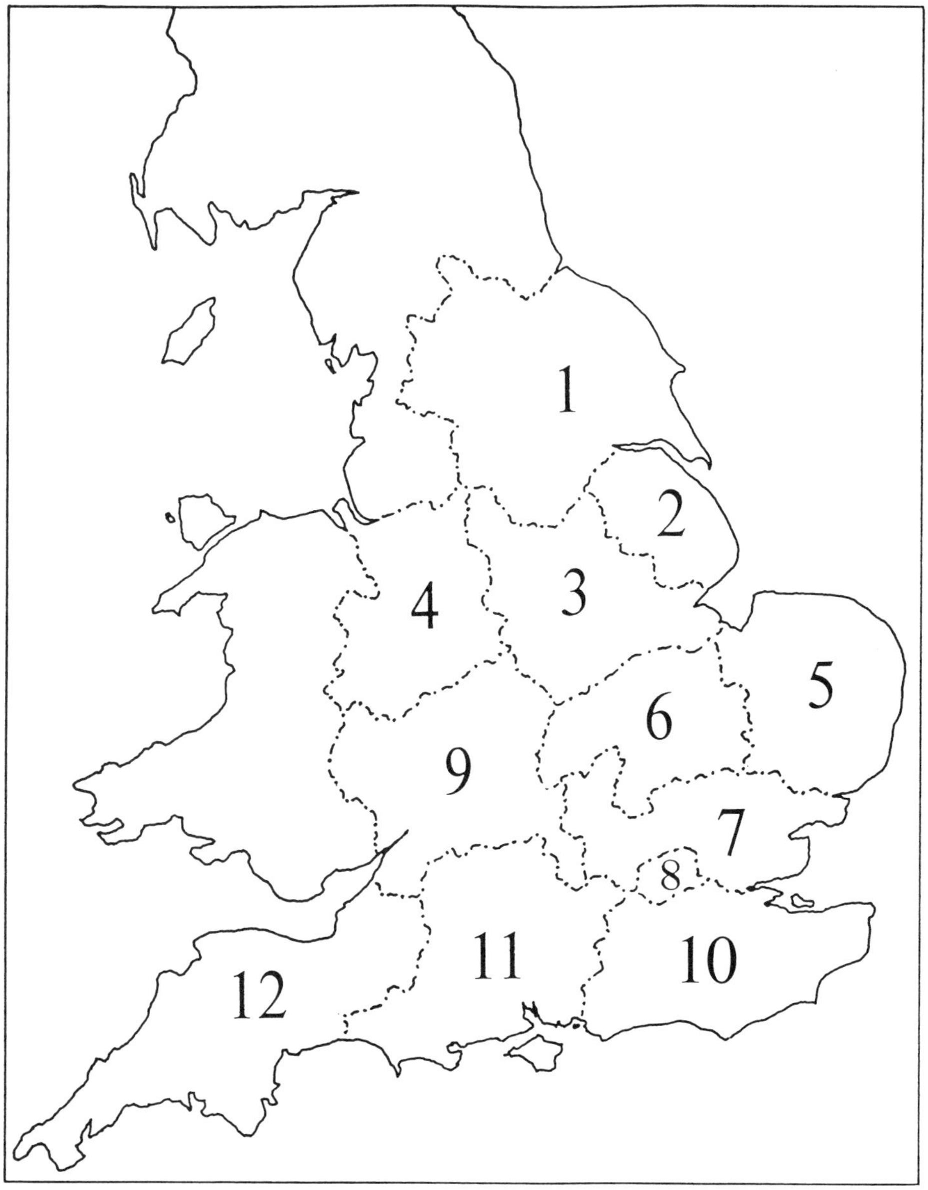

THE REGIONS

Danelaw shires
1. Yorkshire
2. Lindsey
3. Five Boroughs
5. East Anglia
6. Middle Danelaw
7. Southern Danelaw

8. London

Shires under Mercian law
4. The North-West
9. South Mercia

Shires under West Saxon law
10. Kent, Surrey, and Sussex
11. Wessex
12. The South-West

1. YORKSHIRE
Mint-town: York

The currency north of the Humber was to a considerable extent local in origin, in that most of the single finds are of coins struck at the York mint. It was also to a significant extent different from the currency of southern England, in the sense that York coins make up only a very modest proportion of the single finds from the south (see Map 7). Neither the Humber nor the southern boundary of the shire, however, mark an abrupt change, for coins of the York mint are found in Lincolnshire, more than they are elsewhere south of Humber. We may connect that with Domesday Book's mention of tolls collected at Barton upon Humber, Grimsby, South Ferriby, and Winteringham, and of traffic in Nottinghamshire down the Trent and along the Fosse Way towards York.

Even if the Humber was to some extent a natural barrier, that is not necessarily to say that the currency was self-contained. York coins were carried to Scandinavia, and (from what has just been said) presumably most of them were carried direct from Yorkshire, rather than via the south of England. It has been suggested that by the 1060s some 50 million English pennies of the period from *c.*973 onwards had accumulated in Scandinavia: of these roughly 10 per cent were of the York mint. No particular confidence should be attached to the exact figures, but they demonstrate well enough that the currency of Yorkshire was open-ended in that respect.

Likewise if foreign coins, e.g. from Lotharingia, entered the region they will undoubtedly have been melted down and will be invisible in the numismatic evidence.

The city of York itself dominated the monetary affairs of the Northumbrian earldom. Since its capture by the Vikings in 866, and the Danish settlement of Northumbria, it had prospered as the regional capital and as a tidal port with direct access to the commerce of the North Sea. Around the year 1000 it was described by a monk of Ramsey as a place 'enriched with the treasure of merchants who come from all quarters, particularly from the Danish people'. The parallels with Lincoln, another great Anglo-Danish town, and its dominant place in the monetary affairs of Lindsey (q.v., section 2 below) are obvious. By 1066 York had a population probably of 8,000 to 10,000. Through most of the eleventh century, an estimated 8 to 12 per cent of the English coinage was minted in York.

That estimate is Lincoln-based and is derived from the proportion of York coins in Scandinavia. Lean's corpus of the York mint (forthcoming) will permit completely independent and direct estimates, type by type, and should allow us to reconsider the role of Yorkshire in the outflows to Scandinavia, relative to southern England.

Finds are heavily concentrated in York and its vicinity. A recent sample of coin finds of all periods (*Yorkshire Numismatist* 2, 1996, pp. 105-27) lacks material from the late Saxon and Norman period. One suspects a degree of under-reporting from North Humberside, but the Yorkshire dales appear to be an almost coin-less area, as are the broad territories north of the Tees, where a few isolated finds at Jarrow and Jedburgh are very much the exception. From the eastern coastlands of Yorkshire, and from the Wolds, there is a modest handful of finds. The question arises whether the composition of the currency was identical in York itself and in Yorkshire. There is no particular reason to suspect that coinage in the countryside had arrived independently of the money passing through York, e.g. from Lancashire, or from shipping which by-passed the Humber estuary and sailed northwards along the Yorkshire coast. Nor should one expect that town and countryside were other than integrated—particularly the ring of villages within ten or fifteen miles of York which, later in the middle ages, provided not a few of the freemen of the city. But it is probably worth looking at the statistics separately.

York has been, and is, very well served by the activities of the York Archaeological Trust. The number of single finds from in and immediately around the city stands at sixteen, from various sites. Of these, 9 are coins minted up to 1042, and 7 from 1042 to 1086. In the earlier period, 7 out of 9 are York coins, while 2 are of London, and in the later period 6 out of 7 are York coins, with one from Exeter. A larger sample would be welcome, but it seems quite clear that roughly 75 to 85 per cent of the currency in the city was provided throughout by the local mint. That is an exceptionally high proportion in comparison with the other major commercial cities.

The topography of the single finds within York is well documented, but it is probably determined mainly by the choice of sites for archaeological excavation and the intensity of the investigations, e.g. at Coppergate. Most of the finds are from streets within a hundred yards of the river. It is possible that coins from before *c.*1035 are relatively more plentiful on the north-eastern bank of the river, and coins from after *c.*1035 on the south-western side.

It is not possible to work out from the available statistics the scale of the currency within York itself, but one's subjective impression is that it may have been in excess of a figure equal to half the output of the York mint. If the town's population was of the order of 8-10,000, one can see that the available currency in terms of coins per person was a number very roughly half the number of dies.

Although York was the most northerly of the English mints, it was in easy contact by sea with the other east-coast ports: its distance, on the periphery, does not seem to offer a complete explanation for the unusually high degree to which York's currency was self-contained, especially when one sets the hoards alongside the single finds.

The number of hoards from York itself is quite exceptional. They are mostly from the 1060s, and there need be no hesitation in pointing to the harrying of the North as the general explanation for most of them, even if one cannot extend that argument from the general to the particular.

The hoards are of various kinds, and often with a slightly different or very different mint-structure from the single finds. A hoard may reflect a sum of money newly arrived in York, and containing coins from southern mints, which duly passed into the general currency, where the southern coins were statistically submerged—and certainly do not show up in a sample of only 16 single finds. The absence so far of Lincoln coins among the single finds (other than Stamford Bridge) is, however, intriguing. In the Micklegate hoard (see section 4), for example, there were three York coins and two Lincoln coins, in the Minster hoard (section 24) one of York with two others, of Derby and Huntingdon respectively, and at Baile Hill (section 25) two of York and one of Norwich. In the Jubbergate hoard of 1847 (section 31) there were two coins of York, one of London, and one of Lincoln, out of eight. In the larger hoards of Bishophill II (section 25) and Monkgate (section 29) the percentages for York, London, and Lincoln

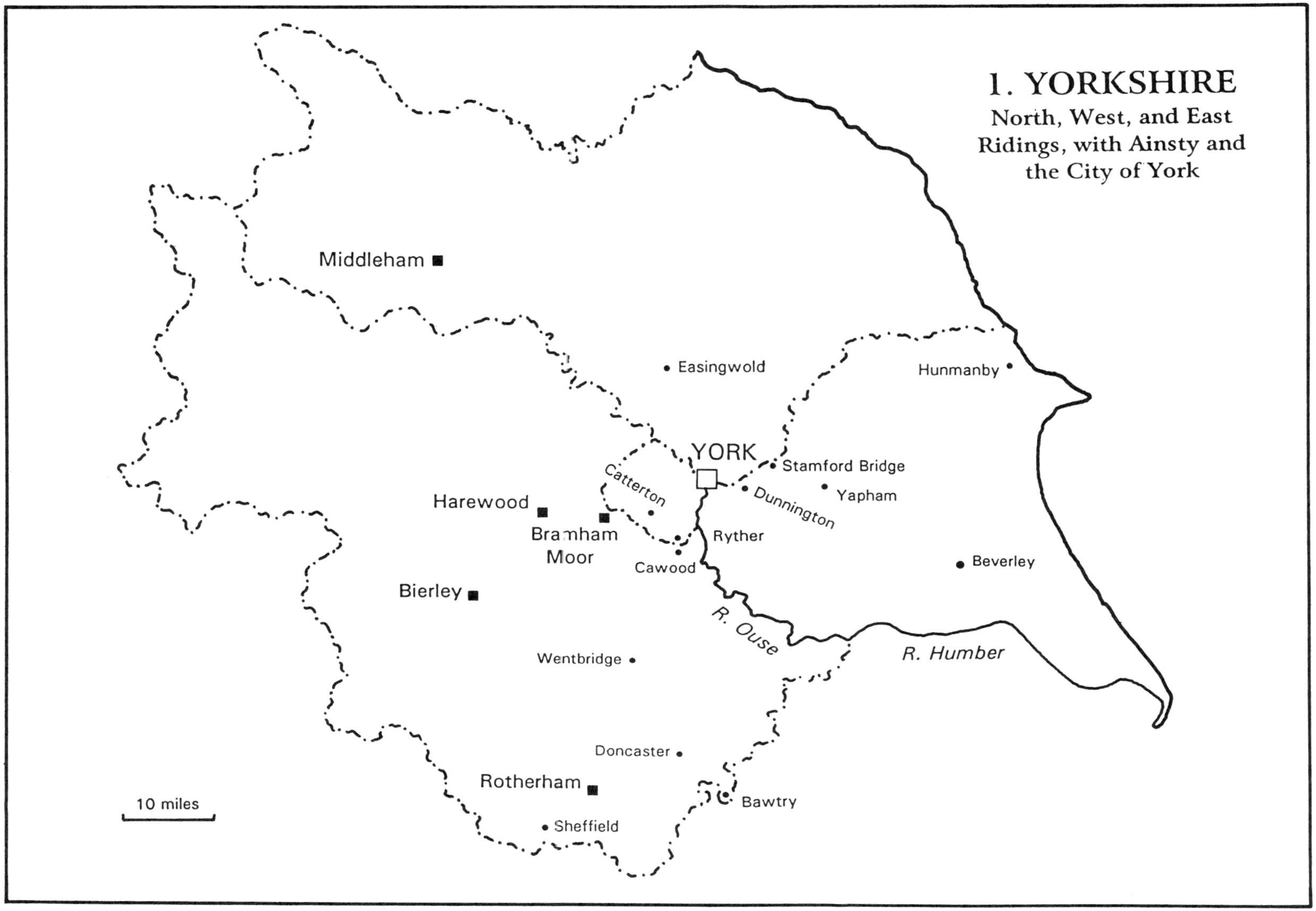
1. YORKSHIRE
North, West, and East Ridings, with Ainsty and the City of York
Middleham
Easingwold
Hunmanby
YORK
Stamford Bridge
Yapham
Dunnington
Catterton
Harewood
Bramham Moor
Ryther
Cawood
Beverley
Bierley
R. Ouse
R. Humber
Wentbridge
Doncaster
Rotherham
Bawtry
Sheffield
10 miles

were 33—21—14 and 45—16—8 respectively.

Bishophill I was a different kind of hoard, in which 97 per cent of the coins were of the York mint. Its owner may have been someone who had frequent occasion to visit the mint.

The single finds from outside York and its immediate surroundings are so few that they hardly permit statistical comparisons. From Catterton, Cawood, Doncaster, Dunnington, Easingwold, Hunmanby, Ryther and Yapton, there are York coins, from Beverley one plus one of Lincoln, from Wentbridge one of Huntingdon, from Sheffield a coin of Canterbury, and from Bawtry one of London and one of Lincoln.

The Harewood hoard, although found in Yorkshire, certainly reflects special circumstances, and belongs to Northamptonshire (section 22). In the Rotherham hoard, which was also virtually a one-type hoard (section 24), Lincoln coins were predominant, in spite of the south Yorkshire find-spot. From Middleham, in Wensleydale, three coins are on record, of which two are of York.

The Castor hoard from Northamptonshire (section 23) was evidently put together in Yorkshire, and carried south to its place of concealment. It resembles Bishophill I in being a multi-type hoard and very probably a savings hoard, but the proportion of York coins, which seems to have been about four-fifths, is not in this case higher than the ratio indicated by the single finds in York.

The Halton Moor hoard, from Lancashire, is also dominated by York coins.

So far as one can judge from limited evidence, the currency in Yorkshire outside York was dominated by York coins, perhaps almost as heavily as in the city itself.

Finally one may mention a few coins from beyond Yorkshire. The excavations at Jarrow have yielded a coin of Edward the Confessor now identified as of the Bedford mint. It is a question whether coins might have reached the monastic site in the hands of travellers from the south of England, either by land or directly by sea, rather than from Yorkshire. From Jedburgh Abbey there is a Last Small Cross penny of Æthelred, from the Lincoln mint. (For Carlisle, see section 4, the North-West, below.)

Single finds from Yorkshire (and northern Northumbria). Bawtry (2), Beverley (2 x ½), Catterton, Cawood, Doncaster, Dunnington (½), Easingwold (2), Ryther, Sheffield, Stamford Bridge (½), Wentbridge, Yapham, York (16). (Jarrow, Jedbury.)

Hoards from Yorkshire (with validity-periods).
A. From York itself: Micklegate (4), Bishophill (22), Minster (24), Baile Hill (25), Jubbergate (25), High Ousegate (25), Bishophill II (25), Monkgate (29), Jubbergate (31).
B. From the rest of Yorkshire: Harewood (22), Rotherham (24), Bierley (25), Bramham Moor (25), Middleham (25).
C. Hoards from elsewhere with a strong Yorkshire flavour: Halton Moor (8), Wellingborough (8), Castor (23). For commentaries on these hoards, see the relevant sections.

Minting at York. Whereas there were very few moneyers at York in the years immediately preceding Eadgar's reform, the Reform validity-period saw no fewer than 32 at work, of whom a dozen were quite active, while the rest are known from only one or two coins today. Thus it appears that York had a particular role in the implementation of the reform, and this is borne out by the die-cutting arrangements, already in the final years of Eadgar's reign (see Q.13). The numbers of moneyers are very similar in the (First) Hand type, and the discrepancy is even more pronounced. In Crux there are some 43 moneyers. The persistence of moneyers from one type through into the next is a topic that has been discussed, particularly in relation to the virtual absence of Second Hand at York (two specimens, of Thormothr and, doubtfully, Eadstan). About half the Reform-type moneyers continue into Hand, half the Hand moneyers into Crux, and half the Crux moneyers into Long Cross. The statistics probably understate the case, because some moneyers are known from very few coins.

Uniquely at York, about three-quarters of the moneyers' names are Scandinavian. This persists until at least 1042. Moreover, the names preserve their Norse forms more closely at York than they do elsewhere. Some are West Norse; some appear to be Norse names coined in England, as they are not recorded in Scandinavia. Celtic personal names, which also make up a significant fraction of the list, almost certainly belonged to Hiberno-Norse immigrants into York: they are largely confined to the early years of the reform coinage. A few old Irish names reappear from Cnut's Helmet type onwards.

Under Edward the Confessor there are still many Norse names. The total of moneyers drifts downwards from about 19 in the early part of the reign, to only ten or 11 at the end. The career moneyers are responsible for the bulk of the output; those recorded only in one or two types are less productive.

Throughout the reign of Edward, York coins are regularly marked with an annulet. It probably signifies that the coins were minted for the financial benefit of the archbishop (cf. the coins attributed to the abbots of Peterborough). The archbishops of York had often held the bishopric of Worcester in plurality, an arrangement which may have had its roots as far back as seventh-century Hwiccia. Archbishop Ælfric Puttoc (1023-51) was given Worcester in 1040-1 in recognition of his support of Harthacnut, but this was discontinued after a revolt by the men of Worcestershire (C.R. Hart, *Early Charters* , p. 266). The Chronicle records that in 1041 Harthacnut had all of Worcestershire harried on account of two of his housecarles who were collecting the heavy tax: the inhabitants slew them inside the minster. If Edward gave Ælfric the profits of minting, it will have been to replace the income he would otherwise have enjoyed from his bishopric of Worcester. The arrangement seems to have come to an end with the death of Edward. There is an exception, in that the Trefoil/Quadrilateral type (*c.*1046-8, i.e. within the pontificate of Ælfric Puttoc) has no additional annulet. No explanation is forthcoming, unless that the brooch on the king's shoulder was thought to be annulet enough.

Under William I the number of moneyers at York was cut from about a dozen, to four. This reduction, in *c.*1070, may be seen in connection with the harrying of the North.

References.

E.J.E. Pirie, *Post-Roman Coins from York Excavations, 1971-81* (The Archaeology of York, vol. 18, The Coins, Part 1), 1986.

E.J.E. Pirie, *Yorkshire Collections. Coins from Northumbrian Mints, c.895-1279; Ancient British and Later Coins from Other Mints to 1279* (SCBI, vol. 21), 1975.

W.M. Lean, *Corpus of Coins of the York Mint* (forthcoming)

P. Seaby, 'Some recent coin finds from Yorkshire and North Humberside', *Yorkshire Numismatist* 2 (1992), 105-27.

C. Briden, 'York as a tidal port', *Yorks Arch. Jl.* 69 (1997), 165-71.

C.R. Hart, *The Early Charters of Northern England*, Leicester, 1975.

D.M. Metcalf, 'Notes on the PAXS type of William I', *Yorkshire Numismatist* 1 (1988), 13-26.

H. Geake and J. Kenny (editors), *Anglo-Saxon Yorkshire* (forthcoming).

2. LINDSEY

Mint-towns: Lincoln, Torksey, Caistor, Horncastle, Louth, (Bardney)

The ancient kingdom of Lindsey was practically an island, cut off as it was by the marshy lands of the lower Trent valley. (The Isle of Axholme, a westwards extension of the kingdom beyond Trent, was an exception.) Lindsey's southern boundary generally followed the course of the River Witham down towards the Wash. Up-stream of Lincoln, the boundary followed the Fossdyke to the Trent at Torksey. Much of Lindsey, east of the Ancholme valley, was occupied by the chalk Wolds. Lincolnshire as it emerged into the twelfth century was composed of Lindsey (with its three ridings), plus Kesteven and Holland, but Holland can hardly have been added to the shire until the East Anglian earldom was dismembered after the revolt of Ralf de Gael in 1075. Kesteven was what remained of the Five Boroughs territory of Stamford, after it had been plundered during the construction of Northamptonshire and by the creation of Rutland (C.R. Hart, *The Danelaw*, pp. 177-203). It seems that for most of the eleventh century the mints of Lincoln and Stamford were not in the same shire, even if Kesteven enjoyed only quasi-shire status.

Lincoln, like York, was an Anglo-Danish city with direct navigational access to the sea and with strong overseas trading connections. At the foot of the hill on which the city stands, the River Witham opens out in to Brayford Pool. South of the river lay the commercial suburb of Wigford. Lincoln dominated the monetary affairs of Lincolnshire, almost to the same extent that York did in Yorkshire. There were second-order regional centres at Caistor, Horncastle, and Louth which, together with Torksey, were given mint status in the time of Edward the Martyr, evidently by an administrative decision to create all four, a year or two later than the implementation of the reform at Lincoln. (In effect, Lincoln too began work under Edward, after a fairly small-scale activity under Eadgar, with dies supplied from elsewhere.) It is doubtful whether a fifth small mint, probably at Grantham, was part of this unrealistic initiative in shire administration: Grantham lay in Kesteven. Caistor and Torksey survived, or rather were resuscitated, in the reign of Cnut, but there was never much demand for the moneyers' services at any of these places. Their combined output, at the height of their activity, was probably only of the order of one-hundredth of that of Lincoln at the same time.

That is not to say that the smaller regional centres lacked the functions proper to towns. Rather, there was no correlation between mint output and urban rank. Domesday Book records that Louth had a market which rendered 29s, and that the market at Partney rendered 10s.

Mint-output at Lincoln was comparable with that at York, especially after *c*.997. It often amounted to 12 or 15 per cent of the national total, if the Scandinavian material can be accepted as random, as between York, Lincoln, and southern England.

The estimated numbers of dies employed at Lincoln are free from that uncertainty, as they can be derived directly from Henry Mossop's fine corpus of the coins of the Lincoln mint. From the 990s until the 1030s it is probable

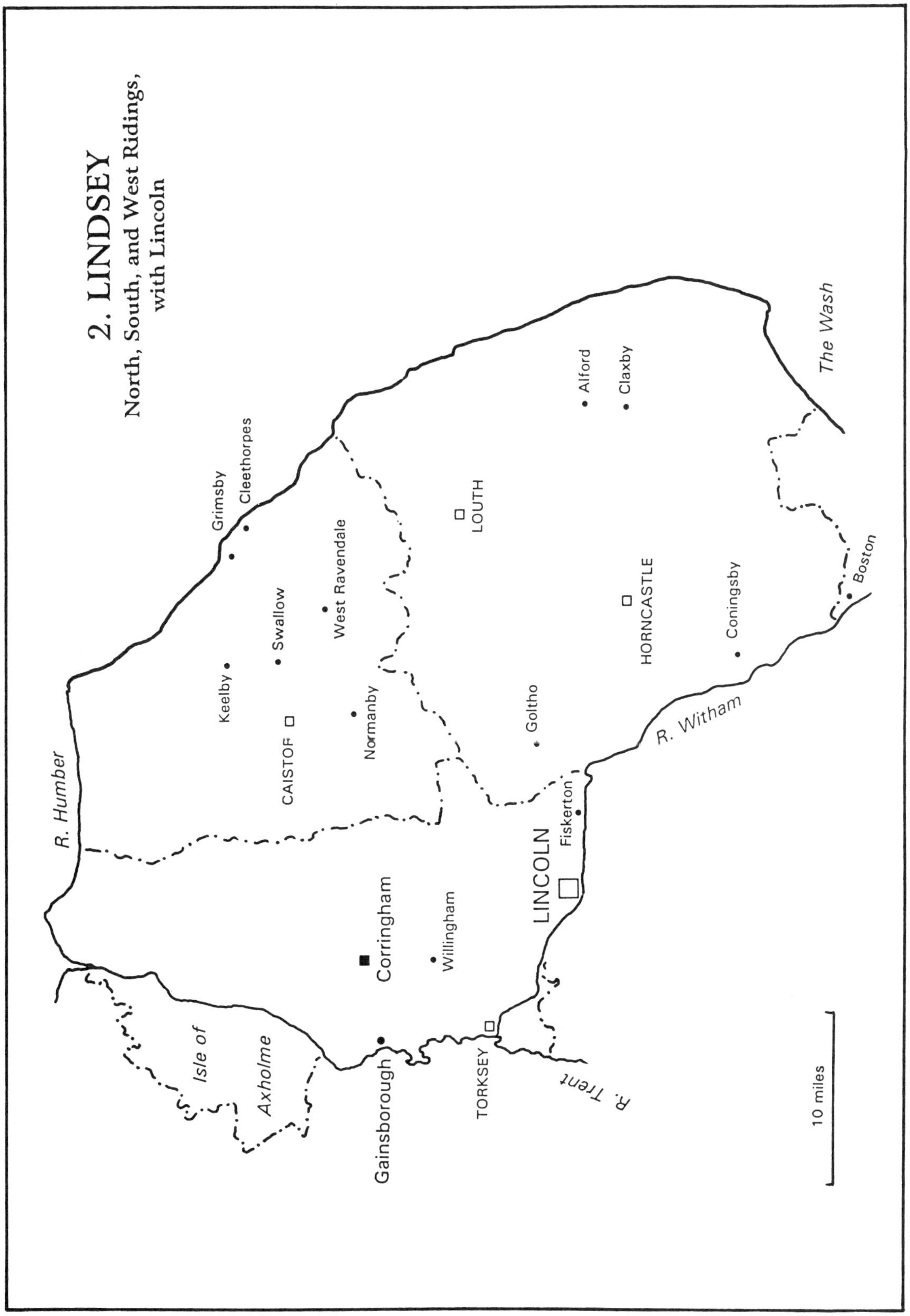
2. LINDSEY
North, South, and West Ridings, with Lincoln
R. Humber
Grimsby
Cleethorpes
Keelby
Swallow
West Ravendale
CAISTOR
Normanby
LOUTH
Alford
Claxby
The Wash
HORNCASTLE
Coningsby
Boston
Goltho
R. Witham
Fiskerton
LINCOLN
Corringham
Willingham
Isle of
Axholme
Gainsborough
TORKSEY
R. Trent
10 miles

that Lincoln moneyers struck upwards of a million coins in each validity-period.

The composition of the currency in the city of Lincoln is well known from single finds from excavations, thanks largely to the activities of the Lincoln Archaeological Trust. Of 19 coins whose mint-attributions are certain, 9 are of Lincoln, 2 of Stamford, 2 of London, with singletons of Exeter, Hereford, Hertford, Thetford, Wallingford. Only 47 per cent, that is to say, are locally minted; two other coins which are identified as either Lincoln or York might push the proportion up to 52 per cent. The figure still seems low. It reflects the dwindling of mint-output under William I. The 14 (16) Anglo-Saxon finds alone give 64 (69) per cent.

One Danish coin and two Norwegian coins of Olaf Kyrre have been found at Lincoln. That represents an unusually high proportion of foreign coins. One wonders whether they could be 'political' rather than purely commercial imports.

The single finds from Lindsey outside Lincoln itself follow a similar pattern. Sixteen out of 31 of which the mints can be identified are of Lincoln (52 per cent), with 3 from Stamford, 4 from York, 4 from London, one from Chichester, one probably from Hastings, and one from Rochester. If we exclude the coins of William I the proportion of Lincoln coins rises slightly.

There is one foreign coin, a Hiberno-Norse issue found at Torksey.

The multi-type Corringham hoard, from near Gainsborough, is composed mainly of coins minted at Lincoln and York. It has been suggested above (section 26) that it may be a savings hoard. The proportions of Lincoln coins (between 35 and 58 per cent, type by type) are sufficiently close to the over-all figure for single finds from Lindsey, for one to suppose that the hoard was put together locally; but the high percentage of York coins among the oldest types in the hoard hints at a particular connection—especially as York coins are otherwise not plentiful in Lindsey.

Single finds from Lindsey. Alford (3), Boston area (1 + ½), Bullington/Goltho (2), Caistor (2), Claxby (½), Cleethorpes, Coningsby, Fiskerton, Gainsborough (2 x ½, 2 x ¼), Grimsby area (½), Horncastle (2 + ½), Keelby, Louth (4 + ½), Normanby, Swallow, Torksey (½), West Ravendale, Willingham (2).

Hoards from Lindsey (with validity-periods). Corringham (26). See above.

Mints: Lincoln. Eadgar's reform was initiated rather timidly at Lincoln, by only four (recorded) moneyers, who obtained their dies from Winchester. Under Edward the Martyr, nearly all dies were cut locally, and the number of moneyers doubled. In its heyday under Cnut, more than 30 moneyers worked, but under Edward the Confessor Lincoln seems to have settled down to a steady complement of ten. Under Harold II the number is reduced to seven, and even fewer under William I, with a reduction to only two at the end of the reign.

Torksey. Although specific evidence is lacking, the Fossdyke, linking Lincoln to Torksey and the Trent, was very probably open to river traffic before 1086, judging by the links between the two places in Domesday. There is a Torksey penny from Nottinghamshire (*NC* 1956, 293-5), and a cut halfpenny from Tamworth. From Torksey itself, a Hiberno-Norse coin is suggestive of the routeway passing through the town.

Torksey later declined to become a place of very little importance, and one may be tempted to think of it as owing its numismatic significance to its role as a staging-post, to an unusual extent. In 1066, however, it had 213 burgesses, which meant that it was by no means the smallest of towns. The appropriate comment may therefore be the opposite of what one might first have thought, namely that mint-output under-stated the general importance of the town.

Caistor. Four specimens are known from the Reform and Hand types, and an equally minimal proportion from the reign of Cnut.

Horncastle. One coin from the short-lived and tiny mint of Horncastle had quickly found its way to Chester in the Pemberton's Parlour hoard, in company no doubt with Lincoln coins.

LV (= Louth?). On the unique coin plausibly attributed to Louth, see the comments in Jonsson, *The New Era*, pp. 146f. The Domesday evidence has been mentioned, above.

Bardney. Hildebrand's attribution of Barnstaple coins to Bardney is made more unlikely by the occurrence of one in the Wedmore hoard, from Somerset.

References

M. Blackburn, C. Colyer, and M. Dolley, *Early Medieval Coins from Lincoln and its Shire, c.770–1100* (The Archaeology of Lincoln, vol. 6, part 1), 1983.

H.R. Mossop, *The Lincoln Mint, c.890-1279*, Newcastle upon Tyne, 1970.

R.H.M. Dolley, 'Three late Anglo-Saxon notes', *BNJ* 28 (1955), 88-105. [Caistor]

I. Stewart, 'A Caistor coin of Æthelred's Hand type', *NC*[7] (1979), 219-21. [Four Caistor coins.]

F.E. Jones, 'A note on the mint of Horncastle', *BNJ* 37 (1968), 191-2. [Three known coins.]

R.H.M. Dolley, 'An enigmatic penny of Edward the Martyr', *BNJ* 28 (1955-7), 499-504. [A circumspect discussion of the coin reading LV... See the commentary in Jonsson, *The New Era*, p. 146.]

R.H.M. Dolley and J.S. Strudwick, 'A note on the mint of Torksey', *NC*[6] 16 (1956), 293-5.

3. THE FIVE BOROUGHS
(other than Lindsey)
Mint-towns: Derby, Leicester, Newark, Nottingham, Stamford, (?)Grantham (GRE)

The Five Boroughs formed a district of Danish settlement with a distinctive administrative character and sense of identity. The confederation is first mentioned in 942, but its origins probably go back to the settlement of the five armies which began in 877. Much later, the Five Boroughs was a jurisdiction: a court sat, and the fines it imposed were double those imposed by the shire courts in the same region. Derby, Leicester, and Nottingham became shire towns, as did Lincoln. Stamford's position was anomalous. Its original territory (Kesteven) was appropriated to Northamptonshire, Rutland, and Lincolnshire. Thus it lay on the very edge of Five Boroughs territory, half in what was to become Lincolnshire, and half (the southern suburbium) in Northamptonshire.

When the Danish soldiers settled down on their conquered territories, the former English land-owners were dispossessed, and the payment of taxes to the English king ceased. A new system of tax liability to the local earl was imposed, characterized by a system of reckoning in eights and twelves, and based on ploughlands (carucates) and wapentakes. It appears that the new system was imposed from the top down, because the total assessment of carucates for each shire was a round number.

The old notion that the Danish settlement was a major stimulus in the development of a money economy finds little enough support from the coin finds of the Five Boroughs. A more circumspect version has it that the lack of royal control over land transactions, and (even more) a custom of partible inheritance fostered a free market in land and stock, which was a major stimulus, etc. The number of stray finds from Derbyshire, Leicestershire, and Nottinghamshire is, however, very modest, and the combined output of the mints of Derby, Leicester, Newark, and Nottingham hovers around one per cent of the national total between *c.*990 and *c.*1030, climbing thereafter to around 3 per cent. Lincoln and Stamford were more active mints, one would judge, not because they were located in Five Boroughs territory and were acting as regional market-places for land and stock, but because they were ports engaged in longer-distance trade. The paucity of stray finds and the low proportion of the currency minted locally may create the impression that the shire-towns were insignificant as towns. At the time of Domesday, however, Leicester and Nottingham may each have had 2,000 inhabitants or more. Leicester had houses *extra murum*, which presupposes a history of urban growth, and Nottingham had merchants' houses (*domus mercatorum*). The needs of inter-regional trade were recognised, in that the waters of the River Trent, and the Fosse Way and road towards York, were both regulated to keep them clear for traffic, under penalty of a heavy fine.

Derbyshire lead-production may have given

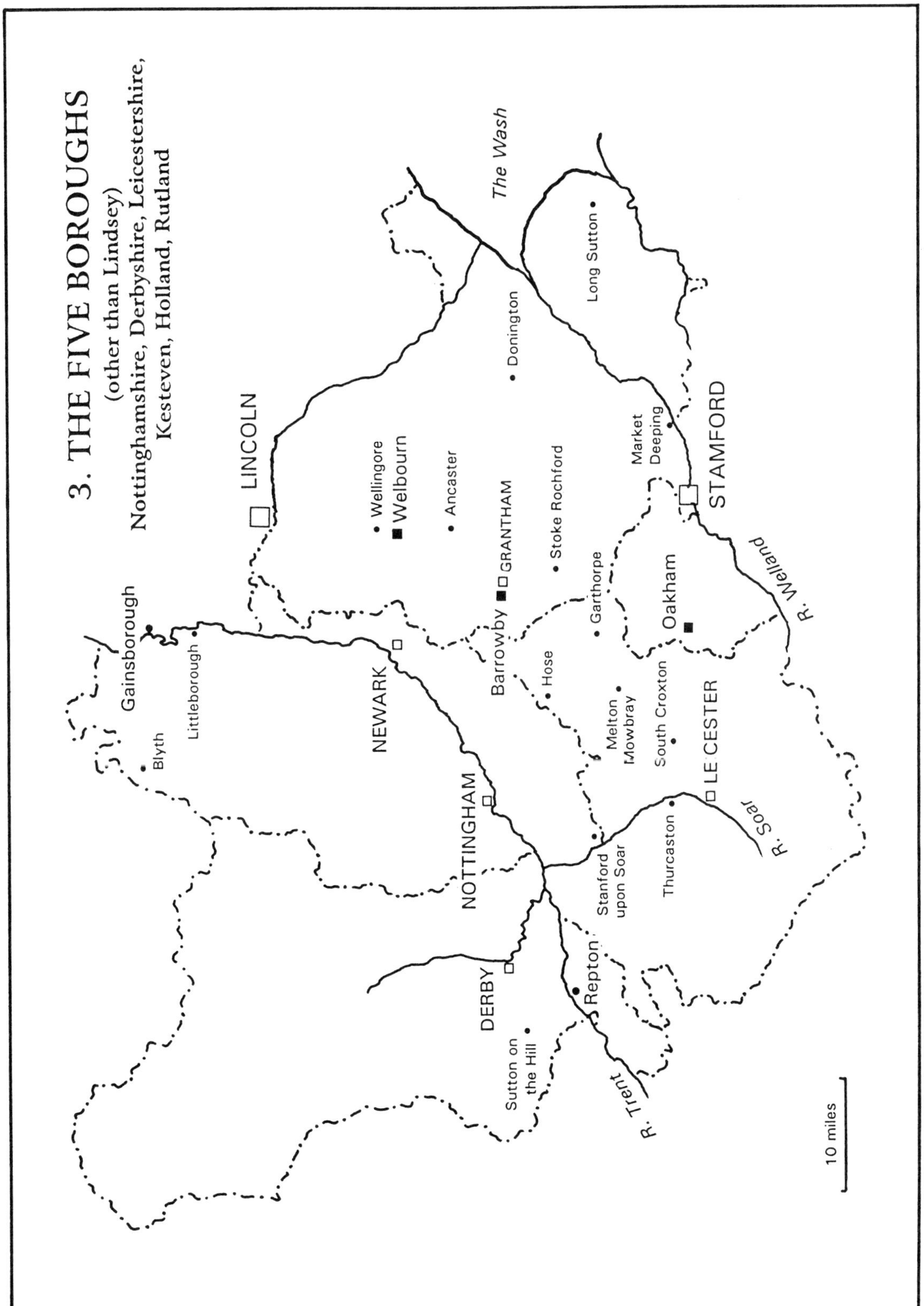
3. THE FIVE BOROUGHS
(other than Lindsey)
Nottinghamshire, Derbyshire, Leicestershire,
Kesteven, Holland, Rutland
The Wash
LINCOLN
Wellingore
Welbourn
Ancaster
Donington
Long Sutton
GRANTHAM
Stoke Rochford
Market Deeping
STAMFORD
Gainsborough
Littleborough
Blyth
NEWARK
Barrowby
Garthorpe
Oakham
R. Welland
Hose
Melton Mowbray
South Croxton
LEICESTER
NOTTINGHAM
Thurcaston
R. Soar
Stanford upon Soar
DERBY
Repton
Sutton on the Hill
R. Trent
10 miles

an impetus towards the monetization of the economy: in 1086, five royal manors rendered £40 of pure silver, not to mention various cartloads of lead. It is to be supposed that the silver was extracted as a valuable by-product of the lead.

If single finds are few in Derbyshire, Leicestershire, and Nottinghamshire, it could be partly because metal-detectorists have searched less assiduously there. Success and failure are reinforcing experiences, in opposite directions, and they may tend to exaggerate regional differences. The proportion of coins of the local mints among the finds from the region, and the source of inflows, are potentially more reliable evidence. Likewise, the distribution of finds of coins of Derby, Grantham, Leicester, Newark, and Nottingham outside Five Boroughs territory will provide information that is completely independent of the Scandinavian sample, which obviously might in principle understate the case.

From Derbyshire there are just five single finds on record (of which four are from Repton). One of them is from the Nottingham mint and one is from either Derby or Nottingham. The five include a cut halfpenny and a cut farthing. From Leicestershire there are six finds, of which one is of the Leicester mint, and two are of Lincoln. The others are from London, Winchester, and Bridport. From Nottinghamshire there are five finds, of Lincoln, Torksey, Stamford, and Dover, together with a German coin. From Kesteven there are five finds, from Lincoln, London (2), Canterbury and Worcester. Thus the local mints seem to have supplied only 15 to 20 per cent of the currency of the Five Boroughs (although if we had site-finds from the towns themselves, the proportion might perhaps be somewhat higher). After making some allowance for outflows to Scandinavia and to other parts of England, the figure of 15-20 per cent allows us to extrapolate a (very) rough total for the scale of the currency within Five Boroughs territory. The wide margins of uncertainty attaching to this exercise underline the need for a larger random sample of stray finds from the region.

It is intriguing that, among 45 site-finds from London and Southwark, there should be four from Derby, Leicester, and Nottingham (2), or 9 per cent, comfortably in excess of the Lincoln-based Scandinavian estimate for those three mints. It is as if the three shires had links (of trade?) direct to London.

The hoards, other than Oakham, for various reasons offer only vague or uncertain evidence of mint-composition. The little Welbourn hoard, from Kesteven, included five coins of First Hand type and one more probably of the Reform type. All were of the Lincoln mint. Even with such small numbers, one may claim a significant contrast with the single finds from Kesteven. One can only hope that the nine recorded coins out of allegedly twenty or more from Welbourn were typical.

The two Nottingham hoards from the late eighteenth century match the single finds as well as can be expected with such limited information—that is, one coin of the Nottingham mint was recorded in each.

In so far as Five Boroughs coins are not plentiful in other regions of England (e.g. from Lincoln, two coins of the Stamford mint, from Meols nothing), it seems to have been a region with net inflows, especially from Lincoln or Lindsey (about a quarter) and from southern England. Stamford seems to have had more of a long-distance function, but only a minor role as a mint supplying Five Boroughs territory.

Single finds from the region. Derbyshire: Repton (4), Sutton-on-the-Hill.
Leicestershire: Garthorpe, Hose, Leicester, Melton Mowbray (2), South Croxton, Thurcaston. *Nottinghamshire*: Blyth, Littleborough, Nottinghamshire, Stanford-upon-Soar (2). *Kesteven*: Ancaster, Donington, Grantham, Long Sutton, Market Deeping, Stoke Rochford, Wellingore.

Hoards from the region (with validity-periods).

Oakham (1), Welbourn (2A, 4), Barrowby (8), Nottingham 1789 (19), Nottingham 1786 (19), Grantham (26).

For a full discussion of the Oakham hoard, see Q.35. There is unpublished evidence among the Ruding MSS in the British Library which suggests that the hoard may have terminated with First Hand.

Mints.

Derby, Leicester, Newark, and Nottingham
Hildebrand confused the mint-signatures of Leicester and Chester. The former was variable, ranging from LIGERCESTE to LIH or LEH, but commonly LIHRA or LEHRA, both versions being used by the same moneyer. The distinction between Newark and Newport is difficult. Coins by Ingolfr signed NIWV or NIEWEN are given to Newark, one of their reverse dies being of peculiar, local workmanship.

Of the four inland mints, Leicester was usually the most active, often exceeding the combined output of the other three. This trend is contradicted in the 1030s, when Leicester for a time takes third place. The deviations, type by type, doubtless could reveal much about administrative cooperation within the Five Boroughs and about the constraints reflected in varying demand for the moneyers' services, if the surviving material were fuller.

Thus, it seems that the reform was implemented, in *c.*973-5, almost exclusively by Leicester, with three moneyers, who were thereafter so far as we know inactive under Edward the Martyr and Æthelred, 975—*c.*979. At Newark and at Derby, single moneyers worked from the beginning and into Edward's reign but produced (it seems from the Scandinavian sample) relatively trivial quantities of coinage. Nottingham seems to have had no moneyer until the Hand type: perhaps Newark's role was transferred to Nottingham.

There are, moreover, pronounced differences between the weight-standards initially employed by the shire-mints. Leicester mints on a whole range of standards, from 1.65-1.69g down to 1.35-1.39g. Newark, meanwhile, operates on 1.45-1.49g and Derby on 1.20-1.24g.

In First Hand Derby suddenly leaps into prominence, when four moneyers produce an output of 61 'equivalent reverse dies'. Was Eadgar's reform not enforced in Derbyshire until six years had elapsed, or were there some special circumstances at Derby in the early 980s? There were certainly several weight-standards, apparently *c.*1.47g, *c.*1.37g, and the earlier *c.*1.22g.

In Cnut's Short Cross type, Leicester had its usual complement of four moneyers, but output fell dramatically from 34 'equivalent reverse dies' in Quatrefoil (from four moneyers) to 3.

Stamford. The River Welland was navigable as far as Stamford. Edward the Elder's fortification developed into a second borough to the south of the river. The two settlements were in due course linked by a bridge. There is nothing to compare with the extensive excavation at York and Lincoln, either north or south of the river. If there were, one imagines that roughly half of the eleventh-century coins found would be of local mintage.

Stamford's contribution to the national total of coinage fluctuated from 2 to 5 per cent, rising in the 1030s to 5 to 7 per cent, but declining under William I.

The reform coinage had been launched ambitiously, especially during the reign of Edward the Martyr, when 14 moneyers worked to produce a large coinage. Stamford's share in the first validity-period was nearly 8 per cent of the national total. (It is significantly higher in the Oakham hoard, from Rutland, at 23 per cent. Lincoln and York accounted for 18 and 11 per cent respectively in the hoard. Whether these two mints would be well represented in an assemblage of site-finds from Stamford is not known; but one suspects not as well as they are at Oakham. See Q.35.) The early promise at the Stamford mint was not sustained, whether because of administrative changes which deprived the town of its quasi-shire town status, or because the unified national coinage somehow worked against the interests of the Five Boroughs.

At the beginning of the Confessor's reign, Stamford still had 11, then 10 moneyers. By the end of the reign, the complement had declined to five.

GRE (Grantham?). A unique First Hand coin from a pair of dies of poor workmanship, with lateral reversal of the bust, is connected by its style with just three others, from Lincoln and (interestingly) Caistor. The borough of Grantham makes a persuasive attribution.

References.

S. Sharp, 'The Stamford mint', *NC*[2] 9 (1869), 327-68; ibid 19 (1879), 153; 'Supplement', ibid., 20 (1880), 205-25.

W.C. Wells, 'The Stamford and Peterborough mints', *BNJ* 22 (1934-7), 35-77; 23 (1938-41), 7-28; 24(1941-4), 69-109.

R.H.M. Dolley, 'The Anglo-Saxon mint at Newark', *NNUM* 1956, 215-19.

K. Jonsson, 'Grantham—a new Anglo-Saxon mint in Lincolnshire', *BNJ* 57 (1987), 104-5.

4. THE NORTH-WEST (AND NORTH WALES)

Mint-towns: Chester, Shrewsbury, Stafford, Tamworth; Rhuddlan

The three shires of Cheshire, Shropshire, and Staffordshire formed the northern half of the region that had been under Mercian law. Each shire had its mint, and there was in addition a mint at Tamworth, the old Mercian capital. Chester, which before Eadgar's reform had been an extremely active mint-town, abruptly declined, but continued to mint 2-3 per cent of the national output of coinage. Shrewsbury also made a steady contribution, of the order of one per cent. Stafford's output was very small, as was that of Tamworth.

From Chester itself there is a growing series of exemplary excavation-reports, but not as yet enough eleventh-century coins among the site finds to provide a useful sample (two coins, both of the Chester mint). From nearby Meols, however, on the sea-coast of the Wirral, there is a good series. There was in effect only one reason for money to reach Meols: it was being used in connection with the Irish trade. Meols seems to have been the port for Chester; and in any case the Chester mint derived most of its tenth-century importance from the city's trade into the Irish Sea coastlands. But it would be simplistic to imagine that there was a direct correlation between mint-output and the volume of trade: the import of Chester ware into Dublin, for example, declines only in the early eleventh century, not abruptly with Eadgar's reform, and the trading connections between Dublin and the Severn estuary become prominent only after the 1020s.

Money in transit is exemplified by the hoards from the time of Cnut, from north-west Wales (which seem to be confined to a brief phase *c.*1020). And the Pemberton's Parlour hoard from Chester itself, which is certainly not typical of the currency of Chester, likewise illustrates inter-regional trade, containing as it does numerous coins from Lincoln, Stamford, and other places far afield, but only nine per cent of Chester coins, less than one per cent from Shrewsbury, and none from Stafford.

At Tamworth there has been a long series of excavations at various sites in the town, published by the South Staffordshire Historical and Archaeological Society. They yielded only one late Anglo-Saxon coin (not of the Tamworth mint) and raise the question whether one is entitled to speak of negative evidence, rather than a mere absence of evidence. But it seems hazardous to conclude that money was not much in use in the town, when it had a mint, and when chance might still reveal a more productive site. Moreover, at Amington, only a couple of miles away from Tamworth, there have been two separate finds of Tamworth mint coins (of the same type, Edward the Confessor's Short Cross, but three fields apart).

The mints identifiable among the Meols finds are Chester (7 coins, or 47 per cent), Shrewsbury, York (2), London (2), Southwark, Winchester, and Shaftesbury.

Single finds from the three shires, outside Chester and Meols, number only six, namely two minted at Tamworth (from Amington), one at Torksey, one at Lincoln, and two at London. With such small numbers it is too soon to judge, but one's provisional impression is that Chester, even more than York, derived its monetary importance from inter-regional trade, and that the use of money in the countryside was on a modest scale.

From Shropshire there is a dearth of evidence, and Staffordshire is not in much better case. Neverthless, Domesday Book informs us that in 1066 Shrewsbury had 252 burgesses; and Stafford, with an estimated population of at least 750, was a walled town.

Single finds from the North-West, and beyond. Amington (2), Chester (1 + ½), Meols (14 + 4 x ½ + ¼), Stafford (2), Tamworth, Wroxeter. *North Wales*: Rhuddlan.
Cumbria: Drigg (Chester mint), Carlisle (2, of the York and Stamford mints).

Hoards from the North-West (with validity-periods). A. From the region: Chester (2A), Mayfield (20), Oulton (25).
B. From beyond the region: Pant-yr-Eglwys (7), Bryn Maelgwyn (8), Drwsdangoed (8), Halton Moor (8), Beetham (25).

Mints: Chester. Immediately after his consecration at Bath, Eadgar took his whole naval force to Chester and received the submission of various rulers in the Irish Sea coastlands. According to Florence's colourful story, he was rowed by his sub-kings on the River Dee, from the palace to the monastery of St John Baptist. The strategic location of Chester is clear. Nevertheless, the suggestion that it owed its importance as a mint-place in the tenth century to the minting of silver given in tribute by Welsh princes has little to recommend it. At the moment of Eadgar's reform the number of moneyers was very sharply reduced, from over 20 to five. The five had all been active moneyers among the 20. This smacks of an administrative reform rather than a 'natural' decline. The other moneyers may have been deprived of their commissions, or they may have voluntarily withdrawn because they judged that the work would be unprofitable. The suggestion that a Viking descent on the Wirral in 980 caused a severe decline (Dolley and Pirie, 1964) is not borne out by the numbers of surviving First Hand and Second Hand coins. (It remains possible that the Chester hoard was concealed in face of the threat.) The numbers of moneyers rise to 12 in Last Small Cross and 24 in Quatrefoil. During the reign of Edward the Confessor the complement of moneyers fluctuated between eight and six.

The Domesday Survey for Chester includes references to shipping and taxes which are unique in Domesday for any English port.

We read that

If ships arrived at the City port or left port without the King's permission, the King and the Earl had 40s from each man in the ships. . . but if it came with the king's peace and permission, those in it sold what they had without interference. But when it left the King and the Earl had 4d from each cargo; if the King's reeve instructed those who had marten-skins not to sell to anyone until they were first shown to him and he had made his purchase, whoever did not observe this instruction was fined 40s.

and

If a merchant reaches the city, bringing a bale of goods, and opens it between Saturday noon and Monday, or on any other Holiday, without permission from the Bishop's officer, the Bishop has 4s fine therefrom; if one of the Bishop's men finds any man loading within the City territory (on a Holiday) the Bishop has therefrom a fine of 4s or two oxen.

Shrewsbury. The Shropshire mint participated in Eadgar's reform, with three newly-appointed moneyers in his reign, but then fell inactive for the rest of the validity-period. It gained momentum only in Long Cross. Under Edward the Confessor the complement of moneyers fluctuated between four and six.

Stafford. Two moneyers were commissioned to implement Eadgar's reform. After his death the mint was inactive for the rest of the

4. THE NORTH-WEST
Cheshire, Shropshire, and Staffordshire

validity-period, —and, indeed until Crux. Stafford continued as a mint with a very small output. The Stafford hoard of 1800 is securely attested, but it mint-composition is, in effect, unknown.

Tamworth. The second Staffordshire mint began to produce reform coins under Edward the Martyr, possibly with an intention that it should replace Stafford. It remained in operation, but with a modest output. One of the two recorded coins in First Small Cross has an added annulet, which may reflect a grant of privileges to Lichfield. The history of the cathedral at this period is so obscure that no supporting evidence can be adduced.

Danson has published a corpus of Tamworth coins, in which there are, for example, 18 coins of Æthelred II from 17 pairs of dies.

Rhuddlan. An Ælfwine minted at Rhuddlan in William's Paxs type. Domesday records that Robert de Roelent held 'medietatem. . . monetae'. The dies are of English workmanship.

References

E.J.E. Pirie, *Grosvenor Museum, Chester. Coins with the Chester Mint-Signature* (SCBI, vol. 5), 1964.

R.H.M.Dolley, 'The Anglo-Saxon coins from Meols sands', *Trans Hist. Soc. of Lancs and Cheshire* 113 (1961), 197-210.

R.H.M. Dolley and E.J.E. Pirie, 'The repercussions on Chester's prosperity of the Viking descent on Cheshire in 980', *BNJ* 33 (1964), 39-44.

P. Rahtz, 'The archaeology of West Mercian towns', in A. Dornier (editor), *Mercian Studies*, Leicester, 1977, pp. 107-29.

P. Carrington (editor), '*Where Deva Spreads Her Wizard Stream*'. *Trade and the Port of Chester: Papers from a Seminar Held at Chester, November 1995*, 1996.

S.W. Ward and others, *Excavations at Chester. Saxon Occupation within the Roman Fortress: Sites Excavated 1971-1981*, (Chester Archaeology, Excavation and Survey Reports, no. 7), 1994.

A. Pownall, 'Coins of the Stafford mint', *NC*[2] 20 (1880) 66-73.

E.W. Danson, 'The Anglo-Saxon and Norman mint of Tamworth, (Staffs.)', *South Staffs. Arch. and Hist. Soc. Transactions* 11 (1969-70), 32-56.

P.H. Robinson, 'The Stafford (1800) and Oulton (1795) hoards', *BNJ* 38 (1969), 22-30.

5. EAST ANGLIA

Mint-towns: Norwich, Thetford, Ipswich, Sudbury, Bury St Edmunds, 'Wilton', 'Dyr' or 'Dernt' and 'Derne'

The Anglo-Scandinavian boroughs of Norwich and Thetford, which were both among England's largest towns in the eleventh century, were the focal points of East Anglian monetary history, just as York and Lincoln were in their respective shires. Like them, Norwich and Thetford had river access to the North Sea and the Wash respectively. The comparison falters, in that the countryside of East Anglia seems to have been more heavily monetized than the Vale of York or Lindsey. Certainly, Norfolk and Suffolk are rich in single finds (and in small hoards). The assemblage so far recorded is already large enough to allow us to establish the composition of the currency by mints of origin, and even to begin to make comparisons between regions within East Anglia, such as the liberties of the fenland abbeys.

Eadgar's reform was implemented at the three mints of Ipswich (already an important wic and mint-place in the eighth century), Norwich, and Thetford. At Norwich there were four moneyers for Eadgar, and most of the output in the first validity-period was in his reign. Ipswich began with two moneyers, and Thetford with only one. Subsequently, Norwich took 2-3 per cent of the national total, and Ipswich was rarely above one per cent, while Thetford, after a slow start, was typically in the range 2.5—5 per cent.

From Thetford there is a very good range of site-finds, from various sites in and near the town. Among 24 coins of which the mints can be identified, 7 are of Thetford itself and another 7 from London (29 per cent each), and 4 are from Lincoln (17 per cent). The rest of the finds are singletons from Norwich and Bury St Edmunds, York, Colchester, Hereford, and Southwark. The proportion of coins of the local mint is thus comparable with Lincoln (47 per cent).

From Norwich there are eight finds and from Ipswich six. Only two of the Norwich finds are of the local mint, the others being of York, Lincoln, Thetford, Cambridge, London, and Canterbury. At Ipswich similarly only one out of seven finds is of the Ipswich mint, the others being from Lincoln, Stamford, Northampton, London, Oxford, and Rochester. It seems that even when a town was active as a mint-place, the local moneyers might supply only a quarter of the coins circulating in the town, or even less.

From East Anglia as a whole (111 finds), London is the leading mint, with 23 per cent, followed in ranking order by Thetford (16 per cent), Norwich (12 per cent), Lincoln (9 per cent), Stamford (8 per cent), York (4 per cent), and Cambridge (3 per cent), and fifteen other mints.

If one quarters the region (west and east Norfolk, west and east Suffolk) the numbers tend to be too small to be statistically useful. London coins are conspicuous in east Suffolk (33 per cent), and Stamford coins in west Norfolk (17 per cent). Norwich coins,

Mint	*Thetford*	*Norfolk* W	*Norfolk* E	*Suffolk* W	*Suffolk* E	*Total*
Thetford	7(29%)	2	6(20%)	1	2	18(16%)
Norwich	1(4%)	4(17%)	6(20%)	2(13%)	-	13(12%)
Ipswich	-	-	-	-	2	2
Bury	1	1	-	-	-	2
London	7(29%)	7(24%)	5(17%)	1	6(33%)	26(23%)
Lincoln	4(17%)	1	2	12	1	10(9%)
York	1	-	2	1	1	5
Stamford	-	4(17%)	2	2	1	9(8%)
Cambridge	-	1	2	1	-	4
Northampton	-	-	-	1	1	2
Other mints	3	4	5	4	4(22%)	20(18%)
Total	24	24	30	15	18	111

TABLE. Single finds from East Anglia, by mints of origin, to show variations within the region.

naturally enough, are most plentiful in east Norfolk (20 per cent). And it looks as if a similar proportion of the currency of Norwich may have entered the town via the east-coast shipping route. One's impression (but the figures are barely statistically adequate to support it) is that Thetford had a more widespread network of contacts than Norwich.

Otherwise, there are no visible local concentrations or unexpected mints which might be significant, except perhaps the four coins of Lincoln among the Thetford finds. Cambridge coins, which might be associated with the abbey of Ely, are not noticeable in the liberties which Eadgar granted to the abbey in East Anglia. (But in the case of the Wicklaw hundreds, the geld was surrendered by Ely to the crown; and the Thingoe hundreds were granted to Bury *en bloc* only in 1043-4.)

How does the mint-representation in the hoards compare with that among the single finds? The available sample from the Ipswich (Buttermarket) hoard has 31 per cent of Ipswich coins. The little Polstead hoard comprised coins from Lincoln, Norwich, Wallingford, and (?)London, thus 25 per cent East Anglian. Bowthorpe falls into a different pattern, as it consisted of three coins, all of the nearby Norwich mint. The multi-type Thwaite hoard(s) are full of interest, with London coins, and East Anglian coins, in proportions which hint at the activities of a merchant using money that was 'close to source' (see the discussion in section 16 above). The Norwich (Garlands) hoard, with 5 Norwich coins out of 9, may fall into the same category. The Cranwich find of Northampton coins doubtless reflects a traveller's hoard.

One may mention, finally, that the 'City' hoard of 1872 (section 21) is another complex multi-type hoard, with distinct East Anglian affinities.

Single finds. Norfolk . Ashwellthorpe, Attlebridge, Bawsey (¼), Bracon Ash, Caister-on-Sea (½), Caistor-by-Norwich, Castle Acre (2 + ½), Castle Rising, Colkirk (½), Congham (1 + ½), Cranwich (3, incl. mini-hoard), Croxton, East Bradenham (2, mini-hoard?), East Harling (1 + ½), East Walton, Great Yarmouth, Hempnall, Holme Hale, Kenninghall, Kirby Cane (¼), Long Sutton, Marham (¼), Merton, Methwold Hythe, Middle Harling (3 + ¼), Mundham, North Lopham, Norwich (8, incl. a mini-hoard?), Oxborough (3 x ¼), Pulham Market, Quidenham, Riddlesworth, Ringstead, Rockland (2), Roydon, Shipdham, Southery,

5. EAST ANGLIA
Norfolk and Suffolk

South Lopham, Surlingham, Swaffham (1 + ¼), Thetford (29, incl. 8 x ½ and 3 x ¼), Tivetshall St Mary, Walpole St Peter, West Harling, West Rudham (½), West Walton (2 + 2 x ½), Weybourne, Wreningham.

Suffolk. Barham (½), Bramford, Brandon (4 + ½), Bredfield (½), Bromeswell (½, ¼), Bury St. Edmunds (2), Coddenham (½), Gosbeck, Ipswich (7 + ½), Ixworth (3), Lakenheath, Mildenhall, Polstead, Stowmarket, Sudbury, Tuddenham St Martin, Wetheringsett (¼), Whepstead, Winston.

Hoards from East Anglia (with validity-periods). Ipswich (2A), Bury St Edmunds 1873 (3), Bury St Edmunds 1993 (3), Thetford (3), Great Barton (4), Polstead (9), Bowthorpe (12), Thwaite (13?, 16), Norwich? (17), Norwich (Garlands) (24), Cranwich (27), East Bradenham? (30)

Mints. Norwich. Although Norwich was the dominant regional mint from the time of the English reconquest of East Anglia (917), its role was shared, from the initiation of Eadgar's reform, with Thetford. Norwich contributed a steady two to three per cent of the national output, from the work of around half-a-dozen moneyers. The destruction of the town in 1004 seems to have caused only a very brief interruption in minting. In Quatrefoil the number of moneyers rises, quite exceptionally, to 14 or 15, but the share remains normal (2.82 per cent). Under Edward the Confessor there is a slight decline, with a virtual intermission in Trefoil and Short Cross (*c.*1046—*c.*1050), after which the complement of moneyers returns to 4 or 5, and relative output rises.

Thetford. It seems that Thetford was newly created as a mint, to implement the reform; the attribution of a couple (only) of pre-reform coins to the mint is uncertain. A single moneyer, Ælfgar, used just three dies under Eadgar (cf. Norwich, where each of four moneyers is known from a single die-combination). From three regular moneyers in Hand, Thetford jumped to 15 at an intermediate date in Crux, although without any equally dramatic jump in their combined share of national output. By the time of Edward the Confessor, Thetford enjoyed a settled régime as a six-moneyer mint. Freeman has argued that on four occasions in the reign, Norwich supplied moneyers to Thetford, in particular from Sovereign/Martlets onwards. There seems to have been some sort of administrative link between the two mints, but its nature is not clear.

Ipswich. At the moment of Eadgar's reform, Ipswich completes a triad of East Anglian mints, with Norwich and Thetford. Like Thetford, it seems to be a new creation. Like Norwich and Thetford, but even more so, it shows a dramatic increase in the numbers of surviving specimens (96), in First Hand: this may partly reflect the Ipswich hoard, on top of a national trend in the quantities of English money hoarded in Scandinavia. Nevertheless, there is also an exceptional number of moneyers at Ipswich in First Hand (9, but only one in Second Hand), suggestive of special circumstances. It is argued above (section 2A, First Hand) that the Ipswich hoard is from no later than 985, whereas the ravaging of Ipswich was in 991. Five Ipswich moneyers in First Hand are represented in the hoard, in proportions which are unremarkable. Many coins in the hoard were fire-damaged, and Dolley suggests that only 100—120 were in good condition. Of these, perhaps 30 or at most 40 were of Ipswich. Ipswich's share of the national output was unusually low in Crux, possibly because the town had not recovered fully.

Freeman makes a case for saying that Ipswich was a four-moneyer mint from the beginning of Expanding Cross.

Sudbury. It is curious that Sudbury was not more important as a mint-place, in view of its borough status and its regional location. At the time of the Domesday Survey its population was substantial, perhaps 700 or more. But it had no access to the sea. The correct attribution as between Southwark (whose coins read either SVDG(eweorc) or SVDB(yrig)) and Sudbury (which can only read SVDB or SVD) has been a stumbling-block and remains to some extent problematic. It seems that in Last Small Cross and Quatrefoil there was a co-ordinated attempt to distinguish the two mints, e.g. as SVG and SVD respectively. It should be possible to draw up a list of Sudbury moneyers. Jonsson gives 8, of whom only Brunman has a namesake at Southwark. On this assessment the mint is almost completely inactive until Quatrefoil (4 moneyers, but only 0.38 per cent of the national output). In the following Helmet type three moneyers are recorded, but the output is trivial. The mint then lay inactive or almost so for a quarter-century, until a moneyer Folcwine struck very small quantities of coins through a succession of types, from *c.*1055 to *c.*1070. Domesday Book refers to moneyers at Sudbury.

Evidently access to the trade of the North Sea, which Sudbury lacked, was the main stimulus to mint-activity.

Bury St Edmunds. The presence of a moneyer Morcere from *c.*1048 to *c.*1065 may reflect the royal grant of abbatial jurisdiction in west Suffolk from *c.*1044. The demand for Morcere's services was minimal.

'*Wilton*'. A rare variety in Last Small Cross is attributed to an East Anglian mint, on the basis of a die-link with Thetford (*SCBI Copenhagen* 1198). Hockwold-cum-Wilton has been conjectured as the location.

'*Dyr*' / '*Dernt*' *and* '*Derne*'. It is probable, but not entirely certain, that these mint-signatures refer to the same place. Suffolk is in any case the most plausible location for both of them. 'Dyr' has been searched for not too far from Ipswich, on the basis of an obverse die-link. Minting was confined to the Short Cross type (*c.*1048-50). 'Derne' and 'Dernt' are also tied to Ipswich, by the shared moneyer Wulfsige, who may subsequently have moved to Norwich. The evidence of the Thwaite hoard (from which the 'Dyr' coins come) for the attribution should be assessed in the context of the hoard's character, on which see section 16, Short Cross. The numismatic evidence, which is complicated, is fully discussed by Freeman.

The location of the mint (Darnford?, Darsham?) is conjectural. Its coins are extremely scarce.

References.

J.C. Sadler, *A History of the Ipswich Mint and its Saxon and Norman Moneyers*, 1976.

R. Seaman, 'The mint of Ipswich'. *NCirc* 85 (1977), 49-50, and cf. ibid., 151-2.

R.A.G.Carson, 'The mint of Thetford', *NC*[6]9 (1949), 189-236; ibid. 15(1955), 243-5.

V. Smart, on the attribution of coins to Sudbury or Southwark: *SCBI* vol 28 (*Cumulative Index, vols. 1-20*), p. 105, s.v. Southwark.

R.H.M. Dolley, 'The sack of Wilton in 1003 and the chronology of the Long Cross and Helmet types of Æthelred II, *NNUM* 1954, 152, 152-6, for the coin of the East Anglian Wilton; and Glendining, 12 May 1971, lot 917 (the F. Elmore Jones collection).

R.H.M. Dolley, 'A new late Saxon mint in Suffolk', *NCirc* 68 (1960), 236.

F.E. Jones, 'The mysterious mint of 'Dernt', *BNJ* 31 (1962), 66-8.

K.A. Jacob, 'The mint of Wilton–in East Anglia?', *Seaby Coin and Medal Bulletin* 1983, 119.

6. THE MIDDLE DANELAW

Mint-towns: Bedford, Cambridge, Huntingdon, Northampton, Peterborough (Medeshamstead); (Stamford)

The four shires governed from Bedford, Cambridge, Huntingdon, and Northampton represent the territory settled by four sections of the Danish army of King Guthrum. Hart groups them together under the term, the 'outer Danelaw', to draw attention to their general dependency on East Anglia. Edward the Elder alienated many estates in Bedfordshire and Huntingdonshire and gave them to English thegns, but in Cambridgeshire and Northamptonshire Danish landowners were permitted to remain (Hart, *The Danelaw*, pp. 10-16).

Each of the four shire-towns had its mint. The English burh of Stamford-south-of-the-river was in Northamptonshire, and it was arguably there that the Stamford moneyers worked, rather than in the Danish burh north of the river. But Stamford was a special case. It has been discussed above (section 3, The Five Boroughs). The minting privileges of the abbot of Peterborough, at Stamford, were probably just a matter of proximity and convenience, and not a proof that the minting activity of Stamford belonged administratively to Northamptonshire. From the time of the reform the four shires of the Middle Danelaw were effectively one-mint shires. Together they accounted for about 3.6 per cent of the national output, with Cambridge and Northampton clearly in the lead. Among 35 single finds, only 4, or 11 per cent, were minted within the region: one Bedford coin from Bedfordshire, among 5, one Cambridge coin from Cambridgeshire, among 12, and two Northampton coins from Northamptonshire, among 11. It follows that most of the coins minted locally left the region in one way or another, otherwise the share of the national currency in the region would have been 3.6 x 35 ÷ 4, or *c*.32 per cent, which is clearly a nonsense.

Of the remaining 31 finds, 9 were from London, 6 from Stamford, and 5 from Lincoln. Only 2 were from south of the Thames.

Hoards from the region are heavily concentrated in Northamptonshire, and show an intriguing York connection, which is not noticeable in the single finds. Apart from the two York coins from Wellingborough, the Titchmarsh hoard, of nine coins, included five die-duplicates by a York moneyer; the Castor hoard was a large multi-type hoard which seems to have contained as much as 80 or 85 per cent of York coins, and which was undoubtedly put together in Yorkshire. The Harewood hoard, from Yorkshire, demonstrates a link with Northamptonshire in the opposite direction.

The Scaldwell hoard, from near Northampton, contained at least 60 coins by the Northampton moneyer Saewine, or a quarter of the hoard.

Single finds from the Middle Danelaw. *Bedfordshire:* Biggleswade, Dunstable, Roxton, Southill (2).

Cambridgeshire: Bassingbourne (½), Cambridge, Ely (1 + ½), Fulbourn (½), Horseheath, Ickleton, Isleham, Knapwell, Papworth (½), Shepreth, Soham, Yelling.

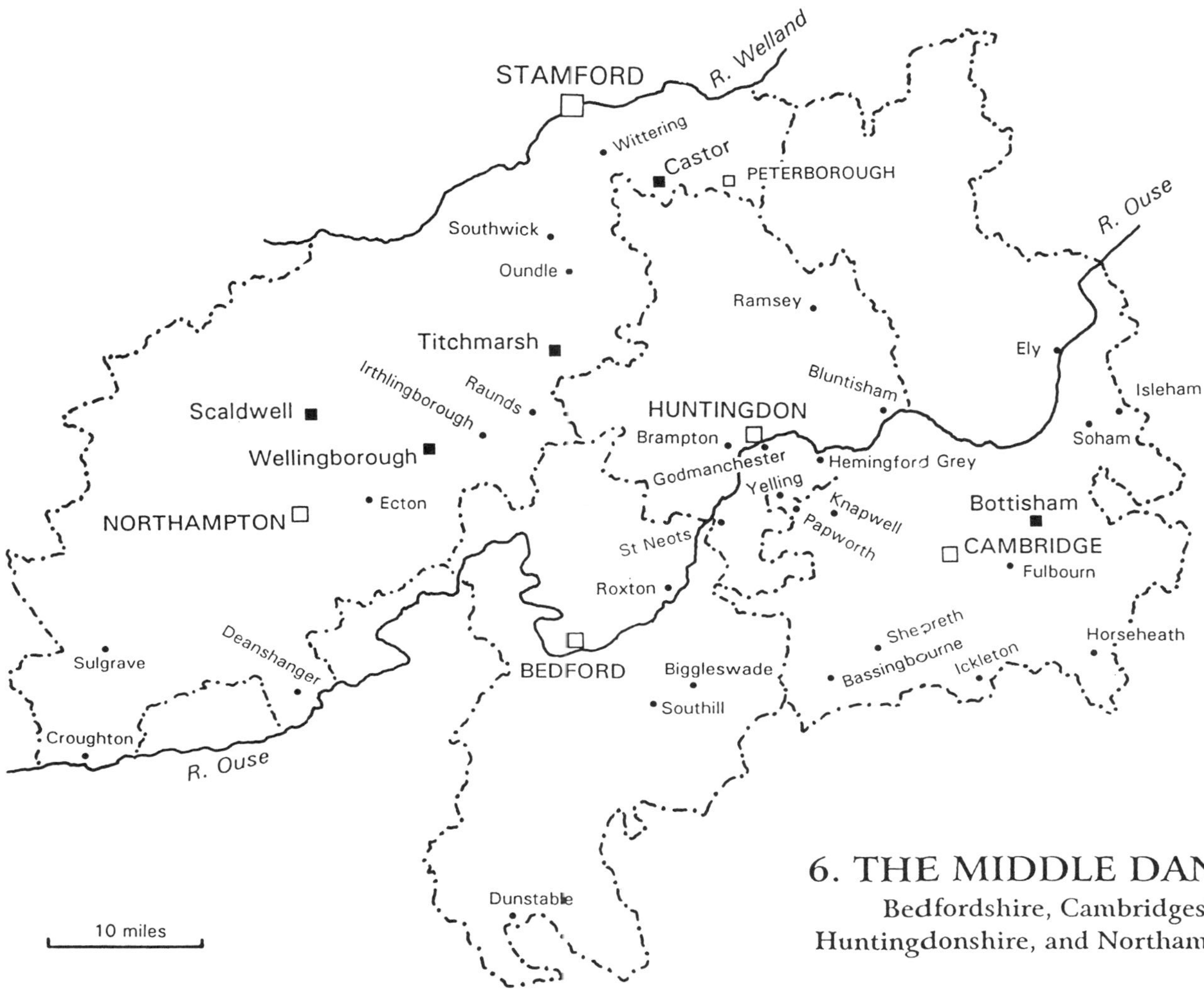

6. THE MIDDLE DANELAW

Bedfordshire, Cambridgeshire, Huntingdonshire, and Northamptonshire

Huntingdonshire: Bluntisham, Brampton, Godmanchester (½), Hemingford Grey, Huntingdon, Ramsey, St. Neots. *Northamptonshire*: Croughton, Deanshanger, Ecton, Irthlingborough, Northampton, Oundle, Peterborough (2), Raunds, Southwick, Sulgrave, Wellingborough (mini-hoard?), Wittering (½).

Hoards from the Middle Danelaw (with validity-periods). Wellingborough, Nth (8), Bottisham, Ca (9), Titchmarsh, Nth (11), Castor, Nth (23), Scaldwell, Nth (28). See also Harewood, Y (22).

Mints. Bedford. Bedford, which had been an active mint-place in the second half of the tenth century, declined somewhat after the Reform validity-period, but still often had three or more moneyers.

Cambridge. Cambridge, of which the urban functions in the eleventh century have been assessed as 'an agricultural community, as primitive as any county borough could be', contributed to Eadgar's coinage reform, but in a very small way. It sprang to prominence part-way through Crux, when the number of moneyers was suddenly increased to 11. A thorough survey of the mint's output has been published by Jacob.

Huntingdon. Huntingdon seems to have begun work only in First Hand, although a Reform coin might, of course, still turn up.

Northampton. Northampton was particularly active in implementing the reform (initially with dies supplied from Winchester, and subsequently partly from Lincoln). Throughout the Reform type, its coins are on average unusually light, at *c.*1.34g or even less. One wonders whether this was something to do with the place, and whether its monetary affairs could have been dominated, e.g. by a market in hides or other cattle products.

Peterborough. The abbot of Medehamstede enjoyed minting rights, granted just before the reform, when Eadgar gave him one moneyer at Stamford. The abbot's coins, bearing the Stamford mint-signature, were evidently distinguished (sometimes or always?) by the addition of an annulet. This hypothesis has been much debated, in particular because during the Reform type not one but six Stamford moneyers (out of 20) strike coins with an annulet (or in one case an erased annulet). In First Small Cross more than half the known Stamford dies are apparently the abbot's. Jonsson comments that the only possible explanation would be to postulate exceptional conditions connected with construction works on the abbey. There is no record of any such works. The church, ruined and desolate, had been rebuilt between *c.*966 and 972, when it was handed over to Abbot Ealdulf, who renounced a worldly career as Eadgar's 'chancellor' to become a Benedictine monk and, eventually (992), archbishop of York. If Medeshamstede enjoyed special monetary privileges, it may have been mainly because Ealdulf was familiar with the corridors of power. When set against the budget of an institution like Medeshamstede, the profits of one moneyer were an utterly trifling contribution.

Under Edward the Martyr, three of the 63 specimens listed by Wells have an annulet. The majority of specimens of Æthelred's First Small Cross type have an annulet, but none is recorded among 47 specimens in First Hand. In that type the Stamford moneyer Hild strikes a (currently unique) coin, of which only part of the mint-signature (*Meth...*) is preserved. Dolley reports an early record of another coin of Æthelred, now missing, with *Methel* or *Methes*, by the Stamford moneyer who signs *Wulstan* at just this time. It seems clear that there was virtually no demand for the moneyer's services at Peterborough itself.

Precedents were not to be lightly relinquished, even if they were not immediately very profitable. An annulet is very occasionally found on Stamford coins of the Long Cross type. The only other coins openly of Peterborough are in Cnut's Quatrefoil type. The annulet reappears after the Conquest.

Part of the case is that annulets at other mints should also be capable of interpretation as ecclesiastical symbols. York throughout the reign of Edward the Confessor almost always adds an annulet. It has been suggested above (section 1, Yorkshire) that the profits of the mint were conceded to the archbishop. Closer to the debate about Peterborough, in First Small Cross, one of the two recorded coins of Tamworth has an annulet, as has the only recorded coin of Worcester.

On the other hand, mints where the bishop is stated in the Domesday Survey to have had a moneyer, such as Hereford or Norwich, did not strike specially identifiable coins.

The only possibly relevant Stamford single find from the Middle Danelaw region is without the annulet, and the two recorded finds from Peterborough are of the Lincoln and London mints.

References.

K.A. Jacob, 'The mint of Cambridge', *Seaby Coin and Medal Bulletin* 1984, 34-43, 72-6.

W.C. Wells, 'The Stamford and Peterborough mints', *BNJ* 22 (1934-7), 35-77; 23 (1938-41), 7-28; 24 (1941-4), 69-109.

R.H.M. Dolley, 'A new Anglo-Saxon mint—Medeshamstede', *BNJ* 27 (1952-4), 263-5.

7. ESSEX, HERTFORDSHIRE, AND BUCKINGHAMSHIRE

Mint-towns: Colchester, Hertford, Buckingham; Aylesbury, Horndon, Maldon, Newport (Pagnell?)

For the relatively short period of a generation or two, the lands of the Danish conquest extended as far as the River Thames and its estuary, in the three shires grouped together by Hart as the 'southern Danelaw'. This region of just over two million acres, in which the traces left by Danish control are lighter than elsewhere in the Danelaw, surrounds London and its environs (discussed separately below).

It seems as if London sucked the adjoining districts dry of money: at least, there are few single finds from north of the Thames within a radius of 25 miles of the city. The recorded finds are mostly from Colchester and eastern Essex, or (at the other end of the region) from the Chilterns and the clay plain beyond.

Among 18 attributable single finds, only one was minted in the region (at Colchester). The others are of London (8), York (3), Stamford, Lincoln, Thetford, Lympne (2) and Christchurch. The proportion of London coins is as high as in London itself, and there is a surprisingly strong representation from York, Lincoln, and Stamford, whereas nearer mints are not represented in the sample. Did the northern coins reach the southern Danelaw by sea, via London? —But the finds from London itself are not overweight in northern coins. Nor are the northern coins chiefly from Essex: find-spots include Tring (Herts) and Stoke Mandeville (Bucks), together with (?)Hambleden (Bucks).

As for the two coins of Lympne, from Aveley and West Mersea, perhaps one should suspend judgement on what may be just a statistical quirk.

The only hoard from the region is the little Welwyn hoard, of four coins, dated by a Winchester coin of Edward the Martyr. The survival in the hoard of two pre-reform coins may be not unconnected with the general emptiness of the monetary landscape in the southern Danelaw.

Single finds. Essex: Aveley (½), Chelmsford, Colchester, Great Wakering, 'North Essex' (4), Rochford, Takeley, Tiptree, West Mersea. *Hertfordshire*: Bovingdon, Much Hadham, Tring, Welwyn, Weston. *Buckinghamshire*: Aylesbury, (?)Hambleden, Little Horwood, Stoke Mandeville.

Mints. Colchester. Minting was initiated at Colchester in the Crux type, by a London moneyer Sweting, striking on the heaviest standard. Part-way through the type there was a dramatic expansion of activity, involving altogether 14 moneyers, and producing 2.7 per cent of the national output. Thereafter Colchester usually produced a half to one per cent of the national total. The historical context of this blip has been explored by Metcalf and Lean, with particular attention to the battle of Maldon. Under Edward the Confessor there were normally four or five moneyers at Colchester.

Hertford. The sole mint-place of its shire, Hertford had a similar history of minting to Colchester. It was a one-moneyer mint in the Reform and First Hand types, and then showed a burst of activity in Crux, with a dozen moneyers. Thereafter its share of the national output was on a par with

7. THE SOUTHERN DANELAW
Essex, Hertfordshire, and Buckinghamshire

Colchester's, or a little lower. In several types Hertford contributed less than a quarter of one per cent. Its complement of four moneyers declined, part-way through Edward the Confessor's reign, to one or two.

Buckingham. The shire town minted on a minimal scale from the Reform type onwards. It showed no special activity in the Crux type. Under Edward one moneyer worked, perhaps intermittently. A corpus of coins of the mint includes 36 specimens, from 24 obverse and 23 reverse dies.

Aylesbury. Aylesbury had two moneyers in Crux and four in Quatrefoil. Under Edward it was a one-moneyer mint-place, possibly sharing its moneyer, Leofwine, with Buckingham. An earlier link with Buckingham is exemplified by a variety of Crux with diadem and sceptre.

Horndon-on-the-Hill. A unique coin of Edward's Sovereign/Martlets type, reading DVDINC ON HORNIDVNE, seems to be genuine. It comes from the St. Mary Hill hoard.

Maldon. Maldon works in the Reform and First Hand types, presumably as the mint for Essex, and thereafter with one, two, or three moneyers and an output similar to or lower than that of Hertford.

Newport (Pagnell?). Half-a-dozen coins exist from a mint-place signing *Niweporte,* in the period *c.*1053-62. Newport Pagnell has been suggested mainly because it was a borough. Newport in Essex has also been canvassed. The arguments for the attribution are set out fully in *BNJ* 1993.

References

D.M. Metcalf and W. Lean, 'The battle of Maldon and the minting of Crux pennies in Essex: *post hoc propter hoc?*', in J. Cooper (editor), *The Battle of Maldon. Fiction and Fact,* 1993, pp. 205-24

R.H.M. Dolley, D.J. Elliott, and F.E. Jones, 'The Buckingham mint', *BNJ* (1965), 46-52.

M.A.S. Blackburn, M.J. Bonser, and W.J. Conte, 'A new type of Edward the Confessor for the "Newport" mint', *BNJ* 63 (1993), 125-6.

8. LONDON AND ENVIRONS

Mint-towns: London, Southwark

No fewer than sixty single finds are on record from London, from a dozen different sites. Many of the coins are from controlled archaeological excavations, and the reliability of the evidence as a random sample is generally very good. The material has been carefully published by Stott.

The bulk of the material is from waterfront sites, along a mile-long zone of land reclamation. Early finds from the foreshore, from London Bridge, and from St Katharine's Dock fall into a context which is now much better understood from recent excavations, particularly on the Billingsgate and Thames Exchange sites.

The chronological distribution of the finds through the eleventh century is difficult to judge. There seems to be a difference of emphasis between the Billingsgate and the Thames Exchange finds. The latter are biassed towards William I, possibly because the reclamation of the site, or the intensity of commercial use, was later than on the Billingsgate site. Even there, coins of Eadgar to Æthelred II are under-represented in comparison with miscellaneous sites (mostly modern excavations) elsewhere in the City. One should hesitate, therefore, to identify any trend on the basis of the single finds, but if one had to guess, one would say that there was a decline in the numbers of stray losses after 1035, Billingsgate and Thames Exchange notwithstanding.

For the period up to 1042 there are 25 finds of which the mints can be identified. Of these, 12, or 48 per cent, are coins minted in London. The rest are from ten different mints, and 8 of them are from south of the Thames. There are 2 coins of Lincoln, and one each of Derby and Nottingham. No coins have so far been recorded from the Southwark mint, none from East Anglia, and none from York. In a sample of 25, mints or regions which took *c*.4 per cent of the national output have an even chance of being represented by one find. Thus, the margins of statistical uncertainty are still quite wide.

From the period after 1042 there are 20 finds, of which only 6, or 30 per cent, were minted in London. Of the rest, 7 out of 14 are from south of the Thames. There are 3 coins from Lincoln, one from Thetford, one from Colchester, one from Maldon, and one from Nottingham. Again, there are no finds recorded from the Southwark mint, nor from York. Thus there is no statistically significant difference between the two periods, and there is no hint, in the list of mints, of any shift in London's regional contacts.

It is really only during the Crux type that one might have expected to see, in a medium-sized sample, Southwark coins mingling with London coins in the currency north of the Thames. In that validity-period the ratio was close to one to two, so that Southwark might be expected to show up among even just half a dozen London site-finds. Otherwise Southwark coins averaged one to twenty or one to thirty London coins. Thus there are not nearly enough London coins in our sample for the absence of Southwark coins to be significant, nor is there any obvious reason for the Scandinavian sample (on which our expectations are based) to be distorted.

From Westminster Abbey there are two single finds, both of German coins. Although they constitute only a tiny sample, they probably reflect a real difference between Westminster and London.

The hoards from London and its environs are numerous and rich, particularly in the later eleventh century. Most of them were concealed almost within a stone's-throw of the river, and reinforce the impression of a waterfront context for intensive commercial and monetary activity. From the reign of Æthelred II there are the Chelsea Reach hoard, Isleworth, Honey Lane, and St. Martins-le-Grand. Isleworth and Honey Lane seem to be more or less typical of the currency of London, as revealed by the single finds, while Chelsea Reach may be incoming money, and St Martins-le-Grand is a special case, with heavy die-linking. From the reign of Edward the Confessor, the Thwaite, Suffolk hoard appears to have a London origin. The Gracechurch Street and 'City' (or Walbrook) hoards (section 21) are multi-type hoards, as is—under William I—the St Mary Hill hoard. These are large or very large hoards of great complexity and interest, which raise difficult questions about the age-structure of the currency. On a simple view one may think of their context as the capital of wealthy merchants trading with, for example, East Anglia. The proportion of London coins in these hoards is generally less than half, and perhaps tends to be below what was typical in the currency of London. They deserve to be studied and compared type by type.

Mints. London. A large number of moneyers worked in London. In types with a high output there were, for example, 47 moneyers operating during the Crux validity-period, 64 during Last Small Cross, and 68 during Quatrefoil. All these men and their supporting staff did not work in a single large factory complex, as they probably began to do in the later twelfth century. Pamela Nightingale comments that 'Cheap, the commercial centre of the city, was an obvious place for a mint and an exchange, and that part of Cheap near St Paul's where it is joined by Friday Street seems a likely moneying quarter since Friday Street was where the goldsmiths were concentrated'.

In contrast with the Anglo-Scandinavian mint-towns of the Danelaw, where a significant proportion of the moneyers have Old Norse names, the London moneyers are overwhelmingly of English background.

London's share of the national output was usually *c.*20 to *c.*30 per cent throughout the late Anglo-Saxon period (with which one may compare *c.*40 per cent in the currency of the city), declining to *c.*10 per cent at the time of Domesday. The exceptions, or apparent exceptions, are the Reform type, where the Lincoln-based Scandinavian estimate is a mere 7 per cent, and Second Hand, where it is 42 per cent. The estimated numbers of dies (and the source of the dies, initially Winchester) go a long way to confirm that the reform was implemented properly at London only in the Hand types: the numbers of dies jump from 70 to 965. Thereafter the share tends to remain fairly steady, whether London's moneyers were using a thousand pairs of dies in a validity-period (as in Quatrefoil) or only 50 to 100 (as in the second half of the century).

Pamela Nightingale has explored the influence on London of the Danish conquest, when Cnut made the city the headquarters of his permanent naval and military forces. 'The need to pay these mercenaries', she suggests, 'made the city the centre of a monetary and tax system which introduced new elements of centralization into the government of the kingdom'. London's status in the kingdom rose, in relation to Winchester's. We may ask ourselves whether these claims are borne out

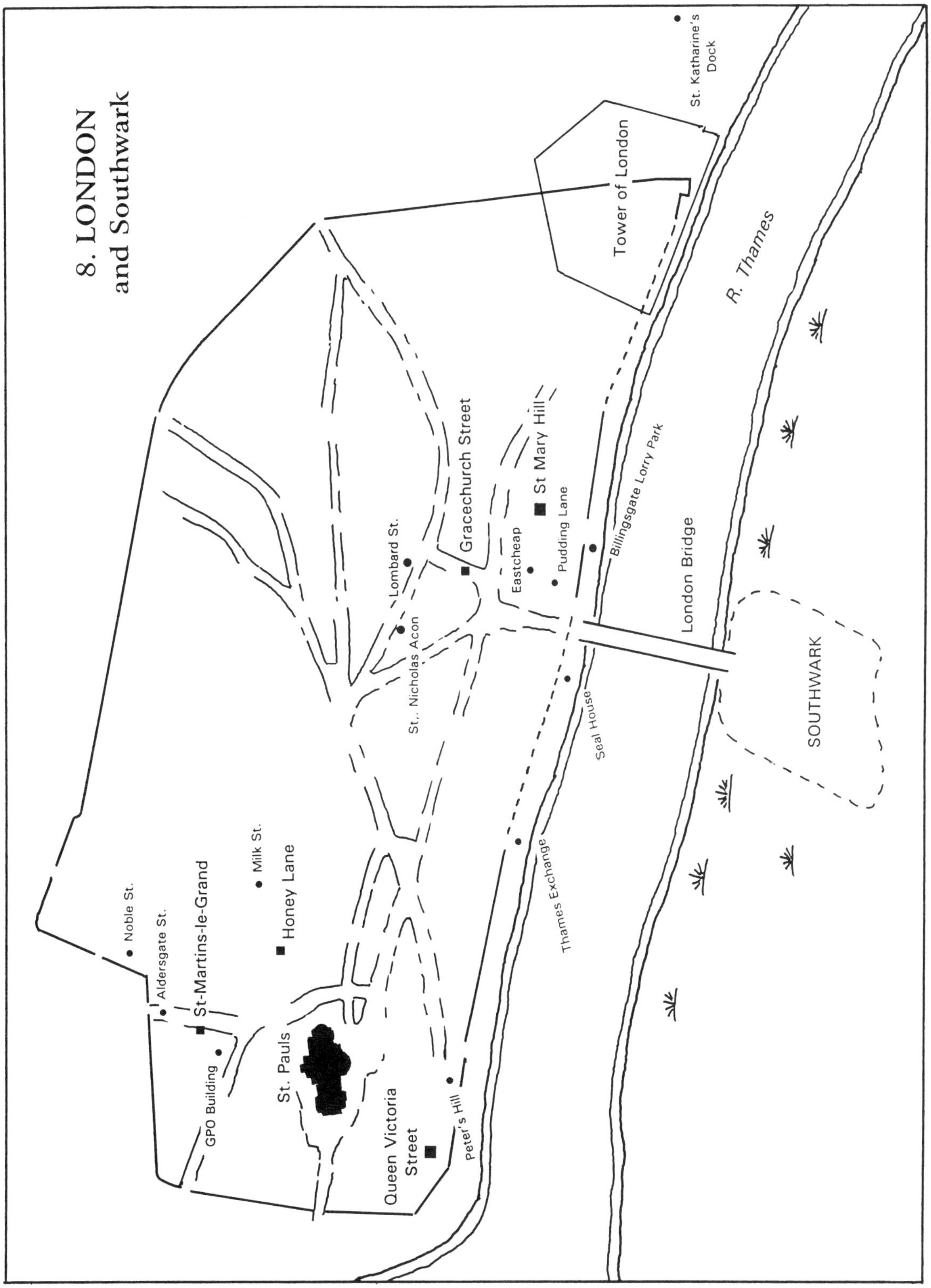
8. LONDON
and Southwark
Tower of London
St. Katharine's Dock
R. Thames
Gracechurch Street
St Mary Hill
Lombard St.
Eastcheap
Pudding Lane
Billingsgate Lorry Park
London Bridge
SOUTHWARK
St.. Nicholas Acon
Seal House
Thames Exchange
Milk St.
Honey Lane
Noble St.
Aldersgate St.
St-Martins-le-Grand
GPO Building
St. Pauls
Queen Victoria Street
Peter's Hill

by, or find a reflection in, the statistics of mint-output. London's share of the national output does indeed rise to 33 per cent in Cnut's Helmet type (*c.*1023-4 to *c.*1029-30), but apart form that one validity-period there is no long-term upward trend (see the Appendix, below), and no significant change in the share before and after 1016. Nor is there any evidence of a significant shift in the circulation-patterns of London coins, or of coins in London, in the short term before and after 1016. Dr Nightingale rightly comments that there is nothing to suggest that the Danes contributed significantly to the economic growth of London or that the kingdom's incorporation into Cnut's northern empire gave a new and more prosperous direction to its trade.

Southwark. For a long time there was uncertainty about the attribution of coins as between Southwark and Sudbury. It is now generally agreed that Southwark used two signatures, Suthgewerc (unambiguously) and Suthbyrig. A few coins reading Suthbyrig belong to Suffolk, but most are certainly from Southwark. There is a long list of moneyers who use both forms, and there are not a few die-links. Southwark is listed in the Burghal Hidage, but later in the middle ages it was notably not a borough.

Southwark was erected into a mint-place in the Crux type, and produced a dramatic 8 per cent of the national output, against London's 18 per cent. This was quite unnatural, in the sense that it did not correspond with the commercial realities (see section 3). Its natural share, thereafter, was closer to one per cent, with a slight tendency to move contrarily to London. Southwark was much busier than usual in Quatrefoil, as many small mints were. The pattern was dramatically modified in William's Paxs type, when Southwark used between 20 and 30 obverse dies, and probably twice as many reverses. Its output may have been half as great as was minted across the river in London, or even more than half. The reason is not yet clear.

References.

P. Stott, 'Saxon and Norman coins from London', in A. Vince (editor), *Finds and Environmental Evidence* (=*Aspects of Saxon-Norman London*, vol.2), London and Middlesex Archaeological Society, Special Paper 12, 1991, pp. 279-325.

P. Nightingale, 'Some London moneyers, and reflections on the organization of English mints in the eleventh and twelfth centuries', *NC* 142 (1982), 34-50.

K. Steedman, T. Dyson, and J. Schofield, *The Bridgehead and Billingsgate to 1200* (Aspects of Saxo-Norman London, vol. 3), 1992.

M.M. Archibald, J.R.S. Lang, and G. Milne, 'Four early medieval coin dies from the London waterfront', *NC* 155 (1995), 165-200.

J. Bird *et al* (editors), *Southwark Excavations , 1972-1974*, 3 vols, 1979-.

P. Nightingale, 'The origin of the Court of Husting and Danish influence on London's development into a capital city', *English Historical Review* 102 (1987), 559-78.

9. SOUTH MERCIA (AND SOUTH WALES)

Mint-towns: Gloucester, Hereford, Oxford, Warwick, Worcester; Berkeley, Bristol, Droitwich, Pershore, Winchcombe; Cardiff, St. Davids (?)

Five shires to the north of the River Thames, and under Mercian law, formed a region of rich agriculture and animal husbandry, where the output of the local mints was nevertheless only moderate, and single finds are relatively few. Gloucestershire, Herefordshire, Oxfordshire, Warwickshire, and Worcestershire include the old territory of the Hwicce. Oxford is the most active of the five shire mints, which together usually account for 4 to 5 per cent of the national output, and it is around Oxford that the single finds are most plentiful. Of the mints outside the shire towns, Bristol was of growing importance in the second half of the eleventh century, but Berkeley and Pershore had a minimal output. Winchcombe was for a time the caput of its own shire, certainly by 1007 and (Finberg suggested) probably from that date. His conclusion relied partly on his view that there was a general administrative revision in that year, by which the west midlands shires were created or formalized. The numismatic evidence is clear that the five shire towns of south Mercia all minted already in the Reform type, and that they were the only mints in the region. But there are Reform coins also, which have been attributed to Winchcombe. (All six except Worcester, curiously, are known to have begun to strike the reformed coins under Eadgar. Worcester had been a major centre of royal administration, and one might have expected it to be at the forefront of the reform. Its early coins could, of course, still turn up.) Bassett has argued that Winchcombeshire had a long prehistory as a *regio* which was the demesne and patrimony of the Hwiccian kings, and subsequently was the private property of the Mercian kings. As regards Winchcombe in the late tenth century, then, (it certainly minted in Crux), it may be that the coins are the best evidence of its administrative status: the date 1007 is in no way sacrosanct, and the attribution of the two specimens of the Reform type reading WENCLES to Winchcombe is not administratively impossible, even if there was no shire as such in 973-5.

The currency of the region was considerably larger than what its mints supplied, being drawn in from Wessex, London, and elsewhere. There seems to have been a gradient from east to west, of declining monetization. There are few finds recorded from Herefordshire; and Worcester stands out in its shire, in a degree of isolation. The paucity of finds from the countryside could be partly because a lower porportion of the acreage was under the plough (see Q.1).

There are unusually few cut halfpennies or farthings among the recorded finds (Worcester excepted). Even though the numbers are large enough for this observation to be statistically reliable, one hesitates over it a little, in case there is some unsuspected systematic explanation at the modern end of the chain which leads through loss and finding. None comes to mind, and if there is none, we can say that the evidence hints at a less pervasive money economy in south Mercia.

Single finds from south Mercia (and south Wales). Gloucestershire: Berkeley, Bristol, Cirencester, Colesbourne, Gloucester (2), Painswick, Stow-on-the-Wold. *Herefordshire:* Hereford, Much Marcle. *Oxfordshire*: Benson (2), Blackthorn, Charlbury, Checkendon, Church Hanborough, Elsfield, Eynsham (1 + ½), Middleton Stoney, Oxford (4), Thrupp, Wheatley, Woodeaton. *Warwickshire*: Coleshill, Great Wolford, Harborough Magna, Shipston on Stour, Warwick, Welford-on-Avon (¼), Wixford. *Worcestershire:* Worcester (1 AV, 2, 2 x ½, lead striking, brooch).
South Wales: Cardiff, Llanstephan, St. Davids, St. Lythans.

Hoards from the region (with validity-periods). Monmouth (3), Penrice (5), Gloucester (7), the 'Hereford' hoard (31??).

Single finds are thickest on the ground in Oxfordshire (although this may result partly from fuller recording) and in Gloucestershire, and certainly they are thinnest in Herefordshire.

Coins originating in the region make up only a quarter of the single finds. Shire by shire that proportion would tend to be a little lower. Roughly another quarter entered the region from south of the Thames (with Wallingford, just across the boundary, a special case), another quarter from London and East Anglia, and the rest from the north-west and the north-east (in roughly equal shares).

London is the most plentiful mint (18 per cent). Half-a-dozen finds from Shaftesbury, Winchester, and (especially) Southampton hint at a north-south route to the Channel coast. The Southampton coins, found at Blackthorn (Oxfordshire) and at Worcester, are stronger evidence than those of Winchester, because they are from further away, from an actual port, and because they were issued in much smaller quantities than the Winchester coins. It was only in First Hand and in Quatrefoil that Southampton had a significant output (after which it ceased to mint entirely). Neither of the finds from south Mercia is of a plentiful type.

Note also a coin minted at Wareham under William I, and found at Cirencester, for which a similar context is plausible.

That such an aspect of the evidence should be visible among the single finds would suggest either that trade through Southampton was relatively important for the south Mercian economy, or that the uses of money in the region were less varied than the scale of the currency suggests.

Worcester is the only shire town of the region from which there is a sizeable sample of single finds. That may be by chance, because more archaeological effort has been expended there, or because coins were recovered more successfully from the excavations. The mint-places of the finds are Worcester itself (2, but one is a lead striking, not a coin), Warwick, Southampton, London, and Lincoln. Note that the Southampton influence was apparently not confined to the southern fringes of south Mercia.

If one attempts to dissect the patterns in more detail, the numbers become far too small to be statistically acceptable. It seems, nevertheless, that the northern inflows are predominantly from before 1042. There are hints, too, (naturally enough) of links with the adjoining regions: coins of the Leicester and Tamworth mints in Warwickshire, Wallingford coins concentrated in Oxfordshire, and so on.

South Wales had a land frontier with south Mercia, and there were special arrangements at the Hereford mint to reflect English political and military involvement in Wales. The few single finds from south Wales include one of the Hereford mint, from St Davids. The Monmouth hoard, of a dozen

9. SOUTH MERCIA

Gloucestershire, Herefordshire, Oxfordshire, Warwickshire, and Worcestershire

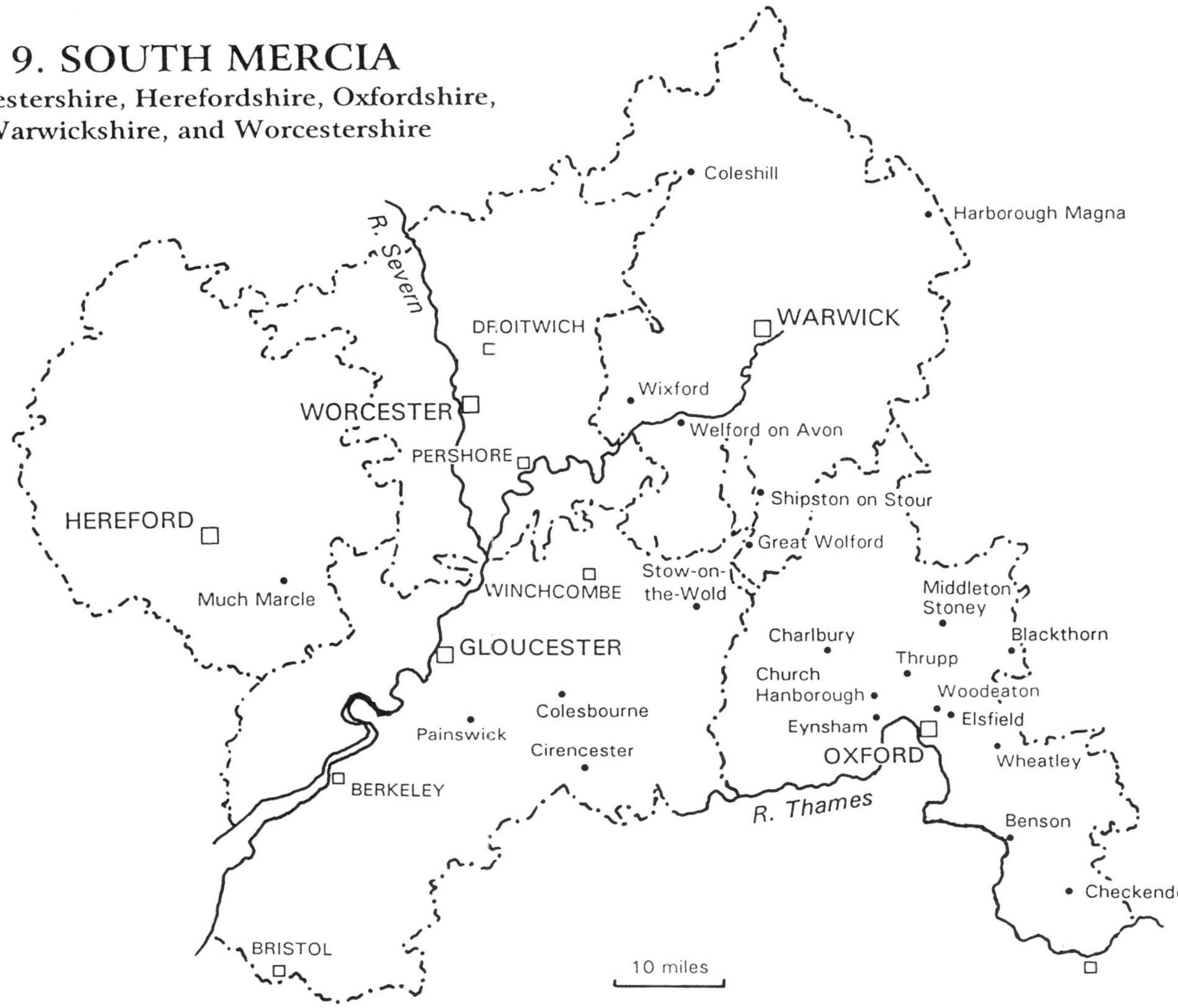

Crux coins, included two of Gloucester and two of Hereford, thus well up to the expected proportion of local coins for south Mercia. Penrice, on the other hand, seems (in so far as its contents are known) to be purely money from the south-west. And the other single finds from south Wales are also probably arrivals from south of Thames (Shaftesbury again, and Lydford).

The composition of the Gloucester (Kingsholm) hoard is not known at all completely, but it seems to have been overweight in the coins of the local mint and of Bath, Langport, Oxford, and Chester.

The 'Hereford' find . A group of coins all of the Hereford mint was offered for sale by Spinks in 1924 (*NCirc*, col. 155-6). A seriously garbled account appears in Thompson's *Inventory*. The coins, described as 'Another find, of the Hereford mint' consists of 12 pennies, ranging from Æthelred's Long Cross (4) and Last Small Cross, through Cnut and Edward the Confessor, to William's Paxs type, plus a coin of Stephen. The mint- and age-structure of the group is thus well-nigh incredible as a hoard or even as a parcel from a hoard, and the information should be accepted with very great reserve, if at all.

Mints. Gloucester. The Domesday Survey records that in 1066 Gloucester rendered £36 together with honey and also iron and iron rods drawn out for making nails for the king's ships. The output of the mint was continuous and essentially steady. Gloucester under Æthelred had two or three moneyers. From Cnut's reign the number grew, but without much effect on the scale of output. It is not clear whether the Scandinavian sample is misleading in this respect.

A detailed survey of the work of the mint is provided by Blunt and Dolley in *SCBI* 19.

Hereford. The Domesday Survey mentions that when the king came into Hereford, the moneyers were to make as many coins for him as he chose—that is, presumably, from the king's own silver and without fee. There may be an echo here of Athelstan's meeting (at Hereford, as Loyn has pointed out) with the Welsh princes, when various kinds of tribute including gold and silver were promised. The Survey adds that the moneyers were also under the obligation to accompany the sheriff on military expeditions into Wales. Whether they went as fighting men or as moneyers is not specified, but the latter seems probable, as we have coins of William I attributable to Cardiff and St Davids, all apparently by the same moneyer, Ælfwine de Turre. In the time of Edward the Confessor, the Survey makes clear, there were seven moneyers at Hereford, of whom one was the bishop's moneyer. From him, the bishop and not the king received the regular 20s. fee when the type was changed.

Eadgar's reform had been implemented at Hereford so far as we know by a single moneyer, Gillys, and it was only in the First Hand type that minting on any scale began.

The coins of the bishop's moneyer are not identifiable by any secret-mark or symbol.

Oxford. Oxford implemented the reform on some scale under Eadgar (using dies supplied from Winchester), and was then almost inactive until the Hand type was introduced. The mint's natural level of activity was evidently lower. It grew gradually during the eleventh century.

Warwick. Warwick minted in almost every type, but on only a small scale. As elsewhere, the numbers of moneyers tended to grow, but without a corresponding increase in output.

Worcester. Worcester was slow to implement the reform, in spite of its old-established administrative importance. Its output was steady, but modest. It signs WIHR, WIHRA, WIHRECE (for *Wihreceastre*) or occasionally WIGR.

Berkeley. Close to the Bristol Channel and 15 miles upstream from Bristol, Berkeley was a mint-place of minimal importance in the period *c.*1048 to *c.*1055, when a moneyer Eadgar worked there, signing BEORC or

BERCLE. Three specimens are recorded. An earlier coin, of the Pacx type (1042—*c.*1045) is of debateable attribution. It is by Ulfketill (a name found at Bedford in the same type) and reads BEO (for BED?) Edward's die-cutters might have been expected to be at pains to use unambiguous signatures for Bedford, Bedwyn, and Berkeley, but the attribution of Ulfketill's coin is perhaps not quite certain.

Bristol. The mint was created essentially for Cnut's Quatrefoil type (although there are rare coins in Last Small Cross). This has been seen as a response to the shifting of the Irish trade away from Chester. The exact timing may also reflect minting policy, in that the output of small and medium-sized mints was exceptional in Quatrefoil. Thereafter the importance of the Bristol mint fluctuated, sometimes exceeding 2 per cent of the national total. In William's Paxs type, it was possibly the most active mint in the south Mercian region.

Droitwich. The importance of Droitwich as the centre of a salt extraction and processing industry, and of the salt-ways along which pack-horses carried the salt, might have led one to expect numismatic evidence to match, in so far as customers are likely to have bought salt for cash. No coins of Droitwich are recorded, however, before *c.*1060, and even then the mint is of minimal importance. The cash that the customers brought was presumably already in the form of English coins, not foreign coins needing to be reminted. For statistical reasons, if no other, its coins do not show up among the stray finds.

A group of just a dozen surviving specimens by the moneyers Godric and Heathewulf with mint-signatures WIC, WICNEH, etc. has been persuasively attributed to Droitwich (which was a Domesday borough) because it includes the rare variant, Edward Type xiv (Pyramids with facing bust) known from Cricklade, Worcester, and Tamworth, and because it links into coins by Heathewulf clearly attributable to Worcester and Hereford.

The first known coin is of Hammer Cross, *c.*1059—*c.*1062. The issues continue through Facing Bust, Pyramids and Pax, and are resumed under William I, in Two Sceptres and Two Stars.

Pershore. Among all the hundreds of Hammer Cross coins that have been recorded there is just one, by Wilfric and with the mint-signature PERESC, attributed to Pershore. Pershore was a Domesday borough (cf. also Droitwich). At the time of the Survey it belonged to St Peter's, Westminster, Edward the Confessor having given it to his great church out of his demesne. Whether the grant of minting rights was somehow connected with the Westminster link, or was a sop to the abbot of Pershore for the loss of many of his abbey's endowments to Westminster, is not clear. Freeman sees a pattern in the concurrent appearance of Droitwich and Pershore as mint-places.

Winchcombe. Winchcombe, in the northern Cotswolds, became for a short time a shire town, as the result of an administrative reform in *c.*1007 or earlier (see above), which was revoked in *c.*1017. Coins signed WINCELE or WINCL (for *Wincelcumbe*) were minted from Crux onwards. Paradoxically, no coins are known from the Last Small Cross validity period, which coincides closely with the period when Winchcombe was certainly a shire town. Having acquired minting status, the town retained it until the end of William's reign, in the person of a moneyer Goldwine, who was at work from *c.*1048 onwards. A thorough survey of the mint by Blunt and Dolley will be found in *SCBI* 19.

An earlier origin for the mint rests upon a variety in Eadgar's reform type, known from two specimens, with the signature WENCLES. In light of the unusual activity at Lympne, an attribution to Winchelsea, in Sussex, seems more attractive, although if one rejects 1007 as the start-date for Winchcombeshire, and envisages six shires in south Mercia already in *c.*973, the only real arguments which remain are the letter S in the mint-signature, and the paucity of early coins. (Carlyon-Britton argued that the S was inconclusive.)

For die-duplicate coins of Winchcombe in the Shaftesbury hoard, see Part 3, Section 4.

Cardiff. A penny of William I's Sword type, found in Cardiff Castle grounds, appears to read HEREIII ON CAIERI, and is plausibly attributed to Cardiff —as is a fragment of the succeeding type, reading CA.D.. Boon endorses the view that these coins are to be associated with the building or re-development of Cardiff Castle in 1081.

Then there are three known specimens of the Paxs type, which have long been attributed to Cardiff. One of them is from a re-cut Bristol die. Another bears the double moneyer's name, Ælfwi Turi. Brooke, in *BMC* comments, 'All of very rough, almost barbarous work, similar in style to the coins of St. Davids.'

St. Davids. Boon endorses Brooke's attribution (*BMC* 883ff.), and connects the coins with William's expedition of 1081, when he marched in force to St. Davids and compelled Rhys ap Tewdwr to accept him as liege-lord, with a fee of £40 a year. Dolley, however, sees difficulties, and would prefer to look towards Montgomeryshire for the location of DEVITVN.

References.

H.P.R. Finberg, 'The ancient shire of Winchcombe', in the *The Early Charters of the West Midlands,* Leicester, 1972, pp. 228-35.

S. Bassett, 'In search of the origins of Anglo-Saxon kingdoms', in Bassett (ed.), *The Origins of Anglo-Saxon Kingdoms,* Leicester, 1989, pp. 3-27 at pp. 6-17 (on Winchcombeshire).

D.M. Metcalf, 'The taxation of moneyers under Edward the Confessor and in 1086', in *Domesday Studies,* edited by J.C. Holt, Woodbridge, 1987, pp. 279-93.

P. Rahtz, 'The archaeology of west Mercian towns', in *Mercian Studies,* edited by A. Dornier, Leicester, 1977, pp. 107-29.

L.V. Grinsell, C.E. Blunt, and M. Dolley, *Bristol and Gloucester Museums* (*SCBI* vol. 19), 1973, (Also for Winchcombe and Berkeley.)

L.V. Grinsell, *The History and Coinage of the Bristol Mint,* Bristol, 1986.

G.C. Boon, *Welsh Hoards, 1979-1981,* Cardiff 1986.

H. Loyn, 'England and Wales in the tenth century: the context of the Athelstan charters', *Welsh History Review* 10 (1980-1), 283-301.

B.H.I.H. Stewart and C.E. Blunt, 'The Droitwich mint and BMC Type XIV of Edward the Confessor', *BNJ* 48 (1978), 52-7.

P. Barker, 'The origins of Worcester', *Trans. Worcs. Arch. Soc.* 3rd ser., 2(1968-9), 3-116.

M. Dolley, 'The first Norman coinage in Wales', in *The Norman Conquest and the English Coinage,* 1966, pp. 30-4.

R.H.M. Dolley 'A note on the Anglo-Saxon mint at Berkeley', *Trans Bristol and Glos. Arch. Soc.* 80 (1961), 80-9.

10. KENT, SURREY, AND SUSSEX

Mint-towns: Canterbury, Rochester, Dover, Lympne, (?) Winchelsea, Chichester, Lewes, Guildford; (Southwark;) Hastings, Romney, Cissbury, Steyning, Sandwich, Hythe, Pevensey.

The three south-eastern shires make up a large tract of land, a hundred miles from east to west, with no single geographical focus. The River Thames is the northern boundary. One can distinguish a number of east-west zones, such as the Thames estuary and valley, the North Downs, the sandy soils and forests of the Weald, and the South Downs. The single finds deserve to be analysed in some regional detail, along those lines, in order to determine whether the list of mints most plentifully represented varies from zone to zone or from east to west.

The south-east had many mint-places, including a number of Channel ports, which may have functioned more as entry-points where foreign silver was recoined, than as market-towns or regional centres for the local economy. That is also something to be borne in mind in considering the detailed distribution of the single finds. Other themes are the occurrence of finds of foreign coins which had escaped reminting; inflows of money from the Winchester area into western Sussex; and coastwise movements of coins from more westerly mints such as Wareham, and beyond.

Out of 69 attributable single finds 16, or 23 per cent, are from London. This approximates to the national average proportion for London. Dover ranks second with 9 finds, and Canterbury takes 8. Mints which take two or three finds are Hastings, Lewes, and Chichester; Wilton; and Lincoln, Chester, and York. There are other northerly mints in the sample which hint at long-distance trade or contacts as providing a component of the currency: Warwick, Leicester, and Nottingham. The same might be said of the westerly mints of Shaftesbury, Bath, Barnstaple, and Totnes.

If we attempt a regional analysis by dividing the south-east into, say, four smaller areas (east Kent, the Thames corridor, east Sussex, west Sussex) the numbers become too small to be statistically valid, and the most that can be offered is a general impression. The Weald is conspicuously empty of stray finds.

East Kent. This small, historic region, which was so rich archaeologically in early and middle Saxon times, provides 26 of the 69 attributable finds, with Dover taking seven, and London and Canterbury six each. There was one other find (of Sandwich) minted within the region, making 14 out of 26, or just over half. When we consider that Canterbury and Dover together accounted for roughly 3 to 5 per cent of the national output, and London over 20, we can see that there was a strong degree of localization of the currency. It may be that that was because coins minted in London and beyond were not carried eastwards to supply the currency of east Kent to the same extent that they were carried elsewhere, but why this should have been so is not clear.

Excavations in the city of Canterbury itself have yielded five attributable coins, of which two are local. From Dover, only two finds are on record, both of the Dover mint.

Of the seven Dover coins, only two were found nearer to Canterbury than to Dover, and there is a complementary tendency for Canterbury coins, which predominate further north. There is thus an unusual degree of localization even within east Kent, and the supply of new coins in and from Dover seems to follow a different pattern from that normally seen in the Anglo-Scandinavian trading boroughs and the shire towns.

The Thames corridor, and Surrey. Fourteen finds include only two from the region (Rochester mint). The others are of London (4), Lincoln (3), Canterbury, Leicester, Maldon, Warwick, and Exeter. The coin losses thus seem to reflect traffic through the south-east towards the continent. There is a clear contrast with east Kent. Note particularly the coins of Lincoln, Leicester, and Warwick.

East Sussex, with Romney Marsh, and parts of Kent. Eighteen finds from the southern coastlands include five minted in the region (Lewes, 3, Hastings, 2), and two of Dover.

From Lewes there are five attributable finds, of which only one is of Lewes. That is more in accordance with what one would expect of a shire town.

West Sussex. Eleven finds include three from London, one minted in the region (Chichester), and singletons from Barnstaple and Totnes. These last suggest coastwise sailing journeys along the south coast of England.

Single finds. East Kent: Bekesbourne (2), Canterbury (3 + 3 x ½), Dover (1 + ½), Great Mongeham (2), Ham, Little Mongeham (2 + ½), Minster-in-Thanet, Reculver (3), Richborough (2), Ringwould, Ripple, St. Nicholas-at-Wade, St Peters (½), Sandwich, Seasalter (2), Worth.
The Thames corridor, and Surrey: Bexley, Darenth, Higham (3), Milton, Rochester (3 + ½), Sevenoaks, South Croydon, Southwark?, Woodmansterne.
East Sussex, etc. Alfriston (3 + brooch), Eastbourne (½), East Dean, Hastings, Hellingly (gold penny), Lewes (6, incl. mini-hoard?), Newchurch, New Romney (½), Old Romney, Rolvenden, Romney, Rye, Seaford.
West Sussex: Bosham, Boxgrove (2), Chichester (2 + brooch), Felpham, Halnaker, Hangleton (2), Steyning, Worthing, Yapton.

Hoards from the south-east (with validity-periods). Harting Beacon (4), ? Hangleton (4), Milton Street (18M), Sedlescombe (21M), ?Little Mongeham (22), Chancton (23M), Ashdown Forest (23?), Offham (23?), Arundel Castle (23?), Oving (23?), Lewes (23), Denge Marsh (24M), Beddington Park (27). M = multi-type hoard.

Minting in the region. Whereas one mint in each shire could be described as the norm to the north of the Thames, east Kent alone had three mints from the Reform type onwards (Canterbury, Dover, and Lympne), and Rochester was a mint-place in west Kent. Sussex also had two or three (Lewes, Chichester, and perhaps Winchelsea). Guildford was an early mint-place in Surrey. Southwark became another mint-place for Surrey in Crux. Various small ports, which subsequently mostly became Cinque Ports, began minting at different dates in the eleventh century.

Canterbury. Shipping which passed through the Wantsum Channel came close to Canterbury, which was a mint-place from the mid-seventh century onwards, largely because it was an entry-point to England for travellers by the short Channel crossing routes. Canterbury retained its mint and its monetary role throughout the middle ages, but its importance in the eleventh century was in fact of a second order, outranked by the Danelaw

10. KENT, SURREY, AND SUSSEX

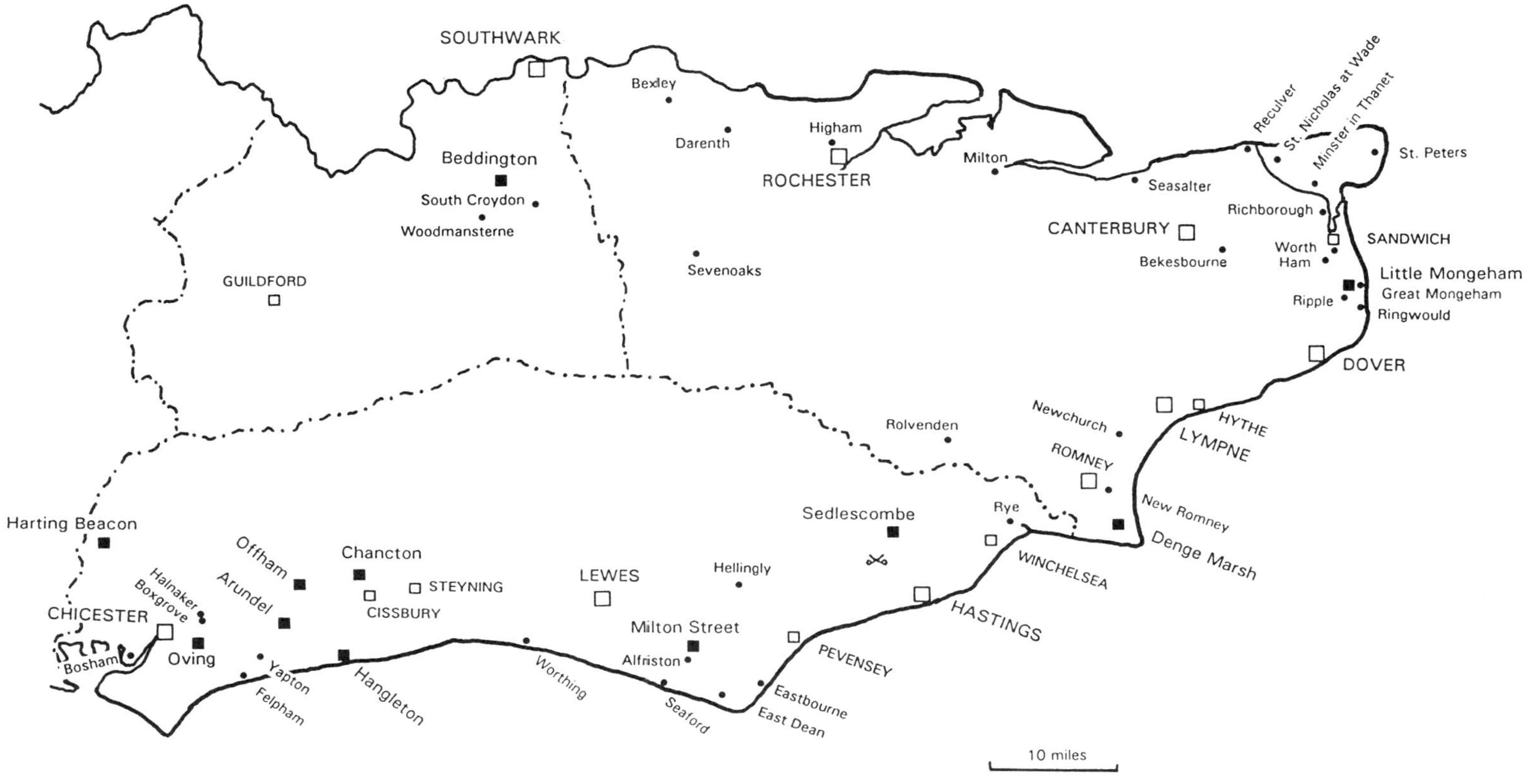

trading boroughs. The distribution of single finds of Canterbury coins, which in other centuries offers a classic example of a local function combined with a long-distance trading function, is surprisingly restricted. They were carried as far as London, but from all quarters north and west of London there are a bare half-dozen single finds. The contrast with London is pronounced. Canterbury in the eleventh century was a wealthy borough, with probably 6,000 to 8,000 inhabitants, and its minting activity has more to do with its role as a shire town and regional centre than with long-distance trade.

Canterbury's share of the Reform type, as estimated from the Scandinavian sample, was *c.*5 per cent. A dozen dies are known. Output rose considerably in the Hand types. Thereafter it fluctuated, generally in the range 2 to 4 per cent. Under Edward the Confessor there were seven regular moneyers or 'workshops' (cf the establishment of seven in the Grateley decrees, of whom four were the king's moneyers, two the archbishop's, and one the abbot's), plus a certain number of single-type moneyers. In the 1060s and 1070s there was a decline, but something like the earlier position was restored in the Paxs type.

Rochester. Rochester was a single-moneyer mint in the Reform type, and was active in the Hand types, but thereafter it declined steadily (even though it was provided with half-a-dozen moneyers in Crux), and in the reign of Edward the Confessor seems often to have been in abeyance. Clearly there was little demand for the moneyers' services.

Dover. Dover played very little part in implementing Eadgar's reform, but gained a modest importance from the Crux type onwards. Cf. Lympne, 12 miles along the coast.

Lympne. From Lympne, an old Roman road led due north to Canterbury. Depending on winds and tides, it offered a swift journey for travellers who could hire horses, but obviously had no advantages for the transport of bulky goods. Lympne had minted on the smallest possible scale before the reform, but in the Reform type it rivalled Canterbury, with a similar share of the national output, a remarkable 5 per cent. Half-a-dozen moneyers are known, and 15 dies were used.

Most of the coins are on very light standards, and one wonders whether that might tell us anything about the purposes for weight-variation. Where did the silver come from? —It is tempting to suppose from abroad: what other function had Lympne than as a port of entry? But in Hand, Crux, and Long Cross there is good evidence of a higher standard, of *c.*1.50g or a little higher. Lympne's moment of glory was soon over, and its production under Cnut was trivial. It is not known to have minted for Edward the Confessor. Whether its activity in the 970s and 980s was prompted by administrative decisions at a national level, or by inflows of foreign money needing to be reminted, and whether the port ceased to be usable, are questions on which no evidence is forthcoming.

Winchelsea. Two specimens from a single die with the mint-signature WENCLES, attributed to Winchcombe, should perhaps be attributed to Winchelsea. The old site of the town (eventually destroyed by storms) lay only two or three miles south of Rye which, curiously in view of its splendid site, lacked a mint. The early decline of Lympne as a mint suggests an analogy with Winchelsea. The attribution remains debateable in the absence of any English single finds. The dies are of Winchester work. One of the two known coins is from the Oakham hoard, while the other is without geographical provenance. The latter weighs 1.60g. (Cf. the very light standard at Lympne.)

Chichester. Chichester struck very regularly, in amounts between 0.5 and 1.0 per cent of the national total.

Lewes. Lewes generally minted between 1 and 2 per cent of the national total.

Guildford. A single coin of the Reform type, with mint-signature CVLEFR, is attributed to Guildford. Later, the mint worked intermittently, striking only very small quantities of coinage.

Southwark. The mint was created in the Crux type, but continued to work thereafter, often contributing 0.5-1.5 per cent of the national total. (See Section 8.)

Hastings. The mint is first recorded in Second Hand, where a single moneyer is known from four specimens, all found in Sweden. Thereafter Hastings often produces 0.5—1.0 per cent of the national total, growing from two-moneyer to three-moneyer status in Edward's Pointed Helmet type. Its coins have had a high survival rate in the Sedlescombe hoard.

Romney. Romney first appears as a mint in Long Cross, and works on a small scale into the 1040s.

Cissbury. Some seven or eight coins with the mint-signatures SITHMES or SITHESTEB (the two forms are die-linked) have been read as Sithestbyrig or Sithmestbyrig, 'the last town', and attributed to the magnificent iron-age hill fort which dominates the South Downs above Worthing. The attribution is supported by the (London) style of die-cutting in Last Small Cross and the Sussex style of the one Quatrefoil die. There seems to be an analogy with the temporary creation of a hill-fort mint-place at Cadbury, also in Last Small Cross, and doubtless for the same general reason of security from Danish attacks. There is an obverse die-link with Chichester, and it may even be that when the expedient was abandoned (the Danish threat having disappeared following Cnut's conquest of England), the moneyer Leofwine transferred to Chichester, taking his obverse die with him. In so far as Cissbury can be said ever to have had a regional function as a mint, that function seems to have been transferred to nearby Steyning.

Steyning. The intermittent activity of the minor mint of Steyning is closely linked with that at Chichester nearby.

Sandwich. Sandwich operates through most of the reign of Edward the Confessor, but only in his first four types at more than a minimal level. The possible connection with Edward's naval expedition has been discussed above.

Hythe. The mint of Hythe, created at much the same date as that of Sandwich, struggled to survive: it was barely viable.

Pevensey. Pevensey was a small Norman mint, attached to the castle.

References.

N. Brooks, *The Early History of the Church of Canterbury*, Leicester, 1984.

I. Stewart, 'The Sussex mints and their moneyers', in P. Brandon (editor), *The South Saxons*, 89-137.

R.H.M. Dolley and F.E. Jones, 'The mints "æt Gothabyrig" and "æt Sith(m)estebyrig"', *BNJ* 28 (1955-7), 270-81.

Glendining, *Coins of the Sussex Mints* (sale catalogue, 14 October, 1985.)

11. WESSEX

Mint-towns: Winchester, Wilton, Shaftesbury, Wareham, Southampton, Malmesbury, Wallingford, Cricklade, Dorchester, Bridport, 'Niwan', 'Brygin', Salisbury, 'Eanbyrig', Warminster, Bedwyn, Reading, Marlborough.

South-central England south of the Thames is here taken to comprise the four shires of Berkshire, Hampshire, Wiltshire, and Dorset. At its heart lay Winchester, from where Eadgar's reform was launched. Selwood, which historically had divided western and eastern Wessex, lay approximately along the eastern border of Somerset with Dorset and Wiltshire, and beyond. Geographically, the region consists mostly of the Hampshire Basin and the chalk downlands further north.

In the Reform type (when the dies for so many mints were cut in Winchester), most of the region's mint-output came from Winchester itself (with an estimated 13 per cent of the national total) and Wilton, with more modest contributions from two Dorset mints, namely Shaftesbury and Wareham. Southampton was a very small mint, and Malmesbury was even smaller, being known at present from only one specimen. The same is true of Wallingford, the only mint in Berkshire at the date of the reform. In effect, the reform was not implemented in Berkshire by the minting of coins within the shire.

In the Hand type, the number of mints is augmented considerably, by Wallingford, Cricklade, Dorchester, Bridport, and the unlocated 'Niwan' and 'Brygin', which are die-linked to each other and to Shaftesbury. 'Niwan' and 'Brygin' were a flash in the pan, and Bridport struggled, but the other three found a role. Because the coins of all these mints are so rare, the possibility exists that specimens from the Reform type could still come to light.

Salisbury (i.e. Old Sarum) took over from Wilton when the latter town was sacked in 1003, and made a regular contribution from then on. Wilton resumed minting within a few years, but on a smaller scale. Warminster also began minting in Long Cross. 'Eanbyrig' is known only in Quatrefoil. Bedwyn and Reading are added under Edward the Confessor, and Marlborough under William I.

From this pattern of development, one can see that to speak of West Saxon shires as having four mints, as if there were some sort of collegiality, is not helpful. It would be better to say that there were many mints in Wessex, for various reasons, mainly perhaps because there were in the region many towns which had evolved from Alfredian fortifications (and which are listed in the Burghal Hidage). Certainly there were a lot of mints in relation to the region's share, characteristically around eight to ten per cent, of the national output.

Winchester dominated the region, although more for national than for regional reasons. As

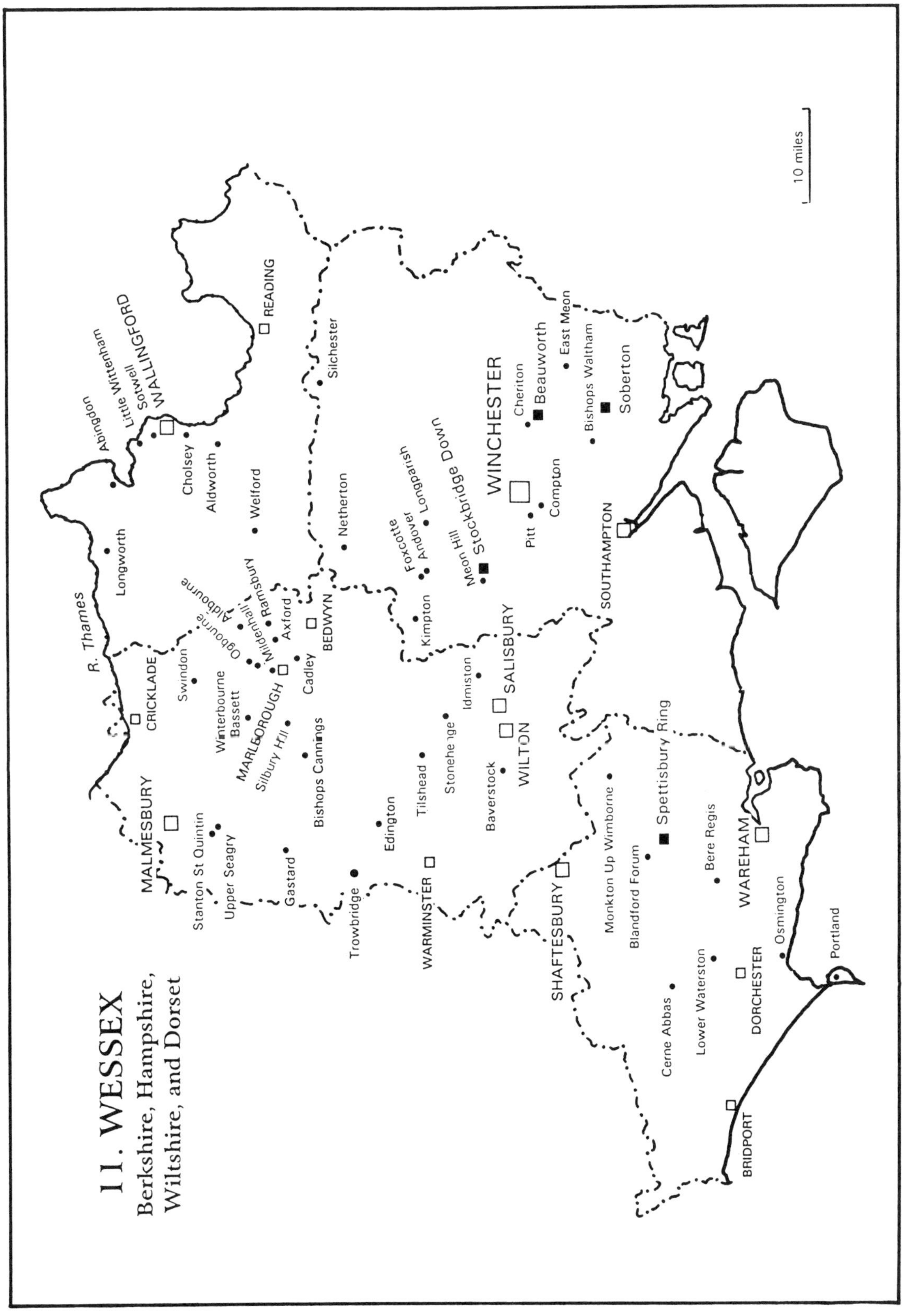
11. WESSEX
Berkshire, Hampshire, Wiltshire, and Dorset
10 miles
R. Thames
Abingdon
Little Wittenham
Sotwell
WALLINGFORD
READING
Cholsey
Aldworth
Welford
Longworth
Silchester
Netherton
Aldbourne
Ogbourne
Ramsbury
Mildenhall
Axford
BEDWYN
Cadley
CRICKLADE
Swindon
Winterbourne Bassett
MARLBOROUGH
Silbury Hill
Bishops Cannings
MALMESBURY
Stanton St Quintin
Upper Seagry
Gastard
Trowbridge
Edington
WARMINSTER
Tilshead
Stonehenge
Baverstock
WILTON
SALISBURY
Idmiston
Kimpton
Foxcotte
Andover
Longparish
Meon Hill
Stockbridge Down
WINCHESTER
Pitt
Compton
Cheriton
Beauworth
East Meon
Bishops Waltham
Soberton
SOUTHAMPTON
SHAFTESBURY
Monkton Up Wimborne
Blandford Forum
Spettisbury Ring
Bere Regis
WAREHAM
Osmington
Portland
DORCHESTER
Lower Waterston
Cerne Abbas
BRIDPORT

regards shire governance, the pattern of mints by the 980s (by when the intentions of the reform were fully visible) was as follows. Berkshire was virtually without a shire mint. Hampshire was served by Winchester, and there was also a small mint at the port of Southampton. Dorset had at least four small or very small mints other than Dorchester, which was likewise very small. Wiltshire had its shire mint at Wilton, and two other small mints at Cricklade and Malmesbury. The north-of-Thames pattern of minting in the shire-town would thus offer a very poor fit with the facts.

The Norman Conquest brought an improvement in the monetary affairs of Wessex. By 1086 its share of the national mint-output had risen to between a fifth and a quarter. Winchester, in particular, seems to have overtaken London, even, to become the country's leading mint. Salisbury rose to far greater prominence than it had known in Anglo-Saxon times, and so did Shaftesbury. Several of the smaller mints seem also to have benefitted.

Out of 91 single finds from the region, 68 are mint-attributable English coins. Of these, 28 (or 41 per cent) were minted within the region, and 15 (22 per cent) were minted within the shire where they were found. If one were to add in the coins of nearby mints, namely by adding Oxford coins to the Berkshire total, and Ilchester coins to the Wiltshire total, 28 would become 32, or 47 per cent. These proportions strike one as a little higher than in other regions. If there is a discrepancy, it may be merely because Winchester was an active mint. In comparison with 13 Winchester coins from the region, there are 16 London coins.

From Winchester itself, from extensive excavations, there are 14 mint-attributable coins, of which only 3 are of the Winchester mint. Three are from London, and the rest have a distinctly West Saxon flavour: Shaftesbury (2), Salisbury, Malmesbury, Gloucester; Chichester; Maldon, Ipswich.

The hoards may be considered against this background of the single finds. The little Spettisbury Ring hoard, from *c.*979, included just two mint-identifiable coins, of Stamford and Totnes. Intriguingly, there are two single finds of the Totnes mint from Wessex (Gastard and Trowbridge), but none of Exeter. The Shaftesbury hoard is obviously a traveller's hoard. The Stockbridge Down find, from *c.*1065, comprises 6 coins all of the Winchester mint, by two moneyers, and includes 3 die-duplicates.

The mint-structure of the Soberton hoard is unfortunately only vaguely known. It was a three-type hoard spanning the years 1065-8, and it seems that more than half of the latest type was of the Winchester mint. The same may have been true of the coins of Harold II. It looks, therefore, as if the proportion of local coins was significantly in excess of that found in the currency at large. A mini-hoard from Wallingford may be postulated on the same argument, although of course one can be sure of nothing when there are only two coins. The Malmesbury hoard contained coins of a variety of mints, but the proportions are inadequately recorded.

The very large hoard of Beauworth, arguably a pious donation of William II for his father's soul, was found some six miles SE of Winchester. It is discussed in Part 3, section 31. The money was presumably withdrawn from the royal treasury (where there was enough coin for a good number of similar donations?) but the proportions of the various mints show a Wessex flavour (Winchester, 26 per cent, London, 12 per cent, etc.). The estimate for Winchester's output is 15 per cent.

Single finds. Berkshire: Abingdon, Aldworth, Cholsey, Little Wittenham, Longworth, Reading, Silchester, Sotwell, Sparsholt, Wallingford (2 x ½, ¼, and a ?mini-hoard), Welford. *Dorset*: Bere Regis, Blandford Forum, Cerne Abbas (2), Dorchester, Dorset, Lower Waterston, Monkton Up Wimborne (½), Osmington, Portland. *Hampshire*:

Andover, Bishops Waltham, Cheriton (3 + ½), Compton (½), East Meon (½), Foxcotte, Hampshire, Isle of Wight, Kimpton, Longparish, Meon Hill, Netherton (1 + ½), Pitt (¼), Southampton (2), Winchester (13, incl. one forgery, + 3 x ½), near Winchester (2). *Wiltshire*: Aldbourne (2), Axford, Baverstock, Bishops Cannings, Cadley, Edington (brooch), Gastard, Idmiston, Mildenhall, Ogbourne St. Andrew, Ogbourne St. George (1 + 2 x ½), Old Sarum (3), Ramsbury, Salisbury, Salisbury Plain, Silbury Hill (¼), Stanton St Quintin (½), Stonehenge, Swindon (1 + ½), Tilshead, Trowbridge (2 + ½ + brooch), Upper Seagry, Winterbourne Bassett.

Hoards (with validity-periods). Spettisbury Ring (1), Shaftesbury (4), Stockbridge Down (22), Soberton (24), ?Wallingford (25), Malmesbury (27), Beauworth (31).

Mints. Winchester. Yvonne Harvey's eagerly-awaited corpus will become a point of reference for the monetary historian, alongside Mossop's Lincoln corpus and Lean's York corpus (see Q.6). Winchester played a major role in launching Eadgar's reform, and struck unusual amounts of coinage for the first decade, possibly because it was associated with the royal treasury. Its coins of these years, however, are not noticeable in the currency at large. The Lincoln-based Scandinavian estimates suggest that Winchester struck 13 per cent of the national output in the Reform type, from 130 'equivalent reverse dies'. These figures can be checked against Jonsson's corpus of 48 specimens from 38 and 37 obverse and reverse dies. Good's formula indicates 101 and 89 dies respectively. Given the sample size, the discrepancy is acceptable, and indeed barely significant. A dozen moneyers launched the reform. The mint was virtually in abeyance during Æthelred's First Small Cross issue, but was very active in First Hand (along with a range of other mints in Wessex). Thereafter, Winchester's share of the national total was usually around 4 to 6 per cent.

Freeman draws attention to a marked structural change at the mint in the latter part of the Confessor's reign, when the number of moneyers was halved from 12 to 6.

Winchester holds a special place among English mints because there is a detailed evidence from Domesday Survey and a later survey showing that moneyers operated in separate establishments, not in an institutional building called 'the mint', until 1158. Their forges can be shown on a plan of the city: they were concentrated in High Street, the busiest street in the city (and outside the precincts of the royal palace). The moneyers, who were of burgess rank, had their houses elsewhere in the city, and these too can be shown on a plan. Biddle and Keene have provided a definitive discussion of the evidence.

Wilton. The shire town which gives its name to Wiltshire played quite an active part in the Reform coinage, and comes to notice again (perhaps for reasons having little to do with the town's monetary role) in Intermediate Small Cross. It was sacked in 1003, in spite of its fortifications. Its failure to strike the Helmet type has been seen as a consequence. The evidence is critically examined in Part 3, section 4, Long Cross. For whatever reasons, Wilton lost its early importance as a mint, and worked only on a small scale from Last Small Cross onwards, showing a progressive recovery from *c.*1045. Under Harold II it suddenly achieved a remarkable, but brief, prominence.

Shaftesbury. Although Shaftesbury was entitled to two moneyers under the Grateley decrees, and its importance as a mint was almost on a par with Wilton until Long Cross, it declined thereafter, until Norman times.

Wareham. Wareham is listed in the Burghal Hidage. Its modest importance as a mint seems to have come from its function as a cross-Channel port. Single finds have occasionally been found far away, e.g. at

Cirencester, of William I.

Southampton. Southampton and Northampton have presented the numismatist with difficult problems of attribution, since the signatures *Hamtun* and *Ham* could apply to either. A canon of moneyers has been established for each place, although still with some residual uncertainty. English hoards and single finds are the touchstone. The mint was closed at the end of Quatrefoil, but reopened in *c.*1068. Clearly it acquired a new locational advantage as a result of the Norman Conquest.

Malmesbury. A Burghal Hidage town well sited on a spur above the River Avon, Malmesbury is known as a mint in Eadgar's Reform type from just one specimen, and one in Second Hand. From then on its contribution was often no more than *c.*0.2 per cent. In 1086 the figure was nearer to 0.5 per cent.

Wallingford. The town enjoyed its locational advantage from an important ford (and later a bridge) crossing the Thames. It is listed in the Burghal Hidage, and minted through much of the tenth century. In the Reform type, however, the mint is known from a single specimen, in Eadgar's name. Its share of the national output fluctuated, usually between 0.5 and one per cent, but in Crux was as high as 2.5 per cent. Thereafter, however, the rival crossing-point of Oxford was always the more active mint-place.

Cricklade. Cricklade, again a Burghal Hidage town, first appears as a mint in First Hand, with two moneyers, and an estimate 0.5 per cent of the national output. One should note, however, that the Scandinavian sample on which the above statement rests contains just two Handcoins of Cricklade. The mint worked on a minimum scale, but very regularly.

Dorchester. A similar caveat applies to Dorchester, except that the sample contains only one coin.

Bridport. Whether Bridport was to any significant extent a Channel port, or merely a market town for its region, is uncertain. Its mint-output follows a similar pattern to that of Dorchester.

'*Niwan*' *and* '*Brygin*'. The die-linked coins in question are illustrated and discussed by Lyon. The only clue to the locality of the places (or place?) is that they may have been in the Shaftesbury area.

Salisbury. The hill-fort of Old Sarum, which was relatively secure against Viking attacks, usurped much of Wilton's role from 1003 onwards, and held the lead over Wilton until *c.*1050.

'*Eanbyrig*', it has been suggested, is a Wessex mint linked to Dorchester by the moneyer's name Swet (and by style). A couple of coins only are known, in Quatrefoil.

Warminster. On the mint of *Worgemynster* see Shortt, and Elmore Jones.

Bedwyn. The moneyer Cild struck in nine successive types, from Trefoil-Quadrilateral through to William's Profile/Cross Fleury.

Reading. The moneyers Beorhtric, and his successor Korf, worked briefly at Reading (possibly for the benefit of the abbot).

Marlborough. The Cild who worked here in the time of William I is probably the Bedwyn moneyer, who had moved his seat.

References.

M. Biddle and D.J. Keene, 'The mint', in M. Biddle (editor), *Winchester in the Early Middle Ages* (Winchester Studies, vol. 1), Oxford, 1976, 396-422.

I. Stewart, 'Reflections on some Wessex mints and their moneyers', *NC*[7] 15 (1975), 219-29.

D.M.Metcalf, 'Notes on the "PAXS" type of William I', *Yorkshire Numismatist* 1 (1986-7), 13-26.

C.S.S. Lyon, 'Historical problems of Anglo-Saxon coinage. 4. The Viking age', *BNJ* 39 (1970), 193-204. [Niwan, Brygin.]

H. de S. Shortt, 'The mints of Wiltshire', *Archaeological Journal* 104 (1947), 112-27, and id., *NC*[6] 8 (1948), 169-87.

F. Elmore Jones, in *BNJ* 28 (1955-7), 217 [Malmesbury, Bedwyn, Cricklade, Warminster].

R.H.M. Dolley, 'A Cnut die-link between the mints of Salisbury and Wilton', *BNJ* 31 (1962), 53-4.

R.H.M. Dolley, 'The emergency mint of Cadbury', *BNJ* 28 (1955-7), at p. 100 (for 'Eanbyrig').

12. THE SOUTH-WEST

Mint-towns: Exeter, Barnstaple, Ilchester, Totnes, Bath, Lydford, Watchet, Launceston, Axbridge, Bruton, Crewkerne, 'Geothanburh', Milborne Port, Taunton, Langport, Petherton, Cadbury, 'Fro'

The south-western shires of Somerset, Devon, and Cornwall were, like Wessex east of Selwood, a region of many mint-places. There are no fewer than 18, of which only half-a-dozen are former Burghal Hidage fortifications. The disparity between provision and need appears all the greater when we see how relatively short the list of single finds is. This thinning out of finds westwards may well reflect a dwindling level of monetization of the regional economy.

The list of mints is cut down to size when we look at the implementation of Eadgar's reform. Coins in Eadgar's name are rare indeed: seven are recorded from Exeter, from six reverse dies, but otherwise there is one from Barnstaple, one from Ilchester, and one from Totnes. Curiously enough, there are none from Bath, where Eadgar was crowned, and where half-a-dozen moneyers had worked in the preceding Type iii. One coin of Edward Martyr is known. The implications of the pattern at Bath for chronology are discussed in Part 3, section 1. All the dies used in the south-west under Eadgar were cut at Winchester. (For Totnes, we must say: presumably.)

It is not just the paucity of coins from the opening years which attracts attention but, even more, the dramatic increase in First and Second Hand. At Exeter, 14 Reform coins are followed by 197 Hand coins (88 + 109), at Totnes, two are followed by 78 (51 + 27), at Barnstaple, one is followed by 40 (20 + 20), and at Ilchester, one is followed by 30 (15 + 15). In effect, the reform only began to be implemented in First Hand, after token issues in the first six or so years. Bath fits into that pattern, with one coin followed by 18, and perhaps Lydford, which is also first recorded for Edward Martyr (four coins followed by 12). Watchet and Launceston are added to the list in the Hand period.

When the reform had been fully implemented in the south-west, the pattern of minting bore no direct relationship to the shires. Exeter was the region's major mint, presumably because of maritime commerce, about which we have disappointingly little knowledge. Totnes presumably enjoyed similar locational advantages, and flourished similarly, on a smaller scale.

In the Reform type, the south-west produces only an estimated 5 per cent of the national output, but in First Hand 13 per cent, and in Second Hand a remakable 17 per cent. This figure is never again matched. Did it represent a peak of commercial prosperity for the region, or is it distorted by technical factors, e.g. the coining of reserves of bullion? Did the south-west have trading links in Normandy and Brittany?

At Exeter, the early weight-standards fall into a classic pattern—successive averages of

1.59, 1.47, and 1.33g in the Reform type, followed by 1.39g in First Hand and 1.18g in Second Hand. These mean values conceal multiple weight-standards, e.g. in First Hand there is a standard of *c.*1.63g, and probably another at *c.*1.42g, as well as the most plentiful standard at *c.*1.30g. Totnes, Barnstaple, and Ilchester also undoubtedly used multiple standards in First Hand. It is not clear that Bath did, but Lydford conforms to the regional pattern.

Taunton begins work on a minimal scale in Crux, but one may probably group it with several other mints which first appear in Long Cross, all working on a very small scale. They are Axbridge, Bruton, Crewkerne, 'Geothanburh', Milborne Port, and Taunton. All these reappear under Cnut. Langport and South Petherton may belong with them, administratively, even though Long Cross coins have not been found.

Cadbury is a special case of an emergency hill-fort mint-place with a short life.

Frome seems to be a late addition to the canon.

The single finds from the south-west are mainly from Somerset (13, cf three in Devon and two in Cornwall). All of them, so far, are whole pennies. Of 18 mint-identifiable coins, six were minted within the region (Exeter, 3, Ilchester, 2, Lydford, 1). A further three are from Winchester. Thus the south-west was much more open to inflows of coins from other regions than was Yorkshire, the other distant region.

In an effort to understand the monetary relations of the south-west with the rest of the country, one may enquire about single finds from south-western mints, found outside the region. There are just a dozen of these (Exeter, 4, Totnes, 3, Ilchester, 2, Barnstaple, Bath, Lydford), of which four are from nearby Wiltshire, a couple (of Exeter and Totnes) are from Sussex and Kent, presumably carried by sea, and one is from south Wales. In short, the counter-flows are on a small scale.

A shadowy hoard from Constantine, near Helston, Cornwall, seems to have contained coins of Harthacnut as well as Cnut. No useful detail is available. St. Austell and Wedmore are the only other hoards from the region. A discussion of the composition and character of the Wedmore hoard will be found in Part 3, Section 13. The proportion of coins from south-western mints is if anything somewhat below the regional average as indicated by stray finds.

Single finds. Cornwall: Padstow, St. Mawgan. *Devon*: Exeter, Plymouth, Stokeinteignhead. *Somerset*: Axbridge, Butcombe, Cheddar (3), Crewkerne, Glastonbury (3), Huntspill, Ilchester, North Curry, Saltford.

Hoards. St. Austell (1), Constantine (10-12?), Wedmore (13).

St. Austell. The Rashleigh sale (Sotheby, 21 June 1909) included ten coins, annotated as having been found near St. Austell, Cornwall. Doubts are expressed about the provenance in *SCBI Fitzwilliam* (623), and the hoard is not mentioned in the standard check-list. The Rashleighs, however, were a well-to-do Cornish family. Jonathan Rashleigh inherited and greatly enlarged an old family collection. Provenances were not a matter of much scholarly attention in the nineteenth century, and Rashleigh's ticketing of these coins as having been found in Cornwall should be seen as local patriotism. Those who are cynically inclined may wonder whether someone sold coins from an Irish hoard to Rashleigh by adding a spurious Cornish provenance; but it seems presumptuous to doubt that they came into his hands because they were found locally. They are of Alfred, Athelstan (2), Eadmund, Eadred, Eadwig, and Eadgar (4). Their mints are mostly difficult to determine, except for two York coins of Athelstan. The Winchester coin was perhaps a late addition, arriving via the south coast, to a sum of money that had reached Cornwall through the Irish Sea coastlands.

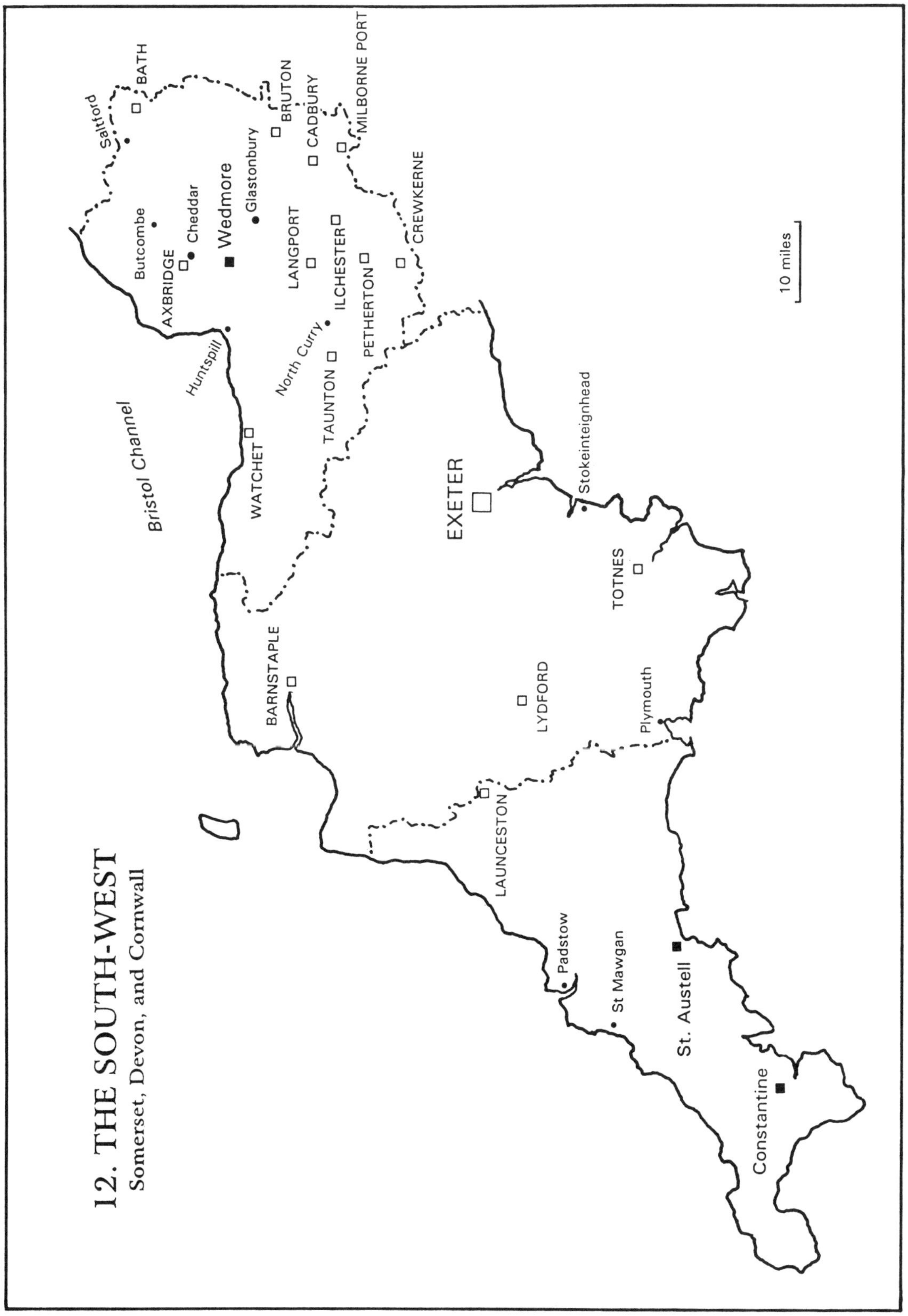

12. THE SOUTH-WEST
Somerset, Devon, and Cornwall

Wedmore. The village, on a fine hill-top site, was an important holding of the bishop of Wells. The hoard, of about 200 coins, was said to have been found in a crock in the churchyard. Its history after discovery is such that not all the coins can be said with certainty to be from the hoard. Its general composition, however, is not in doubt. There was just one coin of Æthelred, and the hoard consists essentially of Cnut's first, second, and third types (128), together with a smaller number of issues of Harold I and Harthacnut (46), and 5 specimens of Edward's first (Pacx) type. A t.p.q. of 1043-4 is indicated. Crucially, the proportion of coins of West Country and west Saxon mints is particularly high in the Quatrefoil type, suggesting a local savings hoard. Exceptional quantities of coinage were minted in the south-west in the Quatrefoil type, and the specimens in the Wedmore hoard are presumably a sample of what remained after the payment of the geld.

Out of a total of 21 Quatrefoil coins, one is from Barnstaple, three from Exeter, four from Ilchester, and one from Taunton. There are also specimens from various Wessex mints —Cricklade, Malmesbury, Shaftesbury, Southampton, and Winchester. In the Helmet and Short Cross types the picture is similar.

Mints. The small mints of the region were quite often served by moneyers of the same name—presumably the self-same men—as worked at another mint or mints nearby. Hunwine strikes in Quatrefoil, for example, at Exeter, Lydford, Watchet, and Axbridge. Ægelwine in Cnut's Short Cross type strikes at Bath, Bristol, Langport, and Cricklade. These links cross shire boundaries. Stewart has drawn attention to them and has discussed the implications, namely that a moneyer may have visited one of the small places for which he had obtained a die very intermittently and only for brief periods.

Exeter. From an establishment of three moneyers in the Reform type, Exeter expanded to a dozen in the Hand types, and 15 in Crux. There was a blip in output in the Arm and Sceptre type. Apart from that, Exeter's share of the national total gradually declined. The number of moneyers had fallen to four by the latter part of the Confessor's reign, in line with national trends, and sank even lower under William I.

Barnstaple. The Burghal Hidage equates Barnstaple and Pilton. A single specimen is known from the Reform type. There were three moneyers in Hand and as late as Quatrefoil, after which output was negligible.

Ilchester. Minting at Ilchester (which was *not* a Burghal Hidage fortification) was transferred to Cadbury in *c.*1010 and did not return until *c.*1017 x 1020. Output shows a strong upturn in Quatrefoil, but otherwise its importance in Hand and Crux was never regained. Two finds of Quatrefoil are recorded, both from Wiltshire (Baverstock and Stanton St Quintin).

Totnes. Totnes, after a strong start in Hand, faded. Unusually, the mint was in abeyance through the reigns of Edward the Confessor and William I.

Bath. Bath had four or more moneyers up to the death of Cnut, and worked quite strongly, as a two-moneyer mint, throughout the Confessor's reign, up to but not including Pyramids. Its importance then declined.

Lydford. Lydford is of interest as a mint which may have coined newly-mined silver. There is as yet very little in the way of chemical analyses to support the hypothesis. The place had other functions, as a Burghal Hidage fortification and regional market. The mint was closed in Edward's Short Cross type, and the sole moneyer, Ælfric, transferred his activity to Barnstaple (via Exeter?). Finds, too, lie northwards: St. Mawgan, St. Lythans.

Watchet. Blackburn's exemplary corpus of the Watchet mint reveals a surprisingly high survival-rate per die, at least up until *c.*1035, which carries the implication that we know virtually all the obverse dies and the great majority of the reverse dies that were ever used. In most types, one or two obverse dies sufficed (and the same is likely to have been true *a fortiori* after 1035). In Long Cross, however, four obverse dies were supplied, and in Quatrefoil, six. There are about 50 Long Cross coins of Watchet, permitting a useful study of the weight-standards die by die. The early cessation of minting in the Crux type, and a notable Hiberno-Norse die-link are discussed in Part 3, Section 3 (Crux), under Evidence for dating.

Launceston. The Cornish mint of Launceston operated on a minimal scale (before Cornwall received full diocesan jurisdiction in 994), in First Hand. One specimen is known. The mint was reopened half-way through the Conqueror's reign. The one available early coin is heavy (1.61g).

Axbridge. A fine study and corpus of the mint of Axbridge (or Axport) was published by Elmore Jones. There are a dozen coins in the Scandinavian sample (0.07 per cent), and no English single finds. Most of the coins with English provenances are from the nearby Wedmore hoard. The mint was served by peripatetic moneyers.

Bruton. The Bruton mint is known from a single coin in Long Cross, by Ælfwine, (who subsequently worked also at Bristol and Ilchester), and from some sixty later coins, mostly of Cnut. Dolley suggested that Bruton was (re-)founded from nearby Cadbury, citing a die-linked pair of coins by the moneyer Ælfhelm (cf. the moneyer's name Wulfhelm at Cadbury, in the preceding type). Bruton, which may have inherited Cadbury's privilege of a mint, is described as a borough in Domesday Book.

Crewkerne. Crewkerne is known from five Long Cross coins, 23 of Cnut, and one of Harold I.

'*Geothanburh*'. The location of this mint, which is die-linked to Exeter, is not known. Philologically, the first sound is Y-, and there is accordingly no justification for thinking of Castle Gotha. Dolley published a corpus of 17 specimens, from 14 obverse and 17 reverse dies, ranging from Long Cross through to Arm and Sceptre.

Milborne Port. No port, but a little market town between Shaftesbury and Yeovil, Milborne Port used the mint-signature MYLE, in Long Cross and in Cnut's Pointed Helmet and Short Cross types. Dolley knew of only 13 specimens, from just three obverse and four reverse dies. Some are by Æthelric, doubtless the same man as an active moneyer at Shaftesbury. Others are by Swetric, possibly a kinsman.

Taunton. Like Ilchester, Taunton shows a pronounced blip in Quatrefoil (with three moneyers). Otherwise, it operates persistently as a single-moneyer mint from Crux through to Domesday and beyond.

Langport. Langport was set up similarly with three moneyers in Quatrefoil, but with only a quarter of the demand for their services compared with Taunton. A very small output continued until the time of Harthacnut, with a final flutter in Expanding Cross (light and heavy).

South Petherton. Like Milborne Port, Bruton, and Bedwyn, South Petherton was located on a royal estate, and in 1066 rendered 'the farm of one night'. Its minting activity was very sporadic and thin: one (very heavy) Quatrefoil coin, and three from early in the reign of the Confessor. This may serve to keep the question of the number and location of mints in the south-west in perspective. Petherton may indeed have been granted a mint because it was the caput of a royal estate; but the need for a mint in connection with a royal estate was absolutely minimal.

Cadbury. The 18-acre Iron-Age hill fort of Cadbury Beacon, near Bruton, was set up as a temporary mint, no doubt as a precaution against a perceived threat of raiding, in *c.*1010, and remained in commission (inconvenient as it must have been to work up there), until *c.*1017 x 1020. Dolley has listed seven pairs of dies in Last Small Cross and two in Quatrefoil. Nineteen and four specimens respectively are recorded, on a range of weight-standards in both types. The moneyers were local men. Winus, in particular, can be traced at Crewberne in Long Cross, at Ilchester in Helmet, then at Cadbury in Last Small Cross and into Quatrefoil, and finally at Crewkerne again, where he continued to work until *c.*1028.

'Fro' The mysterious mint of 'Fro', manned by Brihtwine, is known in various types from Cnut's Short Cross to Trefoil Quadrilateral. An attribution to Frome remains very conjectural.

References.

I. Stewart, *The Exeter Mint and its Moneyers.* (R.P.V. Brettell collection). Glendining, 28 October 1970.

N. Shiel, 'The Saxon and medieval mint', in J. Andrews *et al* (editors), *Exeter Coinage* (Exeter Papers in Industrial Archaeology, 10), Exeter, 1980, pp. 9-17.

I. Stewart, 'Reflections on some Wessex mints and their moneyers', *NC*[7] 15 (1975), 219-29.

J. Stevens Cox, *The Ilchester Mint and Ilchester Trade Tokens*, Ilchester, 1949. (Review in *NC*[6] 9, 1949, 123.)

M.A.S. Blackburn, 'The mint of Watchet', *BNJ* 44 (1974), 13-38, and Appendix, ibid., 46 (1976), 75-6.

F.E. Jones, 'The mint of Axbridge', *BNJ* 30 (1960-1), 61-9.

R.H.M. Dolley, 'The earliest penny of the Bruton mint', *NC*[6] 19 (1959), 183-5.

R.H.M. Dolley and F.E. Jones, 'The mints "æt Gothabyrig" and "æt Sith(m)estebyrig"', *BNJ* 28 (1955-7), 270-81.

O.J. Padel, 'The Saxon mint', *Cornish Archaeology* 21 (1982), 150-2. ['Geothanburh'].

R.H.M. Dolley, 'Three West Country notes', *BNJ* 29 (1958-9), 61-8. [Milborne Port, Langport].

R.H.M. Dolley, 'A note on the Anglo-Saxon mint of Petherton', *NCirc* 69 (1961), 167.

R.H.M. Dolley, 'Three late Anglo-Saxon notes', *BNJ* 28 (1955-7), 88-105 [Cadbury].

L. Alcock, *Cadbury Castle: the Early Medieval Archaeology*, 1995.

R.H.M. Dolley, 'Two Anglo-Saxon mints', *BNJ* 28 (1955-57), 499-508. ['Fro'].

PART FIVE

THE GAZETTEER

Single finds from c.*973–1086*

COUNTY ABBREVIATIONS

(after The English Place-Name Society)

Bd	Bedfordshire
Bk	Buckinghamshire
Brk	Berkshire
C	Cambridgeshire
Ch	Cheshire
Co	Cornwall
Cu	Cumberland
D	Devon
Db	Derbyshire
Do	Dorset
Du	Durham
ERY	East Riding of Yorkshire
Ess	Essex
Gl	Gloucestershire
Ha	Hampshire
He	Herefordshire
Hrt	Hertfordshire
Hu	Huntingdonshire
K	Kent
L	Lincolnshire
La	Lancashire
Lei	Leicestershire
Ln	City of London
Mx	Middlesex
Nb	Northumberland
Nf	Norfolk
NRY	North Riding of Yorkshire
Nt	Nottinghamshire
Nth	Northamptonshire
O	Oxfordshire
R	Rutland
Sa	Shropshire
Sf	Suffolk
So	Somerset
Sr	Surrey
St	Staffordshire
Sx	Sussex
W	Wiltshire
Wa	Warwickshire
We	Westmorland
Wo	Worcestershire
WRY	West Riding of Yorkshire
Wt	Isle of Wight

ABINGDON, Brk (O) (excavations) 1973
Cnut, Short Cross
Lewes, Godfrid. wnr
Oxoniensia 40 (1975), 46

ALDBOURNE, W (North Farm) 1888
Æthelred II, type?
London, Wulfric. wnr
CC P.36; inf. Dr P. Robinson

ALDBOURNE, W 1983
Edward Confessor, Expanding Cross (heavy)
Malmesbury, Ealdwig. 1.78g
SF 2, 1

ALDBOURNE, W 1993
Æthelred II, Helmet
London, Brunstan
brooch, obverse facing
Inf. L. Douglas Wilson

ALDERTON, Sf 1992
Æthelred II, Last Small Cross
Ipswich, Sigeweald. 1.12g *or* 1.37g (frag.)
CR 1993, 220; *Proc. Suffolk IAH* 38/1, 79

ALDERTON, Sf 1992
William I, Bonnet
London, Eadwine. 1.12g
CR 1991, 137

ALDWORTH, Brk 1989
Edward Confessor, Short Cross
mint?, moneyer? (BRIHT ON IO)
Unpublished?

ALFORD, L 1985
Æthelred II, First Small Cross
York, Asketill. 1.29g
SF 2, 2
William I, 'Type xiii' (rectè Type viii, Paxs?)
Chichester, Brunman. wnr
BNJ 1986, 185

ALFORD, L, near 1989
Harold I, Jewel Cross
York, Crucan. 1.09g
CR 1996, 117

ALFRISTON, Sx (E. Sussex) (TQ 526031) (1991)
Æthelred II, Intermediate/Last Small Cross
mint?, Beorhtmær
Sussex Arch. Coll. 129 (1991), 246-7 (illus.)

ALFRISTON, Sx (E. Sussex) 1980
Normandy, Dumas 40 bis, late XI century?
CR 1990, 223

ALFRISTON, Sx (E. Sussex) c.1990
Edward Confessor, Expanding Cross
Gloucester, Leofnoth
brooch
Wilts. Arch. Mag. 83 (1990), 208-10

AMINGTON, St 1993
Edward Confessor, Short Cross
Tamworth, Bruning. 1.02g
CR 1993, 228

AMINGTON, St 1995/6
Edward Confessor, Short Cross
Tamworth, Bruning. 1.05g
CR 1995, 175 (three fields from *CR* 1993, 228)

ANCASTER, L 1981
Edward Confessor, Short Cross
Worcester, Wulfwine. 0.57g
Blackburn et al., *Lincoln and its Shire* II, 28 and Fig. 50

ANDOVER, Ha (near) 1991
Æthelred II, Crux
London, Eadweald. 1.46g
CR 1990, 201

ASHWELLTHORPE, Nf 1994
Edward Confessor, Pointed Helmet
London, Eadræd. wnr
CR 1994, 232

ATTLEBRIDGE, Nf 1995
Æthelred II, Long Cross
York, Sumarlithr. 1.32g (incomplete)
CR 1995, 165

AVELEY, Ess 1985
Eadgar, Reform Small Cross
Lympne, Æthelstan
cut halfpenny, 0.59g
BNJ 1986, 185

AXBRIDGE, So (1918)
Harthacnut, Arm and Sceptre
Ilchester, Godric. wnr
CR 1987, 151

AXFORD, W 1891
Harold II, Pax
mint?, moneyer?
CC p. 36

AYLESBURY, Bk (1912)
Æthelred II, Long Cross
mint? moneyer?
Sotheby 6 Nov. 1912, lot 74 (E.K. Burstall)

BARHAM, Sf 1995
Harold II, Pax
Thetford, Thorgautr
cut halfpenny, 0.52g
CR 1996, 130

BASSINGBOURN, C 1993
Edward Confessor, Pointed Helmet
Thetford, Godleof
cut halfpenny, 0.63g
CR 1993, 223

BAVERSTOCK, W (1979)
Cnut, Quatrefoil
Ilchester, Ælfwine. wnr
Somerset Arch. and NHS 123 (1979), 110

BAWSEY, Nf 1993
Edward Confessor, Facing Bust/Small Cross
mint?, moneyer?
cut farthing, 0.24g
CR 1993, 235

BAWTRY, WRY (S. Yorks) 1984, 1986
Edward Confessor, Short Cross
London, Deorman. 0.90g
CR 1988, 184
Edward Confessor, Short Cross
Lincoln, Asfrøthr. wnr
SF 3, 79

BEKESBOURNE, K 1981
William I, Profile/Cross and Trefoils
Dover, Eadweard. 1.17g
SCBI South-Eastern 1762; *SF* 2, 8.

BEKESBOURNE, K 1991
William I, Paxs
Thetford, Ælfwine. 1.17g
CR 1996, 134.

BENSON, O (1893)
Æthelred II, First Hand
Ipswich, Leofric (moneyer not recorded for Second Hand)
William I, Profile/Cross Fleury
Wallingford
Sotheby 24 Feb. 1893, 56 (Rusher Davies)

BERE REGIS, Do 1986
Edward Martyr, Small Cross
mint?, moneyer? (0.99g, fragment)
SF 3, 80

BERKELEY, Gl 1981
Harold I, Fleur-de-lis
Bristol, Leofwine. 1.02g
SF 2, 9

BEVERLEY, ERY (Humberside) (Lurk Lane) 1979-82
Æthelred II, Long Cross
Lincoln, Wulfric
cut halfpenny, 0.28g (fragment)
Harold II, Pax
York, ...cetel
cut halfpenny, 0.31g
P. Armstrong et al., *Excavations at Lurk Lane, Beverley, 1979-82*, Sheffield 1991, p. 169

BEXLEY, K (in St. Mary's church) 1883
William I, Paxs
Lincoln, Sigeferth. 1.35g
SCBI South-Eastern 1829

BIGGLESWADE (Sheepwalk), Bd (1992)
Edward Martyr, Small Cross
Bedford, Grimr. 1.25g
SCBI South-Eastern 797

BISHOPS CANNINGS, W 1993
Cnut, Short Cross
Lincoln, Leofa or Leofheah. wnr
CR 1993, 222

BISHOPS WALTHAM, Ha (1915)
Edward Confessor, Pointed Helmet
Winchester, Æthelstan. 1.24g
SCBI Mack 1222

BLACKTHORN, O 1989
Edward Martyr, Small Cross
Southampton, moneyer? wnr
CR 1988, 168

BLANDFORD FORUM, Do 1986
Germany, Otto III,? Soest,? *c.*1040-50
SF 3, 82

BLUNTISHAM, Hu (Cambs) (1958)
Æthelred II, Last Small Cross
London, Æthelweard. wnr
SCBI South-Eastern 978

BLYTH, Nt 1985
Æthelred II, Long Cross
Lincoln, Kolgrimr. (1.39g, fragment)
SF 2, 11

BOSHAM, Sx (W. Sussex) 1993
Edward Confessor, Trefoil-Quadrilateral
Lincoln, Godric. wnr
CR 1996, 119

BOSTON, L (general area) 1993
Cnut, Short Cross
mint?, moneyer?
cut halfpenny, 0.49g
CR 1994, 215
William I, Profile/Cross and Trefoils
London, Ælfwine. 1.05g
CR 1994, 241

BOVINGDON, Hrt 1850
Æthelred II, Helmet
London, Sweting 1.38g
Sotheby 21 June 1909, 290

BOXGROVE, Sx (W. Sussex) *c.*1920
Edward Confessor, Short Cross
Chester, Leofwine. wnr
CR 1987, 153

BOXGROVE, Sx (W. Sussex) (1983)
Edward Confessor, Pyramids
Chichester, Ælfwine. wnr
CR 1987, 164 ('apparently found at B.')

BRACON ASH, Nf 1991
Cnut, Short Cross
Lincoln, Svartlingr. 0.92g
CR 1991, 136

Bradenham, *see* East/West Bradenham

BRAMFORD, Sf 1994
Cnut, Short Cross
Dover, Boga. 0.96g
CR 1994, 216

BRAMPTON, Hu (Cambs) 1983
Edward Confessor, Radiate/Small Cross
Norwich, Osmund. wnr
SF 2, 13

BRANDON, Sf 1993
Cnut, Short Cross
Thetford, moneyer?
cut halfpenny, 0.50g (chipped)
CR 1993, 224

BRANDON, Sf 1994
Edward Confessor, Pointed Helmet
Cambridge, Godwine. 1.28g
CR 1996, 122

BRANDON, Sf, near 1995
Æthelred II, Helmet
Stamford, Godwine. 0.87g (chipped)
CR 1995, 168

BRANDON, Sf, a village north of *c.*1991
Æthelred II, Second Hand
London, Wulfstan. 1.14g (pierced)
CR 1996, 102
Edward Confessor, Hammer Cross
Colchester, Wulfwine. 1.14g
CR 1996, 124

BREDFIELD, Sf 1993
Æthelred II, First Hand
London, moneyer?
cut halfpenny, 0.69g
CR 1993, 213

BRISTOL, Gl (Avon) (St. Mary-le-Port excavations) 1962
Harold II, Pax
Bristol, Ceorl. 1.55g
SCBI Bristol 38a

BROMESWELL, Sf 1987
Cnut, Short Cross
London, moneyer?
cut halfpenny, 0.41g
CR 1987, 148
Edward Confessor, Facing Bust/Small Cross
London, moneyer?
cut farthing, 0.24g (worn)
CR 1987, 163

BULLINGTON, L (Goltho manor house) 1971, 1973
Cnut, Helmet
Lincoln, Ulfbjorn. 0.60g (corroded)
Cnut, Short Cross
Lincoln, Leofing. 0.96g (fragment)
Blackburn *et al.*, *Lincoln and its Shire*, II, 22, 23 and Figs. 36, 40.

BURY ST EDMUNDS, Sf 1869
Harold I, Fleur-de-lis
Lincoln, moneyer?
Suffolk Inst. Arch. Jl. 1869, 36

BURY ST EDMUNDS, Sf, near 1994
Edward Confessor, Pyramids
Northampton, Swetman. 1.15g
CR 1996, 128

BURY ST EDMUNDS, Sf, near 1995
Otto-Adelheid Pfennig, *c.*983/991—1040
fragment, 0.48g
CR 1995, 260

BUTCOMBE, So (Avon) (Kingcott Farm) 1990
Æthelred II, Last Small Cross
Winchester, Ordbeorht. 1.43g
CR 1990, 207

CADLEY, W (1889)
William I, type?
mint?, moneyer? wnr
CC p. 36

CAER GYBI (Holyhead), Wales (1976)
Edward Martyr, Small Cross
Northampton, Ketill. wnr
D.W. Dykes, *Anglo-Saxon Coins*, 1976, no. 40

CAERNARFON (*Segontium*), Gwynedd (1976)
Cnut, Quatrefoil
Chester, Gunnleifr
D.W. Dykes, *Anglo-Saxon Coins*, 1976, no. 47

CAERWENT, Gwent
Æthelred II, Crux
mint?, moneyer?
D.W. Dykes, *Anglo-Saxon Coins*, p. 20
Harthacnut, Arm and Sceptre
Chester, Fargrimr. wnr
Dykes, op. cit., no. 52

CAISTER ON SEA, Nf
Æthelred II, Long Cross (? subsidiary)
London(,?) moneyer?
cut halfpenny wnr
EAA 60 (1993), p. 71

CAISTOR-BY-NORWICH, Nf *c.* 1990
Edward Confessor, Pointed Helmet/Hammer Cross mule
Wallingford, Brand. wnr
Unpublished

CAISTOR-ON-THE-WOLDS, L 1984,1986
Æthelred II, Long Cross
Lincoln, Reinald. 1.18g
SF 3, 84
Cnut, Short Cross
Lincoln, Æthelmær (ÆGL-). wnr
SF 1, 2

CAMBRIDGE (Free School Lane) 1886
Æthelred II, Crux
London, Ælfnoth. 1.54g
SCBI Cambridge 662

CANTERBURY, K (Marlowe Car Park site,etc.)
Æthelred II, Long Cross
London, Eadsige. 1.29g (fragments)
Harold I, Fleur-de-lis
mint? moneyer?
cut halfpenny, 0.30g (fragment)
Edward Confessor, Hammer Cross
Canterbury, Ælfræd
cut halfpenny, 0.49g
William I, Two Stars
Sandwich, Ælfgeat. 1.19g
K. Blockley et al., *Excavations in the Marlowe Car Park* (The Archaeology of Canterbury, vol.5), part 2, 1995, pp. 949f.

CANTERBURY, K (St. Augustine's excavations) 1976,1978
Harold I, Jewel Cross
Dover, moneyer? wnr
Edward Confessor, Facing Bust
Canterbury, moneyer?
cut halfpenny, wnr
CC p. 39

CARDIFF, S. Glam ('Sully Moors') 1989
Æthelred II, Last Small Cross
Shaftesbury, Ælfwine, 1.40g
CR 1989, 83

Carisbrooke, *see* Isle of Wight

CARLISLE (Cathedral excavn.) 1985- 8
Æthelred II, First Hand
York? (EFOR), moneyer?
cut halfpenny, 0.36g
SCBI Northern 954

CARLISLE (Stanwix) (Cumbria) 1841
Cnut, Short Cross
Stamford, Maurulf, wnr
CR 1992, 275

CASTLE ACRE, Nf 1980
Edward Martyr, Small Cross
Derby, Asulfr, 1.11g
Seaby 1980, p. 386, E.677
Edward Confessor, Sovereign
Stamford, moneyer? wnr
Edward Confessor, Facing Bust
Thetford, moneyer? wnr
cut halfpenny
CC p. 42

CASTLE RISING, Nf 1980
Æthelred II, First Hand
Stamford, moneyer? wnr
CC p. 42

CATTERTON, ERY 1969
Edward Confessor, Helmet
York, Arngrimr. wnr
Yorks Arch. Jl. 1970, 389 (grid ref.)

CAWOOD, WRY 1980
Edward Confessor, Pyramids
York, Ioketill. wnr
SF 2, 18

CERNE ABBAS, Do 1807
Spain, dirham, Hisham II, AD 999/1000
NC 1957, 242f.

CERNE ABBAS, Do (1943)
Cnut, Helmet
Winchester, Ælfstan. 1.02g (frag.

missing)
SCBI West Country 629 (find-spot)

CHARLBURY, O 1985
Æthelred II, Long Cross
York, Leofstan. wnr
CR 1987, 141

CHECKENDON, O (Hammonds Farm) 1988
William I, Two Stars
Wallingford, Svertlingr. wnr
CR 1988, 196

CHEDDAR, So (palace excavations) 1960-2
Æthelred II, Crux
London/Southwark, Beorhtlaf
cut half, 0.53g (frag. missing)
Æthelred II, Long Cross
Thetford, Osbern. 1.60g
Cnut, Short Cross
Oxford, Ælfweald. 1.02g
SCBI West Country 470, 548, 642

CHERITON, Ha (near) 1993
Æthelred II, Long Cross
London, Godman. 1.19g (clipped)
Æthelred II, Long Cross
York, Sumarlithr. 1.44g
Æthelred II, Long Cross
mint?, moneyer?
cut farthing, 0.42g
CR 1994, 206, 208, 209. A mini-hoard?
William I, Profile/Cross and Trefoils
Wallingford, Svertingr
cut halfpenny, 0.57g
CR 1994, 243

CHELMSFORD, Ess, near
William I, Two Stars
London, Godwine. 1.23g
CR 1996, 133

CHESTER (1-11 Crook Street) 1973-4
Æthelred II, Last Small Cross
Chester, Alsige. 0.74g
S.W. Ward, *Excavations at Chester,* vol. 7, p.27

CHESTER (Greyfriars Court, Dominican friary) 1976-8
Edward Confessor, Facing Bust
Chester, Dunning.
cut halfpenny, 0.3g
S.W. Ward, *Excavations at Chester,* vol. 6,
p.165, cf. vol.7, p.101 ('Chester or Leicester')

CHICHESTER, Sx (Tower St.) 1974
Edward Confessor, Radiate/Small Cross
Barnstaple, Æthelmær. 0.47g (fragment)
William I, Bonnet
Oxford, Æthelwine. wnr
gilt brooch (reverse facing)
SCBI South-Eastern 1139, 1735; A. Down, *Chichester Excavations,* vol. 3, p. 340

CHICHESTER, Sx (Chapel Street) 1971
Æthelred II, Second Hand
London, Leofstan? 1.01g
SCBI South-Eastern 879; A. Down, *Chichester*
Excavations, vol. 3, p. 340 (also another coin of Æthelred II, illegible)

CHOLSEY, Brk (O)
Edward Confessor, Sovereign
Wallingford, moneyer?
Sotheby 24 Feb. 1893, 57 (two specimens?)

CHURCH HANBOROUGH, O 1983
Æthelred II, Long Cross
Oxford, Wulfwine. 1.43g
CR 1987, 140

CIRENCESTER, Gl (St. Mary's Abbey excav.) 1965
William I, Profile/Cross and Trefoils
Wareham, Æthelric. 1.34g (holed)
SCBI West Country 770

CLAXBY-BY-ALFORD, L 1977
Cnut, Short Cross
Stamford, Morulf
cut halfpenny, 0.44g
SF 1, 5

CLEETHORPES, L (S. Humberside) 1983
Æthelred II, Long Cross
mint?, moneyer? wnr
SF 3, 86

CODDENHAM, Sf (Shrubland Hall) 1982
Edward Martyr, Small Cross
York,? Gunnulfr.
cut halfpenny, 0.62g
SF 2, 60

CODDENHAM, Sf 1990-2
Edward Martyr, Small Cross
Bedford, Bealdic. wnr
Proc. Suffolk Inst A. H. 37/4, p. 256

COLCHESTER, Ess 1944
Æthelred II, Crux
Colchester, Eadsige. wnr
CR 1987, 132

COLESBOURNE, Gl (St. James's churchyard) 1959
Cnut, Helmet
Winchester, Leodmær. 0.97g
Trans. Bristol and Glos Arch. Soc. 78 (1959), 92-5 (illus.); *SCBI West Country* 630

COLESHILL, Wa 1983
Æthelred II, Last Small Cross
Winchester, Ælfstan. 1.21g
CR 1988, 175

COLKIRK, Nf 1994
Eadgar, Reform type
Norwich or Cambridge, Leofing
cut halfpenny, 0.66g
CR 1994, 201

COMPTON, Ha 1979
Æthelred II, Long Cross type
mint?, moneyer? (Eadric or Godric, London?)
cut halfpenny, 0.71g
NCirc 1979, 380

CONGHAM, Nf (site 25765) 1995
Æthelred II, Long Cross
Rochester, Eadsige. 1.45g
CR 1995, 163
Edward Confessor, Short Cross
London, Wul-.
cut halfpenny, 0.28g
CR 1995, 174

CONINGSBY, L 1988
Edward Confessor, Radiate/Small Cross
Stamford, Godric. wnr
CR 1988, 183

CRANWICH, Nf 1993
Edward Martyr, Small Cross
Stamford, Boia. 1.26g
CR 1992, 269

CRANWICH, Nf 1994
(presumably a mini-hoard)
William I, Two Sceptres
Northampton, Godwine. 1.29g and 1.28g (die-dupl.)
CR 1994, 237-8

CREWKERNE, So (Barn Street, while laying pipes) 1963
Æthelred II, First Hand
Winchester, Ingalric. wnr
CR 1987, 130

CROUGHTON, Nth *c.*1995
Harold I, Jewel Cross
London, Korf, 0.72g
CR 1995, 170

CROXTON, Nf 1994
Cnut, Quatrefoil
Cambridge, Cniht. 0.75g (incomplete)
CR 1994, 213

DARENTH, K 1989
William I, Two Sceptres
Warwick, Thorketill. 1.31g
CR 1989, 87

DEANSHANGER, Nth (SP 729419) 1990
Eadgar, Reform
Northampton, Baldric. wnr
Northamptonshire Arch. 23 (1991), 112

DONCASTER, WRY (S. Yorks) 1992
Harthacnut, Arm and Sceptre
York, Ælfhere
cut halfpenny, 0.49g (chipped)

DONINGTON, L 1980
William I, Profile/Cross and Trefoils
Canterbury, Godric
cut halfpenny
CC p. 43. Blackburn 31

DORCHESTER, Do 1908
William I, Profile/Cross and trefoils
Wareham, Æthelric. wnr
BNJ 5 (1908), 112

DORSET (site recorded in BM) 1991
William I, Bonnet
Wilton, Sfare. 0.92g (chipped)
CR 1992, 284

DOVER, K 1843
Harthacnut, type?
Dover, Eadsige? wnr
CC p. 39

DOVER, K 1980
Cnut, Short Cross
Dover, moneyer?
cut halfpenny, wnr
CC p. 39

DRIGG, Cu (Cumbria) 1988
Cnut, Short Cross
Chester, Ælfnoth. 1.01g
CR 1988, 177

DRINGHOUSES (York), ERY
Æthelred II, Crux
London, Wulfstan. 1.56g
SCBI Yorks 1028

DUNNINGTON/KEXBY, ERY 1994
Æthelred II, First Small Cross
York, Styr
cut halfpenny, wnr
CR 1996, 107

DUNSTABLE, Bd (near) 1952
William I, Paxs
Winchester, Æthelstan. 1.23g (pierced)
SCBI South-Eastern 1867

EASINGWOLD, NRY 1995
Æthelred II, First Hand
York, Oda. 1.45g
CR 1995, 158
Edward Confessor, Short Cross
mint?, moneyer? 1.04g
CR 1995, 176

EASTBOURNE, Sx (E. Sussex) 1993
Edward Confessor, Pyramids
Cambridge, Godlamm
cut halfpenny, 0.54g
CR 1996, 127

EAST BRADENHAM, Nf 1994
(possibly a hoard)
William I, Profile/Cross and Trefoils
London, Eadwine. 0.99g (incomplete)
Thetford, Godric. 1.39g
CR 1994, 240 and 242

EAST DEAN, Sx (Birling Manor Farm, TQ 559 978) 1991
Edward Confessor, Trefoil-Quadrilateral
Winchester, Godric. wnr
Sussex Arch Coll. 129 pp. 246-7 (illus.)

EAST HARLING, Nf 1982
Harthacnut, Jewel Cross (right-facing)
Canterbury?, Leofnoth?
cut halfpenny, 0.61g.
SF 2, 24
Harold I, Jewel Cross (left-facing)
Thetford, Æthelmær. 0.95g.
SF 2, 25

EAST MEON, H 1990
Æthelred II, Crux
Winchester, Beorhtnoth
cut halfpenny. 0.60g
CR 1990, 204

EAST WALTON, Nf 1992
Edward Martyr, Small Cross
Stamford, Cnapa. (0.72g, incomplete)
CR 1992, 270

ECTON, Nth 1762
Æthelred II, First Hand
Norwich, Folcard
VCH Northants, p.255
'Two Saxon silver coins' found with 'several bones and skulls'. Only one illustrated.

EDINGTON, W 1981
Edward Confessor, Pyramids
Salisbury, Saeboda
Gilt brooch
Devizes Museum

EDWARDSTONE, Sf 1994
Æthelred II, type?
Cambridge, moneyer? (fragment)
Proc. Suffolk Inst A.H. 38/2 (1994), 202

ELSFIELD, O (Royal Oak Farm)

Edward Confessor, Expanding Cross
London, Leofræd. wnr
Inf. DMM

ELY, C (a village near E.) 1983
Cnut, Short Cross
London, Wynsige
cut halfpenny, wnr
SF 3, 89
Harold I, Fleur-de-lis
Lincoln, Kolgrimr, wnr
SF 3, 20
These two coins were from the same site, although found on different occasions. Could they reflect a small hoard?

ESSEX, NORTH (general description) 1987
Æthelred II, Small Crux
London,? Eadsige. wnr
CR 1987, 133
Cnut, Short Cross
London, Godman. wnr
CR 1987, 146
Edward Confessor, Short Cross
London,? Goldsige. wnr
CR 1987, 154
William I, Profile/Cross and Trefoils
mint?, moneyer? wnr
CR 1987, 172

EWELL, Sr (district) 1913
Æthelred II, Helmet
London, Eadmund. wnr
Surrey Arch. Coll. 26 (1913), 137

EXETER, D (near the city wall, Northernhay) 1845
Æthelred II, Helmet
Exeter, Wulfsige. wnr
Cunobelin 10 (1964), 26

EYNSHAM, O (abbey site) 1963
Cnut, Quatrefoil
Exeter, Isengod. 0.97g
CC p. 41. Shown in Ashm. by Vicar of Eynsham.

EYNSHAM, O (abbey excavations) 1991
Æthelred II, First Hand
mint?, Manna
cut halfpenny, wnr
CR 1991, 133

Faccombe, *see* Netherton

FELPHAM, Sx (W.Sussex) 1984
Edward Martyr, Small Cross
Wilton, Boia. wnr
Devizes Museum

FISKERTON, L (Short Ferry Bridge) 1964
Edward Confessor, Trefoil-Quadrilateral
Lincoln, Kolgrimr.
Blackburn et al., *Lincoln and its Shire,* II, 27.

Fortuneswell, *see* Portland

FOXCOTTE, Ha (d.m.v. SU 345 474) 1979
William I, Profile/Cross Fleury
Winchester, moneyer? wnr
CC p. 36

FULBOURN, C 1988
Edward Confessor, Short Cross
mint?, Godwine.
cut halfpenny, 0.51g
CR 1988, 185

GAINSBOROUGH, L before 1995
Æthelred II, First Small Cross
Lincoln, Grind
cut farthing, 0.28g
CR 1996, 101
Cnut, Short Cross
Lincoln, Asleikr
cut halfpenny, wnr
CR 1996, 111
Edward Confessor, Pointed Helmet
Hastings?, Duning
cut halfpenny, wnr
CR 1996, 123
Edward Confessor, Hammer Cross
Lincoln, Authgrimr
cut farthing, 0.29g
CR 1996, 125

GARTHORPE, Lei 1980
Edward Confessor, Sovereign type
Lincoln, moneyer? wnr
CC p. 43

GASTARD, W 1989
Cnut, Helmet
Totnes, Ælfwine
cut halfpenny, wnr
A.H. Graham and S.M. Davies, *Excavations in Trowbridge,* under coin no.7

GLASTONBURY, So (abbey excavations) 1952-4
Æthelred II, First Hand
Ilchester, Ælfsige. wnr
Edward Confessor, Pointed Helmet/Hammer Cross
Wallingford, Brunwine. wnr
die-ident *SCBI Oxford* 894
Edward Confessor, type?
York?, moneyer? (missing)
Proc. Somerset Arch. NHS 125 (1981)

GLOUCESTER (Kingsholm)
Edward Confessor, Short Cross?
York, moneyer?
Trans. Bristol Glos AS 101 (1983), 92

GLOUCESTER 1959
Æthelred II, Helmet
Gloucester, Leofsige. 1.34g
SCBI Glos. 42

GODMANCHESTER, Hu (C) 1995
Edward Confessor, Expanding Cross (heavy)
Ipswich, Brun (ing)
cut halfpenny, 0.74g
CR 1995, 180

Goltho, see Bullington

GOSBECK, Sf 1994
Æthelred II, type?
Ipswich, Lytelman. wnr
Proc Suffolk Inst A.H. 38/2 (1994), 202

GRANTHAM, L (general area) 1989
William I, Canopy
Lincoln, Godric. 1.26g
CR 1989, 86

GREAT MONGEHAM, K 1992
Æthelred II, Last Small Cross
Canterbury, Godman. 1.38g
CR 1996, 108

GREAT MONGEHAM, K 1993
Edward Confessor, Sovereign/Eagles
mint?, moneyer? (0.51g, fragment)
CR 1993, 234

GREAT WAKERING, Ess (towards Shoeburyness), 1994
Edward Confessor, Pacx (var.)
London, Wulfwine. 1.02g
CR 1994, 225

GREAT WOLFORD, Wa 1990
Æthelred II, Long Cross
London, Wulfwine. 1.24g
CR 1990, 206

GREAT YARMOUTH, Nf (Fullers Hill excav.) 1976
Edward Confessor, Hammer Cross
Nottingham, moneyer? wnr
E Angl. Arch 2 (1976), 161

GRIMSBY, L (S. Humberside) (general area) 1984
Æthelred II, First Small Cross
York, Wine... (?Wineman)
cut halfpenny, 0.56g
SF 1, 10

GRIMSBY, L (S. Humberside) (general area) 1986
Æthelred II, First Hand
York, Skaning. 1.35g
SF 3, 105

GUILDFORD, Sr (Saxon cemetery excavn.) 1930
Edward Confessor, Radiate/Small Cross
Lincoln, Godric
cut halfpenny, 0.52g
SCBI South-Eastern 1145

HADSTOCK, Ess 1824
William I, Two Stars
London, Brihtmær
BMC 336

HALNAKER, Sx (W. Sussex) 1988
Edward Confessor, Expanding Cross
Canterbury, Leofstan. wnr
CR 1987, 155

HAM, K 1991
Harthacnut, Jewel Cross
London, Eadric. 1.00g
CR 1996, 118

(?) HAMBLEDEN, Bk 1992-3
Edward Confessor, Radiate (imitation)
(Stamford, Wilgrip) 0.88g
CR 1992, 278 ('Hambledon valley, O ')

HAMMERSMITH (in the R. Thames) 1980
William I, Two Sceptres
Northampton, Sæwine. wnr
CR 1987, 171

HAMPSHIRE 1988
Edward Confessor, Facing Bust
Worcester, Vikingr. 0.86g
CR 1988, 190

HANGLETON, Sx (W. Sussex) 1987 (probably a hoard)
Æthelred, Long Cross
London, Leofric. 1.38g
London, Sweting. 1.35g
CR 1987, 138 and 139. (2 km SE of Angmering)

HARBOROUGH MAGNA, Wa 1991
Cnut, Short Cross
Leicester, Wulfnoth. 1.04g
CR 1992, 274 (*not* Hanborough)

HASTINGS, Sx (E. Sussex) 1936
Edward Confessor, Hammer Cross
Hastings, Duning. 1.25g
SCBI Fitzw. 916

HELLINGLY, Sx (E. Sussex) 1808
Æthelred II, Helmet
Lewes, Leofwine. 3.34g
Gold penny
BMC 1

HEMINGFORD GREY, Hu (Cambs) 1980
Æthelred II, First Hand
London, Cynesige. 1.77g
SCBI South-Eastern 808

HEMINGSTONE, Sf 1995
Italy, Otto I, II, or III, 962 x 1002
0.88g chipped
CR 1995, 271

HEMPNALL, Nf 1989
Æthelred II, First Hand
mint?, Godwine. 0.99g (fragment)
CR 1989, 82

HEREFORD 1965-76
Cnut, Short Cross
Chester, Leofwine. wnr
Hereford City Excavations, vol. 3, 1985
(microfiche 5.F1)

HESLINGTON FIELD, ERY 1868
Edward Confessor, type?
York, Ulfketill. wnr
SCBI Yorks xxxix, no. 17

HIGHAM, K *c.* 1995
Æthelred II, Helmet
Exeter, Dudel. 1.10g
CR 1995, 167
Edward Confessor, Short Cross
London, Ælfw-. 0.90g
CR 1995, 173
Edward Confessor, Sovereign/Eagles
London, Godric. 1.25g
CR 1995, 184

HOLME HALE, Nf 1994
Edward Confessor, Expanding Cross
Norwich, Thorfrithr. 1.55g
CR 1994, 230

Holyhead, *see* Caer Gybi

HORNCASTLE, L 1854
William I, Two Stars
Lincoln, Wi(htric)
Blackburn, *Lincoln and its Shire*, II, 30

HORNCASTLE, L 1976
Æthelred II, First Hand
Lincoln, Theodgild
cut halfpenny
Blackburn, *Lincoln and its Shire,* II, 19 and *NCirc* 1976.
Æthelred II, Long Cross
Rochester, Eadweard.
Blackburn, *Lincoln and its Shire*, II, 21
NCirc. 1976, 365. ('Found on separate sites near Horncastle')

HORSEHEATH, C 1993
Harold I, Jewel Cross
Norwich, Ælfwine. 1.03g
CR 1996, 116

HOSE, Lei (near) 1985
Edward Confessor, Pointed Helmet

Winchester, Godwine. wnr
SF 2, 31

HUNMANBY, ERY 1976
Edward Confessor, Expanding Cross (light)
York, Leofnoth
Trans. Scarborough AHS 3/19, pp. 34-5

HUNTINGDON (near) 1992
Cnut, Quatrefoil
Lincoln, Ulfgrimr. 1.13g
CR 1994, 214

HUNTSPILL, So 1977
Edward Confessor, Pacx
Exeter, Lifinc. 1.07g
SCBI West Country 666

ICKLETON, C *c.*1995
Æthelred II, Long Cross
Oxford, Ælfwine
cut half, in lead. 1.32g
CR 1995, 166 (with discussion)

IDMISTON, W 1949
Edward Confessor, Facing Bust
Wilton, Ælfweald. 0.94g
SCBI West Country 736

ILCHESTER, So 1974
Æthelred II, Second Hand
Exeter, moneyer? wnr
CC p. 39

IPSWICH, Sf 1961, 1975
Æthelred II, Small Crux
Stamford
SCBI East Anglia 1177
Edward Confessor, Trefoil-Quadrilateral
London, moneyer?
CC p.42

IPSWICH (Cox Lane), Sf 1961
Æthelred II, Small Crux
mint?, moneyer?
SCBI East Anglia 1177

IPSWICH, Sf 1991
Æthelred II, Crux
Lincoln, Steinbitr. wnr
CR 1990, 203

IPSWICH, Sf *c.*1980-1995
Eadgar, Reform
Ipswich, Leofric. 0.79g
Edward Martyr, sole type
Oxford, Wulfræd. 0.68g
Æthelred II, First Hand.
Northampton, moneyer?
cut halfpenny, 0.29g
Edward Confessor, Facing Bust
Rochester, Eadwine. 0.25g (fragment)
Ipswich excavations (forthcoming), per J. Newman.

IRTHLINGBOROUGH, Nth 1986
Æthelred II, Last Small Cross
Northampton, Wulfnoth. 1.46g
SF 2, 34

ISLEHAM, Ca 1982
Harold I, Fleur-de-lis
Lincoln, Kolgrimr. 1.11g
CH 7, p. 378

ISLE OF WIGHT 1959
Æthelred II, Second Hand
London, Leofstan. 1.04g (fragment)
SCBI South-Eastern 820 (fd. at Carisbrooke, but in soil from elsewhere on the island)

IXWORTH, Sf 1869
Edward Confessor, Radiate/Small Cross
? Hertford (IEON), Deorsige
Edward Confessor, Helmet (head left)
Lincoln, Godric
Edward Confessor, Helmet
Chester, Leofnoth
Sotheby, 22 March 1869, part of lot 55.
Very probably from a small hoard

IXWORTH, Sf (near) 1994
Æthelred II, Long Cross
London, Leofwine. 1.62g
CR 1994, 207

JARROW, Du (Tyne and Wear) (excavn) 1965
Edward Confessor, Pointed Helmet/Hammer Cross mule
Bedford, Siggautr. 0.43g
SCBI Northern 1046

KEELBY, L, near 1986
Edward Confessor, Pyramids
Lincoln, Ulfr. 1.48g
SF 3, 108

KEELBY, L 1987
William I, Profile/Cross and Trefoils
Lincoln, Thorsteinn. wnr
CR 1987, 173

KENNINGHALL, Nf 1993
Cnut, Short Cross
Stamford, Leofdæg. 0.90g
CR 1992, 277

KIMPTON, Ha 1967
Edward Confessor, Facing Bust
Wilton, Winus
SCBI West Country 970

Kingsholm, *see* Gloucester

KINGSTON-ON-THAMES, Sr (G. Lond) 1888
Æthelred II, Long Cross
London, Eadsige. 1.42g
SCBI Oxford 539

KIRBY CANE, Nf 1988
William I, Profile/Cross and Trefoils
Thetford, Folcard
cut farthing, 0.29g
CR 1988, 197

KNAPWELL/ELSWORTH, C 1995
William I, Sword
London, Godwine. 1.20g
CR 1995, 188

LAKENHEATH, Sf 1983
Æthelred II, Second Hand
Norwich, Branting. wnr
CR 1987, 131

LAKENHEATH, Sf 1990
Cnut, Helmet
London, Godric. 0.84g (chipped)
CR 1993, 221

LEATHERHEAD, Sr 1992
Cnut, Short Cross
Lincoln, Crinan
cut halfpenny, 0.48g
CR 1993, 223 and *CR* 1995, 369

LEICESTER 1980
Æthelred II, Second Hand
mint?, moneyer? wnr
CC p. 43

LEWES (Landport), Sx (E. Sussex) 1975
Edward Martyr, Small Cross
London, Ælfweard. wnr
SCBI South-Eastern 798

LEWES, Sx (E. Sussex) (priory) 1872
Edward Confessor, Hammer Cross
Wareham, Biorn. 1.31g (pierced)
SCBI West Country 968

LEWES, Sx (E. Sussex) 1848
Harold I, type?
mint?, moneyer? wnr
CC p. 39

LEWES, Sx (E. Sussex) 1984
Edward Confessor, Hammer Cross
Nottingham, Wulfnoth
SF 1, 15

LEWES, Sx (E. Sussex), near 1874
Edward Confessor, Sovereign
Chichester, moneyer? wnr
CR 1987, 160
Harold II, Pax
Lewes, moneyer? wnr
CR 1987, 166
Possibly a mini-hoard?

LINCOLN (Bailgate) 1891
Æthelred II, Last Small Cross
Lincoln, Wulfric.
Pecked, and therefore the reliability has been doubted.
Blackburn, *Lincoln,* p. 19

LINCOLN (near S. wall of bishop's palace) 1819
William I, Paxs
London, Godric, wnr
Blackburn, *Lincoln,* I, 37 and Fig. 62

LINCOLN (Danes Terrace) 1974
Æthelred II, Crux
Stamford, Goth... 0.64g (fragment)
Blackburn, *Lincoln,* I, 15 and Fig. 32;
SCBI Lincs 1953
Edward Confessor, Short Cross
Lincoln, Kolgrimr. 0.58g
Blackburn, *Lincoln,* I, 26 and Fig. 49;
SCBI Lincs 1958

LINCOLN (Eastgate excav.) 1959-66
Cnut, Short Cross
York, Beorn. 0.48g
Blackburn, *Lincoln,* I, 21 and Fig. 39;
SCBI Lincs 1737

LINCOLN (Flaxengate excavn.) 1973-6
Cnut, Short Cross
Hereford, Eadstan. 0.90g
Blackburn, *Lincoln,* I, 20 and Fig. 38;
SCBI Lincs 1995
Cnut, Short Cross
Lincoln, Aslakr. 0.37g (fragment)
Blackburn, *Lincoln,* I, 19 and Fig. 37;
SCBI Lincs 1956
Edward Confessor, Pacx
(?) Rochester (or York), moneyer?
cut halfpenny, 0.58g
Blackburn, *Lincoln,* I, 23 and Fig. 45;
SCBI Lincs 1957
Edward Confessor, Pacx
mint?, moneyer?
cut halfpenny or fragment, 0.23g
Lincoln, I, 24 and Fig. 46;
SCBI Lincs -
Edward Confessor, Sovereign
mint?, moneyer? 0.29g (frag.)
Blackburn, *Lincoln,* I, 28 and Fig. 53;
SCBI Lincs 1959
Edward Confessor, Sovereign /Hammer Cross mule
Hertford, Sæmær. 0.83g (frag.)
Blackburn, *Lincoln,* I, 29 and Fig. 54;
SCBI Lincs 1960
Edward Confessor, Facing Bust
Lincoln, Gife. 0.67g
Blackburn, *Lincoln,* I, 30 and Fig. 55;
SCBI Lincs 1961
Edward Confessor, Facing Bust
Lincoln, Ulfr? 0.19g (frag.)
Blackburn, *Lincoln,* I, 31 and Fig. 56;
SCBI Lincs 1962
William I, Two Sceptres
Wallingford, Brand
cut halfpenny, 0.44g
Blackburn, *Lincoln,* I, 35 and Fig. 59;
SCBI Lincs 1963

LINCOLN (St. Mark's excavn.) 1976
William I, Two Sceptres
Thetford, Cyneric. 0.93g
Blackburn, *Lincoln,* I, 34 and Fig. 58;
SCBI Lincs -

LINCOLN (St. Mary's Guildhall excavn.) 1982
William I, Bonnet
London, moneyer? 0.64g (frag.)
Blackburn, *Lincoln,* I, 33 and Fig. 57.
SCBI Lincs-

LINCOLN (St. Paul's excav.) 1974-1979
Æthelred II, First Hand
Lincoln or York, Kolgrimr?
cut farthing, 0.25g
Blackburn, *Lincoln,* I, 12 and Fig. 29;
SCBI Lincs 1951
Æthelred II, First Hand
Lincoln or York, Kolgrimr?
cut farthing, 0.31g
Blackburn, *Lincoln,* I, 13 and Fig. 30;
SCBI Lincs -
Æthelred II, Crux
Lincoln, moneyer?
cut farthing, 0.29g
Blackburn, *Lincoln,* I, 14 and Fig. 31;
SCBI Lincs 1952
Æthelred II, Long Cross
Lincoln, Ælfsige. 1.03g
Blackburn, *Lincoln,* I, 16 and Fig. 33;
SCBI Lincs 1954
Harthacnut, Arm and Sceptre
Lincoln, ...od
cut halfpenny, 0.31g
Blackburn, *Lincoln,* I, 22 and Fig. 41;
SCBI Lincs 1965a

LINCOLN (Stamp End lock?) 1802
Cnut, Quatrefoil
Lincoln, Leofing, wnr
Blackburn, *Lincoln,* I, 18 and Fig. 35

LINCOLN (Usher Gallery grounds) 1973-7
Edward Confessor, Expanding Cross (heavy)
Stamford, Færgrim. 1.68g
Blackburn, *Lincoln,* I, 27 and Fig. 51;
SCBI Lincs 1420
Olaf Kyrre, Norwegian coin, 0.76g
Blackburn, Lincoln, I, 32 and Fig. 65;
SCBI Lincs 1973
Blackburn, p. 32

LINCOLN (West Parade excav.) 1971
Danish coin, *c.* 1045
Blackburn, *Lincoln,* I, 25 and Fig. 42;
SCBI Lincs 1966

LINCOLN (in the R. Witham) 1787

Edward Confessor, Pacx
Lincoln, Ulfr.
BNJ 43 (1973), 168. *BMC* 698

LINCOLN 1854
Æthelred II, Long Cross
Lincoln, Drengr. wnr
Blackburn, *Lincoln*, I, 17 and Fig. 34

LINCOLN (1 mile NW of city centre) 1819
William I, Paxs
Exeter, Sæwine. wnr
Blackburn, *Lincoln*, I, 36 and Fig. 61

LINCOLN (near) 1986
Edward Confessor, Expanding Cross (light)
Mint?, moneyer? 0.29g (fragment)
CR 1987, 159
Norway, Olaf Kyrre, 1067-93
CR 1987, 168 (full discussion)
These two coins were stated to have been found together.

LINCOLN (near), 1992
William I, Paxs
Thetford, Godric. 1.29g
CR 1994, 244

LINCOLNSHIRE, 1993
Æthelred II, Crux
Lincoln, Ubeinn. wnr
CR 1993, 214

LITTLEBOROUGH, Nt (near) 1994
Edward Confessor, Helmet
Stamford, Godwine. 1.23g
CR 1994, 233

LITTLE HORWOOD, Bk 1985
Cnut, Short Cross
London, Sveinn. wnr
SF 3, 112

LITTLE MONGEHAM (near Deal), K 1992
Æthelred II, Last Small Cross
Canterbury, Godman. 1.38g
CR 1991, 132
Edward Confessor, Facing Bust
Wilton, Hereræd
cut halfpenny, wnr
CR 1992, 282
Edward Confessor, Facing Bust/Pyramids mule
Dover, Wulfweard. wnr
CR 1992, 283

LITTLE WITTENHAM, Brk (O) 1867
Æthelred II, Crux
Barnstaple?, DVRASILE (Deorsige?) wnr
NC 1867, Proc., p. 8

LLANSTEPHAN, Dyfed. date?
Æthelred, Last Small Cross
London, Wulfræd (Wulfryd).
Boon (*Welsh Hoards*, p.18; *BNJ* 1993, 85, 'from an ancient ferry terminus'.
Arch. Camb. 1970, 75-82)

LONDON (Aldersgate Street) 1883
Æthelred II, type?
London, Godric. wnr
Stott 92; *JBAA* 1883, 86

LONDON (All Hallows, Lombard St.) 1940
Edward Confessor, Facing Bust
London, Swetman. 0.91g
Stott 125; *SCBI South-Eastern* 1612

LONDON (Billingsgate Lorry Park) 1982
Æthelred II, Helmet
Chichester, Æthelhelm. 0.53g (broken)
Stott 86
Belgium, first half 11th century. 0.75g
Stott 162; Berghaus

LONDON (Billingsgate spoil) 1984-7
Eadgar, Reform Small Cross
Lympyne, Æthelstan
cut halfpenny, 1.30g (!)
Stott 82
Æthelred II, Crux
mint? moneyer?
cut farthing, 0.34g
Stott 85
Cnut, Quatrefoil
London, Eardnoth. wnr
CR 1988, 176
Cnut, Quatrefoil
Winchester, Wine. 0.84g
Stott 102
Cnut, Helmet
Hertford, moneyer?
cut halfpenny, 0.48g
Stott 104
Cnut, Short Cross type
Lewes, Godefrith
cut halfpenny, 0.49g
CR 1988, 180
Cnut, Short Cross
London, Sveinn. 0.75g
Stott 108
Harold I, Jewel Cross
London, Eadwine
cut halfpenny, 0.37g
CR 1988, 182
Edward Confessor, Trefoil Quadrilateral
London, Brunman. 0.96g
Stott 119
Edward Confessor, Expanding Cross, (light)
Lincoln, Godric. 0.99g
Stott 121
Edward Confessor, Sovereign/Eagles
Contemporary copy. wnr
Stott 122
Edward Confessor, Hammer Cross
Hastings, Duning
cut halfpenny, wnr
Stott 123
Edward Confessor, Hammer Cross
London, moneyer?
cut halfpenny, 0.45g
Stott 124
Edward Confessor, Pyramids
London, Wulf...
cut halfpenny, wnr
Stott 128
William I, Pyramids/Profile-Cross Fleury mule
Lincoln, Geirfinnr. 0.73g
Stott 129
William I, Profile-Cross Fleury
London, Wulfgar
coin brooch (uses the reverse). 3.31g
Stott 130
William I, Paxs
Canterbury, Winedæg. 1.14g
Stott 136
William I, Paxs
Canterbury, Ælfræd. 1.20g
Stott 137
Norway, Olaf Kyrre, 1067-93
CR 1987, 168; Stott 164

LONDON (Billingsgate, Thames foreshore) 1986

Harthacnut, Arm and Sceptre (CNVT)
Nottingham, Leofstan (LEASTAN). 0.79g
Stott 118

LONDON (City) 1840, 1854
Æthelred II, type?
mint? Leofwine
cut halfpenny, wnr
Stott 9
Æthelred II, Last Small Cross?
Lewes, Leofnoth
Stott 89
Cnut, Helmet
London, Eadwine. wnr
Stott 103
Cnut, Short Cross
Dover, Boga
Stott 106

LONDON (City, foreshore) 1835-54
Æthelred II, Crux
London, Beorhtlaf. wnr
Stott 84
Æthelred II, Last Small Cross
Winchester, Ælfweald. wnr
Stott 88
Cnut, Short Cross
London, God. wnr
Stott 105
Cnut, Short Cross
London, Wulfræd. wnr
Stott 107
Cnut, type?
mint?, moneyer?
Stott 114 (October 1835)
Harold I, types?
mints? moneyers?
Stott 115-17

LONDON (GPO Building excavn.,City) 1979
Æthelred II, Last Small Cross
London, Leofweald. 0.53g (broken)
Stott 91

LONDON (Gracechurch Street?) 1889
Æthelred II, Agnus Dei
Derby, Blacman. 1.59g
Stott 87; Kluge (1990) for a full bibliography

LONDON (London Bridge) 1824, 1840
Æthelred II, type?
Lincoln, Æthelnoth. wnr
Stott 97
Æthelred II, types?
mints?, moneyers?
Stott 93-4
Cnut, types?
mints?, moneyers?
Stott 109-13
William I, Paxs
Lincoln, Sigeferth. wnr
Stott 133
William I, type?
Canterbury, Ælfræd. wnr
Stott 138

LONDON (Milk Street excavn) 1976
Cnut, Quatrefoil
London, Ælfwig. wnr
Stott 101
William I, Two Stars
mint? moneyer? wnr
Stott 132

LONDON (Noble Street) (1991)
William I, Canopy
London? moneyer?
cut halfpenny, 0.44g
Stott 131

LONDON (Plantation House, Eastcheap) (1991)
Æthelred II, type?
mint?, moneyer? (frag.)
Stott 90

LONDON (Pudding Lane excavn.) 1981
Edward Confessor, Facing Bust
Hertford? moneyer?
cut halfpenny, 0.15g
Stott 126

LONDON (St. Katherine's Dock) 1827
Cnut, Quatrefoil
Canterbury, Leofwine?
Stott 99

LONDON (St. Nicholas Acon) 1967
Cnut, Quatrefoil
mint?, moneyer?
Stott 100

LONDON (St. Peter's Hill excavn.) 1981
William I, type?
mint?, moneyer?
cut farthing, 0.14g
Stott 135

LONDON, Seal House (City) 1974
Germany, Henry IV, 1080-90
Trans London Mddx. A.S. 27(1976), at p.141

LONDON (Thames) *c.* 1850
Æthelred II, type?
London, Leofræd. wnr
Stott 95

LONDON (Thames Exchange site) 1989
William I, Two Stars
Nottingham, Man. wnr.
CR 1988, 195
William I, Sword type
Shaftesbury, Godsbrand. 1.15g
CR 1993, 237
William I, Profile/Cross and Trefoils type
Colchester, Wulfwine. 0.94g
CR 1993, 238
William I, Profile/Cross and Trefoils type
Dover, Leof(r)ic. 1.17g
CR 1988, 198
Byzantine, Constantine X, 1059-67, silver two-thirds miliaresion
T. Curtis, in *NCirc.* 97 (1989), 116

LONDON (Thames Exchange spoil) 1990-1
Harold I, Fleur-de-lis
Lincoln, Sumarlithr. 0.79g
CR 1993, 226
Edward Confessor, Pyramids
mint?, moneyer?
cut halfpenny, 0.49g
CR 1989, 85

LONDON (Thames foreshore) *c.*1995
Æthelred II, Long Cross
London, Æthelweard
cut halfpenny, 0.8g
CR 1995, 162
Edward Confessor, Expanding Cross (heavy)
mint?, Leofwine
cut halfpenny, 0.8g
CR 1995, 181
Edward Confessor, Pointed Helmet

Maldon, Godwine. 1.3g
CR 1995, 182

LONDON (Thames Waterfront excavations) 1990
William I, Profile/Cross and Trefoils
London, Ælfwine. wnr
CR 1993, 240

LONDON? 1854
Æthelred II, type?
London, Leofræd (Crux or later).wnr
Stott 96
Edward Confessor, Short Cross
Canterbury, moneyer? wnr
Stott 120
William I, Paxs
Thetford, moneyer? wnr
Stott 134

London, *see also* Hammersmith, Southwark, Westminster

LONGPARISH, Ha (near Andover) *c.* 1990
Æthelred II, Crux
London, Eadweald. wnr
Inf. Mr Dunford, of Vale Farm, per D. Chick

LONG SUTTON, L before 1967
Æthelred II, Crux
Lincoln, Steinbitr. 1.51g
Blackburn, *Lincoln,* II, 20; *SCBI Lincs* 56

LONGWORTH, Brk (O) 1946
William I, Bonnet type
Oxford, Wulfwig. 1.26g
SCBI Oxford 33

LOUTH, L 1984-6
Harold I, Jewel Cross
Lincoln, Asfrφthr. 0.86g
SF 2, 37 (site A)
Edward Confessor, Pacx
Stamford, Ælfheah. 0.91g
SF 2, 38 (site A)
Edward Confessor, Pacx
York, Grimulfr
cut halfpenny, (0.28g, fragment)
SF 3, 114 (site A)

Edward Confessor, Pointed Helmet
London, Godwig. 1.30g
SF 2, 41 (site B)
William I, Profile/Cross and Trefoils 1986
London, Godwine. 1.31g
SF 3, 116 (site E)

LOWER WATERSTON, Do 1994
Edward Confessor, Expanding Cross, (heavy)
Lincoln, Authgrimr. 1.78g
CR 1994, 229

MANCHESTER ('Castle Hill')
Cnut, Helmet
York, Wulfnoth
Normandy, denier
Both are discussed in *SCBI Merseyside,* p. xx

MARHAM, Nf 1987
Edward Confessor, Hammer Cross
Bury St Edmunds, Morkar
cut farthing, 0.22g
CR 1987, 161; *CR* 1988, 188

MARKET DEEPING, L, near 1993
William I, Bonnet
London, Godwine. 1.03g
CR 1996, 131

Mawgan Porth, excavn., *see* St. Mawgan

MELTON MOWBRAY, Lei 1985
Edward Confessor, Pyramids
Leicester, Godric. 1.08g
SF 3, 119

MELTON MOWBRAY, Lei 1986
Edward Confessor, Pacx
Lincoln, Godric. 1.08g
CR 1987, 152

MEOLS, Ch (Merseyside) c. 1850-1908
Eadgar, Reform Small Cross
York, moneyer? wnr
cut halfpenny
Dolley, *Trans. Hist. Soc. Lancs and Chesh.* 113 (1961), 197-201, no. 6. (Before 1861.)
Æthelred II, First Hand. wnr
Shaftesbury, Æthelstan.
Dolley 7; *SCBI Merseyside* 516. (Before 1861.)
Æthelred II, First Hand
Chester?, moneyer? (fragment). wnr
Dolley 8. (Found 1874.)
Æthelred II, Crux
London, moneyer? (fragment)
Dolley 9. (Before 1861.)
Æthelred II, Long Cross?
York, moneyer?
Dolley, under 9: *JAAHSC* 1908.
Cnut, Quatrefoil
Chester, Ceolnoth. 0.86g
Dolley 10.
Cnut, Quatrefoil
Chester, moneyer? (fragment)
Dolley 11 (*not* London).
Cnut, Helmet
Chester, Gunleof. wnr
Dolley 12. (Before 1861.)
Cnut, Short Cross
Chester, Leofwine. wnr
Dolley 13. (Before 1872.)
Cnut, Short Cross
Shrewsbury, Eadsige. wnr
Dolley 14. (Before 1861.)
Cnut, Short Cross
Winchester, Spilmann. wnr.
Dolley 15. (Before 1861.)
Harthacnut,Arm and Sceptre
Chester, Leofnoth
cut halfpenny, wnr
Dolley 16. (Found *c.* 1870.)
Edward Confessor, Pacx
London, moneyer
cut halfpenny, wnr
Dolley 17. (Before 1861.)
Edward Confessor, Short Cross
Southwark, Ælfwine. 0.45g
Dolley 18
Edward Confessor, Sovereign
Chester, moneyer? wnr
Dolley 19. (Found *c.* 1869.)
Hiberno-Norse coin??
Dolley, p. 200-1.
William I, Bonnet
mint? moneyer? (fragment)
CC p. 45
William I, Two Stars
mint?
cut halfpenny
CC p. 45
William I, Two Stars
mint?
cut farthing?
CC p. 45

MEON HILL, Ha (former earthwork on Houghton Down, ½ m. west of Stockbridge) 1933

Edward Confessor, Pointed Helmet
Winchester, Godwine Ceoca. 1.10g
SCBI South-Eastern 1325; *Hants Field Club* 12 (1934), 132 and 155.

MERTON, Nf 1995
Æthelred II, Long Cross
London, Sibwine. 1.55g
CR 1995, 161

METHWOLD HYTHE, Nf 1985
William I, Profile/Cross and Trefoils
London, Ælfwine. wnr.
CR 1987, 174

MIDDLE HARLING, Nf 1980-3
Æthelred II, Last Small Cross
Norwich, moneyer? 0.23g (fragment)
Edward Confessor, Sovereign
Norwich, Leofric. 1.02g.
Edward Confessor, Pyramids
Oxford, moneyer?
cut farthing, 0.20g
William I, type?
mint?, moneyer. 0.15g (fragment)
EAA 74 (1995), p. 50, nos. 84-9

MIDDLETON STONEY, O 1979
William I, Profile/Cross and Trefoils
London, moneyer? wnr
CC p. 41

MILDENHALL, Sf, near 1995
Æthelred II, Long Cross
York, Sumarlithr. 1.43g (chipped)
CR 1995, 164

MILDENHALL, W 1977
Æthelred II, Long Cross
Lincoln, Sumarlithr. 1.29g
Wilts Arch. Mag. 72-3 (1977-8), 198-9

MILTON, K (near the church) 1939
Cnut, Helmet
Canterbury, Wulfstan. 0.91g
SCBI South-Eastern 1050

MINSTER-IN-THANET, K 1993
Edward Confessor, Pacx
London, Godwig. *c.* 1.1g.
CR 1994, 224

MONKTON UP WIMBORNE, Do 1986
Edward Confessor, Pyramids
Hereford, Earnwig
cut halfpenny, 0.22g.
CR 1987, 165

MUCH HADHAM, Hrt 1957
Æthelred II, Last Small Cross
(Winchester)
contemporary counterfeit (cliché)
BNJ 28 (1955-7), 185-9; Oddy and Archibald, *Scientific Studies in Numismatics* (ed. Oddy), 1980, p. 82.

MUCH MARCLE, He (He and Wo) 1980
Æthelred II, First Small Cross
Lincoln, moneyer? wnr
CC p. 45

MUNDHAM, Nf 1992
Æthelred II, Long Cross
Stamford, Svartgeirr. 1.51g.
CR 1992, 272

NAILSWORTH, Gl (Hazelwood) 1875
Æthelred II, Long Cross
Gloucester, Wihtsige. 1.58g
SCBI West Country 526

NETHERTON, Ha (Faccombe) 1980, 1990
Æthelred II, First Hand
London, moneyer? wnr
CR 1991, 134 (fd. 1990)
Cnut, Quatrefoil
Winchester, moneyer?
cut halfpenny, wnr
CR 1991, 135
Normandy, denier, P.A. 166 (pl. 6, 10)
CC p.38

NEWCHURCH, K 1944
Æthelred II, Long Cross
Bath, Ælfric. 1.11g (chipped)
SCBI Yorks. 1035A

NEW ROMNEY, K 1991
Æthelred II, Small Crux
Dover, Cyneric. 1.08g.
CR 1990, 205

NEW ROMNEY, K 1995
Edward Confessor, Trefoil-Quadrilateral
Hastings, Brid?
cut halfpenny, 0.5g
CR 1995. 178

NORMANBY-BY-STOW, L (½mi N of Stow)
Cnut, Short Cross
Lincoln, Matathan. 1.04g
Blackburn, *Lincoln and its Shire*, II, 24; *SCBI Lincs* 497

NORTHAMPTON (Castle site) 1879-81
Edward Confessor, Trefoil-Quadrilateral
London, Godric. 0.8g (chipped)
SCBI Midlands 368

NORTH CURRY, So (churchyard) 1892
Æthelred II, Long Cross
Winchester, Burhsige. 1.55g
(pierced, chipped)
SCBI West Country 558; *PSomAS* 38 (1892), 76

North Essex, *see* Essex, North

NORTH LOPHAM, Nf 1994
Æthelred II, Helmet
London, ?Eadwine. 1.25g.
CR 1994, 211

NORWICH
Edward Confessor, Short Cross
Canterbury, Brunman, wnr
EAA 58 (1993), p. 206

NORWICH (Magdalen St. excavations) 1987
Edward Confessor, Expanding Cross (heavy)
Lincoln, Godric. 1.45g.
CR 1987, 156
Edward Confessor, Expanding Cross (heavy)
London, Beorhtsige (BRIC-) 1.59g.
CR 1987, 157
(a mini-hoard?)

NORWICH ('in N.') *c.* 1850
William I, Profile/Cross Fleury
Norwich, Guthfrithr. 1.37g
William I, Bonnet
York, Leysingr. 1.42g
William I, Two Sceptres
Thetford, Godric. 1.09g
SCBI Yorks 1111, 719, 1193
(could these coins, ex Goddard

Johnson, be from a small hoard?)

NORWICH (near) 1985
Cnut, Helmet
Norwich, Hwætman. wnr.
CR 1987, 144

NORWICH (3 mi E of) 1986
Æthelred II, Crux
Cambridge, Ælfric. 1.35g.
SF 3, 121

NOTTINGHAMSHIRE 1893
Æthelred II, First Hand
Torksey, Thorketill. 1.69g
BMC 335

OGBOURNE ST. ANDREW, W (towards Ogbourne Maizey) c. 1988
Harthacnut, Jewel Cross, bust right
Oxford, Ælfwine Tosti. wnr.
CR 1988, 181

OGBOURNE ST. GEORGE, W 1991
Edward Confessor, Trefoil-Quadrilateral
London, Leofing. wnr
CR 1993, 229
Edward Confessor, Pacx type
mint?, moneyer?
cut farthing
CR 1993, 230
Edward Confessor, Expanding Cross
mint?, moneyer?
cut halfpenny, 0.23g
ibid. (230)

Old Erringham Farm, *see* Shoreham-by-Sea

OLD ROMNEY, K 1992
Scandinavian imitation of Long Cross type, *c.* 1000
CR 1993, 294

OLD SARUM, W
Eadgar, Reform Small Cross
London, moneyer?
CC p. 38
Utrecht, Bishop Bernaldus, 1027-54. 0.73g
Jaarboek voor Munt- en Penningkunde 44 (1957), 54 (illus); *SCBI West Country* 1010;
Proc. Soc. Antiq. 27(1915), 235.
William I, Sword
Wareham, Godwine. 1.14g
SCBI West Country 769; *AJ* 15 (1935), 184 (in a cesspool in the East Suburb)

OSBALDWICK, Y (2 mi E of York)
Cnut, Short Cross
York, Farthein. wnr
SF 2, 52

OSMINGTON, Do (in a garden) 1969
Cnut, Short Cross
Stamford, Leofwine. 0.82g (fragment)
SCBI West Country 643

OUNDLE, Nth (in the neighbourhood) 1869
William I, Profile/Cross Fleury-Bonnet mule
Stamford, Leofwine. wnr
NC 1869, 354, no. 3

OXBOROUGH, Nf 1993
Æthelred II, Long Cross
Thetford, Osbern
cut farthing, 0.43g
CR 1993, 217; 1994, 368
Harold I, Fleur de lis
mint?, moneyer?
cut farthing, 0.26g.
CR 1993, 225
Edward Confessor, Trefoil Quadrilateral
mint?, moneyer?
cut farthing or broken cut halfpenny, 0.20g.
CR 1994, 223

OXFORD 1962, 1977, 1893
Æthelred II, First Hand
mint?, moneyer? 1.28g
SCBI Oxford 453 (Littlewoods excavn., central Oxford)
Edward Confessor, Pacx
mint?, moneyer?
CC p. 41
William I, Paxs
Wallingford, moneyer?
CC p. 41

OXFORD (half a mile west of city) 1988
Harold I, Fleur de Lis
Wallingford, Wulfwine. 0.83g.
CR 1987, 149

PADSTOW, Co
Æthelred II, Long Cross
Chichester, Æthelstan. 1.56g
SF 2, 53

PAINSWICK, Gl (church) 1879
Æthelred II, Crux
Chester, Æthelmod. 1.62g (chipped)
SCBI West Country 464

PAPWORTH, C (near) 1994
Edward Confessor, Expanding Cross (heavy)
Ipswich, Bruning
cut halfpenny, 0.74g.
CR 1994, 231

PETERBOROUGH, Nth (Cambs) 1983
Æthelred II, Last Small Cross
Lincoln, Asgautr. 1.24g
SCBI South-Eastern 975. (Heavily peck-marked.)

PETERBOROUGH, Nth 1987
Harold II, Pax
London, Godric. wnr.
CR 1988, 191

PITT, Ha (2 mi SW of Winchester) 1992
Eadgar, Reform Small Cross
Stamford, moneyer Ogea (?)
cut farthing, 0.32g.
CR 1992, 268

PLYMOUTH, D 1852
Harthacnut, Jewel Cross
Guildford, Blacman. wnr
BMC 3

POLSTEAD, Sf 1980-90
Æthelred II, Helmet
London, Wulfstan. 1.36g (chipped)
BNJ 61 (1991), 124f.

PORTLAND (92 Fortuneswell), Do
Æthelred II, Crux
Lewes, Oswold. (die-dupl. *BMC* 133)
Proc. Dorset... 105 (1983), 151

PULHAM MARKET, Nf 1995
Edward Confessor, Trefoil-Quadrilateral
mint?, Leofwine. 1.08g
CR 1995, 177

QUIDENHAM, Nf 1994
Edward Confessor, Short Cross
London, Ælfwine. 1.12g
CR 1994, 222

RAMSBURY, W
Æthelred II, First Hand
London, moneyer? wnr
DMM.

RAMSEY, Hu (C) 1966
Cnut, Helmet
York, moneyer?
Seaby 1966, 405

RAUNDS, Nth 1984
Norway, Olaf Kyrre, 1067-93.
CR 1989, 90

READING, Brk (near) 1903
William I, Profile/Cross Fleury
Wallingford, Beorhtmær. wnr
CR 1987, 169

RECULVER, K XVIII century
Edward Martyr, Small Cross
London, Athlestan. wnr
CR 1988, 167
Æthelred II, First Hand
Canterbury, Boga. wnr
CR 1988, 170
Edward Confessor, Expanding Cross
Cambridge ?, Eadweard. wnr
CR 1988, 187

REPTON, Db 1983
Æthelred II, Second Hand
Winchester, Eadsige
cut halfpenny
Edward Confessor, Pacx type
Derby or Nottingham?, Blacman?
Blackburn, *Anglo-Saxon Monetary History*, pp. 130-1

REPTON, DB c1984-5
Harold I, Jewel Cross type
Stamford, Thurulf
BNJ 56 (1986), 24
Edward Confessor, Short Cross type
mint?, moneyer?
cut farthing
BNJ 56 (1986), 24

RHUDDLAN, Clwyd 1976
Edward Confessor, Sovereign
mint?, moneyer?
Dykes, *Anglo-Saxon Coins*, p. 28. no. 10

RICHBOROUGH, K
Æthelred II, First/Second Hand
mint?, moneyer?
CC p. 39
Cnut, Short Cross
Chester, Gunleof. wnr
Cunliffe, *Richborough*, vol 5, 1968, p. 223 (east of Foundation, by Chapel).

RIDDLESWORTH, Nf 1994
Cnut, Short Cross type
Thetford, Brunstan. 1.08g.
CR 1994, 219

RINGSTEAD, Nf 1994
Æthelred II, Helmet
Cambridge, Cniht. 1.10g.
CR 1994, 210

RINGWOULD, K 1991
Edward Martyr, Small Cross
London, Ælfweard. wnr
CR 1991, 131

RIPPLE, K 1995
William I, Profile/Cross and Trefoils
Dover, Leofwine. 1.20g
CR 1995, 189

ROCHESTER, K (general area) 1972
Æthelred II, Second Hand
Rochester, Siduwine. wnr
CR 1988, 173

ROCHESTER, K (near) 1992
Æthelred II, Crux
Maldon, Ælfwine. 1.32g.
CR 1994, 204

ROCHESTER, K (near) 1995
Æthelred II, Crux
Rochester, Leofric. 1.50g
CR 1995, 159

ROCHESTER, K, (near) 1989
Æthelred II, Long Cross
Lincoln, Ubeinn
cut halfpenny, 0.85g

ROCHFORD, Ess c.1988
Harthacnut, Arm and Sceptre
Thetford, Ælfwine. wnr
CR 1996, 113

ROCKLAND ALL SAINTS (*or* ST PETER), Nf 1995
Æthelred II, Long Cross
Chester, Leofwine. 1.58g
CR 1995, 160
William I, Two Sceptres
Norwich, Godwine. 1.33g
CR 1995, 187

ROLVENDEN, K
Cnut, Short Cross
Lincoln, moneyer?
CC p. 40

Romney, see New Romney

ROXTON, Bd 1984
William I, Paxs
Stafford, Godric. 1.24g.
SF 2, 54

ROYDON, Nf 1980
Æthelred II, Crux
Thetford, Leofwine. 1.52g (fragment missing)
CR 1987, 136

ROYSTON Hrt (productive site near R.) 1979-86
Æthelred II, Second Hand
London, Leofwine
cut halfpenny, 0.57g
SF 3, 64

RYE, Sx (E. Sussex) 1904
Edward Confessor, Hammer Cross
York, Authbjorn. wnr.
CR 1987, 162

RYTHER, WRY 1996
Cnut, Helmet
York, Fargrimr
cut halfpenny
YN 3 (1997), 164

ST. DAVID'S, Dyfed 1976
Harold II, Pax
Hereford, Leofnoth. wnr
Dykes, *Anglo-Saxon Coins*, p. 31, no 59.

ST. LYTHANS, S. Glam. 1993
Æthelred II, Helmet
Lydford, Bruna. 1.36g
CR 1993, 218

ST. MAWGAN, Co (Mawgan Porth

excav.) 1949
Æthelred II, Crux
Lydford, Goda. wnr
SF 2, 46

ST. NEOTS, Hu (Cambs) 1961
Harthacnut, Arm and Sceptre
Stamford, Svartr. 1.08g
SF 2, 57

ST. NICHOLAS AT WADE, K 1986
Cnut, Short Cross
Hastings, Brid. 0.80g.
CR 1987, 145

ST. PETERS, K 1993
Cnut, Short Cross
mint?, Ælfwig
cut halfpenny, c. 0.5g.
CR 1994, 220

SALISBURY, W 1866
Edward Confessor, Trefoil-Quadrilateral
Salisbury, Wineman. wnr
NC 1866, Proc., p. 9.

SALISBURY PLAIN, W 1957
Denmark, Magnus the Good, 1042-7
NNUM 1957, 253-6

SALTFORD, So (Avon) (near) 1952
William I, Two Stars
London, Beorhtmær. 1.12g
SCBI West Country 762

SANDWICH, K 1967
Edward Confessor, Hammer Cross
York, Skuli. wnr.
CR 1988, 189

SEAFORD, Sx (E. Sussex) 1987
Æthelred II, Long Cross
Norwich, Ælfric. 1.37g.
CR 1987, 142

Seagry, *see* Upper Seagry

SEASALTER, K 1987
William I, Two Sceptres
Canterbury, Man. 1.34g
CR 1989, 88
William I, Paxs
London, Eadric. (0.69g, chipped)
CR 1989, 89

SEVENOAKS, K 1987
Æthelred II, First Hand
London, Asulfr. 1.35g.
CR 1987, 129

SHEFFIELD, Y 1984
Æthelred II, Long Cross
Canterbury, Ælfræd. 1.58g
SCBI Northern 965

SHEPRETH, C (near) 1993-4
Edward Confessor, Pointed Helmet
Cambridge, Ælfwig (0.91g, fragment)
CR 1993, 232

SHIPDHAM, Nf 1994
Eadgar, Reform Small Cross
London, Wigferth. 1.63g.
CR 1994, 200

SHIPSTON ON STOUR, Wa 1994
Cnut, Short Cross
York, Hrafn. 0.99g
CR 1995, 169

SHOREHAM-BY-SEA (Old Erringham Farm), Sx (W.Sussex) 1963-4
Æthelred II, Second Hand
Canterbury, Leofstan. 1.45g
SCBI South-Eastern 815
Æthelred II, Long Cross
Lewes, Ælfgar. 1.25g
SCBI South-Eastern 918

Shrubland Hall, *see* Coddenham

SILBURY HILL, (1 mi S of Avebury) W 1980
Æthelred II, Last Small Cross
mint?, moneyer?
cut farthing
CC p. 38

SILCHESTER, Brk (near) 1912
Cnut, Helmet
Thetford, Eadwine. 1.07g
SCBI South-Eastern 1067

SOHAM, C, near 1995
Edward Confessor, Pyramids
Lincoln, Ælfgeat. 0.98g
CR 1995, 185

SOTWELL, Brk (O) 1893
Harold I, Fleur-de-lis
Norwich, Leofwine wnr
Sotheby, 24 February 1893, 56 (Rusher Davies)

SOUTHAMPTON, Ha 1968
Æthelred II, type?
mint?, moneyer?
CC p. 38

SOUTHAMPTON, Ha (near) 1810
William I, Profile/Cross and Trefoils
London, Wulfwine. 1.16g
BMC Norman Kings 465

SOUTH CROXTON, Lei 1972
Æthelred II, Second Hand
Bridport, Eadnoth
Inf. Leicester Museums (T. Pearce)

SOUTH CROYDON, Sr (G.Lond.) 1980
French. Sens? P.A. pl. 137, 5
CC p. 41

SOUTHERY, Nf 1995
Edward Confessor, Expanding Cross (light)
London, Leofræd. 1.16g
CR 1995, 179

SOUTHILL, Bd 1987
Æthelred II, Long Cross
Stamford, Svartgeirr. wnr.
CC 1987, 143

SOUTHILL, Bd *c.*1996
Æthelred II, Last Small Cross
Stamford, Æscwig. 1.09g (broken)
CR 1996, 105

SOUTH LOPHAM, Nf 1994
Æthelred II, Last Small Cross
mint?, moneyer? 1.09g (incomplete)
CR 1994, 212

SOUTHWARK?, Sr 1987
Edward Confessor, Facing Bust
Leicester, Æthelwine. 0.58g
Stott 127. (Found in spoil from ? Southwark.)

SOUTHWICK, Nth 1974
Harold I, Fleur-de-lis
Stamford, Vilgrip. 0.74g (fragment)
SCBI Lincs 1375

SPARSHOLT, Brk (O) 1988

William I, Two Sceptres
London, Æthelwine or Ælfwine.
wnr
CR 1988, 194; *CR* 1996, 132

STAFFORD (St. Bertelins) c. 1960?, 1972
Æthelred II, Crux
London, moneyer?
cut farthing , 0.25g
SCBI Midlands 199; A.H. Oswald, The Church of St Bertelins and its Cross. p. 28.
Edward Confessor, Sovereign
London
CC p. 45 (excavn.)

STAMFORD BRIDGE, ERY *c.*1995
Edward Confessor, Facing Bust/Small Cross
Lincoln, moneyer?
cut halfpenny, 0.48g (incomplete)
CR 1995, 172

STANFORD ON SOAR, Nt 1984
Germany, Otto III, 983-96, Häv. 34
SF 3, 127

STANFORD ON SOAR, Nt 1994
Cnut, Short Cross
Dover, Eadwine. 1.00g
CR 1996, 110

STANTON ST QUINTIN, W 1985
Cnut, Quatrefoil
Ilchester, moneyer?
cut halfpenny, 0.44g.
SF 3, 128

Stanwix, see Carlisle

STEYNING, Sx (W.Sx), near 1992
Cnut, Short Cross
London, Brungar. 1.04g
CR 1996, 112

STOKEINTEIGNHEAD, D. 1988
Edward Confessor, Expanding Cross (heavy)
London, Spraecling. 1.32g (piece missing)
CR 1988, 186

STOKE MANDEVILLE, Bk 1986
Edward Confessor, Expanding Cross (heavy)
Lincoln, Manna. wnr
SF 3, 129

STOKE ROCHFORD, L (on the line of Ermine Street) 1920
Edward Confessor, Pointed Helmet
London, Ealdgar. 1.38g
Blackburn, *Lincoln and its Shire,* II, 29 and Fig. 52;
SCBI Lincs 1749 (found with another coin, undescribed)

STONEHENGE, W (excavn.) 1925
Æthelred II, Long Cross
London, Æthelweard. 1.59g
SCBI West Country 536

STONY STRATFORD, Bk 1993
Edward Confessor, Short Cross
London, Eadwig. wnr
CR 1993, 227

STOWMARKET, Sf 1869
Cnut, Helmet
London, moneyer? wnr
Sotheby 22 March 1869 (J. Warren)

STOW-ON-THE-WOLD, Gl (district) *c.* 1900
Eadgar, Reform type,
Shrewsbury, Sigeweald. 1.54g
SCBI West Country 430 (probably a local find, possibly from Lower Swell)

STRATFORD-UPON-AVON, Wa (near) 1949
Harthacnut, Arm and Sceptre
Stamford, Godric. 0.98g
SCBI Lincs 1377

SUDBURY, Sf (on Ess side of R. Stour) 1914
Harold II, Pax
Wallingford, Brandr. wnr
CR 1987, 167

SULGRAVE, Nth (site of Saxon manor) 1963
Æthelred II, Long Cross
London, Leofric. 1.34g
NC 1979, 217

SURLINGHAM, Nf (site 31391) 1995
Edward Confessor, Pointed Helmet
Norwich, Hringwulf. 0.80g
(incomplete)
CR 1995, 183

SUTTON-ON-THE-HILL, Db 1992
Edward Confessor, Short Cross
Nottingham, Blacman. 0.89g (small chip).
CR 1992, 279

SWAFFHAM, Nf 1994
Æthelred II, Second Hand
London, Godwine. 1.11g.
CR 1994, 202

SWAFFHAM, Nf (site TF 81 SW 132) 1995
William I, Profile/Cross and Trefoils
Norwich, moneyer?
cut farthing, 0.29g
CR 1995, 190

SWALLOW, L *c.*1990
Edward Confessor, Trefoil-Quadrilateral
Lincoln, Asfrith, wnr
CR 1996, 120

SWINDON, W (area) 1986
Edward Confessor, Expanding Cross
London, Spraecling. wnr
SF 3, 131

SWINDON area, W 1993
Æthelred II, Last Small Cross
Winchester, Wulfnoth
cut halfpenny, wnr
CR 1996, 106

TAKELEY, Ess 1986
Cnut, Short Cross
York, Crucan. wnr
CR 1987, 147; *CR* 1988, 179

TAMWORTH, St (excavn.) 1960
Edward Martyr, Small Cross
Torksey, Thorketill.
cut halfpenny, 0.82g
SCBI Midlands 180; Dolley in *South Staffs A and HS, Trans.* 1972-3, 42-4

THETFORD, Nf (Brandon Road, site 5756) 1964
Norway, Olaf Kyrre, 1067-93
East Anglian Archaeology, monograph 62 (1993), p. 95 no. 2. See map for

location of site, *c*.500m. NE of St. Mary's church. Now part of the Redcastle Furze housing estate. *CR* 1987, 168

THETFORD, Nf (Brandon Road/London Road, site D) 1979-84
Harold I, Jewel Cross
mint?, moneyer?
SF 1, 27. From the Chase public house site. Coin no longer accessible.

THETFORD, Nf (By-pass spoil) 1993-4
Æthelred II, Crux
Lincoln, Ubeinn. 0.64g (fragment)
Æthelred II, Crux
York, Eadric. 0.84g (fragment)
Edward Confessor, Expanding Cross
London, moneyer? 0.48g (fragments)
Edward Confessor, Facing Bust/Small Cross
Thetford, moneyer? 0.71g (fragment)
CR 1994, 203, 205, 228, 234. From spoil dumped at Lakenheath

THETFORD, Nf (E of bypass, site B) 1979-84
Cnut, Short Cross
Lincoln, moneyer? wnr (fragment)
SF 1, 23. In a field, *c* 500m N of the River Thet.

THETFORD, Nf (Church Trench 2, site 5759) 1969-70
Æthelred II, Crux
Lincoln, Geirfinnr. 1.48g
EAA 62 (1993), 95. For site, 600m SSE of St Mary's,
see map as above.

THETFORD, Nf (Fulmerston Road, site E) 1981
William I, Two Stars
Thetford, Cyneric. 0.85g fragments)
SF 1, 28 = *SF* 3, 132
William I, Profile/Cross and Trefoils
mint?, moneyer? wnr
SF 1, 29
William I, Paxs
Thetford, Ælfwine
cut halfpenny, wnr
SF 1, 30. There is nothing to indicate whether these three coins should be considered as a mini-hoard.

THETFORD, Nf (Icknield Way, site GMK 2) 1948-57
Æthelred II, Crux
mint?, Goda? (London?)
cut farthing, wnr
EAA 22, p. 67, no. 5; *SCBI E. Anglia* 1176
Cnut, Quatrefoil
Thetford, Eadwine. wnr
ibid., no. 6; *SCBI E. Anglia* 1227
The site, within the bend of Icknield Way, is *c*. 300m SW of St Mary's church

THETFORD, Nf (Kilnyard, site 5756) 1966
Æthelred II, Crux
Lincoln, Steinbitr. 1.41g
EAA 62 (1993), p. 95, no. 6. The site is *c*. 100m S of the Brandon Road site

THETFORD, Nf (Redcastle Furze, site 24822) 1988-9
Cnut, Helmet
London, moneyer? 0.37g (fragment)
EAA 72 (1995), p. 87, no. 1
Cnut, Short Cross
Colchester, moneyer?
cut farthing, 0.30g
ibid., no. 2
Harold I, Fleur-de-lis
London, moneyer?
cut halfpenny, 0.52g
ibid., no. 3
Edward Confessor, Expanding Cross (heavy)
London, Ælfwine. 1.60g
ibid., no. 4
Edward Confessor, Expanding Cross (heavy)
mint?, moneyer?
cut halfpenny, 0.56g
ibid., no. 5
Edward Confessor, Expanding Cross (heavy)
London, Beorhtsige.
cut farthing, 0.30g
ibid., no. 6
Edward Confessor, Helmet
Hereford, Wulfwine
cut halfpenny, 0.65g
ibid., no. 7
Edward Confessor, Pyramids
mint?, Godric
cut halfpenny, 0.51g
ibid., no. 8
William I, Paxs
London, Ælfwig
cut halfpenny, 0.58g
ibid., no. 9
The site is *c*. 150m west of the Brandon Road site.

THETFORD, Nf (St. Barnabas Hospital site 1092,) 1977
Æthelred II, Crux
Southwark, Beorhthelm.
cut halfpenny, wnr
EAA 22, p. 68. Just south of the Church trench site, q.v.

THETFORD, Nf 1779, 1789
Æthelred II, Crux
Thetford, Beorhtric. wnr
Harold I, Jewel Cross
Thetford, Brunstan, wnr
Harold I, Jewel Cross
Norwich, moneyer? wnr
NC 1957, 206

THETFORD, Nf (area) c. 1980
Edward Confessor, Short Cross
Bury St Edmunds, Morcar.
Inf. finder

THETFORD, Nf, a few miles east of *c*.1991
Cnut, Pointed Helmet
London, Ælfric. 0.97g
CR 1996, 109
Harold II, Pax
Thetford?, Godleof.
cut halfpenny, 0.53g
CR 1996, 129

THRUPP, O (beside R. Cherwell) 1990
Edward Confessor, Trefoil-Quadrilateral
London, Eadric. 1.05g.
CR 1990, 208

THURCASTON, (near Latimers House) Lei 1945
Æthelred II, Second Hand
London, Ælfgeat. 0.92g (fragment)
SCBI Midlands 191

TILSHEAD/SHREWTON, W 1957
Æthelred II, Small Crux
Canterbury, Leofing 1.33g

BNJ 1955-7, 83

TIPTREE, Ess 1983
Æthelred II, Long Cross
York, Hundolfr. 1.50g
SF 1, 31

TIVETSHALL ST MARY, Nf 1992
Edward Confessor, Expanding Cross (light)
Lincoln, Godric. 1.01g
CR 1996, 121

TORKSEY, L 1992-3
Hiberno-Norse, *c* 1010.
cut halfpenny, 0.58g.
CR 1994, 236

TRING, Hrt 1993
Æthelred II, Helmet
York, Ulfketill. 1.34g.
CR 1993, 219

TROWBRIDGE, W (Town Centre excavns.) 1977, 1986-8
Cnut, Quatrefoil
?Winchester, ?Oda
cut halfpenny, wnr
Cnut, Helmet
Totnes, Ælfwine. 0.69g
Edward Confessor, Expanding Cross (heavy)
London, Epi/Ewi
brooch, uses reverse of coin
Hiberno-Norse, Phase V 0.41g and 0.45g
both originally from back-fill of grave 1696?
A.H. Graham and S.M. Davies, *Excavations in the Town Centre of Trowbridge, 1977 and 1986-88,* (Wessex Archaeology Report, no. 2), 1993, nos. 6-10

TUDDENHAM ST MARTIN, Sf 1988
Dreux, French feudal, *c* 1035-? 1.01g.
CR 1988, 193

(UPPER) SEAGRY, W 1981
Edward Confessor, Expanding Cross (heavy)
London, Godwine. wnr
Wilts. Arch. Mag. 77 (1982), 161 (as *BMC* 936)

WALLINGFORD, Brk (O) (Castle excavn.) 1966
Æthelred II, First Hand
Cricklade, moneyer?
cut halfpenny, wnr
SCBI South-Eastern 803; *Med. Arch.* 1 (1967), 272-319.

WALLINGFORD, Brk (O) (beside the by-pass) 1992
Cnut, Quatrefoil
Winchester, Cynna
cut halfpenny, 0.68g
CR 1992, 273

WALLINGFORD, Brk (O) 1977
Cnut, Short Cross
mint?, moneyer?
cut farthing
NC 1977, 137, n. 1

WALLINGFORD, Brk (O.) 1894
William I, Bonnet type
Wallingford, Svartlingr
CR 1987, 170
William I, Bonnet type
Wallingford, Brandr
CR 1987, 170
Possibly a mini-hoard

WALPOLE ST. PETER, Nf 1994
Edward Confessor, Expanding Cross (heavy?)
London, Godwine
brooch, with reverse of coin facing
CR 1994, 226

WARLINGHAM, Sr 1990
Edward Martyr, Small Cross
Stamford, Oio. 1.22g
CR 1996, 100

WARWICK (Market St. excav.) 1966
Cnut, Quatrefoil
Shaftesbury, moneyer? wnr
SCBI Midlands 315

Waterston, *see* Lower Waterston

WELFORD, Brk (fd. at the church) 1912
Edward Confessor, Pyramids
mint?, moneyer? wnr
SCBI South-Eastern 1681

WELFORD-ON-AVON, Wa 1988
Æthelred II, Long Cross
Norwich, moneyer?
cut farthing, 0.42g
CR 1988, 174

WELLINGBOROUGH, Nth (near) 1971
Cnut, Helmet
York, Hildulfr. 0.97g
Cnut, Helmet
York, Wulfnoth. 1.02g
SCBI Midlands 334 and 336 (probably a mini-hoard)

WELLINGORE, L (near) 1978
Edward Confessor, Radiate/Small Cross
London, Æthelman. wnr
Blackburn, *Lincoln and Its Shire,* II, 26 and Fig. 48

WELWYN, Hrt 1743
Edward Confessor, Short Cross
London, Leofing? wnr.
NC 1958, 93f.; *Num. Jl.* 2 (1837), 252-3

WENTBRIDGE, WRY (near) 1985
William I, Bonnet
Huntingdon, Godwine, 1.15g
SF 2, 70

WESTBURY-ON-TRYM (Bristol), Gl (Avon) (excavn.) 1968
Edward Confessor, Facing Bust
Hastings (or Chester?), Dunning. wnr
SCBI West Country 730

WEST HARLING, Nf 1987
Cnut, Quatrefoil
Norwich, Manna. wnr.
EAA 74 (1995), p. 50, no. 85 (exact grid ref.)

WEST MERSEA, Ess (in a garden) 1986
Edward Martyr, Small Cross
Lympne, Wine. 1.17g
SF 3, 133. Overstruck on a pre-reform coin

WESTMINSTER, (Abbey excavns.) *c*.1975-7
Germany, imitatn of Conrad II, Duisburg mint
Trans. London Mddx. A.S. 28

(1977), 200
Germany, 'probably Henry III' (1039-56)
Trans LMAS. 27 (1976), at p.141

WESTON, Hrt 1993
William I, Profile/Cross and Trefoils
Christchurch, Coleman. 1.15g.
CR 1993, 239

WEST RAVENDALE, L (halet near East Ravendale) 1989
Edward Confessor, Pointed Helmet
Lincoln, Authbjorn. 1.19g (chipped)
SCBI Northern 1038

WEST RUDHAM, Nf (site recorded) 1994
Harthacnut, Jewel Cross
mint?, moneyer?
cut halfpenny, 0.51g
CR 1994, 221

WEST RUDHAM, Nf 1994
Edward Confessor, Expanding Cross (light?)
London, Leofræd. 1.23g
CR 1994, 227

WEST SUSSEX (South Downs) 1991
Normandy, Dumas Group C, late XI century
CR 1990, 223

WEST WALTON Nf 1993
Cnut, Short Cross
mint?, moneyer? wnr.
CR 1992, 276
Æthelred II, Crux
Oxford, Wulfwine. 1.55g
CR 1993, 216
Edward Confessor, Expanding Cross
mint?, moneyer?
cut halfpenny, 0.54g
CR 1993, 231
Two coins from the same site

WEST WALTON, Nf (site 258853) 1995
Harthacnut, Jewel Cross
Norwich?, moneyer?
cut halfpenny, 0.51g
CR 1995, 171

WETHERINGSETT-CUM-BROCKFORD, Sf 1987
Edward Confessor, Expanding Cross (heavy)
Thetford, moneyer?
cut farthing, 0.38g
CR 1987, 158

WEYBOURNE, Nf 1992
Æthelred II, Second Hand
London, Wulfstan. 1.15g
CR 1992, 271

WHEATLEY, O (Mulberry Court) 1964
Æthelred II, Transitional Crux
Oxford, Ælfwine. 1.61g
CR 1987, 134

WHEPSTEAD, Sf 1865
Æthelred II, Long Cross
Stamford, Eadwig. wnr
BNJ 24 (1941-4), 86, no. 96

WILLINGHAM, L 1988
Æthelred II, First Small Cross
Lincoln, Rodbert. 1.17g
CR 1988, 169
Cnut, Short Cross
York, Æ(g)elwine, 0.98g
CR 1988, 178

WINCHESTER, Ha (excavations) 1961-73
Æthelred II, Crux
Maldon, Ælfwine
cut halfpenny, 0.63g
Æthelred II, Last Small Cross
forgery of London, Ælfric. 1.80g
Cnut, Quatrefoil
Ipswich, 'Eldrnt' (Æthelbeorht?). 1.00g
Cnut, Helmet
Winchester, Ælfsige. 0.91g
Normandy, denier, *c.* 1030-40. 0.90g
Harthacnut, Jewel Cross
Gloucester, Wulfnoth. 0.81g (chipped)
Harthacnut, Jewel Cross
Shaftesbury, Æthelric. wnr
Harold I, Fleur-de-lis
London, Leofing. 1.02g
Edward Confessor, Expanding Cross
Winchester, Leodmær. wnr
William I, Canopy
Malmesbury, Beorhtwig 0.93g
William I, Sword
Shaftesbury, Ælfnoth. 1.28g
William I, Sword
Salisbury?, Godric
cut halfpenny, 0.62g
William I, Profile/Cross and Trefoils (*sic*)
London, moneyer?
cut halfpenny, 0.48g
Dolley and Blunt, in *BNJ* 47 (1977), 135-8.

WINCHESTER, Ha (St James Cemetery) 1926
Æthelred II, Long Cross
London, Leofwig. 1.19g
SCBI South-Eastern 934

WINCHESTER, Ha (Cathedral churchyard) 1925
Edward Confessor, Pointed Helmet
Winchester, Godman. 1.23g
SCBI South-Eastern 1323

WINCHESTER, Ha (Lower Colebrook St.) 1992
Edward Confessor, Pyramids type
Chichester, Ælfwine. 1.32g
SCBI South-Eastern 1647

WINCHESTER (near) 1992
Edward Confessor, Expanding Cross (light)
mint?, Ælfwine
cut halfpenny, 0.78g.
CR 1992, 281
William I, Sword
mint?, moneyer?
cut halfpenny 0.47g (fragment)
CR 1992, 285

WINSTON, Sf 1980
Æthelred II, Crux
Exeter, Tuna, wnr
Proc. Suffolk Inst. 34/4 (1980), 292

WINTERBOURNE BASSETT, Wi 1995
Edward Confessor, Trefoil-Quadrilateral
Winchester, Eadwine. wnr.
Inf.

WITTERING, Nth 1996
Harold I, Jewel Cross (early style)
London, Ead...
cut halfpenny, wnr
Inf. finder (DMM)

WIXFORD, Wa 1994
Edward Confessor, Pyramids
Tamworth, Coling. (frag.)
Cr 1995, 186 (with discussion)

WOODEATON, O 1946
William I, Two Stars
Oxford, Heregod. 1.25g
SCBI Oxford 88

WOODMANSTERNE, Sr 1994
Cnut, Short Cross
London, Ælfwine. 0.50g.
CR 1994, 217

WORCESTER (Castle Hill?)
1833
Æthelred II, First Hand
Lincoln, Ubeinn
cut halfpenny, 0.75g
Cnut, Short Cross
London, Leofwine. 0.73g (fragment)
Cnut, Short Cross
Worcester, Æl(f)wine. 0.89g
(fragment)
SCBI Midlands 187, 344, 347

WORCESTER (Nonbury)
Harthacnut
brooch
Svensk Num. Tidskr. 6 (1993), 148-50

WORCESTER (St. Clements church) 1824
Edward Confessor, Expanding Cross
Warwick, Leofing.
gold penny
BMQ 17 (1952), 11

WORCESTER (Deansway excavn.)
1989-90
Æthelred II, Second Hand
Southampton, moneyer?
cut halfpenny, 0.38g.
CR 1990, 200
Æthelred II, Crux
Worcester, Goda
lead striking, 3.09g (broken)
Sharp, fresh condition
CR 1990, 202

WORTH, K 1992
Cnut, Short Cross
Shaftesbury, Æthelric 1.0g.
CR 1994, 218

WORTHING, Sx (W. Sussex)
(Chesswood Nurseries) 1958
Edward Confessor, Pointed Helmet
London, Beorhtmær. 1.35g
SCBI South-Eastern 1293

WRENINGHAM, Nf 1993
Edward Confessor, Short Cross
Thetford, Eastmund. 1.03g.
CR 1992, 280

WROXETER, Sa (near the river)
1993
Harold I, Jewel Cross
Lincoln, Svartbrandr. 0.96g (broken)
CR 1996, 115

WYE, K 1993
William I, Two Stars
Dover, Brunman. 1.26g.
CR 1994, 239

YAPHAM, ERY 1994
Edward Confessor, Sovereign/Eagles
York, Ulfketill
YN 3 (1997), 166

YAPTON, Sx 1991
Æthelred II, First Hand
Totnes, Dodda. wnr
Sussex Arch. Coll. 129 (1991), 246-7
(illus)

YELLING, C 1991
William I, Two Stars
Hythe, Eadræd. 0.99g.
CR 1991, 138

YORK (Bishophill Senior) 1973
Harold I, Fleur-de-lis
York?, Ucede? 0.17g (fragment)
Pirie, *Post-Roman Coins,* no. 66

YORK (Clementhorpe) 1976
Edward Confessor, Facing Bust
York, Authulfr. 0.99g
Pirie, *Post-Roman Coins,* no. 68

York (Clifford Street, Friends Meeting House) 1884
William I, Two Stars
York, Aleifr. 1.57g (base metal)
SCBI Yorks xxxix, no. 18.

YORK (Coppergate excavn.)
1977-80
Æthelred II, First Small Cross
York, Styr. 0.70g
Pirie, *Post-Roman Coins,* no. 62
Æthelred II, First Hand
York, Fastulfr. 0.98g
ibid., no. 63 (fd. 1980)
Æthelred II, First Hand
York, Authgrimr. 0.82g
ibid., no. 64 (fd. 1977)
Cnut, Short Cross
York, Thorgrimr. 0.64g
ibid., no. 65.

YORK (Fishergate) 1880
Cnut, Quatrefoil
York, Bretakollr. 0.90g
SCBI Yorks xxxix, no. 14

YORK, (Minster excavns.) 1970-1
William I, Profile/Cross Fleury
Derby, Kolbeinn. 1.05g
Huntingdon, Godric. 0.69g
(chipped)
York, Authulfr. 1.10g
SCBI Yorks 1106, 1107, and 697.
Undoubtedly a small hoard. See Q. 9, above

YORK (St. Mary's Abbey) 1952
Harthacnut, Arm and Sceptre
London, Brunman
cut halfpenny, wnr
Edward Confessor, Sovereign
Exeter, Sæwine. wnr
York, Authgrimr. wnr
SCBI Yorks, xxxix, no. 15 (both)

YORK (Skeldergate) 1974
Edward Confessor, Facing Bust
York?, Authgrimr. 0.73g
Pirie, *Post-Roman Coins,* no. 67

YORK (Skeldergate Bridge) 1878
Edward Confessor, Trefoil-Quadrilateral
York, Ulfketill. 0.80g (chipped)
SCBI Yorks xxxix, no. 16

York *see also* Dringhouses, Heslington Field, Osbaldwick.

PART SIX

CONCLUSIONS

Millions of pennies and halfpennies circulated across shire boundaries, year in and year out. London and the North Sea ports were the focal points of integrated patterns of circulation which were linked to overseas trade.

PART SIX

Conclusions

Eleventh-century England enjoyed a lively monetary circulation, which involved millions or even tens of millions of silver pennies, halfpennies, and farthings. These coins were struck by moneyers based in upwards of fifty towns all over the country. The currency was renewed every few years, when all the coins were melted down and restruck to a new design. The validity-period for each successive design was originally about six or seven years. From 1036, however, much shorter validity-periods of two or three years became the rule. Because of the repeated *renovationes*, it was the exception for any coins in use to be more than six or seven years old, or even, after 1036, more than two or three years old. The stray coins that were accidentally lost from time to time were therefore on average at most four or five years old, and the average age after 1036 may have been only one and a half to two years. Because of that, and because they originated from so many different mint-towns, they allow us to speak about the rapidity with which coins became diffused and mingled together in use. The distance between the mint-town and the find-spot of a coin accidentally lost was often considerable; and because these finds are random losses in respect of their mint of origin, they are a reliable indicator of the dispersion of the currency as a whole.

Thus, the stray finds from London (of which we can muster a large sample) include only between a third and a half of coins minted in London. More than half are from mint-towns elsewhere, having been carried into London within no more than four or five years, on average. Conversely, London coins were carried far and wide. Because stray losses are undoubtedly random in respect of their mint-town, we can be sure that the stock of currency accumulated in London, which at any particular moment may have amounted to hundreds of thousands or even a couple of million coins, followed quite closely the same proportions, namely between a third and a half of coins minted in London, and the rest minted elsewhere. When we consider that a similar division between local and incoming coins was to be seen in Lincoln, York, Winchester, indeed in every town from which we have evidence, it follows that (up to 1036) millions of coins were being transferred from place to place, year in and year out. What is true of the towns is equally true of their shires. The proportion of local and of incoming coins tends to be the same in a town and in its region. The pattern is maintained quite uniformly throughout England and throughout the eleventh century. This is something that one could hardly have suspected from the written sources, and which one certainly could not have quantified. It is easy enough to imagine that coinage minted locally was used locally, by farmers visiting the market town to buy and sell produce; but one would not have imagined that there were inter-regional transfers of money on such a scale, in every region of England, and in the validity-period of every new coin type.

The broad question of general historical interest is whether all these monetary transfers resulted from commercial activity, or from a geographical redistribution of coinage arising from the processes of taxation and royal expenditure—or from a mixture of both. Our best hope of reaching a judgement on that question lies in a detailed analysis of monetary circulation, dividing England up into regions in order to compare and contrast the currency in each, and dividing the period *c.*973—1086 into the short periods which followed each *renovatio*, again in order to assess the balance of continuity and change. The impression gained from the analysis is overwhelmingly of uniformity and of continuity—as may be judged from the distribution-maps in Part 2. Against that background, any discrepancies or deviations from the trend will be of special interest for the clues they may offer to the political or economic context of the uses of coinage.

The single finds or stray losses which, taken *en masse*, are incomparably our best source of information—much better than coin hoards—reveal how far individual coins have travelled from their mints of origin before being lost. They tend to focus our attention on inter-regional transfers of wealth. The local use of coinage, within the orbit of the nearby market town, is more difficult to measure, but it seems obvious that it will have existed, alongside longer-distance monetary transactions.

With a data-base of nearly seven hundred single finds, it is practicable to divide the country up, for purposes of analysis, into a dozen regions. Because the governance of England was shire governance, to a significant extent, and because questions arise whether the minting and use of coinage were detectable within a framework of shire administration, it makes good sense to define the dozen regions by grouping shires as appropriate, taking account of their Danelaw, Mercian, and West Saxon background and loyalties. The number of single finds from each region varies quite widely. Finds are densest in the south-east, London, and East Anglia, and they tend to thin out westwards. It is arguable that that reflects the amounts of money in the various regions (but not necessarily their natural wealth or prosperity). What is perfectly clear is that the focal points of monetary circulation were the half-dozen major trading centres which lay in the eastern coastlands of England, and looked towards the North Sea—London, above all, and the great Anglo-Scandinavian towns of York, Lincoln, Stamford, Norwich, and Thetford.

For each of the dozen regions one can make an estimate, and for most of them a reasonably good estimate, of the proportion of the region's currency that was minted within the region. It is instructive to tabulate and compare them. Their consistency helps to confirm the general interpretation sketched above. The differences between them may be used to characterize the varying patterns of monetary circulation throughout England, and perhaps to provide ideas about the balance of commercial and administrative uses of money.

Region	*Finds*	*Proportion of local coins*
1. Yorkshire	31	75—85%
2. Lindsey	65	*c.*50%
3. The Five Boroughs	22	15—20%
4. The North-West	27	50—60%
5. East Anglia	111	c.35%
6. Middle Danelaw	35	10—15%
7. Essex, Herts, Bucks	21	5—10%
8. London and environs	61	35—50%
9. South Mercia	43	*c.* 25%
10. Kent, Surrey, Sussex	78	30—40%
11. Wessex	91	*c.* 40%
12. The South-West	18	30—40%

There is a contrast between Yorkshire and all the other regions. Its currency was to an exceptional degree self-contained. Although the coins minted in York were part of the national system, sharing the same designs, fineness, and validity-periods decreed south of Humber, there was not much penetration of southern money into Yorkshire. Nor, indeed, was there much drift of York coins in the other direction, although the balance-of-payments situation within England (which is difficult to quantify accurately) looks to have been somewhat unfavourable to Yorkshire. Distance is the obvious explanation for this isolation: York was more or less the end of the line, for the North Sea trade along England's east coast. But also, the York minters dominated their region partly because they were able to be so active, producing around 10 per cent of the national total of coinage. The disparity between that 10 per cent, and the 75 to 85 per cent of York coins in the currency of Yorkshire, is a measure of the region's isolation, at least as far as inflows from the south are concerned.

In the north-west, Chester occupies a similar position in its region to York in the north-east. Chester coins are (on the evidence of a rather unsatisfactory sample) less dominant, at 50—60 per cent (possibly more in Chester itself?). The difference may well be mainly because Chester was a far less active mint-place. Until we have a substantially larger sample of site-finds from Chester itself, the trends during the eleventh century, and their connection with the shift in contacts with Ireland towards the Bristol Channel ports, will remain unclear.

London, as we have already seen, drew more than half its currency in from elsewhere; and London coins were an important element of the money supply in much of southern England. We may detect differences in the regional make-up of what came in and what went out: it was not a simple exchange. The London finds include a strong component from south of the Thames. They also include a few pieces from the Five Boroughs which, intriguingly, seem to have 'jumped over' the intervening regions, and are over-represented in terms of relative mint-output. Likewise, Lincoln coins are more prominent than those of the East Anglian mints, which perhaps suggests that merchants sailed directly from Lincoln to London. Conversely the distribution of London coins elsewhere is decidedly stronger in East Anglia and the midlands than it is south of the Thames.

In the south-eastern corner of England, the composition of the currency is localized on a small scale, differently in east Kent, in the Canterbury-Rochester-London corridor, and in east and west Sussex. The Weald was a barrier. Canterbury was far less important as a mint-place than it had been in the eighth and ninth centuries, or than it became again later in the middle ages.

In south-central England, the influence of Winchester was strong, and increasingly so after the Norman Conquest. Wessex nevertheless lay within the wider orbit of London. Even the South-West, west of Sellwood, felt the influence of the London mint (perhaps *via* Winchester), although it lay at the farthest edge of the English monetary economy. From Exeter, its main centre, unfortunately we lack a good series of site-finds.

Wales is as usual almost devoid of single finds, except for a few from around the edges of the region, which reflect coast-wise shipping in and out of Chester in the north, and up and down the Bristol Channel in the south. Likewise the Yorkshire Dales, the Pennine uplands, and Cumbria have yielded virtually no finds. One need not doubt that those regions had a virtually coin-less economy.

One could think, then, of a series of 'rooms' opening off the North Sea, each with its port or ports of access. Yorkshire, with York, was the most northerly, and the most isolated. Lindsey, with Lincoln, was already linked into the rest of the Five Boroughs, and into Norfolk, and so was Stamford—another major mint-town from which, unfortunately, we lack a good series of site-finds. Thetford, much more than Norwich, enjoyed some outreach into the midlands. But it was, above all, London that commanded the largest 'room'.

The western ports, and in particular Chester, lacked any significant outreach into the midlands. There is the occasional Hiberno-Norse coin, from Torksey or from Trowbridge, but coins minted in Chester or in the Bristol Channel ports made little progress inland.

The North-Sea 'rooms' cut across the political geography of England, seemingly uninfluenced by the frontier of the Danelaw. There was indeed 'one coinage in all the king's realm'.

South of the Thames, in West Saxon territory, the monetary landscape was rather different, with numerous towns of older foundation (cf. each shire with its shire-town, north of the Thames), and correspondingly numerous mint-places. More specific explanations have sometimes been suggested, particularly with reference to the south-west, where royal manors have been seen as the *raison d'être* of mints. This is a very minor theme, which should not be exaggerated. Exeter normally minted at least twice as much silver as any other mint in the south-west (except in Quatrefoil, when Ilchester was briefly the caput, apparently because of the heavy geld needed to pay the tribute of 1018).

Winchester, from where Eadgar's coinage reform was first implemented, already by *c.*973 evidently had functions in royal government which gave it a certain monetary importance. After 1066 that importance grew. Although Southampton in the eighth and ninth centuries had had a monetary role as a wic and as Wessex's gateway to international trade and travel, that role had almost vanished by the late tenth century. Archaeological exploration of the eleventh-century (and present-day) site of Southampton has been too limited to yield a series of coin finds, but estimates of mint-output make it quite clear that the town's involvement in overseas trade was trivial in comparison with the east-coast ports, and that as the port for Winchester it did not even compare with Meols as the port for Chester. Winchester, therefore, may be contrasted with London, where it seems that the uses of coinage were predominantly commercial. (And London may be contrasted with Westminster.) Winchester seems to have had a 'natural' or regional role westwards of the city, where its coins made up a significant fraction of the currency. Winchester coins north of the Thames are, by contrast, few and far between. Winchester coins among London finds amount to 3 per cent, London coins among Winchester finds, 20 per cent. From the south-western shires of Somerset, Devon, and Cornwall the single finds include three of London, and three of Winchester. (All six could have been carried west from Winchester.)

The regional patterns of minting and of coin circulation strongly suggest that the predominant uses of coinage were commercial, and involved trade between the east-coast ports and their hinterlands, which overlapped, especially south of Humber. If coin circulation had been essentially local, the single finds would have consisted mostly of coins of the local mint, which is far from being the case. If the predominant uses of coinage had been fiscal and administrative, one might have expected minting to be more nearly in proportion to the wealth of each shire, and single finds to reveal a tendency towards coin circulation confined within shire boundaries. There are no signs of such a pattern. Fiscal and administrative uses of coinage may have existed alongside predominantly commercial uses, and may have been blanketed and obscured by them. A combination of the two uses puts a technical difficulty in the way of analysis, namely that coins which had arrived in a shire through trade may subsequently have been used there for fiscal purposes. It is in any case difficult to detect minor themes in the evidence. But the single finds have the merit of summing up the movement of coinage generated by *all* the active uses of coinage in a region (savings and reservoirs of wealth apart). Striking a balance, from the find evidence, between commercial and fiscal contexts is so vague an exercise as to be worthless.

Within the regional currencies, coins which were alike in other respects varied very widely in weight. In each successive validity-period there seems to have been a series of weight-reductions, followed by a return to a heavier standard at the beginning of the next type (or just before). The average weights fluctuated from type to type. These broad patterns conceal great diversity from mint to mint, and the assumption that heavier means earlier within the type, or lighter means later, is by no means a safe basis for historical conclusions, even if it is broadly true. The coins minted in the western shires tend to be heavier. In the east, particularly, multiple weight-standards are found at most mints.

It is extremely perplexing to know who benefitted from the variable weight of the penny. If the customer received new coins from the mint by weight rather than by tale, and spent them also by weight, the weight-standard was immaterial. But payments were also made by tale, and it was the interaction of the two systems which created difficulties. The numismatic evidence is inconclusive as to the intentions of those in authority.

If no clear answers are forthcoming, we may try to conjecture the purposes, and the means, of monetary policy as they might have been decided, or endorsed, by the king and his advisers. Of the decisions taken in *c.*973, the first was to restore the purity of the alloy. There may have been a recognition that England's foreign trade was prospering (because Rammelsberg silver was increasing people's purchasing power in the lower Rhinelands?) and a determination to benefit from it. Eadgar's fixing a minimum price for wool may have had the same general thrust as the coinage reform.

The high quality of the coinage added to Eadgar's dignity and authority. In that respect it revealed a political intention, which was part of the dream of a new era. Secondly, and equally political, the design of the coins was strictly uniform throughout England, whether their mint-towns lay in formerly West Saxon lands, or Mercian territory, or in the Danelaw. Although Eadgar's (discreet) control of the north was not in question, memories of old loyalties were still alive. The coins were valid currency throughout the kingdom, whatever their town of origin. So it was enacted: 'thæt an mynet sy ofer eall thæs cynges onweald'. The currency made propaganda, wherever it went, for English unity under the West Saxon dynasty, by its invariable use of a royal portrait and of the protocol, *Rex Anglorum*. Equally invariable was the naming of the town where the coin was struck. At least 40 mint-towns participated in the reform during the final years of Eadgar's reign, the moneyers receiving their dies from Winchester.

The medieval mind was shrewd enough on the subject of profit and loss, but we must not read back into the eleventh century our own profuse ideas about the management of a national economy through monetary policies. The king and his advisers are likely to have had, by modern standards, only a rudimentary idea of the likely economic effects of their monetary policies—and little or no statistical feed-back to show them whether the policies were working. The chances are that they will instinctively have favoured a bullionist approach; but it may well be that almost whatever they did, England was destined to run a healthy balance-of-payments surplus for two or three generations. The effects of weight-variation, for example, may have been incorrectly guessed, and the government, faced with a gratifying surplus, may have imagined without any rigorous numerical analysis that their policy of weight-variation was working successfully. It may have become the entrenched wisdom, as Keynsian economics did in the mid-twentieth century.

Because the numismatic evidence sends no clear signals, the results of weight-variation, and behind that the intentions of the policy, have defied investigation. The effects are impossible to assess, because they depend upon so many unknowns: first, whether transactions were made by weight or by tale, and secondly whether merchants engaged in trade with the near Continent were the beneficiaries of exchange-rate concessions. A brisk monetary circulation within England ensured that it was only at the point of exchange that concessions could be made. Thereafter, coins on different weight-standards quickly became mingled in use. There was no discernible attempt to prefer heavier or lighter coins in use.

Much freedom was left to the moneyers shire by shire, or mint-town by mint-town, to do as they pleased or perhaps as the shire authorities pleased. We can say with certainty that this was so from the very moment when Eadgar's reform of the coinage was launched. The arrangements established in *c.*973 may have persisted partly through inertia, but it is unlikely that they would have lasted so long, and with little modification until 1036, unless they had been, at the least, fairly harmless and had avoided the creation of sectional grievances. We should be looking, in other words, for an interpretation of weight-variation which recognizes the constraints of history. It is likely, too, that Eadgar's policy was essentially straightforward and probably high-minded, and could be formulated in a sentence or two. Because it is likely to have been simple, one feels that one ought to be able to guess it, or to stumble on it. But so far, Eadgar's vision has proved elusive.

His arrangements were in any case only permissive. They did not ensure that a certain number of coins should be minted in each shire. The facility was put in place, but the use that was made of it was outside royal control. Mint-output was dependent of Adam Smith's 'unseen hand' of individual choice and self-interest. In many places, the moneyers would have eked out a poor living, if they had had no other gainful occupation.

The ebb and flow of England's total monetary resources depended largely on patterns of supply and demand on the Continent, and on what was happening in Scandinavia.

In the end, it is better to defer the quest for an understanding of policy, and to accept the facts of mint-output and monetary circulation as the framework and basis for historical judgement. If the material is examined type by type, that is, in successive periods of about six years, giving way in 1036 to periods of only two or three years, the overwhelming impression is one of regularity, both in the ranking of the mints, and in the geographical patterns of dispersal of the coins. Whether the estimated national total of dies was larger or smaller, whether the validity-periods were longer or shorter, the outcome was broadly the same. That may well be because the volume of the currency was often far greater than was needed to facilitate all the transactions which people wished to make, the surplus functioning mainly as a store of wealth, and because two or three years, never mind six, were enough to generate the characteristic patterns of dispersal, which within that shorter time-span reached something like a steady state. It is puzzling that the massive inflows of the 980s through to *c.*1020 did not distort the share of mint-output taken by the big east-coast ports. Since a command economy is out of the question, one can only supppose that the prosperity of the regions was tightly integrated, and that good fortune was quickly shared by all those who participated in the monetary sector of the economy.

The validity-period of Last Small Cross (*c.*1009—*c.*1017) is a case in point. In spite of the heavy tribute of £48,000 demanded in 1012, in spite of the conquest of almost the whole of England by King Swein, and the subsequently renewed attack by King Cnut, the English currency goes on in its accustomed way with no significant disturbance to the ranking of the mints, nor to the numbers of stray losses, nor to their regional distribution, nor to the distances which coins had travelled before they were lost. English monetary affairs were, so to say, imperturbable.

Again, when England was partitioned between Harthacnut and Harold I in 1036, a *renovatio* was nevertheless organized for the whole country. A single die-cutting centre supplied southern mints with dies which named Harthacnut, while at the same time supplying northern mints with dies reading Harold. Without an agreement between the half-brothers, a national recoinage would have been impossible. The coins of both of them mingled in circulation in both north and south.

The one major disruption of the system occurred in the later 980s, in Æthelred's Second Hand type, when the major mints of York and Lincoln stood idle, or virtually so. The sources do not allow us to reconstruct the political history of northern England in those years in any detail, but there are hints of a crisis of confidence from *c.*985 until *c.*993.

The continuity which we see throughout the period *c.*973—1086 is itself a compelling argument for the predominantly commercial use of coinage. Distortions which can be connected with particular political or military events, such as the involvement of Sandwich in Edward the Confessor's blockade of Flanders, are very few.

The payment of tribute during the reign of Æthelred II has sometimes been offered as an explanation for the great quantities of his coins found in Scandinavia. Estimates suggest that those quantities were so great, that the so-called danegeld can have been only one of the ways in which English money reached the Northern Lands. It seems clear that the money which left England was almost always a mixture of coins of many mints. There is no good evidence that the need to pay tribute disturbed the ranking of the mints, except in 1018 (when the problem may have been aggravated by events during the preceding Last Small Cross type) and to a lesser extent in 1040, when Harthacnut's demand for a tribute of *c.*£32,000 seems to be the reason for an unusual pattern of activity in the Fleur-de-lis type.

The case of Southwark and of various eastern mints in the Crux type has been discussed, as has the 'heavy and severe tax' of 1084. The divergence from the normal order seems to have been initially an administrative innovation, and the big increase in the numbers of moneyers at those mints, which came part-way through the Crux type, was not matched by a corresponding increase in mint-output. The 'heavy and severe' tax of 1084, levied at six shillings per hide, and the apparently unusually large output of Paxs pennies with which to pay it, raise once more the question whether ordinary people throughout the shires held reserves of obsolete coin, which could be clawed back by the mints in dire circumstances, —or perhaps when differing charges were announced, as an administrative device to achieve a clean sweep of the currency.

Substantial inflows of bullion from the lower Rhinelands compensated or more than compensated for the outflows to Scandinavia in Æthelred's reign. The incoming silver, in the form of German coins, is invisible to us because of the strict policy of reminting foreign money. No doubt it underlies the large volume of coinage minted in London and at other east-coast ports, but any hope of identifying the sources of the silver from the scientific measurement of trace-elements (or, more plausibly, of lead-isotope ratios) is for the future.

What other directions may research be expected to take in the future? If the present synthesis has established anything new, it is that single finds can be used to reveal the patterns of monetary circulation, because they can be treated as a random sample. Hoards, which have hitherto enjoyed priority of esteem, are far from reliable for the monetary historian's purposes. Their evidence can be tested against that of the stray, accidental losses—and found wanting. It is clear that often they are not typical, as regards their mint-structure, of the regions where they were found. One may think of such hoards as reflecting an intermediate stage in the process of mixing, in the course of which hundreds of thousands or even millions of pennies were transferred from one region of England to another, year in and year out. Hoards may be money in transit, part of this ceaseless flow. Other hoards, of course, may have been put together in the locality and may be perfectly typical of it—although if they are long-term savings hoards, such as we see especially from 1042 onwards, they may be typical of the local currency not at one particular moment, when the hoard was closed, but at a series of moments extending over several years, or even a decade.

Single finds continue to accumulate year by year. The data-base already contains 685 finds, widely distributed throughout the English counties. New finds, in sufficient numbers, will add greater precision to the numerical assessments that can already be reached, by proportionally narrowing the margins of statistical variability.

Randomness is the *sine qua non* of reliable conclusions drawn from the single finds, and it is desirable to raise awareness of this need among metal-detectorists, to assess new finds from this point of view as they are reported, and to publish whatever remarks can be offered by way of guarantee. Randomness depends on the questions being asked: the same sample of coins may display different degrees of randomness when used for different purposes. Our data-base as a whole should, for example, be a good random sample from which to work out the ranking of the mints. Although it is so much smaller than the Scandinavian sample on which conclusions have previously been based, it escapes any risk that the Scandinavian sample may be un-random because coins were exported selectively, more from the eastern half of England than from the western half. Both samples escape the problem of possible variations in average die-output between large mints and small mints because they are based on counting coins, not dies. Discussing all the evidence step by step, in response to 39 questions, has the advantage of focussing attention on the degree of randomness that is appropriate to that particular question.

By dint of careful consideration it is possible to make good numerical comparisons between the various regions of England. Comparisons between successive validity-periods are not quite as secure, because average die-output may have varied from type to type. There will be many conclusions, even so, for which that is not a hazard. One arrives at a working model of the currency which may not be entirely free from distortions, but which is more than accurate enough to support the broad historical conclusions which it suggests.

A Short Bibliography

An eleventh-century monetary historian marooned on a desert island, and allowed to take only three books, apart from this one, would perhaps choose *Anglo-Saxon Monetary History* (edited by Blackburn), *Studies in Late Anglo-Saxon Coinage* (edited by Jonsson), and *The New Era*, by Jonsson.

The bibliography is arranged under the following headings:

1. Coin catalogues
2. The sequence of periodic types
3. The canon of mint-places
4. Moneyers' names and mint-signatures
5. Statistical estimation of mint-output
6. Weight-standards
7. Metal contents
8. Hoards
9. Single finds
10. Monetary history of England
11. Bibliographies

ABBREVIATIONS

ASE — *Anglo-Saxon England*

Anglo-Saxon Coins — *Anglo-Saxon Coins. Studies Presented to F.M. Stenton on the Occasion of his 80th Birthday, 17 May 1960*, edited by R.H.M. Dolley, 1961.

Anglo-Saxon Monetary History. — *Anglo-Saxon Monetary History. Essays in Memory of Michael Dolley*, edited by M.A.S. Blackburn, Leicester, 1986.

BMC — *British Museum Catalogues.* 1. C.F. Keary and H.A. Grueber, *A Catalogue of English Coins in the British Museum: Anglo-Saxon Series*, 2 vols., 1887-93. 2. G.C. Brooke, *A Catalogue of English Coins in the British Museum: the Norman Kings*, 2 vols, 1916.

BNJ — *British Numismatic Journal*

CC or 'Continuity and Change' — D.M. Metcalf, 'Continuity and change in English monetary history, *c.*973—1086.', *BNJ* 50 (1980), 20-49, ibid. 51 (1981), 52-90.

CNS — *Corpus Nummorum Saeculorum IX-XI qui in Suecia Reperti sunt* (Kungl. Vitterhets Historie och Antikvitets Akademien), Stockholm, 1975-.

Commentationes	*Commentationes de Nummis Saeculorum IX-XI in Suecia Repertis*. Parts 1 and 2, Stockholm, 1961 and 1968. id., *Nova Series*, Stockholm, 1987-.
CR	'Coin Register', *BNJ* (annually since 1987)
Freeman	A. Freeman, *The Moneyer and the Mint in the Reign of Edward the Confessor, 1042-1066*, (BAR British Series, 145), 2 vols., Oxford, 1985.
Hildebrand	B.E. Hildebrand, *Anglosachsiska mynt i Svenska kongliga Myntkabinettet funna i Sveriges jord*, 2nd edition, Stockholm, 1881. The weights of the catalogued coins have now been published by Petersson, in *Studies in Late Anglo-Saxon Coinage* (q.v.), pp. 377-433. See also G. van der Meer, 'Some corrections to and comments on B.E. Hildebrand's catalogue of the Anglo-Saxon coins in the Swedish Royal Coin Cabinet', in *Anglo-Saxon Coins*, pp. 169-87.
NC	*Numismatic Chronicle*
SCBI	*Sylloge of Coins of the British Isles* (published for the British Academy), 1958-. Some fifty volumes have been published to date, giving photographic illustration of many thousands of Anglo-Saxon coins, notably complete publication of the Copenhagen collection (vols. 4, 7, 13-15, 18, and 22), the Hunterian, Fitzwilliam, and Ashmolean collections, and a very full coverage of smaller museums in England. Volumes 28 and 41 are cumulative indexes for vols. 1-20 and 21-40 respectively.
SF or 'Single finds'	M.A.S. Blackburn and M.J. Bonser, 'Single finds of Anglo-Saxon and Anglo-Norman coins', *BNJ* 54 (1984), 63-72; ibid., 55 (1985), 55-78; ibid., 56 (1986), 64-101.
Studies in Late Anglo-Saxon Coinage.	*Studies in Late Anglo-Saxon Coinage, in Memory of Bror Emil Hildebrand*, edited by K. Jonsson (=*Numismatiska Meddelanden* 35), Stockholm, 1990.
The New Era	K. Jonsson, *The New Era. The Reformation of the Late Anglo-Saxon Coinage*, (=*Commentationes*, NS vol. 1), Stockholm, 1987.

BIBLIOGRAPHY

1. Coin catalogues

Many thousands of coins from the period *c.*973—1086 have now been fully published with good photographs and details of weight, die-axis, provenance, etc. The bulk of the material is in *SCBI*. For the full identification of a newly-discovered coin, the numismatist may well wish to have a complete reference library to hand, in order to check for die-duplication. For the general historian, a few volumes of *SCBI* may suffice, e.g. those for the Copenhagen collection. *BMC Norman Kings* may also be needed. Many scarce and interesting coins are illustrated in the *CNS* series.

The older catalogues of Hildebrand and *BMC* are still in constant use. Many individual mints now have a corpus, of which those for the large mints of Lincoln, Winchester (forthcoming), and York (forthcoming) are of special importance.

2. The sequence of periodic types

Hildebrand did not succeed completely in distinguishing scarce varieties which were Scandinavian imitations, from substantive English types. There were, in addition, certain points in the sequence which were slightly out of order. These involved, for example, the coinages of Harold I and Harthacnut, the early issues of Edward the Confessor, and the three different Small Cross issues of Æthelred II. The relative chronology has now been definitively established, and has been codified by Stewart (whose numbering of the types is employed in this book). Two distinguished studies, by Seaby and by Dolley, deserve mention.

P. Seaby, 'The sequence of Anglo-Saxon coins types, 1030—1050', *BNJ* 28 (1955-7), 111-46.

R.H.M. Dolley, *Some Reflections on Hildebrand Type A of Æthelræd II*, Stockholm, 1958.

I. Stewart, 'A numeration of late Anglo-Saxon coin types', *BNJ* 45 (1975), 12-18.

3. The canon of mint-places

Distinguishing the coins of Chester and Leicester, of Southwark and Sudbury, and of Northampton and Southampton has in the past been problematic. Otherwise, any remaining uncertainties concern very small mints. Some new very small mints could, in principle, turn up, but from the view-point of the monetary historian, at least 99 per cent of the currency is mint-attributable.

Much research has been published, in scattered articles, on the mint-signatures of individual problematic coins, and on debateable attributions more generally. Numismatists will often find it rewarding to return to the detail. Bibliographies will be found in each regional section of Part 4, above. For the general student, however, the results are satisfactorily gathered up in standard lists, of which the most convenient is that adopted by Jonsson and also (with numbering, 1-107) by Petersson, both in *Studies in Late Anglo-Saxon Coinage*, Stockholm, 1990. For William I's mints, see *BMC*.

4. Moneyers' names and mint-signatures

Moneyers' names should be normalized, although there may also be a need to record the particular forms as they are found on the coins. A convenient index of normalized names, showing the mint-town or towns where they occur, will be found in *Studies in Late Anglo-Saxon Coinage*, pp. 123-36. The same names are listed mint by mint with tabulation to show the types for which they are recorded, ibid., pp.54-119. Much of the underlying philological research will be found in V.J. Smart, 'Moneyers of the late Anglo-Saxon coinage, *c*.973—1016', *Commentationes* 2 (1968), 193-276 and ead., 'Moneyers of the late Anglo-Saxon coinage: the Danish dynasty, 1017-42', *ASE* 16 (1987), 233-308. For the reign of Edward the Confessor one may consult Freeman's monograph. For William I, the lists of moneyers and tabulation of them by mints in *BMC* are still necessary, although they have been up-dated in some particulars in J.J. North, *English Hammered Coinage*, vol. 1, 2nd edition, 1980. All the evidence has passed under expert review by Mrs Smart for use in her two volumes of *Cumulative Index* to *SCBI* (vols. 1-20, 1981, and 21-40, 1992). The introduction in the first of these volumes gives a valuable survey of the moneyers' names. There are various other, more detailed contributions published as articles by Mrs Smart.

The mint-signatures are generally abbreviated, and expert philological advice may be needed. There is an index of mints in each of the Cumulative Index volumes just mentioned, with a concise commentary wherever appropriate, by Mrs Smart.

5. Statistical estimation of mint-output

Critical surveys of the various methods, with their limitations, will be found in the proceedings of a Table ronde held in Paris and published as *Pact* 5 (1981): *Statistique et numismatique* edited by C. Carcassonne and T. Hackens. One may also consult C. Carcassonne, *Méthodes statistiques en numismatique*, Louvain-la-Neuve, 1987, and W.W. Esty, 'Statistics in numismatics', in *A Survey of Numismatic Research, 1990—1995* (International Numismatic Commission/International Association of Professional Numismatists, Special Publication no. 13). Berlin, 1997, pp. 817-23.

6. Weight-Standards

The evidence is systematically presented in two major works by Bertil Petersson.
H.B.A. Petersson, *Anglo-Saxon Currency*, Lund, 1969: id., 'Coins and weights. Late Anglo-Saxon pennies and mints, *c.*973-1066', in *Studies in Late Anglo-Saxon Coinage*, pp. 207-433.

7. Metal contents

There is only one large-scale, systematic study, analysing 11 elements, in 235 late Anglo-Saxon pennies. It concentrates on four *tranches* of coinage, from *c.*973-91, 997-1009, 1017-24, and 1050-6, and shows that a high silver standard was maintained throughout, while identifying persistent differences between mint-towns, of up to 7 per cent silver contents. Thus, York and Lincoln tended to produce coins of slightly lower fineness.
D.M. Metcalf and J.P. Northover, 'Interpreting the alloy of the later Anglo-Saxon coinage', *BNJ* 56 (1986), 35-63.

The same data for Cnut's Quatrefoil type are also published and briefly discussed in G.C. Boon, *Welsh Hoards, 1979—1981*, Cardiff, 1986, at pp. 10-11 and 32-5.

Lead isotope analysis, without which the historian's questions about the inflows of Rammelsberg silver to England are unlikely to be answered satisfactorily, requires expensive facilities and causes significant damage to the coins analysed. It has not yet been undertaken.

8. Hoards

In the text above, no chapter and verse has been quoted for information about the English (and Welsh) hoards from *c.*973—1086, of which there are some eighty, because details are to be found in the latest revision of the standard check-list: M. Blackburn and H. Pagan, 'A revised check-list of coin hoards from the British Isles, *c.*500-1100', in *Anglo-Saxon Monetary History*, pp. 291-313. This includes bibliographical references. Hoards discovered since 1986 have been published mostly in the pages of *BNJ*.

For chronological lists of hoards from other countries containing Anglo-Saxon coins, see M. Blackburn and K. Jonsson, 'The Anglo-Saxon and Anglo-Norman element of North European coin finds', in *Viking-Age Coinage in the Northern Lands, The Sixth Oxford Symposium on Coinage and Monetary History*, Oxford, 1981, pp. 147-255.

9. Single Finds

The list published above gathers up information from 'Continuity and change', 'Single finds of Anglo-Saxon and Norman coins, 1-3', and the 'Coin Register'published annually in *BNJ*. The material grows year by year. In general it is extremely well attested.

10. Monetary history of England

Attempts to establish the perspectives of the subject will be found in 'Continuity and change', and in various other articles, among which may be mentioned

H.R. Loyn, 'Boroughs and mints, A.D. 900-1066', in *Anglo-Saxon Coins*, pp. 122-35.

R.H.M. Dolley and D.M. Metcalf, 'The reform of the English coinage under Eadgar', ibid., pp. 136-68.

H.B.A. Petersson, *Anglo-Saxon Currency. King Edgar's Reform to the Norman Conquest*, Lund, 1969.

S. Lyon, 'Historical problems of Anglo-Saxon coinage, 4. The Viking Age', *BNJ* 39 (1970), 193-204. id, 'Some problems in interpreting Anglo-Saxon coinage', *ASE* 5 (1976), 173-224.

I. Stewart, 'Coinage and recoinage after Edgar's reform', in *Studies in Late Anglo-Saxon Coinage*, pp. 455-85.

P. Nightingale, 'The evolution of weight standards and the creation of new monetary and commercial links in northern Europe from the tenth century to the twelfth century', *Economic History Review*[2] 38 (1985), 192-209.

D.M. Metcalf, 'The taxation of moneyers under Edward the Confessor and in 1086', in *Domesday Studies*, edited by J.C. Holt, 1987, pp. 279-93.

S. Harvey, 'Taxation and the economy', ibid., pp. 249-64.

11. Bibliographies

An annual bibliography covering Numismatics will be found in *ASE*. Six-yearly surveys have for many years been published in connection with the International Numismatic Congresses, e.g. (most recently) M. Blackburn, 'England, Wales and Scotland: medieval', in *A Survey of Numismatic Research, 1990-1995*, edited by C. Morrisson *et al.* (International Numismatic Commission/International Association of Professional Numismatists, Special Publication no. 13), Berlin, 1997, pp. 323-43. A well-indexed bibliography of the writings of Michael Dolley, compiled by R.H. Thompson, will be found in *Anglo-Saxon Monetary History*, pp. 315-60. There are convenient decennial indexes in *BNJ* and *NC*.

APPENDIX

STATISTICS

The percentage share of the national output of coinage, type by type, for each of the mint-places.

APPENDIX

Statistics

The Table that follows reproduces all the figures from Appendix V in the 1981 paper, 'Continuity and change'. The grouping of the mints into regions has, however, been changed in order to bring it into line with the text of this book.

Two additions have been made. First, the number of surviving specimens from each mint has been added after the mint name. Note that this is *not* the number of coins in the Scandinavian sample used for purposes of estimation (which is printed as Appendix IV in 'Continuity and change'). It is derived from Petersson's Table 4, covering 44,350 coins.

Secondly, an extra column has been added for Type 23 (Harold II), derived from Pagan's corpus of 512 identifiable specimens. Although not procedurally comparable with the figures derived from the Scandinavian sample, it gives a useful view of the ranking of the mints on the eve of the Norman Conquest. An estimate of output for each mint has been derived from Pagan's statistics, yielding an estimated total of 299-343 reverse dies (cf.258 known reverse dies). The percentages in the table are based on figures from the middle of the range for each mint, as percentages of 320.

The numeration of the types follows I.Stewart, 'A numeration of late Anglo-Saxon coin types', in *BNJ* 1975. The numeration of the mints follows H.B.A. Petersson, 'Coins and weights. Late Anglo-Saxon pennies and mints, *c.*973-1066', in *Studies in Late Anglo-Saxon Coinage*, pp. 207-433.

The full list of mints is swollen by a dozen mint-signatures which cannot be interpreted. Only 17 specimens are involved. The early issues which are potentially of historical interest (becaue the national totals are smaller) are, in the Reform type, Luveic (??Chester); in First Hand, Cver, Luthey, and Weingi; and in Crux, Æsthe (?Hastings).

Stewart		1	2A	2B	3	4	5	6	7
		Reform	First Hand	Second Hand	Crux	Long Cross	Helmet	Last Small Cross	Quatrefoil
	1. YORKSHIRE								
107	York (4,805)	8.70	7.82	..	9.42	8.29	12.56	8.62	8.64
	2. LINDSEY								
55	Lincoln (4,342)	5.22	3.77	..	4.86	11.29	8.71	12.63	8.12
94	Torksey (16)	..	..	0.33	..	0.08	..	0.06	0.03
17	Caistor (6)	..	..	..	..	..	..	..	0.10
44	Horncastle (3)	..	..	..	..	..	..	..	..
57	Louth? (1 or 2)	..	..	..	..	..	..	..	..
	3. THE FIVE BOROUGHS								
29	Derby (150)	..	2.96	..	0.08	0.16	0.30	0.23	0.14
53	Leicester (294)	3.48	1.35	1.00	0.54	0.89	0.74	0.51	0.72
65	Newark (9)	..	..	..	..	..	..	0.17	..
70	Nottingham (150)	..	0.27	0.33	0.23	..	0.15	0.17	0.24
87	Stamford (1,712)	7.83	3.77	2.33	1.24	3.01	2.66	4.62	2.65
39	Grantham (1)	..	..	..	..	..	..	..	..
	4. THE NORTH-WEST								
21	Chester (1,550)	4.35	2.16	1.00	0.77	3.82	2.66	2.59	5.20
82	Shrewsbury (359)	1.74	1.08	..	0.46	1.38	0.59	0.28	1.38
86	Stafford (59)	0.87	..	..	0.23	0.32	0.15	0.11	0.10
91	Tamworth (49)	0.87	..	1.00	0.46	0.08	0.15	0.06	..
	5. EAST ANGLIA								
69	Norwich (1,083)	4.35	2.70	2.67	2.01	2.03	2.36	3.27	2.82
93	Thetford (1,485)	0.87	3.23	2.67	3.71	2.27	4.58	4.28	3.20
49	Ipswich (510)	1.74	1.89	1.00	0.85	0.57	1.03	1.47	1.51
90	Sudbury (37)	..	..	..	..	..	..	0.23	0.38
15	Bury St Edmunds (10)	..	..	..	..	..	..	..	..
103	'Wilton' (3)	..	..	..	..	..	..	0.06	..
34	'Dyr' (10)	..	..	..	..	..	..	..	..
30	'Derne'/'Dernt' (4)	..	..	..	..	..	..	..	..

	8	9	10	11	12	13	14	15	16	17-23	23
	Pointed Helmet	Short Cross	Jewel Cross	Fleur-de-lis	Arm and Sceptre	Pacx	Radiate/Small Cross	Trefoil-Quadrilateral	Short Cross	Expanding Cross — Pax	Pax
107	12.03	12.40	10.22	8.81	7.85	9.38	10.26	14.14	5.82	11.65	6.3
55	9.85	13.48	14.43	9.47	11.96	15.86	12.89	12.63	12.70	23.79	4.7
94	0.04	..	..	..		..	..	..	..	..	..
17	..	..	..	..	..	..	..	..	..	..	..
44	..	..	..	..	..	..	..	..	..	..	..
57	..	..	..	..	..	..	..	..	..	..	..
29	0.18	0.51	1.44	1.52	1.31	0.97	1.43	..	0.53	0.49	0.3
53	0.58	0.21	0.48	1.41	1.31	0.32	0.24	2.53	1.06	..	0.6
65	0.15	..	..	..	..	..	..	..	..	..	..
70	0.44	0.72	0.72	0.76	0.93	1.29	0.72	0.51	..	..	1.3
87	3.82	7.05	5.17	5.22	6.36	4.53	3.58	6.57	4.23	2.43	2.2
39		..	..	..	..	..	..	..	..	..	..
21	3.10	2.21	2.64	2.94	2.06	2.59	2.86	2.02	1.59	1.94	1.1
82	0.84	0.82	1.32	0.76	1.50	0.32	1.67	1.52	1.06	..	1.6
86	0.15	..	..	0.43	..	..	..	..	..	0.49	..
91	..	0.05	..	0.22	..	..	..	..	..	..	..
69	1.85	1.75	2.52	2.72	3.36	2.91	3.34	1.01	0.53	4.85	2.5
93	2.58	2.52	2.88	3.48	3.93	4.22	3.82	3.03	5.82	3.88	1.9
49	0.87	0.36	0.96	0.87	0.93	0.65	1.91	1.01	0.53	2.43	1.9
90	..	..	..	..	..	..	..	..	..	..	..
15		..	..	..	..	..	..	..	..	0.49	..
103		..	..	..	..	..	..	..	..	..	..
34		..	..	..	..	0.32	..	..	..	..	..
30		..	..	..	..	..	..	..	..	..	..

		1	2A	2B	3	4	5	6	7
Stewart									
	6. THE MIDDLE DANELAW								
6	Bedford (243)	1.74	0.27	..	0.69	0.65	0.15	0.45	0.79
18	Cambridge (679)	0.87	0.27	..	2.55	1.46	2.36	1.75	3.23
46	Huntingdon (365)	..	1.08	..	0.46	1.71	1.62	0.96	0.86
68	Northampton (359)	3.48	0.81	0.67	1.54	1.87	0.59	0.79	1.10
74	Peterborough (2)	..	..	..	..	..	..	..	..
	7. ESSEX, HERTS, BUCKS								
24	Colchester (378)	..	..	..	2.70	1.22	0.15	0.62	1.27
43	Hertford (272)	..	..	..	2.01	0.24	0.30	0.06	1.20
14	Buckingham (42)	0.87	..	..	0.15	0.16	..	..	0.17
3	Aylesbury (18)	..	..	..	0.15	..	..	..	0.17
45	Horndon (1)	..	..	..	..	..	..	..	..
62	Maldon (172)	0.87	0.27	..	1.39	0.08	0.30	0.06	0.79
66	Newport (5)	..	..	..	..	..	..	..	..
	8. LONDON								
56	London (10,023)	6.96	22.37	42.33	17.53	22.58	28.21	23.96	22.20
84	Southwark (735)	..	..	..	8.26	0.73	0.30	0.51	2.48
	9. SOUTH MERCIA								
38	Gloucester (474)	0.87	0.81	0.33	0.54	1.22	0.59	0.62	1.31
42	Hereford (344)	0.87	1.08	..	0.54	1.38	0.59	0.39	0.89
72	Oxford (754)	3.48	0.27	0.67	1.62	2.03	1.92	0.73	1.93
99	Warwick (202)	..	..	..	0.31	0.97	0.30	0.39	0.31
106	Worcester (245)	0.87	0.81	..	0.77	0.97	0.89	0.23	0.58
8	Berkeley (5)	..	..	..	..	..	..	..	..
11	Bristol (246)	..	..	..	..	..	..	0.11	1.55
33	Droitwich (8)	..	..	..	..	..	..	..	..
73	Pershore (1)	..	..	..	..	..	..	..	..
104	Winchcombe (44)	..	..	..	0.15	0.24	0.30	..	0.17
	10. KENT, SURREY, SUSSEX								
19	Canterbury (1,265)	5.22	4.04	7.67	3.78	3.09	2.07	2.42	1.27
77	Rochester (312)	1.74	1.35	3.00	1.54	0.97	1.15	0.73	0.34
32	Dover (485)	..	0.27	..	0.62	1.06	1.33	1.58	0.72
61	Lympne (86)	5.22	0.81	1.00	0.54	0.24	..	..	0.07
..	Winchelsea? (2)	..	..	..	..	..	..	..	..
22	Chichester (313)	0.87	0.54	1.00	0.77	0.81	0.89	0.28	0.65

	8	*9*	*10*	*11*	*12*	*13*	*14*	*15*	*16*	*17-23*	*23*
6	0.18	0.41	0.12	0.98	0.56	0.97	0.72	..	1.06	..	0.6
18	0.80	0.41	0.60	1.20	2.43	0.32	0.96	1.01	0.53	0.97	1.6
46	1.20	0.46	0.36	0.54	0.93	0.97	1.19	..	0.53	0.49	0.3
68	0.36	0.36	0.60	1.63	0.56	1.29	1.67	..	0.53	1.94	1.3
74	..	..	..	..	..	..	..	..	..	..	..
24	0.47	0.82	0.84	0.65	0.19	0.65	3.10	..	1.06	0.97	1.6
43	0.11	0.98	0.12	1.41	0.19	2.59	2.63	0.51	1.06	0.49	..
14	0.07	0.05	0.24	0.11	0.19	0.32	..	0.51	..	..	..
3	..	..	..	..	..	..	0.72	..	..	..	..
45	..	..	..	..	..	..	..	..	..	..	..
62	0.51	..	0.12	..	..	..	0.24	..	0.53	..	0.3
66	..	..	..	..	..	..	..	..	..	..	..
56	33.33	24.80	23.32	26.33	16.64	25.89	20.53	24.24	28.57	19.42	28.4
84	1.09	0.31	1.20	..	1.50	0.32	1.19	0.51	..	..	0.3
38	1.13	0.77	0.84	1.31	2.80	0.97	0.48	1.01	1.59	1.94	2.2
42	0.91	0.77	2.04	1.31	1.68	1.29	0.72	1.52	1.06	0.97	2.3
72	1.38	1.65	2.16	2.61	2.43	1.62	2.86	3.03	2.12	1.46	3.3
99	0.40	0.36	0.72	0.65	0.75	0.97	0.48	1.01	0.53	0.49	1.3
106	0.87	0.36	0.72	0.98	0.75	0.32	0.24	1.01	0.53	1.46	1.9
8	..	..	..	..	..	0.32	..	..	..	0.49	..
11	..	0.46	1.92	2.18	2.43	0.97	0.95	2.02	1.06	0.97	1.6
33	..	..	..	..	..	..	..	..	..	..	1.1
73	..	..	..	..	..	..	..	..	..	..	..
104	0.15	..	..	..	0.19	..	..	..	0.53	..	0.8
19	2.44	2.62	2.40	1.96	1.31	2.27	2.86	6.06	4.23	3.88	1.6
77	0.25	0.67	0.36	..	..	..	0.24	..	..	..	0.6
32	2.00	4.12	2.40	1.31	1.31	0.97	0.48	1.01	..	0.49	0.6
61	0.04	0.26	..	..	..	..	..	..	..	..	..
..	..	..	..	..	..	..	..	..	..	..	..
22	0.40	0.62	0.36	0.65	0.19	..	0.24	1.01	0.53	0.97	0.6

	Stewart	*1*	*2A*	*2B*	*3*	*4*	*5*	*6*	*7*
54	Lewes (605)	2.61	2.43	0.67	1.24	1.71	1.18	2.31	1.00
40	Guildford (75)	..	..	0.33	0.08	0.41	..	..	0.10
41	Hastings (352)	..	..	0.33	0.24	0.32	1.03	0.23	0.28
78	Romney (94)	..	..	..	..	0.41	0.59	0.23	0.24
23	Cissbury (41)	..	..	..	..	..	..	0.34	0.03
89	Steyning (114)	..	..	0.33	..	..	..	..	..
80	Sandwich (28)	..	..	..	..	..	..	..	..
47	Hythe (7)	..	..	..	..	..	..	..	..
	11. WESSEX								
105	Winchester (2,932)	13.04	11.59	6.67	7.80	4.14	5.32	9.92	6.40
102	Wilton (356)	3.48	1.08	0.33	1.93	1.30	..	0.06	0.14
81	Shaftesbury (307)	0.87	1.35	1.33	0.46	0.97	1.18	0.85	0.83
97	Wareham (142)	0.87	0.81	1.00	1.00	0.49	0.30	0.11	0.03
83	Southampton (89)	..	1.89	0.33	0.31	0.16	0.15	0.17	0.76
63	Malmesbury (99)	..	..	0.33	0.31	0.32	0.15	0.06	0.24
96	Wallingford (480)	..	0.27	1.00	2.55	1.46	0.89	0.34	0.69
26	Cricklade (121)	..	0.54	..	0.31	0.16	..	0.39	0.69
31	Dorchester (95)	..	0.27	..	0.15	0.24	0.30	0.23	..
10	Bridport (37)	..	0.54	1.33	0.31	0.24	..	0.06	0.03
67	'Niwan' (1)	..	0.27	..	..	..	..	..	..
13	'Brygin' (1)	..	0.27	..	..	..	..	..	..
79	Salisbury (293)	..	..	..	..	..	0.89	1.18	0.79
35	'Eanbyrig' (2)	..	..	..	..	..	..	..	0.07
98	Warminster (27)	..	..	..	..	0.24	..	0.11	..
7	Bedwyn (18)	..	..	..	..	..	..	..	..
76	Reading (2)	..	..	..	..	..	..	..	..
	12. THE SOUTH-WEST								
36	Exeter (1,360)	4.35	6.47	9.33	4.09	3.74	4.14	3.55	1.65
4	Barnstaple (161)	..	1.62	1.67	1.00	0.89	0.59	0.11	0.24
48	Ilchester (379)	0.87	1.35	2.33	2.01	0.65	0.44	..	2.58
95	Totnes (260)	..	2.16	2.33	1.24	0.57	0.59	0.28	0.37
5	Bath (476)	..	..	0.33	0.77	1.71	1.33	0.73	0.93
60	Lydford (250)	..	0.81	0.67	0.62	0.73	0.44	1.92	0.45
100	Watchet (103)	..	0.54	0.33	0.08	0.32	0.15	0.06	0.27
52	Launceston (1)	..	..	..	..	..	..	..	..
2	Axbridge (16)	..	..	..	..	0.08	..	..	0.14
12	Bruton (62)	..	..	..	..	..	..	..	0.34

	8	*9*	*10*	*11*	*12*	*13*	*14*	*15*	*16*	*17-23*	*23*
54	0.73	0.87	0.84	0.65	2.06	0.97	0.48	1.01	1.59	0.49	1.3
40	..	0.68	0.12	0.11	..	..	..	..	..	..	0.3
41	1.09	1.29	0.96	0.76	0.56	..	0.48	0.51	..	0.49	0.9
78	0.36	0.31	0.12	0.33	..	0.32	..	..	..	..	0.3
23	..	..	..	..	..	..	..	..	..	..	..
89	0.15	0.36	..	0.33	..	0.65	..	..	..	0.97	0.3
80	..	..	..	..	..	0.65	0.48	0.51	0.53	..	..
47	..	..	..	..	..	..	0.24	..	..	..	..
105	4.40	5.09	4.57	4.03	6.17	5.18	5.25	3.54	7.94	1.46	4.1
102	0.22	0.31	0.24	0.65	0.56	..	0.95	1.01	1.59	3.40	6.6
81	0.69	0.93	0.48	0.33	0.37	0.32	1.43	..	1.06	..	1.3
97	..	0.05	..	0.22	0.19	0.65	..	..	..	..	1.3
83	..	..	..	..	..	..	..	..	..	..	..
63	0.25	0.10	0.24	0.22	0.56	..	..	0.51	0.53	..	0.8
96	0.69	0.77	0.72	2.07	2.24	..	0.48	0.51	0.53	0.97	2.8
26	0.36	0.26	0.24	0.32	0.37	0.65	0.24	..	..	..	0.6
31	0.15	0.21	0.48	0.87	0.56	..	..	0.51	..	..	0.3
10	0.07	0.05	0.12	..	0.19	..	..	..	..	..	0.3
67	..	..	..	..	..	..	..	..	..	..	..
13	..	..	..	..	..	..	..	..	..	..	..
79	1.20	1.29	1.32	1.74	1.12	0.65	0.95	0.51	1.59	..	..
35	..	..	..	..	..	..	..	..	..	..	..
98	0.04	0.15	0.12	..	..	..	..	..	..	..	..
7	..	..	..	..	..	..	..	..	1.06	..	..
76	..	..	..	..	..	..	..	0.51	..	..	..
36	2.29	1.65	2.04	1.41	2.99	0.65	1.67	0.51	1.06	1.46	1.6
4	0.11	0.15	..	0.11	..	..	0.24	..	..	..	..
48	0.44	0.31	0.36	0.11	0.37	0.65	..	..	..	..	0.9
95	0.58	..	0.12	..	0.19	..	..	..	..	..	..
5	1.02	0.87	0.84	0.65	0.75	0.97	0.72	..	1.06	..	..
60	0.11	0.10	0.12	0.11	0.37	..	0.24	..	0.53	..	..
100	0.07	0.15	0.24	0.22	..	..	0.24	..	1.06	..	..
52	..	..	..	..	..	..	..	..	..	..	..
2	0.04	0.05	0.36	..	0.37	..	..	..	..	..	..
12	0.25	0.31	0.12	..	0.19	0.65	0.24	..	..	..	..

	Stewart	1	2A	2B	3	4	5	6	7
25	Crewkerne (29)	..	..	..	..	0.24	..	..	0.31
20	'Geothanburh' (43)	..	..	..	..	0.24	0.74	0.17	0.24
64	Milborne Port (14)	..	..	..	..	0.16	..	..	..
92	Taunton (79)	..	..	..	..	0.16	..	0.06	0.62
51	Langport (23)	..	..	..	..	..	..	..	0.17
75	Petherton (4)	..	..	..	..	..	..	..	..
16	Cadbury (23)	..	..	..	..	..	..	0.56	0.03
37	'Fro' (6)	..	..	..	..	..	..	..	..

	8	*9*	*10*	*11*	*12*	*13*	*14*	*15*	*16*	*17-23*	*23*
25	0.04	0.15	0.12	..	..	..	..	..	..	..	..
20	..	..	0.12	0.22	0.75	..	..	..	..	..	..
64	0.04	0.10	..	..	..	..	..	..	..	..	..
92	..	..	..	0.11	0.37	0.32	..	0.51	..	..	0.3
51	0.07	0.05	0.72	..	0.19	..	..	..	..	0.49	..
75	..	..	..	..	..	..	0.24	0.51	..	..	..
16	..	..	..	..	..	..	..	..	..	..	..
37	..	0.05	..	..	..	0.32	..	..	..	..	..

Index

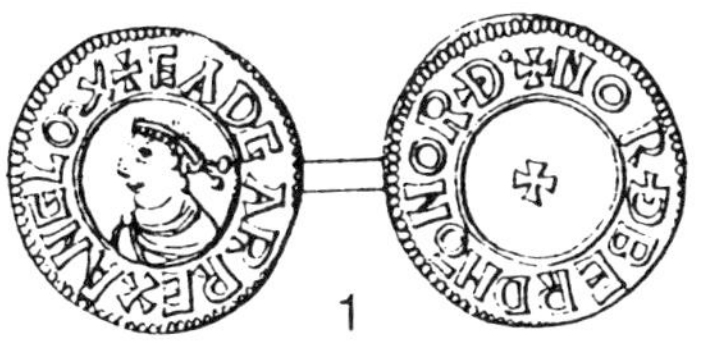
1

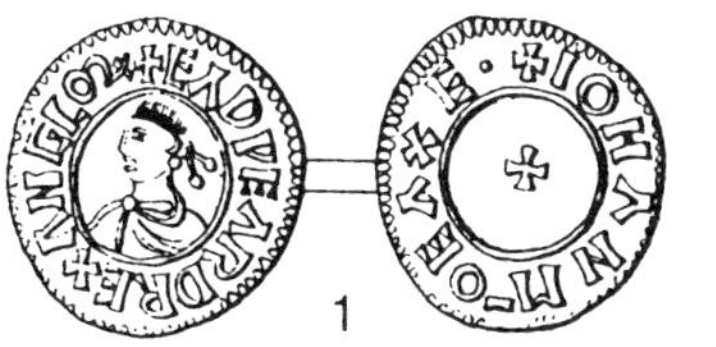
1

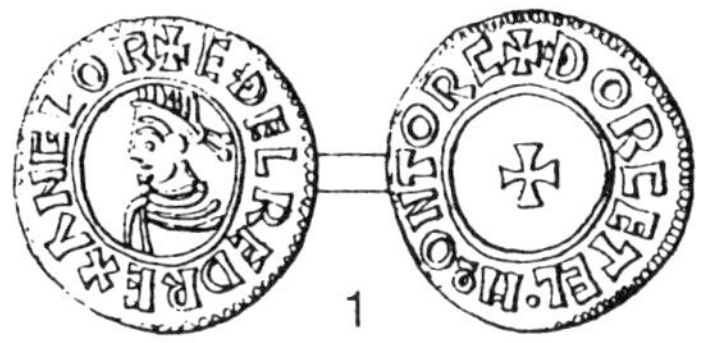
1

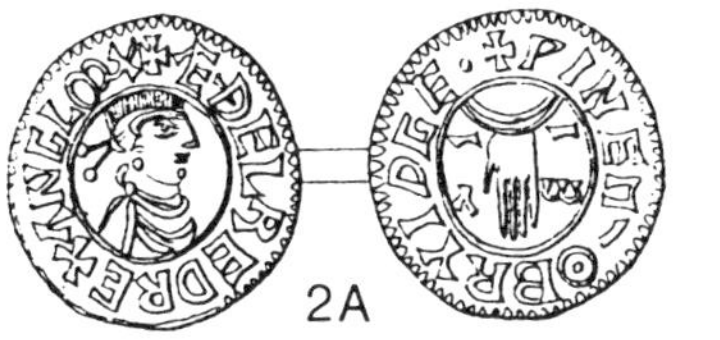
2A

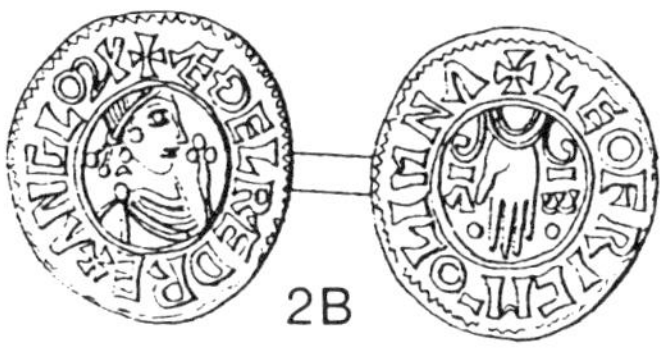
2B

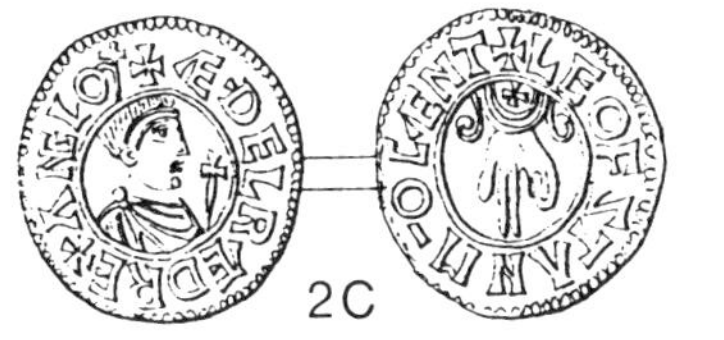
2C

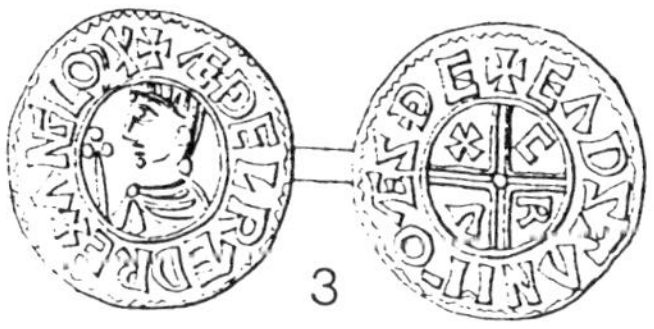
3

4

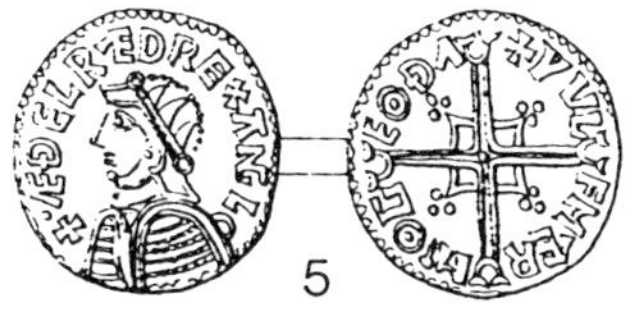
5

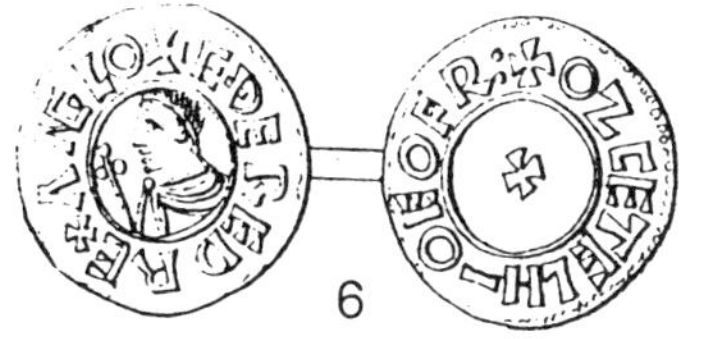
6

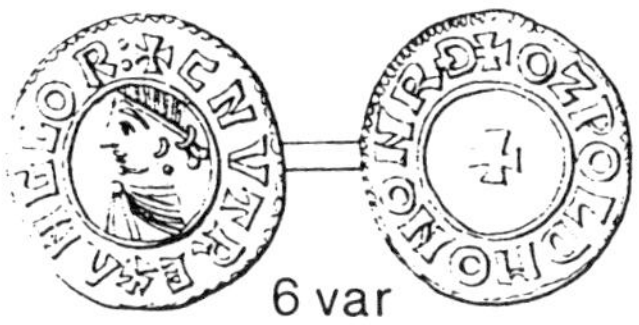
6 var

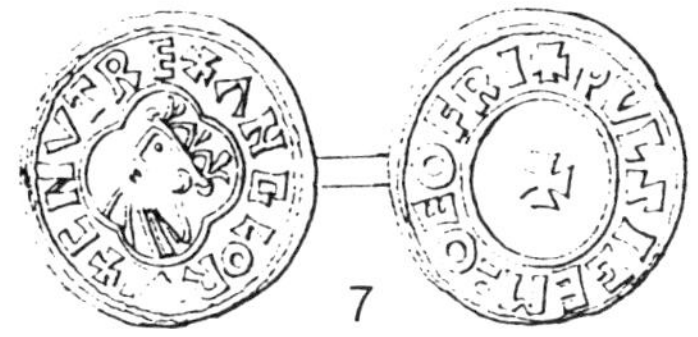
7

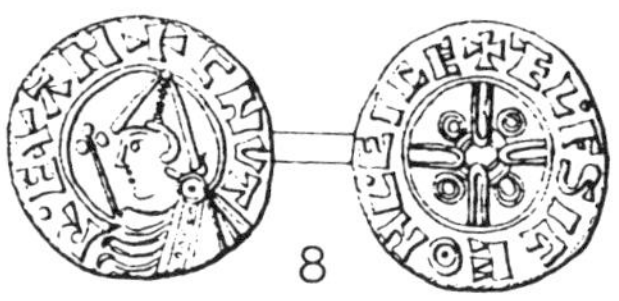
8

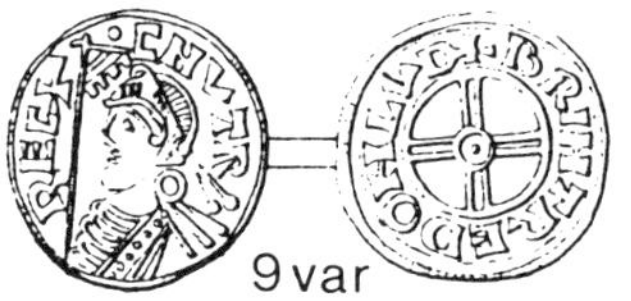
9 var

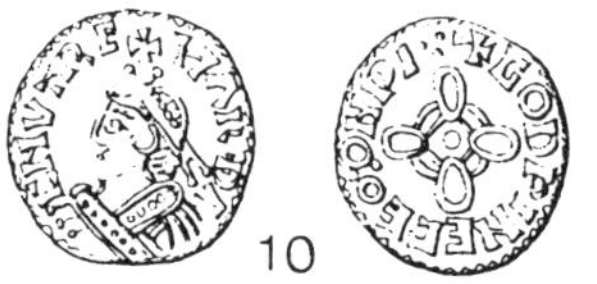
10

10

11

12

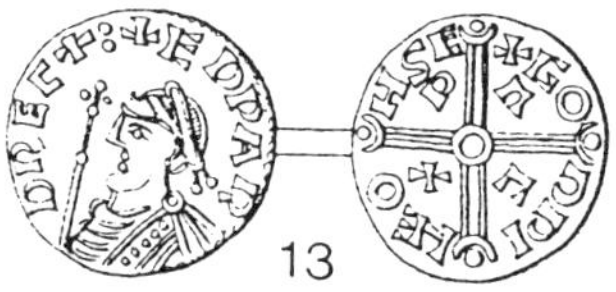
13

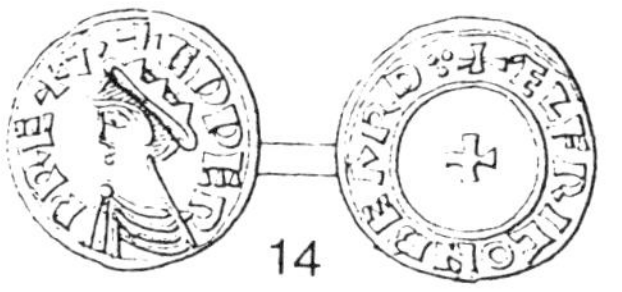
14

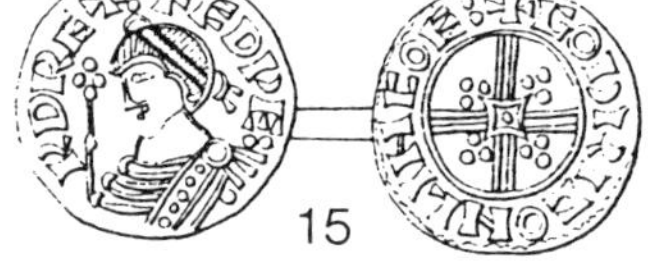
15

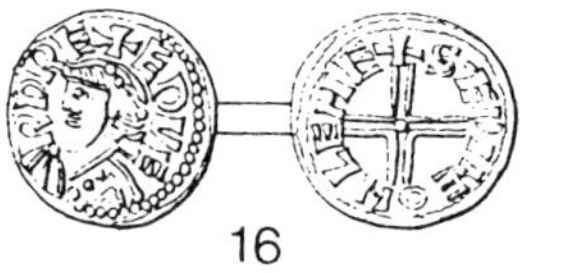
16

17

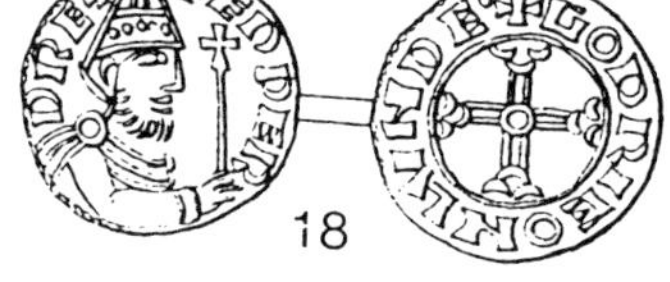
18

19

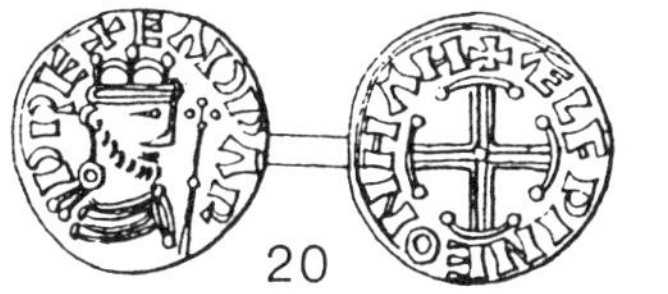

20

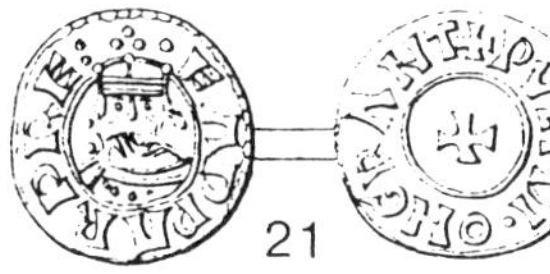

21

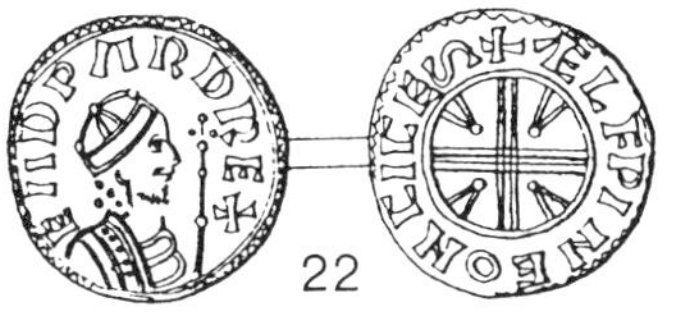

22

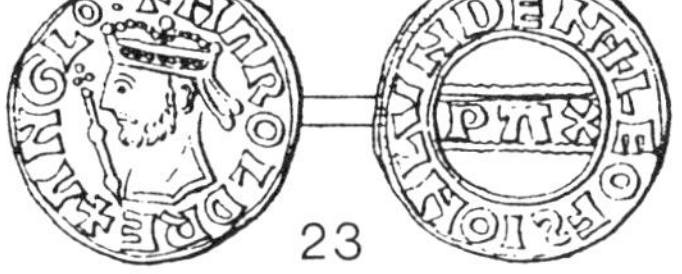

23

24

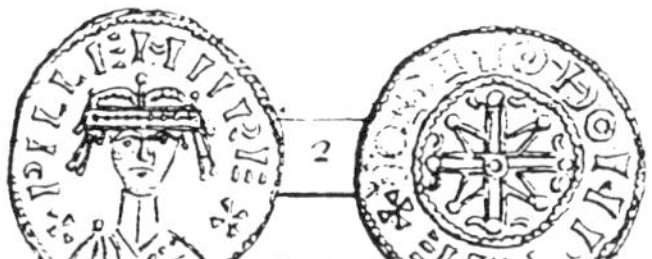

25

26

27

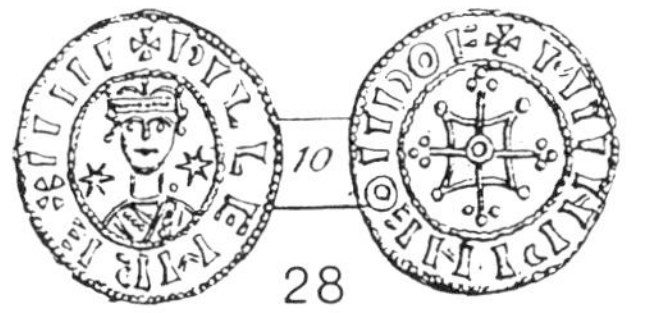

28

29

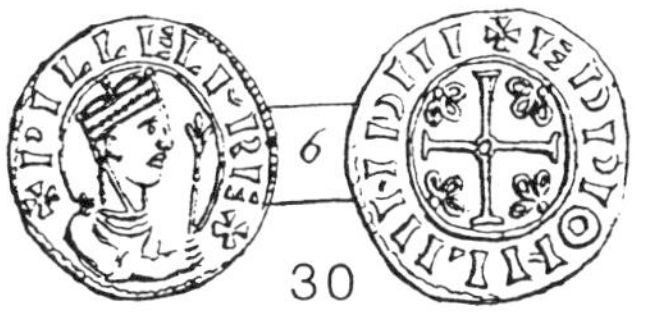

30

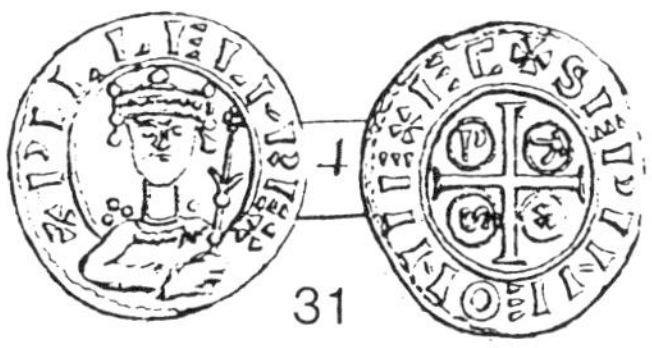

31